# PARTIES AND
# POLITICAL CONSCIENCE

# KTO STUDIES
# IN
# AMERICAN HISTORY

*Consulting Editor: Harold M. Hyman*
William P. Hobby Professor of History
Rice University

# PARTIES
# AND
# POLITICAL
# CONSCIENCE:
## American Dilemmas
## 1840–1850

*William R. Brock*

kto press

A U.S. Division of Kraus-Thomson Organization Ltd.

Millwood, New York

First printing

Printed in the United States of America

Library of Congress Cataloging in Publication Data

Brock, William Ranulf.
   Parties and political conscience.

   (KTO studies in American history)
   Bibliography: p.
   Includes index.
   1.  Political parties—United States—History.
   2.  United States—Politics and government—1841–1845.
   3.  United States—Politics and government—1845–1849.
   I.  Title.   II.  Series.
   JK2260.B75 1979      329'.02      78-32174
   ISBN 0-527-11800-1

# CONTENTS

# ACKNOWLEDGMENTS

The preparation of this book began as long ago as 1965 in the Henry E. Huntington Library, San Marino, California, and was completed —after many interruptions and other projects—in the Charles Warren Center of Harvard University. My thanks are due to the authorities of these two distinguished institutions for the financial support that made the work possible. I am indebted for help to many libraries on both sides of the Atlantic. The collections of American material in the university libraries of Cambridge and Glasgow and in the Institute of Historical Research in the University of London have been invaluable for a scholar who has had to do the bulk of his research on this side of the Atlantic.

The quotation from the papers of Gideon Welles on page 23 is reprinted by permission of the Trustees of the Huntington Library. The quotation on page 150 from the papers of William Henry Seward is reprinted by permission of the Rush-Rhees Library, University of Rochester, Rochester, New York.

WILLIAM BROCK

*Glasgow, August 1978*

# INTRODUCTION

Between 1834 and 1840 the various groups opposed to Andrew Jackson and Martin Van Buren fused together to form the nationwide Whig party. Throughout the next decade the two parties fought each other in every state of the Union in a period of high voter participation. On most issues the parties displayed remarkable solidarity in Congress, and were able to retain stable support in the country. Though short lived this party system came to be regarded as the normal way of organizing political life in American society. Sectional parties were treated as unfortunate aberrations, and one-part states or regions as symptoms of poor political health; third parties were considered as abnormal, and more than three as a step towards chaos.

It is a major premise of this book that the rise of the two-party system cannot be explained merely as the outcome of local power struggles or its perpetuation by the vested interest of party machines. The behavior of individual politicians cannot explain the preference and motives of thousands who have to be attracted to the polls if any party is to survive. Nor is it sufficient to explain party rivalry exclusively by reference to religious or ethnic differences. These have their part in forming the character of parties, but their political role is defensive and cannot account for enthusiasm or the pursuit of positive aims. Though study of these factors has made an important contribution to the literature of political history, the roots of party loyalty are best revealed by the self-evident fact that people support a party because they believe that it has better policies, a better grasp of the long-term interests of the country, and more correct attitudes toward public responsibility. An admirable statement of this simple truth comes from George Bancroft. In 1836 he was already a politician, something of a philosopher, and about to embark on his life-work as a historian. In a carefully prepared July 4 Oration he said,

> No party can be held together and succeed except by an honest principle. Men rally to nothing else: and if ever a party should fail to have a great truth for its central point that party could not long be held together; it would have no vitality.[1]

Working from this premise this book examines the framework of ideas within which the parties existed, and argues that both represented broad but distinct channels through which could flow material aims, political hopes, conservative fears, and concepts of national character. If the differences have been obscured by subsequent historical analysis, they were clear to contemporaries.

There are conditions which affect the survival of parties. However strong their initial impulse they may flag and eventually disintegrate if they achieve nothing. The Whigs never recovered momentum after the disastrous failure of 1841–42 and were particularly vulnerable when they had to encounter new problems presented by nationalism and the expansion of slavery. The Democrats were in better shape for survival and managed to circumvent some of the problems of a rapidly changing society by resorting to their traditional policy of throwing responsibility to the states; yet this evasion of major questions meant that their ideas became increasingly stale. The dynamic character of the early Jackson movement faltered and Democrats flourished only because the sterility of their opponents was even more clear.

It is a characteristic of modern democracy that much is expected of government. These aspirations become manifest in parties, and it is inevitable that many of them will be concerned with material gains, welfare, and class relations; but there come points when solutions have to be found to moral problems. No society can exist if its members believe that its basic principles are unjust, and sooner or later conscience demands that moral questions must be faced and answered. Conscience governs personal conduct, but becomes political when public ends have to be achieved.

As political history is never simple, the emergence of political

---

1. George Bancroft, *An Oration to the Democracy of Springfield* (Springfield, 1836), 30.

conscience must be discovered by a close study of the interplay between events and ideas. For this reason much of this book examines the effect of specific issues and events on the minds of individuals or groups, but beneath this detail run the three great currents of nineteenth century thought—religion, rationalism and romanticism. The impulse for moral betterment, the conviction that problems could be solved by constitutional argument, and the urge to grasp large truths intuitively, are recurrent themes of the period. The wish to do good was concerned with the whole field of human endeavor but inevitably fastened upon slavery as the greatest of evils. Rationalism generated the optimistic hope that difficulties could be met, and many believed that slavery need not be attacked because it was doomed by progress. Ironically, reasoned argument readily provided support for slavery, though rejected by Northern thinkers, and Southern political conscience demanded national responsibility for an institution apparently justified by scientific observation, essential for the well-being of a society of two races, and sanctioned by the Constitution. The catalyst that made morality and rationality explosive was romantic nationalism. As the nation ceased to be merely an association of states and became a corporate person, with the will to act, it was inevitable that its character and actions must be made acceptable to political conscience.

The rival claims could not be fully satisfied, but the political system still had enough resilience to make agreement possible. What was essential was not a compromise worked out as a treaty between hostile powers but the reestablishment of an arena in which men could argue, cooperate, agree to differ, and accept majority decisions. The compromise reached in 1850 made no more than a temporary repair to the system, while alienating the men who claimed to be the keepers of the American political conscience. It did not satisfy the most active, and, in some ways, most clear-headed men in the South. It was an abomination to a small but articulate element in society which could draw upon the deep wells of universal Christianity and revolutionary American tradition. The consequences are too well-known to require further comment.

The annexation of Texas and the Mexican War persuaded some Americans that their nation had acted and might continue to act immorally. Subsequent events convinced many Southerners that the nation would not and could not protect their essential interests. It was always possible that even at this late stage some revolutionary event would have changed the course of history, but hypothesis does not alter the fact that the damage done was not repaired. It can never be known whether wounds would have healed if the parties had retained their vitality, but at least we know that their failure coincided with the deterioration of national life. Political conscience had broken one party and debilitated the other; perhaps they had always been too weak to stand the strain, but the strong bases which each had built in every state suggest that wiser leadership might have preserved organizations which were durable, resilient, and capable of satisfying moral or material aspirations

Looking at events as they were and not as they might have been, crucial importance attaches to the formation of a political tradition that was to influence the future. For this reason more space than some would think justified is devoted to the minority among Massachusetts public men who accepted the appellation "conscience Whig." Attention is also given to dissent within the Democratic party, from the introduction of the Wilmot proviso to the nomination of Martin Van Buren as the Free Soil candidate for president. Abolitionism, especially in its Garrisonian form, is not treated directly. There are several excellent, stimulating and diverse studies of abolitionism, and, as many Southerners believed, a generation of teaching and preaching had prepared a majority in the North for total rejection of Southern society. But the Northern men of political destiny were not abolitionists; they disliked slavery, but their opposition became active only when they saw danger in the proposition that slavery was permanent and national. The moment of decision came with the realization that, if tendencies were not checked, a citizen of the United States, wherever born and bred, would stand before the world as a man who paid taxes, fought wars, and obeyed laws in order to extend and perpetuate slavery.

For similar reasons the Liberty party is given no more than incidental treatment. Some of its members, such as Salmon P. Chase, came to play an important part in public affairs, but as an independent political force its influence was severely circumscribed. The Liberty party might have gone on to gather more support, attract able leaders, and survive as an independent third party; but it did not do so. Despite the increase in the Liberty vote between 1840 and 1844, the party was losing momentum and attempts to broaden its base as a party dedicated to the rights of all races made little public impression. Political abolitionism became significant only when the Liberty party lost its identity in the broad-based Free Soil movement. It was fear of the extension of slavery, and identification of the slave power, which changed the character of American politics when nine years of effort were about to lead the Liberty party into a dead-end street.

Less space is devoted to the evolution of Southern thought, but it is essential to emphasize two aspects of the change which took place during this period. The first is already well-known. Dominant ideas about slavery moved from acceptance of inherited evils to positive defence of an institution which ought to be preserved. In this transformation religion, humanitarian argument, economics, science, and medicine were enlisted in the common cause. The second aspect has been less fully investigated. This was the collapse of opposition to slavery by non-slaveholders, and its replacement by positive support. Both developments are linked to nationalism, expansion, and the attempt to prevent the extension of slavery. The positive defence of slavery by the upper class had slowly gathered strength for some years, but Northern opposition to the annexation of Texas and the Wilmot proviso brought forth a flood of pro-slavery writing in journals and pamphlets. Most of this literature was written by slaveowners for large slaveowners, but it was the plain people of the South who would suffer material disadvantage if prevented from improving their lot in the traditional way by moving with slaves to new land. Moreover the Free Soil emphasis was not on the evil of slavery itself but on condemnation of the white society that slavery had created. This was a reproach which few Southerners could tolerate, and their reactions were predictable.

A chapter is devoted to the Compromise of 1850, in which it is argued that it was a symptom of political degeneration and a cause of more that followed. This is likely to be a controversial judgment since generations of Americans have been brought up to believe that the Compromise was worth the effort, and that blame for its subsequent failure rests with a new generation of lesser men. The basic assumption of the Compromise was that it was better to adjust political mechanism rather than face fundamental issues, and its effect was to perpetuate the idea that the country was divided into two separate societies which could remain in union only by refusing to discuss the future of slavery. This involved the further demand that men who disliked slavery must accept black servitude as the price of white union. Events would quickly show that the Compromise itself provided fresh fuel for the fires of political conscience. The basic error lay in the use of methods which were of proved success in dealing with the normal stuff of politics—patronage, struggles for power, and economic disputes—to satisfy men who were not content merely with the preservation of the Union but wanted to know what kind of Union it was to be.

The book closes with observations on some Northern reaction to the Compromise of 1850. The separation between conservatives and radicals became clear, but the latter, despite defeat, had a sense of history on their side. They were heartened when men of books and religion were moved to public declaration that the nation could not progress so long as the slave power flourished. For those who believe that politics can be understood exclusively in terms of power struggle, ethnic rivalry, religious difference, and status anxiety, the conclusions of intellectuals are of little significance. For those who believe otherwise, the new note struck by Ralph Waldo Emerson's lectures or Henry Ward Beecher's sermons was the most significant outcome of an unhappy decade.

The party system existed within a federal, constitutional, and democratic framework. This Introduction may therefore conclude with some brief observations on the way in which institutions conditioned controversy. A federal society may develop in one of two directions, toward greater local autonomy or stronger central authority, and controversy is likely to arise whenever new issues force a choice between the two. Growth and change in the economy presented new questions that could not be answered without exposing tension between local and central government. Familiarity with arguments did not lessen the intensity with which they were pressed. When the subject was new—such as federal responsibility for new territories—the argument became deeply involved in semantic and historical rhetoric. The federal principle was universally accepted but its application generated heat that threatened to damage the whole structure.

The Constitution defined powers, and when disputes arose the first remedy was to examine its provisions. The Constitution was the product of a period when balance between powers was regarded as the safeguard for freedom. An equilibrium of force was envisaged, and statesmanship demanded its preservation; but the static ideal was disturbed by the dynamics of change, and each new development became the occasion for controversy. Appeal to the Constitution meant that the most frequent arguments were retrospective and in American rhetoric the word 'conservative' acquired quite unusual emotive force.[2]

The Constitution commanded respect, and though it could not

2. John C. Calhoun, *Works,* ed. R. K. Crallé, 6 vols. (New York; 1853–55), I. In his *Disquisition on Government* John C. Calhoun defined the "conservative principle" as that by which governments are "upheld and preserved."

cover all contingencies, its interpretation all too readily became a substitute for realistic appraisal of social and political issues. It was assumed that the Constitution contained untapped reserves of meaning, and hours or days were exhausted in minute (and usually incompatible) accounts of what the Founding Fathers intended.

In practice these exercises in constitutional logic invariably applied external criteria. The most fervent appeals for adherence to the Constitution meant loyalty to concepts that were not found in the document. William Henry Seward encountered much abuse when he invoked 'the Higher Law' in 1850, but at the same period Calhoun declared that the Constitution should be amended to preserve an equilibrium between slave and free states. Seward placed the Constitution under the arch of civilized opinion, Calhoun judged it to be inadequate because it did not conform to his individual idea of what it ought to be. In fact, Seward did not suggest that the 'Higher Law' might justify individual defiance of the Constitution, but that external criteria must be applied when the Constitution was silent or ambiguous. In effect he asked that men should do consciously what they had normally done implicitly, and interpret the principles of the Constitution in the light of their social or moral philosophies. Arguments which began with examination of what the Constitution said could never stop short at that point.

Democracy meant two things: defence of individual rights and the expression of collective will. Within the constitutional framework, voters had ample opportunity for protecting their interests; but when every power was checked, the implementation of collective will was more difficult. In practice the national will was always elusive, because the national majority was the product of many local majorities. In the states and districts the collective will of the majority might be clearly expressed, and often in the form of a mandate to Senators and Representatives to do their best for their constituents. Roads, canals, harbors, railroads, and grants of public land were the normal currency of this democratic exchange. The conglomeration of local aspirations in a national policy was necessarily irregular in outline and cemented by platitudes rather than promises.

Politicians were dependent on votes and, in conflicts between local and national aims, the former usually prevailed. When local issues were embarrassing there was a temptation to make the most of emotional appeals which could sublimate them; but when politicians took a moral line the pressure frequently came from below. It did not require more than a minority of dedicated men to persuade the majority, and in Washington, presented with sudden demands for action, congressmen were likely to think of their most articulate supporters, and respond to their imagined demands.[3] Even so it was most unusual for a single measure to gather massive support, when no party whip was applied to bring doubters into line. The unusual happened when Northern representatives, by large majorities in both parties, voted to prohibit slavery in the territories acquired from Mexico.

Federalism, constitutionalism, and democracy were recipes for conflict as well as harmony, and the choice lay in the hands of men at the center who were acutely sensitive to popular pressure. The Washington establishment was smaller and subject to more frequent change than that of other national capitals, and the few men with long experience of public life were likely to be advanced in years. Their views had been formed in the early years of the century, and the era of good feelings had been the apotheosis of their republican ideals. This meant that the political leaders whose words carried most weight were out of touch with the currents of thought which gave vitality to the two parties.

This explains in part the failure to achieve a durable settlement in 1850. Compromise recognized the need to restore conditions in which agreement to get on with the government of the country was possible, but this was achieved by sacrificing political conscience to expediency. In the South many drew the conclusion that their society was regarded as inferior by the Northern majority. A substantial minority in the North believed that the government of their country was committed to injustice. This was the point from which there was no return—perhaps for the nation, certainly for the national two-party system.

3. The ultimate need of a politician to retain or enlarge popular support was often obscured by his immediate dependence upon local party workers. An anonymous writer in *Hunt's Merchants' Magazine* observed in 1843 (Vol. IX: 532ff.) that "by the introduction of the system of ward committees and party conventions, the old electoral franchise has been changed. The majority of the members of the lower house attribute their election, not to the voluntary choice of the people, embracing within its limits each of the various interests which possess the country; but to a self-constituted caucus which represents but one interest and that the basest of all. Political adventurers, office seekers or office-keepers, tavern politicians, form in fact, the constituents of a large part of the lower house." Without denying the force of the criticism (which recurs in every period) it is also true that men who sought to survive in politics had to establish a good reputation among their constituents at large.

# PARTIES AND
# POLITICAL CONSCIENCE:

## ABBREVIATIONS
## USED IN NOTES

The following abbreviation is used for references to the *Congressional Globe*: *Congressional Globe* 30. 1. 123 = *Congressional Globe* 30th Congress, 1st Session, Page 123.

If the word "Appendix" is included in the reference this indicates that the source is the Appendix to the *Congressional Globe* (usually printed as a separate volume) in which revised versions of speeches were printed. For many important speeches an abbreviated text is given in the *Globe*, and the full version appears only in the Appendix.

Congressional documents are referred to in the same way, e.g., Senate Documents 30. 2. V. No. 20. 15 = Senate Documents 30th Congress, 2nd Session. Volume V, Document No. 20. Page 15.

# Chapter 1

# TWO
# PARTIES IN
# ONE NATION

Early in 1840 the Whigs of Ohio called a convention at Columbus for February 21, and for weeks the party newspapers urged attendance even from distant parts of the state. "Let no young or middle-aged Whig speak of rough or bad roads," declared a Cleveland editor, and on February 17 he recorded with approval that a large number had set out. Indeed response exceeded expectation, and by the evening of February 20 many thousands filled the streets of Columbus, and to the east a "dense and uninterrupted stream of the REAL DEMOCRACY" advanced along the national road, while twenty-seven canal boats arrived from the southern counties. On the following morning delegates from the north and west marched in with a band playing the "Marseillaise." One estimate, perhaps exaggerated, put the assembled number at twenty thousand.[1]

Two days of speeches and songs reached a climax with a grand procession such as had never been seen in Ohio or "in all the nation's existence," and enthusiasm was little damped by rain toward the close of the second day. This was the first of many mass meetings organized by the Whigs during 1840. In May the Young Men's Whig Conven-

---

1. The account of the Columbus convention is taken from John C. Miller, *The Great Convention* (Columbus, 1840) and supplemented by information from the *Annals of Cleveland* (A digest and abstracts of the Newspapers of Cleveland undertaken by the Works Progress Administration in Ohio), Vol. XXII, 192–93. See also *Ohio Archeological and Historical Quarterly*, 50 (1941), 135–36. Letters of John M. Woodbridge, 21 and 22 February 1840, to Willis Woodbridge. "Truly this is a movement of the people," wrote Woodbridge, who was a delegate to the convention, "Never since the days of '76 was there so much rejoicing."

tion met at Baltimore, in August Henry Clay was the orator of the day at Nashville, as was Daniel Webster at Richmond in October. At Baltimore, after the close of official proceedings, impromptu meetings continued far into the evening and as "each knew his neighbours to be good Whigs, it was not long before cordial fellowship united all in excellent concord and good humor." At Richmond "the dense mass" of male Whigs was "flanked by galleries of beauty, and of true, sincere, and devoted Whigism of the fairer portion of our species."[2]

The meeting at Columbus presented most points of interest, because it was the first and drew men from so far afield. As one reporter observed, "In crowded cities or in the populous districts of older countries the assembling together of many thousands of persons is neither uncommon nor wonderful. In this country, however, with its sparse and busy population, the voluntary congregation of [such] a throng . . . is indeed, both strange and wonderful."[3] Unlike the urban crowd, rural gatherings could not be spontaneous or accidental, but required planning, publicity, and a multitude of individual decisions to arise and go to a distant place. The Cleveland Whig editor declared enthusiastically that delegates "had left their homes under the solemn conviction that it was their duty to act at once, if they would preserve the stability and purity of their liberties."[4] February might be a slack time for farmers but hardly the month to travel for pleasure in midwestern America. What impulse persuaded men to make the journey? What did they think had been accomplished when the speeches and singing were done? How did "good Whigs" recognize others of the same species? What meaning, indeed, did they attach to the name that their banners carried?

The campaign of 1840 has been fair game for historians, who have been inclined to agree with Andrew Jackson that "by Coon, Coonskins, Sour Cider, and big balls"[5] the people were "led into the destruction of all good Morals and religion." It should rather occupy a significant place in the emergence of modern democracy: it was keenly fought by two parties organized in every state; generated an unpre-

2. Citations from A. B. Norton, *The Great Revolution* (Mount Vernon, Ohio, 1888).
3. Miller, *The Great Convention*.
4. *Annals of Cleveland*, Vol. XXII, 193.
5. Jackson to Francis Blair, 5 March 1844, Blair Papers, Library of Congress, Washington, D.C. "Coon" became the symbolic animal of the Whigs, and Henry Clay was often called "the Old Coon"; the Sour Cider was the hard cider reputed (incorrectly) to be the favorite drink of W. H. Harrison. The "big balls" were rolled along the roads plastered with anti-Democratic emblems. Jackson forgot to mention the log cabin, best-known symbol of Harrison's republican simplicity.

cedented amount of partisan literature; and drew to the polls a proportion of eligible votes higher than in any previous or subsequent presidential election. This was a new dimension in popular government and, despite the crudity of much of the rhetoric, the level of information was often high. If some of the speeches and pamphlets contained nonsense and vulgar abuse, others discussed issues rationally. If Martin Van Buren was the target of much vicious slander, this masked a genuine concern over recent trends in executive authority. If many Whigs spent more energy in singing down their rivals than in arguing with them, this was a symptom of real frustration in an economic depression which Democrats seemed unable or unwilling to remedy.

The operation of a two-party system requires a high degree of political sophistication. There must be an underlying assumption that the varied interests and ideals of a modern society cannot be adequately represented by one party but can be contained in two; that conflicts can be formalized without becoming unreal; and that party organization does not stifle but expresses popular aspirations. However wrongheaded the minority believes it to be, the party winning an election has the right to govern; but the opposition has a legitimate right to proclaim the superiority of its policies and principles. A smooth transition from one government to another must follow the swing of the electoral pendulum, and though partisanship is the lifeblood of a two-party system, it must operate within a framework established by law, institutions, and unwritten conventions.

In a majority of countries, where authority derives its "just power from the consent of the governed," a one-party system has been preferred. In others a multi-party system seems to be the natural pattern, and the character of the government is not determined by popular majorities but by intricate negotiation between party groups at the center. The first experience of a national two-party system in mass democracy is therefore worthy of study in its own right.[6] The knowledge that its breakdown helped precipitate catastrophe has colored the political history of the period, but it is worth remembering that experience between 1840 and 1850 set a pattern to which men tried to return in later years. After the Civil War both parties attempted once more to become national, and it was not the fault of Republicans that the South became a one-party society. After 1945 the solid South began to crack, and the restoration—at least in more developed

---

6. The "second party system" is the first true two-party system. Between 1790 and 1800 neither party accepted the party struggle as a normal and permanent condition.

areas—of a lively two-party system has been welcomed as a return to normal health, even by those with little love for new-style Southern Republicans. Yet in fact normality was fixed by the comparatively short experience of rivalry between Democrats and Whigs.

\*        \*        \*

The beginning of the new party system can be dated with some precision. The name "Whig" was first used as a contemporary label during the year 1833, as an expression of the alarm raised when Jackson, after defying the Senate and dismissing two secretaries of the Treasury, removed government deposits from the Bank of the United States. Traditional associations quickly won the name wide acceptance, and advanced the claim that the new Whigs were lineal descendants of the Revolutionary Whigs in opposition to executive usurpation.[7]

Having originated in opposition to Democratic ascendancy, much of the early Whig rhetoric condemned all parties and did not call for the formation of a new one. In 1835 John Bell, architect of the anti-Jackson movement in Tennessee, proclaimed "Guard against the excesses of party" as a universal maxim for statesmen. Party was "the only source whence destruction awaits our system," and when its spirit received "an organic existence" designed "to control the natural operation of the regular, lawful, and constitutional government . . . the evil which is in party is predominant."[8] Many of the original Whigs echoed these warnings against the excesses of party.

In 1840, with Whig victory imminent, it was the turn of the Democrats to condemn party. The *Democratic Review* deplored "the condition of political demoralization" which seemed to pervade the country. What caused "this frightfully morbid and corrupt state of things," asked the *Review* and, without giving a direct answer, concluded that it was somehow connected with "the detestable poison of *party spirit*."[9]

7. There is sound logic in the observation by Elliott R. Barkan that "in a sense, the name created the party and politicians lost little time in capitalizing on it." (*Portrait of a Party: the Origin and Development of the Whig Persuasion in New York*. Unpublished Ph.D. dissertation, Harvard University, 1968, 213).

8. This speech was made at Vauxhall, Tennessee, and was widely circulated as a pamphlet. It was a principal factor in promoting the candidacy of Hugh White in opposition to Van Buren. Weston A. Goodspeed, *General History of Tennessee* (Nashville, 1887; reprinted Nashville, 1973), 766.

9. *U.S. Magazine and Democratic Review* VIII (September 1840): 199. Hereafter cited as *Democratic Review*.

A closer examination of anti-party rhetoric will show that in 1834 and 1835 it was a protest against one-party rule, and in 1840 a last-ditch stand against the permanent division of the country into two organized parties. The *Democratic Review* could not accept the idea that government should alternate between the two parties, and argued that while Democratic victory would restore national harmony, a Whig victory would perpetuate conflict and damage the country by continued competition for power.[10] There could not be two versions of political truth, and if the Whigs succeeded, they could do so only by misleading the people. This might give them the power to govern, but not a legitimate right to do so.

Were there reasonable grounds for the Whig repudiation of one-party government? Andrew Jackson's domination had become a very personal matter and, in the eyes of his critics, the removal of the deposits was a vindictive sign of autocracy to come. Martin Van Buren, his designated successor, was a man of different temperament but the leading exponent of party regularity. Disciplined majorities might undermine the constitutional checks on executive authority. In the nullification crisis Jackson had won widespread support in the North, but in exceptional circumstances, and by the end of 1834 Philip Hone—an archetypal Whig who may have been the first to use the name in public—retracted his good opinion of the president, and linked abuse of power with party. "Some of his late experiments, . . . must have satisfied him that he may take whatever power he pleases," and "depending upon his popularity with the Jackson party" he could ignore "the petty trammels which restrained the Washingtons, the Jeffersons, and the Madisons of former times."[11]

The prospect of Martin Van Buren's succession suggested that the system of party management perfected in Albany would become national and, ironically, the clearest evidence and most outspoken complaint came from the radical or Loco-Foco Democrats of New York who subsequently became Van Buren's devoted supporters. Their secretary and historian recalled that in New York wards a caucus composed of the "oldest and wisest" decided "the course necessary to be pursued for the good of the whole." The leaders selected a committee and instructed office holders to be present at a meeting of "independent Democratic Republican electors." Following this "the sovereign people were again called upon to approve or disapprove"

10. *Ibid.*, 204.
11. Philip Hone, *Diary,* ed. Bayard Tuckerman (New York, 1889), I: 123.

nominations at a county meeting. A favorite tactic was to have the committee seated on the platform before the public were admitted; names nominated for office would immediately be read over; a voice vote was called for and declared to be affirmative. Then, said "a sagacious politician," "the farce is over, the meeting is adjourned, and the 'regular ticket' is announced next day to those who always submit to the majority and never vote any other."[12]

From precinct to Congress regularity and obedience to majority decisions were cardinal principles of the Democratic party. In 1843 James Buchanan wrote that when the Pennsylvania Democrats in Congress went into caucus, they invariably accepted the result. "Such has always been the practice of the Democratic party in this State and they have always denounced as deserters those who refuse to abide by the decision of the majority."[13] The penalty was proscription, loss of office, and even violence. When William Cullen Bryant's *Evening Post* endorsed the Loco-Focos, he was not only denounced but also lost the public advertising. "The despotism of the Republican Party," wrote the Loco-Foco historian, ". . . was so energetic and pervading in those days, that it required both moral and physical courage to openly attack a dynasty of monopolies, with its vassal office-holders and political committees."[14]

The attempt to impose this discipline upon public men led to one practice with grave constitutional objections. The Constitution decreed that United States Senators should have a six-year term and intended to insulate them from the changes and chances of public opinion; yet it became firm Democratic doctrine that state legislatures could instruct their Senators and demand compliance or resignation. In this way a Whig Senator could be humiliated or a vacancy created. Instructions were defended because a Senator was chosen by the legislature, but in reply it was argued that members of the legislature acted, in this instance, as agents of the people and had no greater claim to be his constituents than any other respectable body of citizens.[15]

12. F. Byrdsall, *History of the Loco-Foco or Equal Rights Party* (New York, 1842), 16.
13. Buchanan to Barnwell Rhett, 25 September 1843, Buchanan Papers, Historical Society of Pennsylvania, Philadelphia, Pa.
14. Byrdsall, *Loco-Foco Party*, 16.
15. This was the argument used by the Whig minority in the Georgia legislature in 1842 when Senator John M. Berrien was instructed to vote against the tariff bill of that year. The protest was written by Alexander H. Stephens, and was used by Berrien in his reply. He also sent a copy to Judge Joseph Storey who promised to incorporate it in the next edition of his *Commentaries*. Berrien voted for the tariff, refused to resign, and was vindicated at the next election, which the Whigs won.

Nevertheless the right to instruct became a fundamental doctrine of the Democratic party. In 1834 Jackson himself wrote instructions that were to be sent to Tennessee Senators, but by the time they were received the Whigs had won a majority which ignored them. Subsequently instructions became a major issue when Thomas Hart Benton moved that the 1833 resolution censuring Jackson should be "expunged" from the journal of the Senate. Some Senators stood by their earlier votes; others declared that they would not reaffirm it, but could not vote to remove the record of what had occurred. Jackson took a personal interest, and several Democratic legislatures were instructed to instruct. John Tyler of Virginia resigned rather than obey, and thereby contributed to a reputation that won him the vice-presidential nomination for 1840. Willie P. Mangum of North Carolina would not obey instructions, but resigned when the Democrats won the state elections and gave that rather than the instructions as his reason. In 1837 the Whigs won control in North Carolina and requested their Democratic Senators to represent the wishes of the people; they refused on the ground that the letter was not framed as an instruction, but resigned when the majority of the electorate rejected the right to instruct at a subsequent election. Thus the controversy came near to establishing the precedent that a Senator, despite his six-year term, was bound to follow the election returns.

The increase of executive authority, the manufacture of public opinion, and public pressure on critics have been familiar steps in the establishment of modern one-party states. There was an equally familiar ring about the Jacksonian habit of branding all opponents as "Federalists" and implying that they were an aristocratic or monied conspiracy against the people. Neither Jackson, Van Buren, nor any of their supporters set out to establish authoritarian rule, but the experience of modern times suggests that the fears of their critics were not groundless.

This association between the origin of the Whig party and opposition to executive influence based upon one-party rule became a familiar and persistent theme in Whig rhetoric. In 1844, John Pendleton Kennedy, a leading exponent of Whig policies, wrote that "it was a poor device of the enemy to complain, in 1840, that the Whigs were a party without principles. . . . Every man in this nation who had given his mind to public affairs, was aware that the Whig party was organized in 1830, as in 1776 it was organized, to resist Executive encroachment."[16] Four years later he claimed that there was one thing

16. *Defence of the Whigs* (New York, 1844), 48.

to which the Democrats had "been invariably true, and that was to the encouragement and extension of the Executive power of the Government."[17] In 1844, William H. Seward placed first among Whig principles the "jealousy of executive power and strict adherence to a system of firm and equal representative legislation."[18] And in 1848 Tom Corwin, probably the leading Whig west of the Appalachians, claimed that the policies of the party—tariff, currency, and internal improvements—were mutable and responded to changing circumstances, but "the principles upon which that party is founded are older than all these. . . . Look back for centuries, and across the water, and you will find that John Hampden was the first Whig and laid down his life in defense of their principles. *It was opposition to the one man power*."[19]

\*        \*        \*

While fears of executive authority and party despotism were the principal themes of the new party, popular response indicated widespread disquiet. The majority of voters were less likely to be concerned by the exercise of power than by the purposes for which it was used. The speculative boom of 1835 and 1836, followed by the financial panic of 1837, the uncertainties of 1838–9, and the depression that gathered full force in 1840, all contributed to the rising tide of criticism. The Whigs inherited National Republican policies, and Henry Clay was anxious to vindicate "the American system." Though most large manufacturers were reconciled to the falling scale of duties under the Compromise Act of 1833, small manufacturers and craftsmen associated their economic difficulties with diminished protection. The financial panic of 1837 caused many failures, a subsequent cutback in credit, and the depreciation of notes issued by many state banks. The metropolitan banks of the East charged a high premium on bills from more remote parts of the country, and might refuse to accept them if the source was suspect or unknown. During the years of expansion several states had embarked upon ambitious canal and road programs; the depression caught them with heavy debts and no prospect of a return on investments for many years to come. In addition the plight of manufacturers and the cutback on

17. *National Intelligencer,* 18 October 1848.
18. *Niles' Register*, 23 March 1844 (from a speech to the Whigs of Cayuga and Cortlandt Counties).
19. *National Intelligencer*, 2 July 1848.

improvements led to unemployment, while depression drove many societies dedicated to social, moral, and philanthropic reform into deep financial difficulties. Thus depression had a direct effect upon banks, state governments, industrial labor and high-minded members of the middle class.

There were, therefore, ample reasons why the party that had been in power since 1829 should bear the weight of complaint, particularly as critics could make a strong case that Jackson's anti-bank policy, the placing of government deposits in state banks, and the specie circular of 1835 were major or even fundamental causes of the economic difficulties. Democrats were more likely to blame intervention by state governments, unwise speculation, and the erosion of moral values in business enterprise. The pressure of business on state governments was denounced as corrupt, and further ills were prophesied if the national government intervened to save states and individuals from the consequence of their folly. In 1848 a Democrat attempted a general definition of his party's character which deserves quotation:

> The Democratic Party seeks to reach the whole people, and to secure equal rights to all, without unjust sacrifice to any. It stands upon the basis of the Constitution, and yields none of its safeguards to construction. It sustains the humble citizen in all his rights, and the States in their prerogative of sovereignty. It favors simplicity of life, the elevation of the people, and rigid economy in the administration of government. It acts from itself outwardly, and seeks to extend the greatest good to the whole people.[20]

Many years later, when memory of the Whigs was almost erased from the public mind, Robert C. Winthrop, who had played a leading part in their councils, asked rhetorically, "What was the party of which Henry Clay and Daniel Webster were so long the leading lights, and of which Abraham Lincoln, to name no other, was so long one of the lesser luminaries?" It was, he said, a Constitutional Union party, a "law and order party, which tolerates no revolutionary or riotous processes of reform." It was conservative, yet also a party of progress, and it was a party of peace at home and abroad. "It was, above all things, a National Party, extending over the whole country,

---

20. Nahum Capen, *The Republic of the United States* (New York, 1848), 169.

and systematically renouncing and repudiating all merely sectional organizations and issues."[21]

In 1841, Horace Greeley, fresh to his task as the self-appointed philosopher of the Whig party, fastened upon the famous sentence, "The best government is that which governs least," which appeared on the title page of every issue of the *Democratic Magazine*.

> Just think of it! What a stupendous, a fatal mistake our revered fathers must have made in forming and adopting our federal Constitution! What palpable mistakes have since been made by the Free States in establishing, fostering and endowing our common schools! They ought to have "governed least" to please the *Democratic Review,* and let the children of ignorance and vice grow up ignorant and vicious in sad succession forever! And so of roads, bridges, and all those common conveniences which make up the advantages and comforts of civilized life. All these should have been left to individual enterprise and caprice.[22]

This was to be a persistent theme and seven years later Greeley summed it up by saying that "the great fundamental principle" of the Whig party was that "government is not merely a machine for making war and punishing felons, but is bound to all that is fairly within its power to promote the welfare of the people—that its legitimate scope is not merely negative, repressive, defensive, but is also affirmative, creative, constructive, beneficent."[23] This may seem an overstatement in view of the meager Whig record in federal legislation, and the known reservations by some Southern Whigs on the extent of federal power, but it becomes a statement of hard fact when one looks at the record in the states. Not, of course, that the Whigs had succeeded in everything they intended nor that all Democrats opposed roads, canals, and railroads, but across the nation in most states the Whigs sought to employ government to promote economic and social development.

This positive view of the general government was important in Whig rhetoric. When in 1844 leaders of the party realized somewhat tardily the need for a monthly of intellectual distinction, they spon-

---

21. Robert C. Winthrop, *Memoir of Henry Clay* (Boston, 1880), 21.
22. *New York Tribune*, 2 September 1841.
23. *Ibid.*, 2 June 1848.

sored the *American Whig Review,* which made an enlarged view of the government of the United States its persistent theme. The *Review* invariably referred to the "National Government," and observed in 1848 that Loco-Focos never mentioned the government "without prefixing the word 'federal' . . . to convey the idea of its being a mere federation of States."[24] Many Southerners had come into the party by the State Rights road, and in Georgia, which became for a short time the principal bastion of Southern Whiggery, the name "Whig" did not replace "State Rights" until 1842. There is however considerable confusion over what was understood by State Rights doctrine. It meant a belief that states retained their sovereignty over most activities affecting the daily lives of citizens, and that this area of responsibility should not be diminished by federal encroachments; it implied that ultimately a state possessed the right to decide whether it would remain in the Union, but not that this right should be used as a constant threat; it was usually combined with strict construction but not with the abdication of public responsibility for social problems.

In the nullification crisis many of those who subsequently became Whigs in Georgia found themselves in an equivocal position. They disliked the tariff of 1828, but did not think it unconstitutional; they believed that a state had the right to protest against federal action, but regarded nullification as a great folly; they thought that a state had the right to be wrong, but not at the expense of the Union; they refused support to South Carolina, but disliked Jackson's threat to coerce a state. Nevertheless these difficulties were not common to all Southerners. A sizeable minority had been elected as National Republicans, and several others who had entered Congress as Jackson men were strongly nationalist. As Charles G. Sellers pointed out many years ago, the voting record of Southerners in Congress from 1833 onward shows that "a majority of southern anti-Jackson men were far from being state rights doctrinaires."[25]

Moreover even Whigs who did incline toward State Rights were often active promoters of state participation in economic activity; and, though a sizeable minority had opposed rechartering the Bank of the United States in 1833, the crisis of 1837 and the depression caused them to reconsider the case for a national institution to regulate the currency and provide credit. With relatively weak banking institu-

24. *American Whig Review,* New Series VII (July 1848): 11.
25. "Who were the Southern Whigs?," *American Historical Review,* XIX, no. 2 (January 1954): 339.

tions the Southern states were acutely embarrassed when regulation at the center faltered, and the Democratic separation between government and banks destroyed what confidence remained. Hard money was an even more severe threat to an economy short of easily realizable assets. In 1841 the *National Intelligencer* observed that a great change had taken place in the South in views on financial policy, and anticipated that "from some of the States hitherto most opposed to a National Bank" there would be in Congress a "nearly unanimous expression of sentiment in its favor."[26] This expectation was fulfilled, for with very few exceptions Southern Whigs gave solid support for both abortive bank bills in the special session of Congress in 1841. It was the Whig misfortune that one of the exceptions was President John Tyler.

Southern Whigs were less happy about the tariff, but in the circumstances of 1841 they knew that the government revenue had to be increased and were prepared to allow discrimination in the duties to favor American manufactures.[27] John M. Berrien, Senator from Georgia, was at first in some trouble in his state for supporting the Whig tariff but triumphantly survived attacks. In a progressive state such as Georgia it was not beyond hope that manufactures would take hold, and there was much support for the protective system in the upper South. Moreover, if Southern Whigs were divided over the tariff, most of them were positively attracted by a proposal to distribute the revenue from the sale of public lands to states in proportion to their population. This was the keystone to the Whig arch that Henry Clay was trying to build and in 1842 Willie P. Mangum, an influential Whig Senator from North Carolina, wrote to him: "I am glad to find the Northern and Eastern men generally holding on tenaciously to the Land Law—the Southern Whigs will go very far to gratify them in a tariff if they shall stand by the Land Law."[28] Mangum eventually voted against the tariff of 1842, but only after Tyler's veto had killed the distribution of land revenues.

Whigs learned to talk the same language in Washington because it continued a debate to which they were already accustomed. In Georgia the well-to-do lawyers and planters of the State Rights–Whig party had vigorously prompted the building of railroads to give the upland cotton planting region access to the sea. Nor were Whig

26. *National Intelligencer,* 11 May 1841.
27. Southern Whig attitudes toward the tariff are discussed in Chapter 3.
28. Mangum to Clay, 15 June 1842, Clay Papers, Library of Congress, Washington, D.C.

policies in the South solely the concern of the prosperous. In North Carolina an exceptionally conservative group of planters, led until his death by Nathaniel Macon, had held back the development of the state, to the dissatisfaction not only of commercial interests in the east but also of the poor but populous farming counties of the west. In 1834 a split in the ruling elite led to the emergence of the Whig party, which is described by the most recent historians of the state as "strongest wherever slaves were fewest" and "preeminently the party of the democratic small farmers, merchants and businessmen who desired the economic development of the state."[29] It controlled the state government for an unusually long period (1836–1850), and did much to bring North Carolina into the nineteenth century. Money received from the national government when the surplus was distributed was invested in banks, railroads, and drainage schemes with anticipated profits to form a fund for public education. A public school of law of 1839 was intended to build schools, which would be free to all whites; it did not work as well as hoped but 2,657 schools were in operation by 1850.

Louisiana was unusual in having a group of prominent sugar planters who favored protection and, in combination with the major part of the business community of New Orleans, they formed the backbone of the Whig party, with popular support in the poorer counties, and won an easy victory in the state elections of 1838. They were more concerned with national than local issues but had a direct interest in the possibility of federal aid for the improvement of river and harbor facilities.[30]

Tennessee played a notable part in the rise of the Southern Whigs for the home state of Jackson and Polk witnessed the first major Southern revolt against Jackson's leadership, in which John Bell was the leading spirit and Senator Hugh White presidential candidate in 1836. Then as now the state was sharply divided into western, central, and eastern sections, and the emergent Whig party depended upon an alliance between the old but poor "white" counties of the east and the comparatively prosperous but recently settled counties of the west. East Tennessee had a paramount interest in internal improvements with much to gain by links with the Atlantic and with the Mississippi River system. In 1836 the Whig legislature passed an act by which the

29. Hugh T. Lefler and Albert R. Newsome, *North Carolina: the history of a Southern state,* 3rd ed. (Chapel Hill, 1973), 357.
30. William H. Adams, *The Whig Party of Louisiana* (Lafayette, 1973), 15–16, Chap. II *passim.*

state was to subscribe one-third of the stock for all new railroads and turnpikes, and in 1838 a state-owned bank was set up and enlarged aid plans for internal improvements were authorized. The bank was to contribute a part of its profits to a common schools fund. The depression meant that both acts failed to achieve their purposes, and the only tangible benefits were a number of comparatively expensive turnpike roads in middle Tennessee where a majority had been opposed to the whole scheme. The political balance was too close to permit much bold experimentation, and it was not until the later 1840s that state aid for railroad building was revived.[31]

Looking at the South as a whole there is much to support the argument advanced by Charles G. Sellers that the Whig party in the South was "controlled by urban commercial and banking interests, supported by a majority of the planters, who were economically dependent on banking and commercial facilities"; but to this one must add that much of the voting support came from poorer, backward counties where improved communications and credit were major issues, and make some qualification about the "majority" of planters.[32] Only in Georgia and Alabama were the small farmers of the "white" counties predominantly Democratic. Sellers is certainly correct in saying that "the southern people divided politically . . . over much the same questions as northern voters, particularly questions of banking and financial policy," and recent studies by economic historians make it clear that the South was not a stagnant region dominated by economically conservative planters, but developing as fast or almost as fast as other parts of the country. Economic expansion stimulated intense political activity both among those who had gained, and could see the prospect of further gain, and those who were conscious of being denied their fair share and demanded action to redress the balance. In some areas the rise of the Whig party was also associated with a revolt against leadership by old-style planting gentry for whom a secure social status, low taxes, and local autonomy were major political virtues. The Whig party in the South therefore contained the two principal ingredients for successful political action: an educated leadership with clear economic interests at stake, and a popular base composed of men who believed that money and effort were necessary to bring them benefits that they deserved.

31. Stanley J. Folmsbee, Robert E. Corlew, and Enoch L. Mitchell, *Tennessee: a short history* (Knoxville, 1969), 251–55.

32. "Who were the Southern Whigs," p. 346.

What is often overlooked is the extent to which Whig leader-
ship, in its heyday, was Southern. Henry Clay was both Southern and
Western; his close friend and ally John M. Berrien was a Georgian and
former member of the State Rights party; Willie P. Mangum was from
North Carolina, William Archer from Virginia, and John Bell from
Tennessee. They made a powerful Southern group in the Senate; in the
House party leadership was more Northern, but even there the South
was prominent.

In several northern and western states there is a similar unwritten alliance between the more ambitious financial, commercial, and
manufacturing groups and the less developed regions with most to
gain from economic development. One should beware of interpreting
these categories too rigidly, and it will be suggested later that there
were traditional and emotional reasons why men in the same social
and economic situation reacted differently. There are also complicat-
ing factors which destroy a clear-cut division along the lines of
economic interest. In New York the success of the Erie Canal meant
that government aid for internal improvements was not a major issue,
and the argument—which cut across parties—was over which towns
or districts should be served by new schemes. In the newer western
states internal improvements were equally popular, and both parties
strove to make political capital by serving local needs. In Pennsylvania the state had become heavily involved, and heavily indebted,
through investment in canals and roads, and neither party could claim
credit for success or escape blame for failure. In all states, however,
depression did make the treatment of public debts a major issue—
with Whigs arguing the need to keep up confidence and Democrats
favoring ways to ease the burden on taxes—and made the distribution
of public land revenue a popular issue. Here again there is a qualification, because in western states both parties maintained that if any
revenue was to be distributed the states containing public lands
should get a larger share.

The tariff issue was also somewhat complicated. In Pennsylvania
both parties were equally committed to protection, and in New York
and New England many Democrats favored it. In the West, as in the
South, the Whigs argued for future and national benefits rather than
for immediate gains, so that argument over the tariff tended to be an
abstract rather than a concrete question. In the Great Lakes area,
where small local manufacturers felt competition from imported
goods, there was more active interest in protection and Whigs reaped
political gains. Eastern Ohio was a center of the woolen textile indus-

try, which always had a strong interest in protection against imported British products. On the other hand there were wealthy shippers and importers in the eastern ports who favored free trade, as did many of the bankers handling international payments. Bankers who were interested in raising capital from European sources—some of them as correspondents for the great London firm of Baring Brothers—were not much concerned either way by the tariff but had a direct interest in the distribution of public land revenues, which might enable the indebted states to meet payments on bonds placed abroad.

As one might expect in a society of growing complexity attitudes toward economic issues in the North were mixed. There were good reasons why men should favor a party though not agreeing with all its policies, and there were equally good reasons why they should agree with some of its policies without giving it political support; but on banks and currency almost all Whigs made common cause. For all who were interested in economic growth a stable but flexible currency was essential; it had to be uniform in value in all parts of the country, command international confidence, and yet be able to meet demands for credit in an expanding economy. Jacksonian monetary policies failed to meet all three criteria. The deposit of government funds in state or "pet" banks had encouraged excessive issues of paper and no one could be certain whether a bill from a distant part of the country deserved acceptance. Uncertainty over the value of American money meant embarrassment in meeting external debts and difficulty in attracting foreign investment.

For Whigs the democratic remedies—the Independent Treasury and hard money—were almost worse than the disease. Large sums of money would be withdrawn from private banks and placed in the Treasury where they could not provide security for commercial credit, while the need to find specie would prevent bankers from taking legitimate risks when making advances to clients with good prospects. The *Democratic Review,* while admitting the need for some banks, thought that they should issue no small notes and few large ones; their function should be to receive deposits, deal in exchange, and act as agents between lenders and borrowers.[33] In other words, bankers themselves could not take the initiative in deciding what enterprises they would back and to what extent. Most Whigs believed that the only real solution was a return to some form of national bank, which could make commercial advances, receive deposits from other

33. "Currency Reform," *Democratic Review* VII, no. 27 (March, 1840): 195–208.

banks, regulate issues by deciding the rate at which it would accept notes, and set up branches in the main commercial centers.

Analyses of party leadership have revealed little ethnic or socio-economic differences between the leaders of the two parties, but contemporaries were able to perceive other differences.[34] Shared endeavors, social intercourse, and the use of a common rhetoric molded character, so that the response to events was usually predictable. From the national capital to the urban ward or rural county, Whigs and Democrats might be expected to give different answers to all questions about the responsibilities of government, presidential power, banks, public aid for internal improvements, and relief for indebted states. These differences extended down the social scale, and local circumstances decided which should be dominant at any one level. Maps showing voting preferences can be misleading unless supplemented by the figures. For instance, the Whigs were strong in the "black" counties of Georgia, but even a "black" county contained many white voters and the majority would probably be men of fairly small property. Old feuds, which went back to colonial days, could become identified with the contemporary party conflict, and traditional rivalries were often a more reliable indicator of party allegiance than contemporary economic interest.

In December 1844 the *Democratic Review* offered some thoughtful observations on what people voted for and what was decided by elections. "There is one broad, paramount issue, strongly drawn and universally made up all over the country, and very apt to swamp many of the partial questions which the discussions of the general controversy may introduce into the canvass. It is simply this—*Which of the two great leading parties shall be placed in power?*" There might be many minor and some major issues but "many a vote—perhaps a majority of votes—is given, one way and the other, by those who, on the whole, in view of all the considerations involved, prefer the ascendancy of their *party*, even though there may be one or more points, in its present policy, which they do not approve, and do not mean to be understood as approving."[35] This statement would be generally ac-

34. But the data relied upon by Lee Benson in his *Concept of Jacksonian Democracy: New York as a Test Case* (Princeton, 1961) to prove this point may not be entirely typical. The long tenure of power by Van Buren's "Albany Regency" meant that an unusually high number of banking and commercial interests were attached to the Democratic party. Sellers stresses the commercial and transportation interests of many Southern Whig leaders which distinguished them from men engaged exclusively in planting.

35. *Democratic Review* XV, no. 78 (December, 1844): 531–32.

ceptable to most modern political scientists who have studied the vexing problems of party affiliation and voter support. It points to deeper wells of support for parties than the analysis of groups, interests, and issues can reveal. It does not demonstrate irrationality in politics, for it may be as rational to support men because their records and tradition will incline them to act in a certain way, as it is to declare support because specific commitments have been made.

Democrats believed that their men, when faced with specific issues, would think first of protecting the rights of individuals, then of giving effect to majority decisions with the reservation that government must be "wise and frugal," and finally reacting with suspicion and alarm to the designs of monied men. Whigs believed that government had a responsibility to initiate some improvements that were beyond the capacity of individuals to undertake, and support others that seemed to be useful to the public. Development, protection, and promotion were the themes. The differences were accentuated by a depression during which Democrats argued that states and individuals must be left to endure the consequences of their folly, while Whigs argued that states should be helped by a distribution of the revenue for public land rates, and individuals by a bankruptcy act.

Though the contrast in attitudes was clear, there was a continuing doubt about names. To the Whigs every Democrat was a "Van Burenite" or, better still, Loco-Foco with its hint of raving egalitarianism. To Democrats every Whig was a Federalist serving the monied power while deviously claiming support from the people. In 1838, campaigning in Tennessee, James K. Polk claimed that he had been abused and slandered because he had had "the temerity stubbornly to refuse to betray the old-fashioned Republican constituents," whom he represented, and had resisted the "covert, selfish and concealed designs, to transfer them, with their principles, to the embraces of their Federal opponents."[36] He would call the Whigs "Federalists" to his dying day. Real or imagined association with the Hartford Federalists could be anticipated whenever Democratic orators launched an attack on their rivals.

In 1844 the Address of the Whig Convention of Virginia declared that "the advocates of Martin Van Buren will assume to themselves exclusively the name of republican, whilst they will endeavour to cast odium upon the Whigs by attaching to us the name of federalist."[37] Occasionally Whigs wondered whether their name had

---

36. Quoted Charles G. Sellers, *James K. Polk: Jacksonian* (Princeton, 1957), 348.
37. *Niles' Register*, 2 March 1844. Reporting the Address of the Whig Convention of Virginia.

sufficient magic for the voting masses, but the *Tribune* told them to
hold fast for "it is short, pithy and implies resistance to Executive
Despotism" and also resistance "to that baleful, blighting Jacobinism
which seeks to array the poor against the rich, the laborer against the
capitalist, and thus embroil society in one universal network of
jealousies and bitter hatreds."[38]

Whigs resisted for long the general acceptance of the word
"Democratic" to describe their opponents. As late as 1845 Thurlow
Weed complained bitterly of the way in which Whig congressmen
and the Whig *National Intelligencer* had yielded the point, and observed that "we have only been able to stand our ground, with chances
of success, for the last seventeen years, by denying our opponents'
right to this designation, and by showing that they were false to
Democratic principles."[39] Confusion often reigned in localities where
Whigs were trying to woo traditional Jeffersonian Republicans, and
in 1840 all kinds of designations were being used to describe the
anti-administration forces, while even as late as 1843 the Whigs in
Pennsylvania were still calling a "Democratic Harrison Convention."[40] In 1844 Calvin Colton, a Whig pamphleteer, writing under
the pseudonym "Junius," asserted that "there is scarcely a feature of
resemblance between the democracy which preceded the amalgamation of parties under Mr. Monroe, and the self-styled Democracy that
has sprung up since." The people, he said, had had nothing to do with
this "democracy" which was "strictly a disciplined party under *one
Chief* . . . it had a military character in its organization, discipline,
and effect."[41] But Horace Greeley had no wish to "enter into a scuffle
with the Loco-Focos about the possession of a name which they have,
to a great extent, desecrated. The name of Whig, under which our
ancestors achieved the independence of the country, has an odor of
patriotism about it that we like, and will do well enough for us."[42]

Argument over who might claim to represent what, and under
which name, continued, but the election of 1840 brought men face to
face with the fact that division of the nation into two parties was more
than temporary. The dawn of recognition may be traced in the pages of
the *Democratic Review*. Before the election the *Review* argued that the
conflict between parties should be allowed to die. If the Whigs won

38. *New York Tribune*, 11 November 1844.

39. Weed to Granger, 12 February 1845, Francis Granger Papers, Library of Congress, Washington, D.C.

40. Henry J. Mueller, *The Whig Party in Pennsylvania* (New York, 1922), 89.

41. "Junius," *Democracy* (New York, 1844), 7.

42. *New York Tribune*, 11 November 1844.

"the flames of party spirit would continue to rage throughout the country as violently as before," but Democratic victory would lead to "a new era of repose and harmony—the old opposition dissolving itself, and an interval of tranquility ensuing, to be followed by a gradual recombination of future parties on new grounds of division."[43] This implied that two parties were called into existence by particular crises, but once these were resolved the normal condition of one-party government should be resumed. An organized opposition party was a temporary expedient, not a permanent feature of the political system. This may be contrasted with a Whig view that

> The two great parties of this country will always remain nearly equal to watch each other, and every few years there must be a change. This is essential to the preservation of our liberties. If power stays always in the hands of one party, the leaders would ruin us.[44]

Faced with the election returns, the *Democratic Review* made a discreet but significant change in emphasis. After rehearsing predictable comments on Whig misrepresentation of the issues, the writer went on to admit that long tenure of office was in itself an argument for change:

> Three terms of possession of the Administration constitute alone a strong reason for allowing the Opposition half of the nation to take a fair turn at the helm of government. . . . However, earnestly and conscientiously as we may have deprecated such a national calamity as the success of the Whigs . . . we are not so ill-satisfied with the result, after all as may probably be supposed . . . and probably the day is not distant when we shall all recognize it as the best thing that could have happened for the true and permanent interests of our party and our cause.[45]

In this there were two essential contributions to the theory and practice of two-party government. There was recognition that the "opposition half of the nation" had a right to take a turn at government, and

43. *Democratic Review* VIII, no. 33 (September 1840): 204.
44. "Junius" [Calvin Colton], *The Crisis of the Country* (New York, 1840), 15.
45. *Democratic Review* VIII, nos. 25 and 36 (November and December 1840): 397.

the belief that any party might be healthier for a period out of office.

Some years later Gideon Welles, an ardent Democrat from Connecticut and a somewhat disgruntled office-holder in President Polk's administration, attempted a broad definition:

> In a country like ours where the people are generally intelligent, there must inevitably be differences of opinion on almost all important questions, and these differences extending through a succession of measures resolve themselves into parties. One man looks to the government for assistance, his neighbour relying on his own energies asks only for protection. The former desires special privileges, the latter only equal and exact justice. One believes that general and individual prosperity will be promoted by fostering legislation, the other has no doubt the sum of human happiness and their best and truest interests will be attained by simple and general laws made for the common good of all and the particular benefit of none. One would have the government exercise the ultimate control, the other believes that men are governed too much. Differently constituted and differently nurtured their fundamental opinions, when reduced to practical experience, distinguish between the democrat and the anti-democrat.[46]

The distinctions may appear to be commonplace, but they mark an important stage in the development of democratic theory. A tough Democratic partisan could recognize that the views of his opponents —to whom he would not concede an inch—were grounded on differences of opinion which would be found at every level of society.

In July 1848 another ardent Democrat, Howell Cobb of Georgia, delivered a speech in Congress, which was published as a pamphlet with "The Necessity of Party Organization" as its title, attacking the Whig nominee, Zachary Taylor, for running as a "no party" candidate.[47] What, asked Cobb, was a party? Was it "a mere catchword used to delude, deceive and impose upon the honest people of the land?" Or was there "something in that word of principle, which commends it to the intelligence and integrity of the country."

---

46. Gideon Welles Papers, Huntington Library, San Marino, California. Undated, but probably written in 1847.

47. *Congressional Globe,* 30. 1. Appendix, 775.

Perhaps with conscious echoes from Burke, Cobb went on to define party as "an association of men acting in concert with each other, to carry out great fundamental principles in the administration of Government." However strongly people might feel on specific issues they were powerless unless they were "enabled to manifest themselves in the practical workings of the Government." Party was the instrument of popular will, and attacks on party organization were "a blow at the corner-stone of our whole political system . . . [and] at the fundamental principle of self-government." This was, in a sense, special pleading against Whig attempts to attract Democrats by discrediting party organization, but it carried the implication that both parties should stick to their organization and appeal to the people as party men. By 1848 party had ceased to be a temporary association to get bad men out of government, and had become a permanent organization to promote political principles, while even stern partisans were prepared to admit that there should be two such organizations, with equal claims to legitimacy provided they could win an election.

\*    \*    \*

The argument that political division represented real and abiding differences of attitude and opinion is reinforced by evidence of stable party affiliation, which first became evident in 1836, was still apparent in the twilight of Whig hopes, and not entirely obliterated by subsequent events.[48] In 1836, 1,051 counties made returns in the presidential election, of which 322 went for Van Buren and remained Democratic in the next three presidential contests. A further 89 were Democratic in two, with most defections explained by Harrison's personal success in carrying a block of Indiana counties or the Free Soil intervention of 1848 which lost the Democrats some counties in Pennsylvania and all but two in New York. In other words 322 were consistently Democratic, and a further 89 were lost only in exceptional circumstances. In 1836 Van Buren's three rivals carried between them 381 counties that remained Whig in three and 94 in two subsequent elections. Most of the latter were explained by Whig losses in the South in 1844 and the loss of several Ohio and some New England counties to Free Soil in 1848. Only in 105 of the counties voting in

48. In an essay contributed to *The Nation Divided* (ed. George M. Frederickson, Minneapolis, 1975) I have shown that many of the Southern "white" counties, which voted Whig in 1852, were Republican during and after the Reconstruction years.

1836 did the winning party carry one, and lose two of the succeeding elections, and most of them were in states in which population increased very rapidly during the period.[49] There were few marginal counties in the older settled and more stable regions; no more than three in all New England, four in Pennsylvania, one in New Jersey, five in Virginia, and two in Alabama.

In 1840 there was a very large increase in the numbers voting, and this meant that an abnormally high proportion of those voting did so for the first time in a presidential election. Of the 897,000 increase in the total poll, the Whigs took 534,829 or 59.6 percent. It is a common observation that a man's first vote has a strong influence on his future party loyalty, so the Whigs probably held the majority of those drawn to the polls for the first time in 1840. But the Democrats did better in recently settled areas, and of the counties making returns for the first time in 1840 forty-one became consistently Democratic and only eighteen consistently Whig. In subsequent years the Democrats were far more successful than their rivals in winning new voters: between 1840 and 1844 they increased their vote by 210,683, while the Whig increase was a mere 25,473. In 1848 the Democratic vote was down by 100,000, but this is explained largely by losses to Free Soil of whom a large number returned to the fold in 1852. In the same year the Whigs, with a popular candidate, increased their vote by 60,000 but this was far below the number they should have won to keep pace with population. The Whigs were more troubled than the Democrats by competition from the Liberty and Native American parties, while fusion with the latter in many local elections ensured that every new immigrant Catholic voter would side with the Democrats.

This trend away from the Whigs does not alter the general conclusion that party allegiance became exceptionally stable from 1836 onward, and in happier circumstances the Whigs might well have recovered with new leadership after 1850. A study of county voting shows a very large number of close results, and the persistence of large Whig minorities where the Democrats were in the ascendant. It would not, therefore, have taken much to reverse the trend, just as Republicans were able to reverse it in northern and western states from 1854 onward. A hidden factor in party fortunes may have been an aging Whig leadership still drawn from men who came to the fore before or during the Jacksonian period, while the Democratic setback

49. Indiana (14), Illinois (11), Mississippi (10), Kentucky (8), Georgia (7), Missouri (6).

in 1840 and an internal party revolution in 1844 cleared the way for younger men. This seems to have been true in several states, as well as of the parties in Congress.

The stability of the two-party system is also demonstrated by small swings in the popular vote. In 1836 the parties were almost level, with 50.85 and 49.15 percent; in 1840 the Whigs reached their peak by adding just over 2 percent to their total, while in 1852 the Democratic "landslide" was won with 50.95 percent of the vote. In 1844 and 1848 neither major party had a majority, the balance being held by the Liberty party with 2.3 percent in 1844 and by Free Soil with 10.1 percent in 1848. There was no state in which one of the parties had negligible strength, with Vermont as a possible exception in the Whig camp and New Hampshire in the Democratic, and in all the minority party could count on some wins in local and state elections.

Stability has also been shown by studies of Congressional voting behavior.[50] On all issues save those involving slavery party regularity was very high. Even on some votes that did involve the contentious question men in Congress sought consciously or unconsciously for a formula that would preserve party solidarity. As will be seen, the final vote on the annexation of Texas (perhaps by accident rather than design) followed party lines with few defectors. In the House there were some significant changes in party strength, but these swings were not greater than might be anticipated in a stable political situation in which small shifts in voter preference tend to produce large effects. The period from 1834 to 1840 was one of steadily rising Whig congressional strength; the election of 1842 brought the Democrats a decisive majority, which was not reduced in 1844. Disputes over the Mexican War restored Whig strength, and for four years the parties were near equality with the balance held first by Native Americans and then by Free Soilers; 1850 gave a blow to Whig fortunes from which the party never recovered. In conformity with voting patterns in more recent times, new phases were inaugurated at mid-term rather than at presidential elections.

The stability revealed by figures is confirmed by political geography. In New England the Democrats held Maine and New Hampshire; the Whigs were impregnable in Vermont and Massachusetts,

50. Thomas B. Alexander, *Sectional Stress and party strength: a study of roll-call voting patterns in the United States House of Representatives 1836–1860* (Nashville, 1967); Joel H. Silbey. *The Shrine of Party: congressional voting behavior, 1841–1852* (Pittsburgh, 1967).

## PARTY STRENGTH IN CONGRESS
### 1835–1853

| Congress | Date Elected | D. | W. | Other | |
|---|---|---|---|---|---|
| 24th | 1834–5 | 145 | 98* | — | |
| 25th | 1836–7 | 108 | 107 | 24 | (Calhounites, Anti-Masons, Independent) |
| 26th | 1838–9 | 124 | 118 | — | |
| 27th | 1840–1 | 102 | 133 | 6 | (Whigs supporting Tyler) |
| 28th | 1842–3 | 142 | 79 | 1 | |
| 29th | 1844–5 | 143 | 77 | 6 | (Native Americans) |
| 30th | 1846–7 | 108 | 115 | 4 | ( "         "      ) |
| 31st | 1848–9 | 112 | 109 | 9 | (Free Soilers) |
| 32nd | 1850–1 | 140 | 88 | 5 | ( "     "   ) |
| 33rd | 1852–3 | 159 | 71 | 4 | ( "     "   ) |

*In the 24th Congress the Whig opposition includes several Anti-Masons, States Right Democrats, anti-Jackson Democrats, and some still describing themselves as National Republicans. Source: *Historical Statistics of the United States* (Washington, 1975), 691. It is not possible, in all cases, to reconcile these figures with data derived from the *Congressional Globe*. They must therefore be treated as approximations, but can be used to demonstrate the trend of party fortunes. Some discrepancies can be explained by changes in membership during the life of a Congress, caused by resignations or death. For an example of discrepancies see the vote for the Speakership in the 31st Congress described in Chapter 10.

and strong but not safe in Connecticut and Rhode Island. The Democrats could usually win some congressional seats in western Massachusetts and southern New England. In New York the Democrats normally carried the city, most of Long Island, and all the central counties, while the Whigs were solid in the western part of the state and in several counties in the Hudson valley. New Jersey and Delaware were Whig by safe margins. Pennsylvania was safely Democratic, but there were groups of Whig counties around Philadelphia and Pittsburgh, and along the Maryland border. Ohio was very evenly balanced. The Western Reserve and other counties on the south shore of Lake Erie were Whig, with a large block of Whig counties in the west central part of the state. There were more Whig counties along the Virginia border but the rest of the Ohio valley and the northwestern counties were Democratic. Indiana was a patchwork and one of the few states to make a decided change in its political allegiance during the period: Harrison swept it into the Whig camp, but almost half the counties that he carried went Democratic in 1844 and 1848. Michigan was predominantly Democratic, though there were Whig counties in the developed area on the Indiana border and on the recently settled frontier. Illinois had a number of Whig counties in the center and the northwestern corner. Looking at the Midwest picture as a whole one can generalize by saying that most areas of Whig strength were associated with commercial centers, manufacturers, and New England settlements, but there were also some counties in newly settled or remote areas where the need for internal improvements was probably a decisive issue.

There was a marked difference between the distribution of parties in the upper and lower South; and it is almost correct to speak of two separate party systems. In the lower South the Whig party was associated with plantations, large slave population, and commercial development in the ports and inland centers. By no means all the "black" counties were Whig, but almost all the "white" counties were Democratic. Central and southern Georgia, southern Alabama, the Mississippi valley, southern Louisiana, and the city of New Orleans provided the Whig hard core, while few slaves, no large towns, and many small farms were an almost certain index of Democratic strength. In the upper South the pattern is reversed. There were indeed some Whig counties in the tidewater and prosperous piedmont areas, but "white" counties of the Shenandoah and other inland valleys were Whig. In North Carolina a solid block of western counties made it a predominantly Whig state. Over the mountains Kentucky was solidly Whig except for the northeast and southwest. In Tennessee the east was predominantly Whig, so were most counties in the recently settled west, and there was enough Whig strength in Nashville and the central counties to put the state of Jackson and Polk into the Whig camp in every presidential election, though by the closest of margins. Maryland was overwhelmingly Whig, but an exception to the rule because three western "white" counties were Democratic.

This evidence of stability in the country might lead one to expect continuity in Congress. Nothing could be more untrue. The persistence of a few elderly men in the Senate has given a false impression, for Congress as a whole was a constantly changing body. Of the Senators at the close of the 27th Congress in March 1843, only nine were members of the 31st Congress when it assembled six and a half years later in December 1849. Two Representatives in the 27th were in the Senate of the 31st, and they were joined by one other appointed to fill an unexpired term in June 1850. Twelve Representatives in the 27th were elected to the 31st, and two Territorial Delegates in the 27th were Senators from newly admitted states in the 31st. In all only twenty-six members of the 31st could claim a legislative experience that went back to 1842.[51]

To this short list of experienced congressmen should be added a small number who served both in Congress and the Administration during the decade. Of them the most distinguished were Daniel Webster, John M. Clayton, J. J. Crittenden, R. J. Walker, James Buchanan, and Millard Fillmore. Several of the long-term congressmen were of little influence, leaving a group of perhaps twenty men whose experience in the executive and legislative branches set them apart from their contemporaries. The record is in sharp contrast to that of the British House of Commons where election was for seven years (though in practice the interval between elections was less), and many members were reelected several times. A man appointed to the British Cabinet had probably fifteen to twenty years' service in Parliament, and once appointed to high office was likely to be a member of at least two administrations. This is not to suggest that long tenure was in itself an asset, but to emphasize the point that the Washington "in group" of public men with long experience of national government was always small.

Nor did the parties evolve a central machinery to provide continuity and control. There was no permanent secretariat, and the party caucus in Washington did little more than fix the date for the national convention. Individuals tried to maintain their own network of friends, who were expected to influence events in different parts of the country. Henry Clay was particularly assiduous as a letter writer,

51. Senators in 27th and 31st Congresses: W. R. King (Ala.), J. M. Berrien (Ga.), H. Clay (Ky.), T. H. Benton (Mo.), W. L. Dayton (N.J.), J. W. Miller (N.J.), W. P. Mangum (N.C.), J. C. Calhoun (S.C.), S. S. Phelps (Vt.).

Representatives in 27th and Senators in 31st: J. A. Pearce (Md.), B. Rhett (S.C.) from June 1850, R. M. T. Hunter (Va.).

Representatives in 27th and 31st: T. B. King (Ga.), L. Boyd (Ky.), J. B. Thompson (Ky.), R. C. Winthrop (Mass.)—to Senate, July 1850—J. Thompson (Miss.), E. Stanly (N.C.), E. Deberry (N.C.), A. H. Shepperd (N.C.), J. R. Giddings (Okla.), I. Holmes (S.C.).

Territorial Delegates in 27th and Senators in 31st: A. C. Dodge (Iowa), H. Dodge (Wis.).

Not all of these had unbroken service: Stanly did not serve in the 28th, 29th, or 30th Congresses; Deberry did not serve in the 29th or 30th.

with regular correspondents among influential men in all parts of the Union. Martin Van Buren also wrote a large number of letters (which even frequent correspondents may have found hard to decipher) but relied more upon Democratic regularity to preserve his personal following. Daniel Webster confined his correspondence largely to New England, New York, and Ohio. John C. Calhoun wrote and received many letters, but by far the largest part of his correspondence was with friends from South Carolina, other lower South States, Virginia, and occasionally from Pennsylvania and New York. Judge John Mc-Lean, a less well-known but perennial aspirant for the presidency, maintained a regular correspondence with political friends in Ohio and New York. Of all those who used personal correspondence as an instrument of political leadership, Clay alone won a presidential nomination and he lost the election. There was no party bureaucracy to capture or control; organization sprang to life when a candidate had been nominated, and died after his election.

The rapid changes on the Washington stage were indicative of a general condition in the national political system. The fluidity of congressional membership gave added weight to the few who stayed the course, but there was no continuity in executive leadership and most of those who came to occupy executive posts had little experience of national affairs. Until 1841 all the Presidents had come from an inner circle of men with long experience of public service, and if Jackson seems to be an exception it should be remembered that he had been a judge, Senator, and Territorial Governor, as well as winner of the battle of New Orleans. Indeed his insistence that Van Buren should be his successor confirmed the view that a President should be a man of long political experience.

The nomination of Harrison changed this, and if Polk was not quite so dark a horse as his detractors proclaimed (he had, after all, been Speaker of the House) his experience could not match that of Van Buren whom he replaced. The political ignorance of Zachary Taylor was a byword, and in 1852 the Democrats swung the pendulum back only a little way by nominating an ex-Senator who had made little mark in that body. Political outsiders in the White House tended to put political novices into their cabinets. Harrison did, indeed, choose Webster as his Secretary of State, Polk chose Buchanan, and Taylor appointed Clayton, but all three Presidents filled other offices with men who were little known in Washington.

There is therefore a contrast between continuity in the constituencies, and its lack in Congress and the Executive. Stability was not secured by firm direction at the center, but by local organizations employing traditional ideas and modes of speech enabling like-minded men to communicate with each other and move from chance acquaintance to working partnership.

In most states the parties were rigidly controlled, and office holders provided a core of professional politicians who would carry on through slack times and good. State parties were prone to faction, but they strove to capture the loyal party following rather than to create it. Once in command a faction would pour out a stream of stereotyped propaganda and loyal editors sounded the clarion call to action, but this was effective only when addressed to men already conditioned to believe the party precepts. The party presses might occasionally discover a new application for familiar ideas, but most of the time their success depended upon saying emphatically what was already accepted as true.

The majority of legislators and executive heads had some things in common. Almost two-thirds were trained as lawyers. Among those who carried their education beyond the elementary stage Latin had provided the backbone for the curriculum. Most had a reasonable knowledge of the history of their own country since the Revolution, and this was often extended to seventeenth-century England. Nearly all professed some form of Protestant Christianity, and attended Sunday worship as a public act if not with conviction. These common experiences help to explain a certain monotony in congressional debates, where the same arguments recur though the actors depart and are replaced by others. Common experience, shared knowledge, and similar religious belief also supplied the material for discourse between public men and their followers.

The secrets of party loyalty may therefore be found deep in these common traditions, in different interpretations of similar concepts, and in contrasting response to circumstances and change. One need not expect to find a clear-cut division, separating man from man or class from class, but a large number of different attitudes which collectively—and allowing for many exceptions and qualifications—produced contrasting attitudes toward the problems of man in society. These persistent attitudes, which Gideon Welles and others diagnosed as a perennial argument over the role of government, were deeply rooted in American ideas about the character and purpose of their society.

*Chapter 2*

# THE INTELLECTUAL FRAMEWORK OF THE NEW PARTY SYSTEM

Men who lived in the first half of the nineteenth century were conscious of change in a way that none of their predecessors had been. Material change was an outward and visible sign, but men who pondered the meaning of the times were more impressed by shifts in moral and social attitudes which seemed to press upon the foundations of American life. In 1844 Dr. Walter Channing, an eminent physician of Boston much engaged in works of social reform, pictured civilization as a landscape which seemed so fixed but, under the eye of the geologist, moved from its depths. "The hard crust which has slowly gathered over the soul, the heart of man, of society, is swelling and heaving with the living fire below."[1] As early as 1812 Lyman Beecher, the famous Congregationalist preacher and theologian, viewed change in a different light but was acutely conscious of the contrast between past and present, promise and fulfillment. "No other portion of the human race ever commenced a national existence as we commenced ours. Our very beginning was civilized, learned and pious. The sagacious eyes of our ancestors looked far down the vale of time." This was a retrospect to the close-knit New England community—dominated by Church, school, and selectmen—rather than to the turbulence of the Revolution when Deism, infidelity, and threats to social order had crept in, and helped powerfully to work the mischief. "Our vices," declared Beecher, "are digging the graves of

1. Walter Channing, M.D., *My Own Times or 'Tis Fifty Years Since* (Boston, 1845), 30–31.

our liberties, and preparing to entomb our glory. . . . The mass is changing. We are becoming a changed people."[2]

Over twenty years later George Bancroft—fresh from the influence of German Idealism and already embarked upon his great historical project, but also an active Democratic politician—saw the conflict of the times in a different light. In a Fourth of July oration he developed the theory that modern civilization was the battleground for three rival principles—Tory, Whig, and Democrat. For Tories, the law was the expression of absolute will, for Whigs the protection of privilege, and for Democrats the declaration of right. The conflicts of the age were inescapable, because the three principles could not live together. The Tory principle had been defeated in America when the Revolution rejected monarchy and hereditary rule, leaving the other two struggling to control the nation. This could have but one outcome, for democracy once unchained was by far the more powerful. "Its energy is derived from the will of the people; its object is the welfare of the people." The opponents of democracy said "it is established" rather than "it is right," and this "by its very nature, can apply to nothing but material wealth; because the mind is always in motion."[3] Numbers and moral judgment were on the same side. In his History Bancroft traced the conflict of principles from colonial times, and in contemporary America he saw approaching a time of decision which would be as significant as the Revolution.

William Ellery Channing, influential as a Unitarian minister and a man of letters, was equally convinced that great changes were afoot. In 1841, toward the end of a life which had touched upon all the religious, intellectual, and social excitement of his time, Channing saw that the "commanding characteristic" of the age had been "the tendency for all its movements to expansion, to diffusion, to Universality." The "spirit of exclusiveness, restriction, narrowness, monopoly," which had prevailed in the past, was passing away. Philosophic thought was no longer the privilege of the leisured few, because education, religious controversy, and political action presented to the whole people "great subjects of thought, and bring multitudes to earnest discussion of them."[4] Unlike Bancroft, Channing saw conflict as an unwelcome product of generally beneficial change, and not as the

---

2. *A Reformation of Morals practicable and indispensable: A Sermon at New Haven.* 27 October 1812 (Reprinted. *Lyman Beecher and the Reform of Christianity*, New York, 1972).

3. *Oration, to the Democracy of Springfield,* 4 July 1836, 9.

4. *The Present Age: An Address delivered before the Mercantile Library Company of Philadelphia,* 11 May 1841.

essence of the historical process. There was a danger that conflict debased the mind by concentrating on material advantages, and then "the spirit of collision, contention, discord . . . breaks forth in religion, politics, in business, private affairs." These controversies were the necessary but harmful result of "the selfishness which prompts the endless activity of life." In 1844, Ralph Waldo Emerson, reflecting upon the experience of the preceding quarter century in New England, observed that it had been a period of "great activity of thought and experimenting." "Ardent religion" had been "falling from the Church nominal," and had become manifest in "temperance and non-resistance societies, in abolitionist and socialist movements, in Sabbath and Bible conventions, and in assemblies of ultraists, of seekers . . . and of all the soldiery of dissent." In old age he returned to the theme and placed the turmoil in the context of general theory. There were "always two parties, the party of the past and the party of the future, the Establishment and the Movement"; and sometimes "the schism runs through the world and appears in literature, Philosophy, Church, State, and social custom." Such restless ages were difficult to date precisely but one "made itself remarked, say in 1820 and the twenty years following."[5]

George Bancroft saw his conflicting principles made manifest in the party battles of his time; William Ellery Channing and Emerson saw political conflict as a distraction. Channing was left with the paradox that the trend toward "universality" was accompanied by acrimonious debate and damaging divisions, and evaded the problem by claiming that competition and conflict were explained by the pursuit of "the sensual and material, for gain, pleasure and show." Emerson was more profound in his retrospective comment that there were "always two parties"; but he regarded contemporary political battles as trivial, and largely irrelevant to the great battle of principles that molded nineteenth-century American civilization. Both Channing and Emerson believed that the fundamental question was the nature of authority in religion, philosophy, and government. Traditional authority had been under attack from every quarter, and even where it survived was now so weak that it provided neither moral nor political guidance. Emerson and his fellow Transcendentalists sought a new source of authority in a universal spiritual force which directed the world and yet was present in every man. In this majestic yet vague

5. *New England Reformers* (1844); *Historic Notes of Life and Letters in New England* (first published 1884).

concept there was no room for argument over banks or tariffs or the next election, but awareness of basic conflicts between "Establishment" and "Movement."

Men who had neither Channing's broad and optimistic tolerance nor Emerson's detachment, were more likely to explain their partisanship by identifying it with adherence to "principles" which were invariably vague but not meaningless. The changes of the time caused a disposition to attach value and significance to political conflicts even when their origins could be clearly discovered in personal ambition or resentment, competition between factions for the possession of office, and the crude pursuit of material gain. The significance of party is not explained away when these petty issues have been exposed. It should rather be said that whatever its origin a political movement acquired significance when it was seen as the instrument by which moral and material aspirations could be fulfilled. It would be too much to suggest that each party became a transcendental phenomenon, but it is impossible to explain the durability of party loyalty without recognizing that, despite the hypocrisy of individual politicians, the mass of voters saw in "principles" something more elevated than a horse race or a faction fight.

The minds of men provided the battleground for three great forces of nineteenth-century civilization: rationalism, romanticism, and religious revival. Calvinism was the most rational of religions, and no one can read theological expositions by Cotton Mather or Jonathan Edwards without being impressed by the powerful logic which derived a universal philosophy from a small number of simple precepts; but the rationalism derived from seventeenth-century science and eighteenth-century inquiry was of a different order. Its central concept was that man was master of his world and with knowledge could make it as he wished. God remained as the prime mover and universal spirit of reason, but was no longer a personal Deity, made manifest in Christ, speaking directly to the individual conscience though omniscient and omnipotent.

Scientific rationalism, with its optimistic faith in the power of knowledge, its impatience with the supernatural, and its confidence that man could shape his own destiny, implied a conflict with a deeply rooted Calvinistic tradition that he could do nothing without God and that there were frontiers beyond which human understanding could not venture.

This conflict seldom became explicit in America, as it did in some European countries. There was no need for anti-clericalism, when everyone was free to break off from one Church, join or form another, or cease to worship in any way. Religion in education was an issue, but never of the magnitude that it became in Europe. If there was some pressure to ensure conformity in public schools with a generalized Protestant faith, anyone could and several did establish denominational colleges for higher education. There was deep concern over "infidelity," but it was characteristic of America that it was likely to be detected in respectable Protestant congregations which stoutly maintained their adherence to Christian principles.

The belief that man was master of his world did not produce a major rift in American civilization but, for this very reason, its influence was pervasive. It was evident in revived controversy, within the Churches, over predestination and free will. It divided traditional Churches into old and new schools. It divided the older Universities into those adhering to strict Calvinism, and those accepting less rigorous doctrines. It led to a large number of break-away Churches, and in Massachusetts one of them—the Unitarian—became the dominant force in intellectual life. It even influenced the revivalist movements which might seem to be its antithesis.

In politics the influence of rationalism was profound and the making of the Constitution was a supreme example of rationalist achievement. The Revolution had repudiated metaphysical concepts of authority, and constitution making—first in the states and then in 1787—had worked on the assumption that rational men were not bound by precedent and could select institutions of government best suited to their needs. In a way characteristic of advanced eighteenth-century political thought, it was assumed that a somewhat mechanical balance of forces was the best guarantee for liberty and the pursuit of happiness. In the intervening years Americans had come to revere the work of the "founding fathers" in a way that inhibited political experiment, and the rationalist achievement stood as a barrier against the continuation of rational inquiry. Yet the great work of 1787 had left unanswered some of the fundamental questions about popular government.

There was a contradiction between consent embodied in a Constitution, ratified by the people but binding until amended, and consent embodied in the will of the people revealed at frequent elections. There was no clear distinction between tacit agreement on the spirit and rules of public life, and decision by a majority on specific issues. James Madison in Federalist No. 10 had wrestled with the problem of securing the "permanent and aggregate interests of the community" against the violence of "faction" especially when it formed a majority; but since Madison's day Americans had lost the taste for thinking philosophically about political problems, and contempt for "abstractions" was part of the common wisdom of the day. Yet potential conflict between "faction" (now able to control national government by party apparatus), and the larger interests of the people was the heart of the matter. When one party had become dominant, did not the Madisonian principle require another to restore the equilibrium? Or should one speculate (as did John C. Calhoun) upon ways in which a concurrent or local majority might check the power of the numerical or national majority? This quest for a definition of authority and a redefinition of political balance formed the core of political controversy.

To Europeans the American Revolution had appeared (for good or ill) as rationalism in action. This reputation survived and European reformers continued to regard Americans as pioneers in the substitution of rational for obscurantist principles. Yet the experiment never completely broke with the past, but was deliberately placed in a tradition which ran from Aristotle and English mediaeval constitutional practice to Locke and Montesquieu. This conservative strain, now enshrined in popular regard and intellectual acclamation, prevented the development of a radical critique. The separation of powers, the division of sovereignty between national and state governments, bicameral legislatures, and written constitutions became axiomatic and a whole range of political enquiry became irrelevant. Great Britain, laboring still with antiquated institutions, developed a tradition of rational reform while political thought in the United States sank to the level of constitutional logic chopping. There were no philosophic radicals, no pressure group of ardent utilitarians, and no impulse to investigate in order to reform.

The irrelevance of criticism by intellectuals was accentuated by the environment of a national capital which lacked both commerce and culture. American intellectuals had no metropolitan forum comparable to London or Paris and men of letters preferred New York, Philadelphia, Baltimore, and Boston to Washington. In quality Boston literary culture was unmatched in the English-speaking world, but remained by choice compact and deliberately provincial. A good deal of European rationalism had flowed into the New England mind through the influence of the Scottish philosophers, and this contributed to the reputation, among American readers, of the contemporary *Edinburgh Review*. New England writers were all too aware that none

of their efforts could emulate the influence of the Reviewers whose
trenchant articles might affect government policy. American men of
letters could have no such hope.

The strength of British intellectuals in the nineteenth century
lay in their journals, clubs, and personal contacts with public men.
The London *Times*, the *Edinburgh Review*, and the *Quarterly Review*
were read by everyone of importance and everyone else who wished to
be informed. This was the "public opinion" respected by British
politicians. Criticism was pontifical but caricature could be vicious,
and from 1841 *Punch* made the weaknesses of public men familiar to
the educated middle class across the land. Paradoxically the politicians in democratic America were treated with more deference and
lived more sheltered lives than their aristocratic British counterparts.
They were exposed to polemics but not to ridicule or dissection by first
class minds. It was a part of conventional wisdom that common men
were better judges of policy than experts, and opinion on Main Street
was more significant than the *North American Review*.

It was at this point that the Romantic movement, with its insistence that simple truth was superior to sophisticated reasoning, affected political behavior. George Bancroft epitomized Romantic
thought at the highest level, disliked Locke and eighteenth-century
rationalism, and believed that observation of men in action, not pure
reasoning, would reveal the great moral forces in history. Toward the
end of his very long life he wrote that "the individual who undertakes
to capture truth by solitary thought loses his way in the mazes of
speculation, or involves himself in mystic visions, so that the arms
which extend to embrace what are but formless shadows return empty
to his breast."[6] And at the outset of his career as historian and politician he quoted with approval a passage from Jonathan Edwards:

> Moral truth is from God. Nothing the creature receives is so
> much a participation of the Deity; it is a kind of emanation of
> God's beauty, and is related to God as light is to the sun. It is
> not a thing that belongs to reason; it depends on the sense of
> the heart. . . . Not many wise men, men after the flesh, not
> many mighty, not many noble, are called. But God hath
> chosen the foolish things of the world.[7]

6. George Bancroft, *History of the Formation of the Constitution*, 3rd ed. (New York, 1882), 5.
7. *Oration to the Democracy of Springfield*, 4 July 1836, 18.

Much romantic thought was no more than sentimentalism, but it represented a powerful current. If Bancroft invoked Jonathan Edwards (when speaking to a New England audience) he might also have quoted Rousseau if he had not already classed him as an apostle of revolutionary violence. Rousseau's chains, which bound naturally free men, were forged by kings, priests, aristocrats, lawyers, and the whole apparatus of so-called civilized society. Man could not be free until he had found his way back to first principles and rebuilt on the solid consensus of moral truth. Under proper conditions man's real will was to do good and collectively the moral consensus became the General Will which was the only possible sovereign in a just state. Every other sovereign must, by definition, represent the particular will or selfish interest of a minority. There could be no "just powers" derived from anything less than the moral will of a whole people. If Americans did not read Rousseau, the problem which he posed was implicit in their controversies.

One characteristic of romantic thought was to wrap up complex ideas in large packages, endow them with collective personalities, speaking as though they could will and act. Of all romantic concepts of this kind "the nation" was the most powerful. Nations had been the dominions of a king drawn together by dynastic accident, living perhaps in a single area, but not necessarily of the same linguistic group. Countries had been bound together by common allegiance, but nations (or those who claimed to speak for them) claimed the right to exist as self-conscious political entities; men who did not belong to the dominant culture had to conform or suffer, ethnic character became pronounced, and alien rule was by definition unjust.

There was an inherent tendency in American discourse to fall into this mode of expression. "The people" became a convenient way of describing a majority of the people, and once the idea of a collective people became established it followed that "the people" could decide, act, and command. The Constitution itself became a romantic concept which acted upon men without their intervention. The "Union" became larger than the confederation of states, acquired character and moral responsibility, and when it acted unjustly all were involved in the guilt.

The collectivization and personalization in romantic thought affected the way in which men regarded the sections. It was still customary to say that a man lived "at the South," in much the same way as one might say that he lived in America, but by 1850 it was more common to speak of "the South" as a collective entity, providing each

Southerner with an identity that transcended differences of class, occupation, or political affiliation. Even more extraordinary was the way
in which men came to speak of the whole varied region that stretched
from New England to the western prairies as "the North." As soon as
one came to assume that "the South" and "the North" had separate
collective wills, acting toward each other on hostile principles, the
road to disunion lay ahead.

While romantic thought endowed large entities with simple
personalities, it also praised the individual who was larger than life.
The romantic hero stood for all the good principles against all the bad
principles. Sometimes he was doomed to die while fighting for the
truth, but on other and more glorious occasions his triumph brought
peace and happiness to the virtuous. In this character Andrew Jackson
challenged and overthrew the forces that threatened to corrupt the
nation and, as the hero must have an adversary, it was "federalism"
aided by "the money power" against which he fought. Jackson had
rallied the people against those who claimed the right to govern on
grounds of superior intelligence, and in this new form the struggle of
the centuries was to be renewed. In 1840, John A. Dix, a highly
intelligent supporter of Van Buren, drew a picture of the perpetual
struggle by "those who were in favor of a less popular form of government . . . to obtain for the government, by construction, powers
which are not expressly conferred by the constitution." The principles
were the same as those of 1800, but there was the added danger that
the people were now confronted by "the money power of the
country—aided, possibly, by the money power of England." The
popular claims of the Whigs were false and dangerous for "our attention may, by artful appeals to our pecuniary interest, be turned away
from the great principles which concern our freedom and happiness."[8]
The "people" should recall the principles of the "old hero" whose
followers might save the nation from its own worst enemies. If the
Democrats as politicians could accept the verdict of the polls in 1840,
the romantics among them saw Whig triumph as a temporary rever-
sion to the age of darkness.

Romantic influences were tenuous and diffuse, but Protestant
religion had an immediate and powerful effect. It engaged the most
active minds of the age, promoted reflection on the condition of society, and introduced new variations on old themes. Though it may be
argued that the year 1840 marked the moment at which politics

8. *Address before the Democracy of Herkimer County*, 4 July 1840.

superseded religion as the principal cause of popular excitement, there is little doubt about the primacy of religion before 1835. The religious press included a large number of widely circulating periodicals, at a time when the lights of the political press though numerous were dim and mainly of local influence. Revivalism made religion a matter absorbing popular interest, and intense competition among the denominations for new coverts west of the Appalachians made every village a hothouse breeding the fruit of faith.

Late in the nineteenth century a Baptist recalled the years between 1824 and 1839 when his father had been a minister in Ohio.[9]

> Preaching was far more theological than it is at present. . . .
> The denominational debate supplied an intellectual want to which the platform lecture, the editorial, and the review article now minister. The champions of the Baptists and the Disciples, or the Methodists, would meet in friendly controversy, and spend a week or ten days in keen battling in the presence of the assembled people. The whole town would be aroused, as it is now only by a political campaign, and men, women, and children would throng the scene of contest. . . .
> Usually some lawyer or judge would preside, preserve excellent order, and require courtesy towards each other from the contestants. The hearers went home to search the Scriptures, and the Baptists made great gains.

The intervention of civil power to moderate religious controversy is perhaps testimony to the involvement of whole communities in doctrinal debate.

In many isolated parts of the country, church membership alone provided a link with distant communities, participation in a nationwide organization, and a chance to hear reasoned argument between educated men. The pulpit provided a model for the platform, party organizers learned their lessons from itinerant evangelists, and the style and intensity of political debate in the middle of the nineteenth century followed closely the pattern set by the contest between denomination and denomination or revivalism and sin.

Given the ubiquity of religion, the topics of controversy were of considerable importance. In one way or another the more contentious

---

9. Justin A. Smith, *A History of the Baptists in the Western States* (Philadelphia, 1896), 132, quoting from the reminiscences of Franklin Johnson.

questions explored the familiar ground of free will and original sin. Was man damned without the gift of grace from God? If man was predestined to eternal punishment or divine election, what was the incentive for benevolence? In answer William Ellery Channing declared that enlightened Christianity must display "a sensibility to the abuses and evils which deform society, a faith in man's capacity of progress, a desire of human progress, a desire to carry to every human being the means of rising to a better condition and a higher virtue." In the modern age he proclaimed, "It begins to be understood that to be Christian is to be a philanthropist, and that, in truth, the essence of Christianity is a spirit of martrydom in the cause of mankind."[10] Calvinists might claim that it was a travesty of their doctrine to imply that they rejected benevolence. Cotton Mather had argued that if God gave an individual the capacity to do good, it must be used for the benefit of others. Jonathan Edwards said that moral responsibility came from God; man was unfree only in the sense that no living thing could go beyond the limits set by its nature. Nevertheless a rigid and unintelligent interpretation of Calvinist theology might conclude that a man defied the will of God if he sought to improve the condition of others. An extreme example was provided by the Anti-Mission Baptists of the South who solemnly declared that "we have no Christian fellowship for those who advocate the Missionary, Bible, Tract or Temperance societies, Sunday School Union, anxious seats or anything of the kind as a religious institution or means of grace; nor with any person who communes with a church which advocates any of those institutions."[11] In a debased and secularized form this spirit still survives among those who use "do-gooder" as a term of abuse.

Educated divines of strict persuasion dismissed the Anti-Mission Baptists and their like as deluded men, but would still argue that men who believed they could change the world by benevolent action misunderstood the nature of sin. The Bible enjoined charity to the poor, but no one could *save* the poor unless they were chosen by God for salvation. Still less could a man hope to win salvation for himself by doing good works for others. Unlike Anti-Mission Baptists they would argue that if a benevolent enterprise was undertaken it must be part of God's purpose that it should be done, but that the human instrument earned no remission of sins by doing what he was com-

10. William Ellery Channing, *The Philanthropist: A Tribute to the Memory of the Rev. Noah Worcester D. D.* (Boston, 1837). And in all editions of Channing's collected works.
11. Garnett Ryland, *The Baptists of Virginia* (Richmond, 1955), 253.

manded to do. However broadly this doctrine was interpreted it might lead to the conclusion that men who claimed a call to reform the world were deceiving themselves.

In 1824 an earnest, scholarly, and deeply devout Presbyterian, Albert Barnes, reopened the old controversy in a sermon entitled "The Way of Salvation." He argued that God had given every man the opportunity of salvation and the will to take it; those who refused to exercise this will remained sunk in sin, and this was the state of the vast majority of mankind, but those who could be persuaded to use the will that God had given them might win forgiveness.[12] The distinction may seem fine, but was of vital importance to men trained to relate belief to action and led, in 1837, to a formal separation between Presbyterians of the Old and New Schools.

In 1852 Albert Barnes, by then leader of the New School, explained that "Presbyterians were not sworn to a cold, cheerless and rigid system of mere opinion." While holding to the great truths of Calvinist doctrine they wished "to preach a free Gospel," promote "glorious revivals of religion," move forward "with the progress of true mental philosophy," and be "identified with the great movements of the age for the conversion of the world." The New School wished to join with others "in promoting the great purposes of Christian benevolence."[13] The social implications of the doctrinal distinction were clear. Christians were not merely permitted but enjoined to work for the improvement of society, and God's will could be invoked to further the cause of reform.

Rigid Calvinists were suspicious of revivalism when salvation was promised as a reward for confession and a show of repentance under emotional stress. Revivalists believed that if a man or woman could be persuaded to take the first step, full regeneration might follow, and offered to converts the blessings of eternal life but this, to a believer in divine election, was not theirs to give. Charles Grandison Finney, the greatest of the revivalists, carried this emphasis on human agency in the conversion of souls to extreme but practical limits.[14] A revival could not begin unless the preacher knew his business, and

12. Albert Barnes, *The Way of Salvation* (New York, 1824).

13. Albert Barnes, *Our Position* (New York, 1852), 20. Barnes admired Jonathan Edwards, and one reason for the separation of the New from the Old School was to allow fuller cooperation with New England Congregationalists, whom he regarded as more liberal than those who took their Calvinism direct from Scotland or Northern Ireland. The New School and the Congregationalists should work together in "systematic enterprises for the conversion of the world."

14. Finney was full of sensible advice. The following is an amazing but typical example: "People should leave their dogs and very young children at home. I have known contentions

its momentum could not be maintained unless converts were given opportunities to show their faith by works. They should never be allowed to withdraw from the world but must commit themselves to its improvement.

"Politics," said Finney, "are a part of religion in a country such as this, and Christians must do their duty to the country as a part of their duty to God." This did not imply the formation of a "Christian party," which might do harm by alienating existing political organizations, but the use of influence within parties to ensure that all candidates were "honest and upright . . . and to be trusted." Converts should not "rest satisfied with being merely useful, or remaining in a situation where they can do *some* good. But if they see an opportunity where they can do more good, they must embrace it, whatever may be the sacrifice to themselves."[15] It was immaterial whether a man was Democrat or Whig, Bank or anti-Bank, Jackson or anti-Jackson; Christians should vote for men who appeared to be doing most good. It was a creed for political activity and, though intended to promote individual benevolence or voluntary association, did not sit well with the Jeffersonian maxim that the best government governed least.

In eastern Massachusetts, and with outposts in several cities in other states, Unitarianism provided another but very different inspiration for reform. Many young men, who rejected both the rigidity of orthodox Calvinism and the exuberant emotionalism of revivalism, found in this relaxed denomination an outlet for their idealism. In 1833 James Freeman Clarke, then a minister in Louisville, Kentucky, and destined to play an important part in the reform movements of his time, expressed his gratitude to Unitarianism for its "mental freedom," and for the "higher atmosphere of religious freedom" to which it had led him. The essence of orthodox Calvinism was, in his view, the belief that sin and punishment were not personal matters, but part

---

arise among dogs and children to cry, just at that stage of the services that would most destroy the effect of the meeting. If children are present and weep, they should *instantly* be removed. . . . As for dogs, they had infinitely better be dead, than to divert attention from the word of God. See that deacon; perhaps his dog has in this way destroyed more souls than the deacon will ever be instrumental in saving." Charles Grandison Finney, *Lectures on Revivals of Religion*, ed. William G. McLoughlin (Cambridge, 1960), 239. The suggestion that a dog might destroy an individual's chance of salvation would be highly offensive to the Old School; if God willed that a man should be saved he would be saved—dog or no dog—and if the dog appeared to intervene between man and God it could only be because this was, in some mysterious way, a part of God's purpose.

15. *Ibid.*, 297, 404.

of a providential plan. This was the spirit that discouraged attempts to improve the world, and should be the principal target of Unitarian attack.[16]

In 1832 Martin Luther Hurlbut, a more conventional Unitarian than James Freeman Clarke, contributed a series of articles to the *Unitarian Advocate* on the prospects of American society. He argued that civil institutions had advanced faster than religious knowledge, with the consequence that men had more freedom than they knew how to enjoy "with safety or innocence." Society could not survive unless this condition was remedied, but revivalism was not the remedy for "the tumult of the passions and the wild play of the imagination" were too easily mistaken for divine inspiration. The age demanded "a rational and liberal religion or none at all."[17]

In 1840 Orville Dewey, later to become president of the American Unitarian Association from 1845 to 1847, argued that true civil liberty was not "a boasting and blustering, nor proud and self-sufficient, nor a reckless and licentious principle," but implied greater service to others and willing acceptance of responsibility. It was the intention of Jesus "to draw all men to him . . . in sympathy, in imitation, in love . . . to win the world for a noble spirit of self-sacrifice." This was a "renovating power" which worked upon the whole civilized world, and was "fast spreading to the end of the earth."[18] This gentle yet active faith inspired James Freeman Clarke with the conviction that everywhere men wanted "a more spiritual philosophy and a more living religion," and for men of his generation this meant a religion that lived in the world and accepted responsibility for its improvement.[19]

In Boston and Cambridge Unitarianism was accepted by the majority of influential congregations, and ruled the Harvard Divinity School. But if it liberated the spirit, its combination of calm rationalism and acceptance of Biblical authority could also provide a cloak for civilized conformity. "All the young and ardent rebel, and raise the war cry of freedom," wrote Clarke, "but in middle life, seeing lawlessness to be worse than slavery, they patiently reassume the old fetters."[20] The tension between conservative and liberal Unita-

16. Clarke to W. H. Channing, 10 February 1834, Clarke Papers, Houghton Library, Harvard University, Cambridge, Mass.

17. *Unitarian Advocate* VI, no. 1 (1832): 134, 167.

18. Orville Dewey, *Discourses and Discussions in Explanation and Defence of Unitarianism* (Boston, 1840), 131.

19. Clarke to W. H. Channing, 10 February 1834, Clarke Papers.

20. *Ibid.*

rians became acute when some of the latter became associated with Transcendentalism.

In seeking a universal principle of divinity in all men, Transcendentalists seemed to be moving away from Biblical revelation to some mystic but man-made rule of conscience. In 1838 Emerson's address to the graduating class at Harvard substituted universal Deism for a personal God, denied the authority of the Scriptures, and advanced radical criticism of conventional preaching. This raised alarm, persuaded more conservative Unitarians to define the limits of their liberal faith, and may have inspired Orville Dewey to draw his firm distinction between rational and anarchic Christianity. Conservative Unitarian congregations looked askance at young ministers associated with Transcendentalism, and Theodore Parker, the most dynamic and learned of their number, could find no pulpit in Boston until 1846.

Age and temperament divided the Unitarians, and some of the liberals would become independent or Universalist, but there was no separation into old and new schools. Conservative Unitarians, though reluctant to embark upon new intellectual ventures or endorse radical schemes of social reform, gave generously to existing projects for moral improvement. In politics the great majority of Unitarians became Whigs and imparted to the new party an element of high-minded benevolence that was characteristic of middle-class liberalism on both sides of the Atlantic. Divergent attitudes toward political anti-slavery in 1845 would bring on a furious quarrel with enduring consequences, but until that time the Unitarians included social conservatives and restless reformers, Harvard professors and active politicians, merchant princes and enthusiastic young ministers.

For this harmony much credit was due to William Ellery Channing, of whom Theodore Parker declared that "No clergyman ever exercised such dominion among men."[21] His congregation covered the whole spectrum of Boston Unitarian society, and his sermons instructed young reformers, conservative merchants, and "lords of the loom." "There was scarcely a good work or liberal thought in his time," said Theodore Parker, "which he did not aid and powerfully aid," and his views deserve careful scrutiny.

In 1822, speaking at Harvard on *The Evidence of Revealed Religion*, Channing said that the Epistles bore "all the marks of having come from men, plunged in conflicts which the new religion excited, alive

21. Theodore Parker, *The American Scholar* (Boston, 1907). This and the following quotation, 143, 146.

to its interest, identified with its fortunes. . . . They are written on real business, intended for immediate effects, designed to meet prejudices and passions, which such a religion must at first have awakened."[22] Throughout his life he saw himself as an actor in just such a world, with an interest in everything that seemed to break new ground, from romantic poetry to the labors of his friend, Joseph Tuckerman, as "minister at large" to the Boston poor. No one insisted more frequently or more emphatically upon improvement as a Christian duty. In a eulogy on Tuckerman he wrote:

> "Society has hitherto employed its energy chiefly to punish crime. It is infinitely more important to prevent it. . . . Society ought not to breed Monsters in its bosom. If it will not use its prosperity to save the ignorant and poor from the blackest vice, if it will even quicken vice by its selfishness and luxury, its worship of wealth, its scorn of human nature, then it must suffer and deserves to suffer, from crime."[23]

The meaning that Channing gave to "society" was never quite clear; it might be "all Christian men," or the community as a whole, or the government that men elected. He was not a clear prophet of the welfare state (though often coming near to it) but expressed a typical nineteenth-century faith in the contribution of educational and material progress to the improvement of morals.

> No man has seized the grand peculiarity of the present age, who does not see in it the means and material of a vast and beneficent social change. The revolution which we are called to advance, has in truth begun. The great distinction of our times is a diffusion of intelligence, and refinement, and the spirit of progress, through a vastly wider sphere than formerly. The middle and laboring classes have means of improvement not dreamed of in earlier times; and why stop here? Why not increase these means where now enjoyed? Why not extend them, where they are not possessed?[24]

22. *The Evidence of Revealed Religion: a Discourse before the University of Cambridge*, 14 March 1822.

23. *A Discourse on the Life and Character of the Rev. Joseph Tuckerman*, 31 January 1841.

24. *The Obligation of a City to care for and watch over the Moral Health of its members with remarks on the life and character of the Rev. Dr. Tuckerman* (Glasgow, 1841), 9. The impulse given the quest for improvement amongst the Unitarians was not ephemeral; five years later, in an address to the

Channing was no party man. He was equally critical of those Boston Whigs who were complacent, conservative, and socially exclusive, and of the clique of Federal office holders who controlled the state's Democratic party. He became an open opponent of slavery because he believed that it damaged the moral character of master and slave and raised formidable obstacles to national improvement, but he was never an abolitionist and gave no hint of sympathy for Garrison. Yet his belief that bad conditions despressed the spirit, bred crime, and deadened conscience, meant that his influence was always cast on the side of those who believed in public responsibility for social ills. It was the young Whig reformers who learned most from his teaching, and his ideas would appear in secular guise in the editorial columns of Horace Greeley's New York *Tribune.*

The bridge between Protestant faith and eighteenth-century rationalism had been erected by the Scottish philosophers. Channing was impressed by the argument of Adam Ferguson that regeneration was a gradual process, and that the enlargement of knowledge and the refinement of human sympathy should bring each generation nearer to moral perfection. Above all he was influenced by Francis Hutcheson, whom he read as a student at Harvard and continued to regard as "the master light of all his seeing." Hutcheson wrote that there were "two calm natural determinations of the will"; the first was "an invariably constant impulse toward one's own perfection and happiness of the highest kind"; the second was "toward the universal happiness of others."

> That disposition therefore which is most excellent and naturally gains the highest moral approbation, is the calm, stable, universal good-will to all, or the most extensive benevolence. And this seems the most distinct notion we can form of the moral excellence of the Deity.[25]

This concept of benevolence as a universal characteristic might seem to bring Channing close to Bancroft's romantic conviction that "the many are wiser than the few," but there were important differences between them. Hutcheson, anticipating Rousseau, defined two

---

American Unitarian Association, George Hillard said that "the great problem for the Christian world now to accomplish is to effect a closer union between religion and politics. . . . We must make men do good and be good, with that energy and intensity with which they now pursue wealth or political distinction, or make love, or seek revenge." *Boston Whig,* 13 July 1846.

25. Francis Hutcheson, *Moral Philosophy* (Glasgow and London, 1755), I: 69.

kinds of will and the "calm natural determination" was often at war with anger, lust, or other irrational impulses, "sometimes the passion conquering the calm principle, and sometimes being conquered by it." Though the conflict occurred in all men, those with trained minds and the opportunity for reflection were best able to understand and act upon the "calm impulse of the soul." Educated men had therefore a moral obligation to lead, instruct, and improve. Progress could not be left to decision by the masses, among whom passion might prevail for, as Hutcheson observed, "the constant impulse toward one's own perfection" operated "in the bulk of mankind very confusedly," and more general benevolence might be still harder to grasp.

Translated into everyday American terms this meant that although Channing believed that men were naturally equal, social circumstances made the will of the majority a very imperfect guide. Fortunately, salutory checks were imposed by the Constitution, and should be observed in spirit as well as letter. Individuals should recognize their duty to society, but society should look to enlightened individuals for a calm understanding of the Divine impulse to good in man. There were merits in both parties, but as a reformer, intellectual, and leader among men, Channing was of Whig rather than Democratic persuasion.

The opposite view was expressed by an anonymous contribution to the *Democratic Review*, which the editor printed with reservations "for the sake of some good thoughts contained in it."[26] According to this writer, the democratic doctrine recognized God "as the immediate and sole Governor of the Universe of which He is literally, not figuratively, the life and soul—ordering the affairs of man in infinite wisdom and love and directing him in every thought and action that he may attain to the true ends of his being—indeed that he may be at all." God had given men intelligence "without any reference to what is termed Education." This was a fundamental doctrine of Democracy. The uneducated many might avail themselves of the services of the educated few, "but as instruments only, subject to their directions." It was, he noted "the hot house system of education introduced by infidel aristocracy, which has produced so many sickly and poisonous plants in our intellectual garden." Thomas Jefferson would hardly have agreed, but he might have endorsed the argument that the pretentiousness of an elite had produced "derangement in the whole machinery of society."

Some earnest and pious men believed that the great campaign to

26. *U. S. Magazine and Democratic Review* VIII (October 1840): 360ff.

reform the world on Christian principles could best be advanced by
voluntary association. A mighty host of societies sprang to life to convert the heathen, distribute tracts and Bibles, reform fallen women,
promote temperance, and abolish slavery. "Anniversary weeks" in
New York, Philadelphia, and Boston became the occasion for meeting, planning, and launching appeals by all these diverse societies (of
which many had overlapping membership), but by 1840 the
momentum was slackening and the centralizing tendency in benevolent enterprise became an object of suspicion.[27]

The pious elite came under direct attack from Calvin Colton,
later to become an assiduous Whig pamphleteer and editor of Henry
Clay's papers, who identified the national directorate of Christian reform as the religious equivalent of one-party rule and "executive
tyranny." Others saw untold dangers in the innocuous Sunday School
Union, which had begun with purely educational objectives, had
been taken over by Christian reformers as a weapon in the war against
immorality and infidelity, and now presented an infringement upon
the separation of Church and State.[28]

There were other reasons for the slackening of Christian
reform—notably the financial panic of 1837 which dried up funds—
but it left its mark upon the conscience of the age. Indeed the decline
of national association under voluntary leadership strengthened the
case for action by secular authorities. This was especially true of the
great temperance campaign, which originated in humanitarian concern over the social consequences of alcoholism, became the hallmark
of Protestant moral reform, and pressed for restraint that could not be
achieved without legislation. Other crusades against vice, violence,
and depravity also argued for enlarged public responsibility.

The Christian crusade found its greatest challenge in two very
different areas—the overcrowded eastern cities and the thinly settled
areas of the West—where the political establishment was likely to be
Jacksonian and professional politicians regarded amateur reformers
with little favor. There were Western areas where missionary fervor

27. As early as 1832 Martin Luther Hurlburt remarked that there was a "Strong tendency at
the present time, in society, to run into masses. . . . Benevolent objects of every sort are now
affected by joint stock operations." The danger was that charity became associated with money
and "the vulgar elements of worldly" and a divination of private charitable activities. *Unitarian
Advocate* VI (1832): 18.

The whole story of the benevolent "international" is studied in Charles I. Foster, *Errand of
Mercy: the Evangelical united front, 1790–1837* (Chapel Hill, 1960).

28. Foster, *op. cit.*, chapters XII and XIII *passim*.

went hand in hand with Democratic politics, but in 1840 the Whigs —as the party of change—were more likely to benefit.

There is no clear national correspondence between denominational and political allegiance, but locally the identification could be marked and where this occurred religious enthusiasm was a powerful stimulus for political activity. Northern Baptists, who inclined to modified Calvinism, New School Presbyterians, Congregationalists, and Unitarians were likely to be anti-Jacksonian. Methodists were divided. In the West they generally inclined toward Democratic politics, particularly in congregations opposed to the authority of trained itinerant ministers, but in eastern cities and old settled areas they were more likely to be anti-Jacksonian, especially where Democratic strength lay among Irish or German Catholics or low-paid urban workers who seemed beyond the reach of all religion. Old School Baptists or Presbyterians were not invariably Democrats, but in New Hampshire, Maine, and throughout the lower South they seem to have been. In the upper South Whig politics in the white counties were often found in association with theologically liberal forms of Calvinism. Episcopalians, North and South, tended to be Whig because of their traditional belief in social order.

Religious controversy contributed to the intellectual and political ferment. Factional rivalry or economic interest might provide the immediate incentive, but contending sides sought moral justification, religious debate provided the rhetoric, and Christian enthusiasm elevated the issues to the level of high principle.

On a philosophic plane religion highlighted the problem of authority. To whom had God entrusted the right to hold dominion over men? In the Churches this might become an organizational debate over the power of assemblies, synods or congregations, over the need for a trained ministry or the right to preach for all who studied their Bibles and felt the Spirit move within them, or between denominations dominated by clergy and moral reform societies directed and financed by laymen. In politics the nature of authority was the unacknowledged theme as orators charted a course through the powers of nation and states, legislatures and executives, popular majorities and constitutional restraints. Where lay the ultimate right to decide when every power was checked?

Despite George Bancroft's appeal to Jonathan Edwards to demonstrate the superiority of moral sense among ordinary men, the majority of Protestant churchmen agreed that constitutional restraint was a necessary barrier against ignorance and depravity. This was not a doctrine of class rule (though it might justify an educated elite), but rather a profound belief that the forces of evil were always abroad and could be defeated only by constant vigilance. In secular terms this came to mean that Democrats were most likely to see danger in the concerted power of wealth and government sanctioned privilege, the Whigs in demagogues and mass emotion. Democratic rhetoric claimed that the people demanded the destruction of Federalism or curbs on the money power, while Whigs sounded the alarm when a President claimed to speak for the people or politicians were too successful in the enforcement of party regularity. Not that the Whigs scorned popular support or deplored popular indignation when they deemed it to be righteous. Indeed most dramatic protest against elitist government of the Jacksonian period was made by the Anti-Masons, and the great majority of them passed over into the Whig party carrying with them their special brand of moral fervor. It was no coincidence that this movement flourished first in the districts where Finney and other revivalist had scored their most spectacular successes.

\*       \*       \*

The Anti-Masons attained strength in the early 1830s in the small towns and farms of western New York. Their movement spread into neighboring states and was strong for a time in Massachusetts and Pennsylvania. Though their existence as a political party was short, they launched into public life men of the future, among whom Thurlow Weed and William H. Seward were preeminent in New York and Thaddeus Stevens in Pennsylvania. The movement was moralistic, democratic, and egalitarian, and its political leaders soon moved from the narrow ground of anti-Masonry to the broad theme of popular resistance to the secret designs of the rich and influential.

The Address of the Anti-Masonic Convention of the state of New York declared in 1831 that

> All just governments are contrivances of the people, for their own security and aid, in the great work of their common improvement and happiness. All the people, upon whom they are to operate, are, therefore, equally interested in them; and have an equal right to interfere in their institution and conduct.[29]

29. *Address of the Anti-Masonic Convention of the State of New York, 17 February 1831*, New York.

In Massachusetts Anti-Masons stressed the paramount need for morality in politics, and saw the Jackson administration as the embodiment of vice. "The greatest of these evils is the degeneracy of public morals, the outrages committed upon freedom of debate, the passionate violence of the Executive, the substitution of his will for the will of the people, and the character of the partisans by whom he is surrounded."[30] Anti-Masons also pictured themselves as the champions of Christian principles against the aristocratic rationalism. "Masonry in its whole length and breadth is as Anti-Christian as it is Anti-Republican. Its tendency is to corrupt, and, ultimately, to undermine and destroy all our civil and religious institutions, and to spread infidelity, despotism, and misery through the earth."[31]

The moralistic tone of political Anti-Masons attracted ex-President John Quincy Adams and in 1832 he accepted their nomination for Governor of Massachusetts. He ran second but, as no candidate had an overall majority, withdrew to avoid a fight with the National Republican candidate when the election went to the legislature. In announcing his withdrawal he defended Anti-Masonry as "founded upon a pure, precise, and unequivocal principle of morals," and claimed that it "sprang from the bosom of the people themselves . . . a cry of horror from the unlearned, unsophisticated people."[32]

Anti-Masonry failed to make headway as a separate political party, but most of its leaders and rank-and-file transferred their support to the anti-Jackson movement which blossomed as the Whig party in and after 1834. This added a new dimension to the Northern Whig party, and one which was to be of immense significance. In New York it provided a large rural constituency straddling the route to the Great Lakes and the West, and responsive to plans of New York entrepreneurs for the development of communications.[33] It also brought into the Whig mainstream Thurlow Weed, who was to be the party's most active organizer. In 1830 prominent Anti-Masons contributed funds to launch his Albany *Evening Journal* which had by 1840 the largest circulation of any political paper in the state. As editor Weed was also the principal political reporter and his constant

30. *Address of the Anti-Masonic Convention to the People of Massachusetts, 5 and 6 September 1832*, Boston.

31. *Proceedings of the Anti-Masonic State Convention of Massachusetts, 19 and 20 May 1831*, Boston.

32. John Quincy Adams, *Letters on the Masonic Institution* (Boston, 1832), 271.

33. Elliott R. Barkan observes of the Whig party that its "funds would flow from New York City, Albany, Rochester, Utica, and Buffalo, but its votes would come from Canadaigua, Auburn, Binghamton, Ithaca and countless other villages and small towns." *Portrait of a Party: the Whig Persuasion in New York State* (Unpublished Ph.D. dissertation, Harvard University, 1968).

presence in the capital during sessions of the legislature gave him ample opportunity to practice the art of management. One of his major purposes was to promote the fortunes of his friend and fellow Anti-Mason William Henry Seward, who was elected Governor as a Whig in 1838 and may justly be reckoned one of the wisest and most farsighted statesmen of the age.

Even more important than votes and leaders were the new dimensions which Anti-Masonry brought to the Whig alliance. Flourishing in areas where evangelical revivalism had been most active, Anti-Masonry brought the Northern Whigs into intimate association with all kinds of movements for moral improvement by voluntary action and association or—if it became necessary—by legislation. Gerrit Smith and Myron Holley had been original members of the Anti-Masonic committee and, though their later support for the Liberty party did not endear them to Whig leaders, Seward and Weed retained close links with Northern anti-slavery. Further afield they found common ground with the Adams family and anti-slavery sentiment in New England. In Pennsylvania Thaddeus Stevens entered politics as an Anti-Mason, and would fight a lifelong battle against racial discrimination.

In 1840 the Whigs of reform temperament found a spokesman. Horace Greeley had been too young and too obscure to be an active Anti-Mason, and in 1840 he was an unsuccessful and penniless free-lance journalist (having failed to impress the austere William Cullen Bryant of the *Evening Post*). His talents were spotted by Thurlow Weed, and in 1840 he was commissioned to edit a campaign journal, *The Log Cabin*. This was not great journalism but gave Greeley a claim on the generosity of Whig leaders who helped him to found the *Tribune* the following year. It was soon apparent that Greeley was an editor of genius. He made the *Tribune* an influential political organ and one of the best newspapers in the English-speaking world. Greeley aimed to capture a wide readership but never let his standards lapse; he wrote for the educated middle class and intelligent workingmen in language that was clear and simple but also sophisticated. He included excellent literary features as well as political comment, foreign and domestic news, and also compiled a great deal of political and economic information. Through Greeley conservative Whig readers were introduced to a variety of reform movements, including Fourierism and plans for workingmen's associations. His interest in exotic reform movements was not welcomed by Thurlow Weed and ultimately led to the dissolution of the "firm" of Seward, Weed, and

Greeley but, for a time, the triumvirate did much to give a new direction to the Northern Whig party.[34]

Greeley's enthusiastic—one might say fanatical—support of protection was consistent with his other reform interests. High tariffs secured the living standards of American workingmen, and the promotion of American industry was essential for the advance of welfare, education, and respectability. Turning the flank of the Democratic attack on privilege accorded to economic interests by government legislation, Greeley converted economic progress into a moral crusade. The revivalist legacy was apparent in his urge to preach reform and in the emotional language of his editorials when iniquity or free trade seemed to be riding high.

The Whig as social and moral reformer became manifest in 1839 when Seward, as governor of New York, made the improvement of public education a major aim. He told the legislature that "the advantages of education ought to be secured to many, especially in our large cities, whom orphanage, the depravity of parents, or other forms of accident or misfortune seem to have doomed to hopeless poverty and ignorance."[35] Some educational reformers, such as Horace Mann in Massachusetts, tried to separate moral education from denominational influence, but Seward, realizing that the Catholic masses of New York City would be as unwilling to accept secular as Protestant teaching, recommended that the poor of the city should be "instructed by teachers speaking the same language and professing the same faith." This did not endear Seward to Nativists or evangelical Protestants, but he remained unshaken in his belief that available and acceptable education was the necessary condition for social improvement. Another echo of the Anti-Masonic resentment of social exclusiveness was the support given by many Whigs to the anti-rent movement in upper New York state. Man should inherit the earth, and enormous estates in single ownership were an offense in the eyes of God, whatever the courts might say.

Thus revived religion did much to arouse disquiet and suggest remedies. Religious reform was not partisan, but when existing conditions were brought under critical review the party in power received most of the knocks, while the benefits accrued to their rivals. Re-

34. In August 1844 Henry Clay wrote to Epes Sargent that he regretted "the eccentricities of the *Tribune*" but otherwise it deserved high praise. "On statistics and the state of elections and public opinion throughout the Union I regard Mr. Greeley as surpassed by no other editor in the country." (Epes Sargent Collection, Boston Public Library).

35. W. H. Seward, *Works*, ed. George E. Baker, 5 Vols. (New York, 1853–1889), II:75.

vivalism provided rhetoric with which to condemn the present, recall a happier past, and look to a better future. A Cleveland editor, writing in 1835, offered a good example of the Whig debt to revivalist thinking.

> Everyone must acknowledge that political honesty has become a thing of the past, that the love of country and the love of the constitution . . . have become mere by-words. Americans have come to regard with more anxiety the success of a mere party, than of liberty and law; have ceased to select their rulers for character and talents, but choose those who have given their adhesions to certain political opinions, and have pledged themselves to support these opinions. . . . We here record that the existing government of the country is working to overthrow our constituton, which has been the pride of the whole world, and that a majority of the American people are supporting and encouraging those who are thus depriving them of their glorious birthright.[36]

The force of these comments explains the rapid rise of the Whig party. For thousands who flocked to the polls in 1840 it was the party of moral, social, and political regeneration, in opposition to upstart Jacksonian politicians or Old Republican oligarchies in the South who had done little to improve the condition of the people. The attack became more intense as the country experienced first a financial crisis and then a deep depression.

\*    \*    \*

The Democrats fought back and were forced to rationalize their ideas about government by the revolt, within their own ranks, of the Loco-Foco or Equal Rights movement. Democratic theory, hitherto vaguely defined, began to assume greater coherence and vigor, and if party members shared with the Whigs a strongly moralistic flavor they owed more to humanistic and rationalist traditions than to religious revivalism.

36. *Annals of Cleveland* (W.P.A. Project 16823) Vols. XVIII and XIX, Part I, 77. The same editorial exclaimed rhetorically, "May the people awake from the delusion that enthrals them, and rising in their might, hurl from the high places of the land those rulers whose abuse the authority entrusted to them, and who would destroy those who bestowed it. May they come forth and maintain that the constitution is holy and shall be sustained inviolate."

In 1840 the *Democratic Review,* in the course of a long and thoughtful article on Jeremy Bentham, commended him for doing much "toward establishing the true functions of government."[37]

> Unless . . . he who proposes a law can prove that there is not only a specific reason in favor of it, but a reason stronger than the general reason against it, he transcends his province, and invades the rights of the individual.

This principle would "simplify government until it became what it ought to be, a mere instrument for the protection of person and property." All partial legislation, all exclusive privileges, all monopolies, and all unequal laws would stand condemned "and this is all for which the great democratic party, the party of progress is striving." The people should be left "free to act, and untaxed, untrammelled, and uncontrolled, except so far as may be required for a strict public economy, the preservation of peace and order at home, and our national independence and security abroad." If a community wanted improvements "private enterprise would supply them, and on the safest and best possible terms; but government must not, ought not, and . . . could not, in any way interfere with the private occupations of the people." This may appear to anticipate Herbert Spencer, but the premise was not that free competition was the key to economic progress but that privilege was contrary to public morality.

Early in 1840 the Sub-Treasury Act divorced government from private banking and set the course of financial policy toward hard money. This might be regarded as a logical sequel to Jackson's war with the Bank of the United States, but by 1840 it was backed by a refined social and economic theory. Originating as a critique within the Democratic ranks, and providing theoretical ground for the Loco-Foco revolt against Tammany control, its adoption as official policy was recognized when Van Buren appointed William Gouge as a clerk in the Treasury.

Gouge proved to be a hard-working civil servant who performed a useful task by imposing logic and order upon Treasury reports to Congress, but his best known achievement was the publication in 1833 of *A Short history of paper-money and Banking,* to which was prefixed *An Inquiry into the Principles of the System with consideration of its effects on Morals and Happiness.* The title was significant, for

37. *Democratic Review* VIII (1840): 251–71.

though he discussed at length the operation of central banking and paper currency, his principal concern was with moral rather than economic consequences. Gouge was a careful rather than popular writer, but his work attracted sufficient notice to warrant a second edition in 1835, in the same year a London edition published by William Cobbett, and in 1840 the New York *Evening Post* printed another as an exposition of Democratic views. Transferred from the study to the forum the arguments were calculated to appeal equally to radical opponents of the money power and rural Calvinists of the old school.

The burden of Gouge's argument was that paper money had diverted profits to the wrong people. The country's increase of wealth had been "principally for the benefit of those to whom an increase of riches will bring no increase of happiness, for they have already wealth enough."[38] Paper money encouraged rapid expansion and equally rapid reduction of credit with economic instability as its inevitable consequence. "The vicissitudes of fortune . . . will tend to increase the inequality of social condition, by throwing the wealth of several rich men into the hands of one." This result might not be felt in remote areas for years to come, but meanwhile others would "exhibit all the splendor and licentiousness, and misery and debasement, of the most populous districts of Europe." The rich might practice benevolence, diffuse the blessings of education, and attempt to promote moral and religious improvement. "But these efforts will only alleviate our social evils; they cannot cure them." Indeed paper money actually encouraged men to seek a legal remedy for each social evil. "They are willing to leave nothing to nature; the law must do everything." Paper money would never circulate freely unless governments gave the banks corporate privileges and evils created by law required further legislation as a remedy. In this way, and steering a course between excessive private wealth and unnecessary legislation, Gouge provided the Democratic party with a doctrine which would dominate its economic and social thinking until the Civil War.

The political impact of the doctrine might have been less marked had it not caught the imagination of William Leggett, the powerful though erratic journalist who was William Cullen Bryant's assistant editor on the New York *Evening Post*. In 1835 Leggett turned his editorial pen against the banks and other corporations that owed their existence to the Tammany party machine in New York City, and (in

38. William Gouge, *A Short History of paper-money and Banking* (Philadelphia, 1833), 124–27.

the words of an admirer) "the coming forth of his paper was looked for daily with the most eager desire, for it was well-known that no functionary however high, no party however strong, no editor however subtle, could escape the deep-toned thunder of his invective."[39] Though himself too unwell to take an active part, Leggett was the prime mover of the Loco-Foco or Equal Rights party.

At the first meeting of the Equal Rights men—the famous occasion on which Tammany agents turned off the gas and business was conducted by the light of loco-foco matches—resolutions declared that gold and silver should be "the only legitimate, substantial, and proper circulating medium," that "perpetuities and monopolies were offensive to freedom," and that "all bank charters granted by individual states . . . [were] founded on . . . principles of speculation and gambling, at war with good morals and just and equal government, and calculated to build up and strengthen . . . the odious distribution of wealth and power against merit and equal rights."[40]

Two years later, after the experience of financial panic to prove their point, the Loco-Focos of New York issued a manifesto consciously modeled on the Declaration of Independence. "Banks have fostered extravagant speculations in real estate, and consequently enormous increase of rents. Their extraordinary issues and accommodations have enabled forestallers to buy up and hoard up all the provisions in the land, and consequently to extort any price their horrible avarice demands." The delusion of wealth through paper money was the parent of "all those odious monopolies, and iron bonds upon the free exercise of our liberty by which we are bound, robbed, oppressed and insultingly derided."[41] William Leggett summed up the new doctrine:

> The remedy is easy. It is to confine government within the narrowest limits of necessary duties. It is to disconnect banks and state. It is to give freedom to trade, and leave enterprise, competition, and a just sense of right, to accomplish, by their natural energies, what the artificial system of legislative checks and balances has so signally failed in accomplishing.

He argued that the federal government need do nothing but "hold itself entirely aloof from banking," while state governments should

---

39. F. Byrdsall, *History of the Loco-Foco or Equal Rights Party* (New York, 1842).
40. *Ibid*.
41. *Ibid*.

repeal their laws imposing restraint on the free exercise of capital and credit.[42]

In 1835 Leggett and the Loco-Focos were cast out by the ruling powers in the Democratic party, but in October 1839 a special meeting at Tammany Hall formally expunged the resolution refusing recognition to the *Evening Post,* and Leggett's doctrines were incorporated into the central dogma of the party. Leggett himself had died earlier in the year but, according to the *Democratic Review,* "four short years had sufficed to effect a change and a progress in political opinion amounting to a revolution."[43]

How does one account for this change? The Loco-Focos had had no success in elections, and had made no progress toward winning a national constituency. Attempts to explain the new course by the need to seek support from urban labor, to offset losses in the South and West in the election of 1836, are unconvincing. Even less satisfactory are "explanations" which discover the fine hand of *laissez faire* capitalism. The voters whose allegiance the Democrats had to retain were in the countryside and small towns. Banks that had advanced paper for the purchase of land were blamed for the bubble that burst in 1837. Speculators had taken their profits and left the purchasers to face a falling market. In this situation hard money could not make every man honest, but would remove some of the worst temptations, keep honest savings where they belonged, and deprive rich men of at least one reason for bringing pressure to bear upon state legislatures. Though the original Loco-Focos were small storekeepers, clerks, and craftsmen, it was entirely appropriate that the leading congressional spokesman of hard money, in season and out, was Thomas Hart Benton, the formidable Senator from Missouri and representative of western farmers.

When Congress was called into special session in September 1837 to deal with difficulties arising from the financial crisis, President Van Buren made nonintervention, the Independent Treasury, and hard money the cornerstones of his policy. His message declared that government "was not intended to confer special favors on individuals or on any classes of them, to create systems of agriculture, manufactures, or trade, or to engage in them either separately or in connection with individual citizens or organized associations."[44] Nor

42. *Democratic Review* VII (January 1840): 15.
43. *Ibid.,* VI: 443.
44. J. D. Richardson, *Messages of the Presidents,* III: 324.

was it intended to make men rich or to recompense them for losses not
incurred in the public service.

> Its real duty—that duty the performance of which makes a
> good government the most precious of human blessings—is
> to enact and enforce a system of general laws commensurate
> with, but not exceeding the objects of its establishment, and
> to leave every citizen and every interest to reap under its be-
> nign protection the rewards of virtue industry and prudence.

Specifically Van Buren urged that the Treasury alone should receive and disburse public money—without the intervention or
agency of any private bank—and should receive and pay only in gold
or silver (except for occasional Treasury drafts issued as a matter of
convenience and redeemable in specie at an early date). These recommendations finally became law early in 1840, with 1842 fixed as the
year in which the Treasury would cease to receive paper currency issued by banks.

In 1840 Democrats were aware that Van Buren's administration
was under attack for inaction in the face of distress caused by depression. This forced them to define their position more precisely. When
Calvin Colton, writing under the pseudonym "Junius," accused the
government of destroying the credit system, which benefited poor
men as well as rich, the New York *Evening Post* sponsored a reply
asserting that Whigs wanted a privileged bank while Democrats denied "the natural right of government to grant special rights to a few."
It was "a vital, all-essential condition in [the Democratic] political
creed" that government should act upon the principle of equal legislation and equal rights. John A. Dix, a prominent New York Democrat, called Van Buren's proposal for the divorce of government from
commercial banking a "Declaration of Financial Independence"; but
for Junius it was "like a bolt from heaven that shivers the oak." He
accused the government of having told the people, "Since you will
abuse credit, you shan't have it." This simple political rhetoric
provided symbols for a sophisticated argument over the role of government in society.[45]

The new Democratic orthodoxy went beyond the separation of

45. "Junius" [Calvin Colton], *The Crisis* (New York, 1840); Anon., *The Crisis Answered* (New
York, 1840). The argument became somewhat involved because Junius represented the refusal
to extend credit to those in distress as an example of government interference while Democrats
argued that their policy was based on the principle of nonintervention in private affairs.

bank and state and hostility to paper currency to embrace a whole theory of nonintervention in economic and social affairs. The axiom that the best government is that which governs least had been coined at a period of history when even the most active of governments did very little, and emanated from a deep suspicion of aristocratic government rather than from economic or social theory. Now there emerged a new concept that society was a self-regulating mechanism which would operate best if left to itself. In 1840 Samuel J. Tilden, then a young rising star in the Northern Democratic party, defended administration policy in a speech which attracted much attention. Most nations, he said, had been taught to assume that privilege and monopoly were necessary, but "the American people have tried the principle of equal freedom in nearly every branch of business; and they have found all those branches better regulated than under any other system." They had unfortunately departed from these principles by legislating for banks and "assumed to substitute for the laws of Trade which Nature has ordained." State governments had caught the infection and set up a "system . . . subject to all the dangerous impulses of private business, but exempted, under the pretense of government regulation from the laws of trade by which these impulses would be restrained."[46]

While Democratic spokesmen echoed the moral precepts of rural society they were aware that progressive economic thought in Europe and especially in Britain endorsed their views. Classical economists had little political influence in America, and even Adam Smith was treated with more respect than understanding; but from the pages of the *Edinburgh Review* and other British publications, Democratic writers learned that their suspicion of government was based on sound economic principles, while bank men, protectionists, and advocates of government aid for internal improvements were uninformed, old fashioned, and erroneous. This intellectual respectability was an asset to Democrats, while Whigs were handicapped by lack of an acceptable theory. The men who claimed to argue from experience in manufactures and banking were told that their cause was selfish and their economic theory contemptible. Henry Carey had yet to establish his reputation and was not even, at that stage, a full-blown advocate of protection. Nor were the spokesmen of the New England elite unanimous, and at Harvard Francis Bowen taught classical economics in a way that made no con-

46. Samuel J. Tilden, *The Writings and Speeches of Samuel J. Tilden*, ed. John Bigelow (New York, 1885): "Currency, Prices and Wages," I: 144.

cession to American experience. Many Whigs accepted the academic case for a self-regulating market economy but defied theory and supported a party that advocated the incorporation of banks, protective tariffs, and public aid for canals, highways, and railroads.

\*     \*     \*

There was little or no difference in economic or social status between leaders of the two parties, but each accused the other of fomenting class warfare. Democrats used the rhetoric of class conflict and then denied that they meant it; Whigs pictured themselves as holding the gate against mob rule and then invited every respectable workingman to come in. In this argument over which party represented which class—or whether class was irrelevant—Whigs admitted that they had the harder task.

In 1835, when the two-party system was enduring its birth pains, William H. Seward reflected upon the Whig failure in their first New York contest and wrote to Thurlow Weed that it was utterly impossible to defeat Van Buren because the people were for him or, rather, "for the principle they suppose he represents. That principle is democracy. . . . It is with them the Poor against the Rich." The opposition had a tremendous task if they were to win the poor "while the rich we have always with us." Seward and Weed did not see themselves as representatives of the rich, and had risen as leading representatives of the anti-elitist, anti-monopoly, Anti-Mason party which flourished in the small towns and farming districts of western New York; but they could not disguise the fact that much of the talent and most of the money in their new party came from the wealthy classes in New York City.[47]

The elite of the cities felt themselves under attack, and it is in their testimony that one hears most plainly the language of class conflict. In 1840 Philip Hone of New York wrote that "scenes of violence, disorder and riot have taught us in this city that universal suffrage will not do for large communities." He believed that things were better in rural districts where a large proportion of the voters were Americans, "born and brought up on the spot."

> But in the heterogeneous mass of vile humanity in our population of three hundred and ten thousand souls the men who decide the elections are unknown. . . . They left their own

47. Seward to Weed, 12 April 1835, Seward Papers, University of Rochester, Rochester, N.Y.

country for ours to better their condition, by opposing everything good, honest, lawful, and of good report, and to effect
this they have banded themselves into associations to put
down, at all hazards, the party in favor of order and good
government.[48]

In 1844 the Whigs were even more disturbed by the evidence of class
hatred. "No man who noted the scowling brows, the clenched fists,
the exhibitions of demoniac rage and hatred by the Loco Foco masses,"
wrote a *Tribune* reporter, "would fail to observe that a great change has
come over the character of our people. They met us not as differing
citizens but as enemies."[49]

When in 1844 William Cullen Bryant in the *Evening Post* assured
businessmen that they need not be alarmed by Democratic victories,
the *Tribune* replied that he "never listens to speeches on his side of the
house. . . . If he will but go into a Town or Ward gathering of his
party he will see how industriously his colaborers strive to create envy,
jealousy and hatred between the Employer and the Workingman.
Wealth is regarded as proof presumptive of fraud, and profit as the
amount swindled from the hard earnings of the workmen."[50] After
the election of that year John Pendleton Kennedy, novelist and Whig
pamphleteer, claimed that open war had been declared against "every
substantial interest in the nation with which the Whigs could in any
manner be connected." He noted with alarm that "the *bonnet rouge*, fit
emblem of this intolerable scheme of social mastership, has been
hung, during the whole of this canvass, from the headquarters of
democracy in this city."[51]

The *Tribune* saw "this fell spirit" as a direct result of "the deadly
Jacobinism inculcated through the last twelve years" since Jackson's
vote message in 1832. "The war cries of 'The Rich against the poor!'
and the like, have done this dreadful work."[52] Thus the threat of class
conflict was seen as a symptom of decadence, and the venerable Judge
Storey wrote privately to Judge John McLean that he had "long de-
spaired as to the future of our country."

We are too corrupt, imbecile, slavish in our dependence upon
and under the auspices of Demagogues to maintain any free

48. Philip Hone, *Diary*, ed. Allan Nevins, I: 508, 3 November 1840.
49. *New York Tribune*, 1 November 1844.
50. *New York Tribune*, 12 November 1844.
51. *Address to the Clay Association of New York* (in *Niles' Register*, 7 December 1844).
52. *New York Tribune*, 1 November 1844. The conclusion was that "A terrible social Anarchy
seems to be the pervading spirit and the unfailing reliance of the Loco Foco Party."

constitution, and we shall sink lower and lower in national degradation. Who now will talk of the intelligence of the people to guard and protect their rights and understand their duties?[53]

On other occasions Whigs denied that class divided the country. Horace Greeley believed that character drew the line between parties: one was "most likely to win a majority in localities where the people are notoriously most intelligent and moral, while the other is pretty sure of the ascendancy in localities where the mass of the people are debased by ignorance and vice." Whigs grew strong when a community gave increased attention to religion and education, while Democrats flourished "where groggeries are multiplied and dissipation is rampant." A typical Democratic ward in New York City was "in good part given up to brothels, gambling dens and other haunts of wickedness." Continuing the disassociation of Whigs from class, Horace Greeley asserted that "the Whigs are by no means all wealthy, nor are the wealthy all Whigs." By their advocacy of free trade the Democrats had won the support of "the foreign importing interest, and with that the votes of a large number of merchants, of clerks, and almost the entire body of seamen." The shipping interest fancied "free trade in everything *but* shipping" and "hundreds of voters have on this ground been transferred from the Whig to the Loco-Foco tickets." The impression that Greeley intended to leave with his readers was that the virtuous in all classes were Whigs while the unprincipled were Democrats.[54]

Democrats resisted the accusation that their popularity with the poor indicated a commitment to radical egalitarianism. "We must not be misunderstood," said the *Democratic Review* in 1839, "neither must our meaning be perverted. We are no agrarians—no levellers. It would be as practicable to produce an absolute equality of condition among men as it would be to produce an absolute equality of stature; and if it were practicable it would not be desirable."[55] Organization of the poor was justified only because the rich had organized against them. Of the New York City campaign in 1834 William Cullen Bryant wrote:

Well, be it so. If the rich will, by their own acts, and their own choice, thus draw the line of distinction, between the

53. Storey to McLean, 23 November 1844, McLean Papers, Library of Congress, Washington, D.C.
54. *New York Tribune*, 3 May 1848.
55. *Democratic Review* VI (December 1839): 461.

two great classes of mankind, and provoke the people into self-defense by declaring war against them, they must meet the consequences. The people must make common cause against them, since they have made common cause against the people.[56]

Ten years later Lucius Lyon, a prominent Michigan Democrat, elaborated this theme when he wrote that "the ordinary political contests in the United States . . . have been little more than a struggle between the capital and labor of the country, the former seeking by means of legislation to obtain more than its just and natural share of the joint earnings of the two in the production of wealth, and the latter resisting the selfish and unhallowed attempt." In an ideal world he believed that the mutual interest of the two would be recognized, but "whenever the laborer seeks, by means of agrarian laws, to possess himself of the wealth of the capitalist, or the capitalist seeks through legislation to obtain exclusive privilege . . . a conflict must commence between them."[57] This abstract analysis was far removed from the emotions behind "the exhibition of demoniac rage and hatred by the Loco-Foco masses," but the message was the same.

Even in social intercourse the rich were alleged to erect barriers. Senator Linn, a Jacksonian stalwart from Missouri, "knew very well that the Democratic Party was considered the dregs of the earth by the favored few who contrive to rule everything," and whose doors "were shut against the best young men in the country, if they were known to entertain Democratic notions, as if they were something beneath the notice of good society."[58] In Boston young George Bancroft did not invariably find the doors of the social elite shut against him, but was made to feel that his Democratic opinions were unacceptable to his hosts and debarred him from the most exclusive circles.

Much of this evidence can be discounted. In western New York the Anti-Masons turned Whig were the social upstarts. In North Carolina and Tennessee Whigs championed the poor against the planter elite. In many parts of the South Whigs were as likely to be

56. Quoted Albert F. McLean, *William Cullen Bryant* (New York, 1964). In 1846, at the dedication of Jackson Hall Frank Blair and William C. Rives sent a message that "Associated wealth can only be arrested in its strides to absolute power by associated labor. . . . The slavery of Europe consists in the powers of the higher orders to despoil the producing classes." Washington *Union*, 8 July 1846.

57. Letter to the Democrats of Grand Rapids, 31 August 1844. Lucius Lyon Papers, William Clements Library, University of Michigan, Ann Arbor, Mich.

58. *Congressional Globe*, 27.1. 185.

found among self-made businessmen as in plantation great houses. In the newer western states the Whigs might hope to make money, but the social tone was set by leading Democratic families. Skilled workers in Eastern industries were as likely to be Whig as Democrat, and in the towns recent immigrants tended to divide along ethnic and religious rather than class lines.

Class conflict was a factor in party battles and cannot be ignored. It was crucial in areas where the results were usually most in doubt, and particularly in the City of New York from which most of the evidence has been drawn. Nevertheless there are qualifications to be made before accepting class struggle as an explanation of party divisions even in those areas where it was most evident. The resentment of recent Catholic immigrants (both Irish and German) can be readily understood, and so can the fears of long-established and wealthy families as their influence seemed to decline, but both parties were anxious to appeal to all classes and both accused their opponents of fostering class hatred. If Whigs claimed to represent "character" they meant to include not only the rich but also the mass of hard-working, respectable mechanics and thrifty workingmen, and they seem to have had much success among New Englanders and recent immigrants from England, Scotland, and other Protestant countries.[59] If Democrats claimed to speak for the poor they did not reject the leadership of well-to-do lawyers or financial support from bankers and merchants. Ethnic and religious backgrounds had greater influence than social and occupational categories on the choice of party. There was a complex pattern of party affiliations, and the major battle for support was fought among the heterogeneous mass of storekeepers, innkeepers, clerks, skilled tradesmen, and (in country districts) the smaller landowners. In this stratum the Equal Rights party won its following in New York City but in western districts the prize went first to Anti-Masons and then to Whigs. Both parties insisted that no industrious man need remain poor, but Democrats blamed conspiracies among the rich, and the Whigs disastrous Jacksonian policies, for disappointed hopes.

Both parties claimed to diagnose the cause of class conflict and to provide cures, but the interesting aspect was the extent to which both accused government of responsibility for a condition that they de-

59. In *The Concept of Jacksonian Democracy: New York as a Test Case* (Princeton, 1961), Chapter VIII *passim*, Lee Benson demonstrates the probability that most recent immigrants from the Protestant countries voted Whig, while Yankees who had moved into New York were equally divided (but not along class lines). The few free Negroes who had the suffrage voted Whig.

plored. For Democrats the great evil was privilege conferred by legislation; this had been the theme of Jackson's veto of the Bank Bill, the
inspiration of William Gouge and William Leggett, the mainspring
of the Loco-Foco revolt and, from the moment that Van Buren entered
the White House, the guiding principle of orthodox Democratic
thought. If the major demand was that government must be divorced
from private enterprise, it nevertheless recognized the powerful role
played by government in determining the character of society. Con-
versely the Whigs argued that only positive action by the federal
government—so far as the Constitution allowed or implied—could
overcome the obstacles that prevented men in all ranks from enjoying
the just reward for their efforts. With variations caused by local needs
and traditions the same arguments were repeated in the states.

The claim of both parties to unite classes constituted as powerful
an argument in their favor as their concurrent claim to unite sections.
Class conflict was seen as an unwelcome departure from the democratic way of settling disputes by working for victory at the polls. In the
light of subsequent American history this observation may appear too
commonplace to deserve notice but when viewed against the history of
other advanced societies during the nineteenth century its fundamental importance can be appreciated.

*         *         *

The focus of debate upon government action or inaction raised other
interesting questions. The great forces of nineteenth-century political
life demanded more of government than ever before. It was no longer
enough to govern; the question was now what part government
should play in the wide-ranging changes that were taking place in
society. This debate seldom took the shape of a clear-cut argument
over the powers of government but this was implicit in all the major
controversies. It was the habit of the age—and perhaps a laudable
one—to translate material issues into moral terms, and this gave
significance to the arguments of religious and romantic reformers. In
Europe a tradition of respectable antiquity had maintained that governments served a moral purpose and that rulers were ordained by God
as instruments in the divine plan. In the United States the Revolution
had replaced this sanction for authority by the assertion that governments derived their just powers from consent of the governed, that
their primary purpose was the protection of rights that could not be
abridged, and that utility and expediency were the sole tests that

should be applied. Now the idea that government had a moral character, and should have a moral purpose, was reentering American life.

Once the moral purpose of government was recognized, it became imperative to ensure that its actions met the standards set by
conscience. If government could promote the good life, it could also
protect or foster wickedness. To this was added the romantic view that
nations had a collective personality, and that all citizens shared in the
guilt of unjust government. In more prosaic terms the question was
whether citizens should pay taxes to support actions that they regarded as immoral. This dilemma would shortly be brought into
sharp focus by the annexation of Texas, the war with Mexico, and
territorial extension of slavery. Men who were offended by these acts
demanded from government the same moral standards as from individuals. Nor was moral shock purely Northern, for in the South white
men of all classes were profoundly disturbed by threats to their social
order. There is no reason to rehearse or justify the pro-slavery
arguments in order to understand why Southerners resented criticism
of their society, regarded abolitionist attacks as immoral, and fought
desperately to prevent their endorsement by the national government.
In both sections men who had influence and thought most deeply
insisted that government had a higher purpose than the reconciliation
of competing material interests. The imperatives of individual
morality were transmitted to the wider stage of national affairs, and
the new and disruptive force that emerged can best be described as
"political conscience." This transformed the quarrel between Jackson
and his critics into a contest over fundamental principles, or so it
appeared to many sincere partisans. In course of time political conscience would also attack the structure of the new parties, destroying
one and draining away the vitality of the other.

As great events unfolded, the misfortunes of the Whigs may
seem to be of small significance, but a basic assumption of party
government was nullified by the demonstration that the men who
had carried an election could not enact the policies which had won
them support. The idea of two-party government rested on the assumption that when a party won a majority in the country and in
both houses of Congress it should be able to direct the course of government. Men had learned, in preceding years, to see important principles at stake in the controversies over banks, internal improvements, public lands, and protection, and the failure of the
Whigs in 1841 and 1842 could not be treated merely as the loss
of a few measures designed to serve special interests. The Whigs

had proclaimed their principles as materially and morally superior, but in 1841 it was demonstrated that even a convincing electoral victory was of no avail. This shook the hitherto untested assumptions of the two-party system and threw doubt on the thesis that an American government should accept the mandate of political conscience. For these reasons it is now necessary to turn to a close examination of political events in 1841 and 1842, and to ask how far the Whig failure was caused by personal or institutional factors.

## Chapter 3

# PARTY GOVERNMENT— EXPERIMENT AND FAILURE

The inauguration of William Henry Harrison in March 1841 was expected to open a new era in the methods and aims of American government. The aims went beyond immediate remedies for depression and contemplated major changes in the relationship between government and national life. Depression called for measures to restore credit, regulate the currency, rescue indebted states, salvage schemes for internal improvements, and save manufactures from the threat of foreign competition. The number of business failures also prompted demands for a national bankruptcy act which would permit voluntary liquidation, save honest but unfortunate traders from debtors' prisons, and permit fresh starts without perpetual indebtedness. These remedies, called forth by the trials of the times, took their place in larger plans to stabilize currency, finance economic expansion through collaboration between government and private banking, and use revenue from the public lands to provide funds for internal improvements administered by the states. The enterprising businessmen of the country would be given security and working capital, but economic policy combined with political wisdom to emphasize the arguments for aiding the poorer regions, giving the more prosperous incentives for further development, curing unemployment, maintaining or raising the level of wages, and eliminating injurious conflicts between capital and labor.

Subsumed within these plans for recovery and growth were conservative fears over the trends in democratic society and widely diffused hopes for moral improvement and social betterment. The movement toward mass democracy could not be reversed, but its dangers might be appreciated and corrected, so that the best traditions of the early Republic could be preserved. If one side of this coin was "conservative" the other bore the clear imprint of the great religious and rationalist ideals for the betterment of social life. Government might not be asked to initiate but should provide the necessary aid and encouragement for schemes of improvement undertaken by voluntary effort.

The extent of Whig failure in 1841 must be measured by the magnitude of these expectations. There was to be a revolution in the style and purpose of government, and the spirit of early days would be restored in order to advance from a firm base in the days of recovery, expansion, and change that lay ahead. The subsequent misfortunes of 1841 and 1842 left the Whigs with a meager legislative achievement, and bequeathed to their supporters frustrations with far-reaching implications. Among the casualties was the belief that a party which had won an election could control national policy through its majority in Congress. Success would have meant a significant step toward party government, as distinct from party as an organization for local power and a quadrennial alliance to elect a president.

*            *            *

The irony of 1840 was not that Whig victory was won by avoiding issues, but that expectations ran so far beyond the possibility of rapid achievement. Immediately after the election one friendly critic observed that "there never was a President elected who has a more difficult task imposed upon him than General Harrison. Too much is expected of him. Many expect his election to bring about immediate relief to the people, which time alone can secure to us."[1] Moreover, the Whig denunciation of executive tyranny involved a political paradox. An election could be won only by stressing the honesty, integrity, courage, and public spirit of Harrison; yet it was implicit in Whig rhetoric that once this paragon was in the White House he must abjure executive influence and confine himself to the faithful execution of the laws. Political initiative must be restored to Congress.

It is at this point that a singular lack of realism enters the debate. The Whigs proposed to enact a series of important measures and to alter the balance of power in the national government with little ap-

1. J. Mitchell to McLean, 28 November 1840, McLean Papers, Library of Congress, Washington, D.C.

preciation of the administrative tasks involved. Too often it was assumed that Congress would enact principles while the details would look after themselves. One can compare the impatient optimism of the American Whigs in 1841 with the caution of British Whigs after 1832. There had been pressing demands for wide-ranging changes in British social policy—in the Poor Law, in municipal government, in factories, and in education—and, at the same time, a need to adjust to the new constitutional situation, abolish slavery, grapple with the problems of rapidly expanding economic life, and absorb a host of new ideas advanced by economists and social thinkers. With varying success these tasks were accomplished, but the first wave of reform took four years and involved intensive investigation by two Royal Commissions (which included experts without official position), several major Parliamentary committees, and exhaustive public discussion. In the United States the tasks were comparable, but Whig leaders expected to take all the major steps in one short special session of Congress called during the summer of 1841.

Historians have often implied that the election of 1840 was a riot of nonsense and blamed the Whigs for debasing the standards of politics.[2] The campaign did indeed produce some fine specimens of demagogic art and introduced methods of electioneering that were then unfamiliar, but the major speeches were not mere declamation, and Harrison was not a nonentity, but a man whose experience of public life went back to the beginning of the century. He conducted his own campaign and his important speeches—widely circulated as pamphlets—contained intelligent though general discussion of issues. His adroit blend of humor, reminiscence, and serious argument made him a good campaigner, but what he could not do—because contrary to Whig philosophy—was to commit Congress to accept his policy.[3] Henry Clay claimed that "the present distressed and distracted state of the country may be traced to the single cause of the action, the encroachments, and the usurpations of the executive branch of government." General Harrison agreed that his major task was to cut the presidency down to the size intended by the makers of the Constitution. He recalled that he had been "brought up after the strictest manner of Virginian anti-federalism" and "taught to believe that, sooner or later, that fatal catastrophe to human liberty

2. Perhaps the most important aspect of the campaign was that people enjoyed it—if they were on the winning side—and why not?

3. The major campaign speeches are printed in Anthony B. Norton, *The Great Revolution of 1840: Reminiscences of the Log Cabin and Hard Cider Campaign* (Mount Vernon, Ohio, 1888). The quotations that follow are taken from this publication.

would take place—that the General Government would swallow up all the State governments, and that one department of the government would swallow up all other departments." In 1840 the latter danger was apparent, and Harrison invited the people to revive "the old republican rule, to watch the administration and control all its acts which are not in accordance with the strictest code of republicanism." The qualifications of Harrison for the presidency had to be stressed, yet once elected he would hand over political initiative to the majority in Congress. He would be the instrument of change, but should not decide its direction. Typically he expressed personal doubts about a national bank, but added "if the people deem it necessary to the proper discharge of the function of their government to create a national bank, properly guarded and regulated, I shall be the last man, if elected President, to set up my authority against that of the millions of American freemen."

Henry Clay made specific proposals for the reduction of executive power: The President should be limited to a single term; the veto power should be more precisely defined; bills passed within the last three days of a session should become law if the President failed to sign them or return them; vetoes should be overridden by simple majorities; the power to dismiss from federal office should be restricted and the President bound to communicate his reasons to the Senate; control over the Treasury should be vested exclusively in Congress and the right of the President to dismiss or suspend the Secretary should be "rigorously precluded." Finally no member of Congress, during his term or in the subsequent year, should be appointed to federal office. These proposals would have drastically revised the balance of power in the national government, and moved the United States a significant step toward parliamentary government with the executive wholly responsible to Congress. Clay could hardly expect the passage of a whole series of constitutional amendments, but probably hoped that voluntary observance of these limitations would establish precedents which future Presidents would find it difficult to break. Harrison's promise not to veto measures passed by clear majorities in both Houses might establish a convention, and Clay may have recalled that in England the royal veto had dropped out of use without formal alteration of the law.

If Congress were to capture the initiative from the Executive, it would require organization and leadership. Organization must build on party which could alone provide continuity, loyalty, and regularity in voting. Congress already had party caucuses, but they must become more frequent, reach binding decisions, avoid embarrassing differences in public, regulate day-to-day business, assign work to committees, and declare the party line on amendments or procedural questions. Committees would have to stick to the timetable agreed by caucus, while instructing the executive departments rather than awaiting their proposals.

Leadership offered a difficult problem. No one could claim to be the "leader" of a party except the elected President. It had been customary for some Representatives and Senators to act as Administration spokesmen, but there were no officially recognized majority and minority leaders. The party caucuses might recognize the responsibility of individuals for particular bills, but were reluctant to give any one man overall responsibility. Henry Clay was determined to lead the Whigs in the Senate, and there was no one of sufficient eminence to contest his claim once Webster became Secretary of State, but his authority depended upon personality not on received congressional practice. In the House the chairman of the Ways and Means Committee was recognized as being, next to the Speaker, the leading man of the majority party, but he was no more than a *primus inter pares* without authority to issue directions except on financial business, and in 1841 there was no Whig of sufficient stature to take the lead.

In the Senate the committees were elected but allowed for minority representation. The Senator of the majority party with the largest number of votes became chairman for the two-year term of Congress. In the House committees and chairmen were appointed by the Speaker, but once appointed made their own decisions subject to the rules of the House. The committee system worked well enough when scrutinizing proposals from the Departments or submitted by individuals, but was less effective when required to formulate policy. One problem was timing. The membership of committees was not known until after Congress had been organized, and though there was usually some continuity of membership (especially in the Senate) this was not guaranteed. In 1841 the committees would have new Whig chairmen and a majority of inexperienced members, but would be expected to produce quick results. For instance, House rules required the Ways and Means Committee to report on appropriations thirty days after appointment, so that much detailed business would be hurried and members flounder amid undigested figures.[4]

Congress was therefore ill-equipped to handle quickly a number

---

4. Millard Fillmore Papers, Buffalo Historical Society, Buffalo, N. Y., 18 December 1841. The Ways and Means Committee met daily at 9 A.M. For a description of congressional procedure see Luther Stearns Cushing, *Elements of Law and Practice of the Legislative Assemblies of the United States* (Boston, 1855).

of legislative innovations; yet this was required if the Whig commitment to change were to be implemented. In 1846 James K. Polk would demonstrate what could be done, even against resistance within his own party, when a President was determined and active departmental heads were ready to feed detailed proposals to Congress, but this was precisely the pattern of behavior that the Whigs had foresworn. There was nothing intrinsically wrong with government by party in Congress, but it was going to be very difficult to put into practice.

Party leaders might hope to control the situation in Congress, but only the President could make an administration or supply the faithful of the party with their expected share of federal offices. In choosing his Cabinet the President-elect had to observe the need for sectional and factional representation, and when these requirements had been met the appointees were likely to be unfamiliar with the Departments they were supposed to direct and lack personal acquaintance with the congressmen whose help they would have to seek. Recommendations for the lesser appointments might come through individual politicians, local party organizations, or by personal application. In the preceding ten years the number of offices had increased— from 11,491 in 1831 to 18,038 in 1841—and so had the difficulties of an incoming President. Leading a party with innumerable demands for patronage, he had to evolve his own rules and weigh the contribution each appointment would make to solidarity or factionalism in the party. Congressional leaders clamored for the recognition of those upon whom they must depend for support, and awaited with apprehension decisions which might make or mar their political careers.

Formal appointments were only part of the story. The real decisions would be made by the comparatively small number of men who enjoyed influence at the national capital. There were forty-five Senators and two hundred and forty-one Representatives; the departmental heads and their more important subordinates numbered perhaps fifty; men without official position, but with influence, numbered perhaps twenty or thirty. One might add a few high-ranking members of the armed services, some influential lobbyists, and a handful of experienced newspaper reporters, but the whole Washington "establishment" did not add up to more than five hundred. In practice the inner group upon which the working of the system depended was much smaller. A majority of the Representatives were on the periphery, and perhaps a third of them might not reappear after the next biennial election. Senators were likely to be around for

longer, but some were obscure, some idle, and several primarily concerned with maintaining power in their states. In both Houses few
were willing, available, or competent to accept responsibility for
day-to-day business or participate fully in arduous committee work.
In the cabinet probably not more than two or three wielded effective
influence outside their own Departments, and most departmental officials lived apart from political circles and steered clear of involvement in controversy.

As a purely administrative capital Washington lacked the cultural and social life of London, Paris, or Vienna. In the older capitals,
which had grown naturally around medieval institutions, the political
structure was buttressed by men for whom the capital was the natural
center of national life. In London the prestige of the hereditary aristocracy, the strength of a professional upper middle class, the close association between Church and State, and developing links between politics and letters all made for a large and intellectually varied "establishment." If real decision was confined to a small number, many more
were closely involved in the discursive life of politics because of social
position, professional function, or intellectual merit. The ancient
universities, the Church, the armed services, and London society
provided a common background, and men who entered the charmed
circles from middle-class backgrounds hastened to assimilate themselves into the upper class environment. The Washington political
elite was smaller, had a weaker fund of common experience, and
lacked continuity. The presidential years marked phases in Washington society in a way that changes of government in London did not:
when the Democrats went out and the Whigs came in, it was like a
change of dynasty in a monarchical state; the faces changed, the manners changed, and the topics of conversation changed.

In this changing scene leading Senators and the few Representatives who survived from election to election could achieve a reputation
out of proportion to their talents. Survival marked them as exceptional, and often imposed upon them more than a fair share in the
time-consuming pursuit of legislative business. During the session,
day in and day out, there was an enormous volume of work to be done
which attracted no publicity and earned no partisan advantage; the
reward was the esteem of Congress and a place among the small
number of men who influenced national policy.

Members of Congress not of the inner circle might be obscure in
the capital, but each represented a combination of friends and allies in
a state or district. This was the reality of party for most politicians,

and its preservation was their major concern. Federal office or the promise of office was an important counter in the local game, and it was inevitable that politicians looked to the President rather than to the congressional leaders, and sought to establish reputations as the men most likely to influence presidential or departmental appointments. Whatever the Whigs might have said about "executive usurpations" the character of the party in the country would be molded by presidential patronage, and the cohesion of the party would depend upon a close rapport between the President and the inner circle of congressional leaders. Within days of Harrison's inauguration Henry Clay had deeply offended the President, and was complaining bitterly that he had no way of satisfying the numerous men who sought his influence in their quest for office.

\*     \*     \*

At sixty-four Henry Clay was regarded by his admirers as the leading statesman of the age. He had been a member of the House for fourteen years, and Speaker for eleven of them. He had been twice a candidate for the presidency, Secretary of State for four years, and since 1831 a Senator. His name was prominently associated with the movement for war in 1812, the Missouri Compromise, the Tariff of 1833, and opposition to Jackson that had brought the Whig party to birth. As author of the phrase "American System" he had given high-sounding patriotism to the protectionist cause. In debate he impressed by incredible vitality, which continued into old age, and by fluency rather than by elegance or profundity of thought. It was often difficult— since the magic touch of personality was absent—for admirers to describe exactly why they thought Clay great. Perhaps the best impression was that given by Robert C. Winthrop in old age, recalling an incident in 1833 when Clay was presented with some silver pitchers by a gathering of young National Republicans in Boston.[5]

> The rooms were not spacious. He had not a note for reference, nor had he contemplated any thing but the briefest and most formal acknowledgment of the gift. But, whatever had kindled it, "the fire burned, and he spoke with his mouth." No

---

5. Robert C. Winthrop, *Memoir of Henry Clay* (Boston, 1880), 30–31. Winthrop also admitted that "his prepared speeches were generally his least successful." *Ibid.,* 28.

lava from a long-closed crater could have rushed in a more impetuous torrent, and he recalled to me at once John Adams's description of James Otis as a "flame of fire."

After speaking of the Compromise Tariff, he "depicted the danger of civil war which it had averted," and "dwelt on the Union of the country as the best hope of freedom throughout the country."

After the lapse of forty-six years, I dare not attempt to recall the precise words or thoughts which were addressed to me on that occasion. But the tones still ring in my ears, and I can only bear witness to an impressiveness of speech never exceeded, if ever equalled, within an experience of nearly half a century, during which I have listened to many of the greatest orators on both sides of the Atlantic.

The man who could leave so abiding an impression—not on a great public occasion but with an impromptu speech to a semiprivate gathering of fifty or sixty young men—was no ordinary man.

If the quality that convinced contemporaries of his greatness is elusive, it is equally difficult to explain why a man with his record achieved so little. It is true that his name was forever associated with the compromises that saved the Union or deferred its dissolution, but these were negative achievements in which he yielded points that he would have preferred to sustain. It was his fate to fight defensive battles, and throughout his long career no permanent and positive measures were associated with his name. He failed to save or restore the national bank. Internal improvements under national direction foundered, and the distribution of the public land revenue (intended to salvage the improvements policy) was still-born. The battle for protection was lost with the low tariff act of 1846, and America advanced toward wealth without the aid of measures Clay had deemed essential. Were there elements in Clay's personality that made bad luck inevitable?

Clay was at his best face to face with an audience, but his words carried neither the majesty of Webster nor the penetration of Calhoun. To modern readers his speeches appear prolix, imprecise, and often shallow; the same impression must have been left with some contemporaries, and little of the essential Clay could survive the small blurred print of early nineteenth-century newspapers. There were also defects in judgment. In argument personal asperities often went too far and even when redeemed by subsequent courtesy, indicated a temperament that was too emotional and too impatient for political achievement of the highest order. The man who made his reputation as the architect of compromise was often insensitive to the feelings of others, and his fondness for bold oratorical pronouncements concealed an ignorance of detail. Though much of his public life was absorbed by the bank question, he seems never to have understood how the credit system worked in practice. There was force in the criticism that he proposed to hand over the financial business of government to private bankers because they knew how to handle matters which he could never bother to master.

The immediate cause of the quarrel between Clay and Harrison was the former's insistence that Congress should be called into special session during the summer of 1841. The normal lapse of nine months between the inauguration of a President and the first meeting of the new Congress allowed departmental heads time to learn their business, while the President took stock of the situation after the rush of first appointments, matured his ideas, and established personal relations with his cabinet and party leaders. The alternative of calling Congress into special session has seldom commended itself to new Presidents, though in 1841 there were some arguments for taking this course. The Whigs had promised remedies for economic distress and their main target, the Independent Treasury, would remain operative until removed by act of Congress and replaced by some other institution to handle the public money, currency, and expanding credit. These reasons for calling a Special session reinforced Henry Clay's personal determination to direct policy.

In his campaign speech at Taylorsville Clay had spelled out the measures that Congress ought to adopt, and during the lame duck sessions of December 1840 to March 1841 he and his friends had brought forward proposals in Congress. There was no hope of legislation at that stage, but the object was to familiarize Whigs with the tasks ahead and prepare the ground for hard work in the summer. Immediately after the inauguration he pressed Harrison to call a special session, and even sent him a draft of the proclamation that he was to issue. Harrison was furious, told Clay that he was too impetuous, that others would have to be consulted, and that he preferred to communicate in writing rather than argue the case face to face. Clay was equally angry and more than ever determined to gain his point. The spectacle of two elderly men in violent altercation might be mildly ridiculous, but the dispute raised a question of fundamental impor-

tance. How and upon whose terms could the Whig principle of congressional governmenl be made to work?[6]

Millard Fillmore of New York, who was marked down for an
important position in the House, confided to Thurlow Weed that he
had been "strongly opposed to an extra session, and am still if it can be
avoided, but the course of events had unfortunately precipitated us
upon the discussion of the supposed measures of the incoming administration in a way to give our opponents the benefit for anything
that is odious and to give us the benefit from anything that is popular."[7] In other words the Whigs led by Clay had committed themselves to the proposition that there would be no improvement without
Whig measures and could not risk delay. "The whole discussion,"
Fillmore thought, "has been fraught with much mischief, and it has
done much to render an extra session indispensable or at least politic."
Clay had committed the party to action, and like it or not they had to act.

Clay got his special session, but before it met the well-
intentioned Harrison was dead and his place had been taken by Vice-
President John Tyler of Virginia, who was known for his somewhat
unimaginative adherence to old-style Virginian politics. He had little
in common with Whigs who were wedded to economic growth and
social change, and had opposed a protective tariff and the recharter of
the Bank of the United States. He had broken with Jackson over the
President's excessive use of presidential authority, and Clay pinned his
hopes on Tyler's acceptance of the Whig view of executive power. To
John M. Berrien, his principal Southern lieutenant, Clay wrote that
Tyler's acceptance of the vice-presidential nomination implied "an
obligation . . . to stand by, and carry out the measures of the Whigs."
He added, "I shall repair to Washington with all the confident hopes
of the success of our measures, which I expressed to you before the late
separation at Washington."[8] Undeterred by the doubts of supporters,
the warning notes sounded in the quarrel with Harrison, or by lack of
information about the new President's views, Clay was resolved to put
his policy and the whole issue of government by party in Congress to
the test.

6. Clay to Harrison, 13 March 1841, Clay Papers, Library of Congress, Washington, D.C.
Clay suggested "the propriety of a definitive decision" on the special session; abandonment of the
idea would lead to "the imputation of vacillating counsels." Harrison replied, "You are too
impetuous," and said that there were others to consult. March 15: Clay was "mortified by the
suggestion you made . . . that I had been represented as dictatory to you."

7. Millard Fillmore Papers, 6 February 1841.

8. Clay to Berrien, 20 April 1841, Berrien Papers, Southern Historical Collection, University
of North Carolina, Chapel Hill, N.C.

The main features of the Whig program could be anticipated. The Independent Treasury would be replaced by a "fiscal agent," which would act as the government's banker, regulate the currency, and facilitate commercial transactions. Like the old Bank of the United States it would be a private corporation chartered by congress. This might have been legislation enough, but in addition the proceeds from public land sales would be distributed to all the states according to a formula yet to be devised, and an increase in the tariff was necessary because the government was running at a deficit and would lose a further $2 million of revenue in July 1841 when the final reduction under the Act of 1833 became effective. Clay had been evasive on the question of protection, but his personal views were well known. As the author of the Compromise of 1833 he claimed to interpret its spirit, and in his Taylorsville speech had argued that protection for manufactures could be obtained under the 1833 Act, by home valuation of imports, and by putting some items used by industry on the free list. If arguments over the tariff were prolonged, it would be necessary to take immediate steps—either by loan or by postponing the reductions under the 1833 Act—to meet the government deficit. There was also considerable support for a national bankruptcy act. Finally many Whigs came to Washington with frequently voiced but largely illusory hopes that public expenditure might be reduced. All this was a heavy program for a new Congress, and could succeed only if the Whig leaders showed unusual skill in drafting measures to unite their followers and circumvent the opposition.

Clay did not conceal his conviction that real leadership must come from his seat in the Senate. Before the end of the old Congress in March he had had discussions with his colleagues, planned strategy, and perhaps considered means to overcome the perennial difficulty of limiting opportunities for obstruction and curbing the apparently unlimited verbosity of Senators. On Monday, June 7, a week after the special session had assembled, Clay proposed resolutions "in compliance with suggestions thrown out at the last sitting of the Senate." The first stated that no business ought to be transacted "but such as, being of an important nature, may be supposed to have influenced the extraordinary convention of Congress." This gave notice that the Whig leaders would give no time for the private or local bills which would normally deluge a new Congress. The matters designated as important and urgent were the repeal of the Independent Treasury, the incorporation of a national bank, the provision of adequate revenue by new duties, a temporary loan, the distribution of the proceeds of the public lands, the necessary appropriation bills, and a modification of the banking system in the District of Columbia (which was an innocuous way of announcing the incorporation of a national bank). Finally, he said, "it is expedient to distribute the business proper to be done at this session, between the Senate and House of Representatives, so as to avoid both Houses acting on the same subject at the same time." The resolutions were not discussed but printed and laid upon the table. In the allocation of responsibility the Independent Treasury repeal, the new bank, and distribution were initiated and first discussed in the Senate; under the Constitution revenue measures had to originate in the House, and Clay intended to leave them there until the bank and distribution measures had been cleared in the Senate.[9]

The plan was clear-cut but the execution was necessarily difficult. The House of Representatives had elaborate rules (which could be adopted, modified, or abandoned at the beginning of each session) designed to cut short debate without encroaching too much upon freedom of speech. John Quincy Adams urged that debate should be closed by majority vote, and reminded Southern Democrats, who contended for freedom of debate, that the rigid restriction of discussion on abolitionist petitions—the 21st or "gag" rule—had been imposed by a simple majority. The House preferred not to alter the rules which already allowed party leaders to decide the Order of the Day, move the Previous Question or motions for reconsideration, and limit speeches to one hour's duration. The Order of the Day fixed the day and hour for consideration of a motion, which then had precedence over all others. If other business was proceeding at the appointed time a member could move that the Order of the Day be read, but if this motion was lost, the Order of the Day was suspended. In other words a majority could force discussion of a particular motion, close debate on other matters, or (by failing to accept the Order of the Day) keep some other question in debate. The Previous Question was derived from the British Parliament where it was used to avoid a vote, but in Congress it was used to force a vote on the question under discussion. The question (normally moved by the majority member in charge of a bill) was "Shall the main question be now put?" The Previous Question had to be seconded by a majority of those present, but the motion could not be debated, no call for "yeas and nays" was allowed, and the Speaker decided whether it was carried. Once the

9. *Congressional Globe*, 27. 1. 319.

Previous Question had been accepted no further debate on the main question was allowed except that the member in charge of a bill had the right of reply to points made. Until 1841 the Previous Question was not used in the Committee of the Whole—when debate ranged more widely than in formal sessions—but it was so applied in the special session. By a majority decision a future date and time could also be fixed to terminate debate and proceed to vote. Finally a motion to reconsider brought to the House, for final determination, a decision that had already been taken, and thus rendered snap votes ineffective.

Then as now a vital part was played by the congressional committees, which were appointed in the House of Representatives by the Speaker (or occasionally by ballot). The member named first by the Speaker (or, in a ballot, the member with most votes) became chairman. The committees were bi-partisan, but the majority and the chairman always belonged to the majority party. Legislative proposals were referred to the appropriate committees, which could examine witnesses, call for papers, and make reports which could be arguments for discussion or a draft bill. In the House a motion to receive a report had priority over all other business except points of order.

The key man in the House of Representatives was the Speaker, who was elected, usually on a straight party vote, at the beginning of each Congress. He influenced, if he did not decide, the Orders of the Day, and accepted or rejected motions for the Previous Question or reconsideration. A Speaker who kept a tight grip on the House could either limit severely the opportunities for obstruction, or connive at delay if it happened to suit his party. At the same time his power was not unlimited. By frequent procedural motions, and demanding roll-call votes, the minority could make life uncomfortable for a Speaker who appeared to be administering the rules unfairly, and his situation became more difficult if members of his own party were likely to defect or disappear when crucial votes were called. In 1841 the Speaker was John White from Kentucky. One can assume that Henry Clay had had a hand in the choice, and with a substantial and almost united Whig majority his task was comparatively easy.

The Senate offered a more severe test for party management than the House of Representatives. In 1841 the Whig majority was small, and two or three were in the party but not truly of it. Senators enjoyed a six-year tenure, and their careers depended far more upon their personal standing in their states than upon proceedings in Congress or the goodwill of party leaders. Freedom of debate was unlimited, and Senators could and did speak at enormous length with little regard for relevance. Once recognized by the Chair a Senator could not be silenced until he concluded his speech or yielded the floor to another. Prior agreement on a course of action was therefore essential if any business was to be completed. On the bank bill the Whig Senators "had a caucus for four or five consecutive days and the whole measure was gone through most carefully." A little later they "adopted in Caucus, a pledge, for every Senator to vote on every occasion—to vote down amendments without discussion," but only twenty-two senators attended and there were doubts about the absentees.[10]

Fear of obstruction by frequent and lengthy speeches prompted Clay to suggest that the Senate should copy the House in adopting "a rule in the nature of the *Previous question*." This caused much bad temper. On July 13, Senator King of Alabama asked whether it was the intention to introduce "a gag law," and the following conversation ensued:

> *Mr. Clay:* I will, sir; I will.
> *Mr. King:* I tell the Senator, then, that he may make his arrangements at his boarding house for the winter.

King went on to say that he "was truly sorry to see the honorable Senator so far forgetting what is due to the Senate as to talk of coercing it by any possible abridgment of its free action."[11] This was followed by Thomas Hart Benton with a furious speech which proclaimed that

> Senators have a constitutional right to speak; and while they speak to the subject before the House, there is no power anywhere to stop them. The previous question, and the old sedition law, are measures of the same character, and children of the same parents, and intended for the same purposes. They are to hide light—to enable those in power to work in darkness—to enable them to proceed unmolested—and to permit them to establish ruinous measures without stint, and without detection.

With equal determination Calhoun maintained that the freedom of debate had never been abused. "Speeches were uniformly confined to

10. Willie P. Mangum, *Papers*, ed. Henry T. Shanks (Chapel Hill, 1950-56), III:184.
11. T. H. Benton, *Abridgment of Congressional Debate* XIV, 316 (not in *Congressional Globe*).

the subject under debate. There could be no pretext for interference. There was none but that of all despotisms." Deterred by the arguments, the narrowness of the Whig majority, and the possibility of defections on this issue, Clay took no action and the Senate remained ungagged.[12]

Clay was king of the Whigs, but a limited monarch who occupied no constitutional position. His leadership depended upon personal ascendancy; the possibility of "dictatorship" worried sensitive Whigs, while strong-minded men were unwilling to take instructions from a man whose title and status was no higher than their own. In the Whig senatorial caucus Clay "was put almost *hors de combat*, not only on account of an imputed dictatorial spirit, made by our opponents, but beginning to be pretty openly insinuated by our friends." According to one estimate he did not speak, in several caucus meetings for more than five or six minutes in all, and his claim to lead had merely demonstrated the capacity of Senators to maintain their individual and collective rights.[13]

Despite these difficulties the Whig Senators displayed remarkable solidarity, and the House majority remained intact. Against every kind of harassment from the opposition, and later from the executive, the Whig majorities held together and carried their measures. In the Senate some part of this success may have been due to Willie P. Mangum of North Carolina, who was a devoted adherent of Clay and one of those patient, adroit men whose skill is essential to the success of any legislative assembly. The one advantage that accrued to the Whigs from John Tyler's translation to the White House was that it made Mangum, as president *pro tempore*, the presiding officer in the Senate, while his work as chairman of the Whig caucus did much to preserve harmony and party effectiveness. In later years a characteristic melancholy, copiously relieved by alcohol, diminished the effectiveness of a man who, with better fortune, might have left a greater name in history.

In spite of near unanimity among the Whigs the odds were against Clay and congressional government even before Tyler used his veto. The nature of Congress, the conventions it had evolved, and frequent needs to conciliate touchy and erratic men, frustrated initia-

---

12. *Ibid.*, 317, 319. The project seems to have been revived later. Willie P. Mangum wrote to W. A. Graham on 10 July 1841 that he was on a committee set up by the Senate Whigs "to prepare a rule in the nature of the Previous Question" (Mangum, *Papers* III:193). Nothing came of this.

13. Mangum, *Papers* III:184.

tive and disorganized strategy. Moreover the program itself was too ambitious. Nevertheless one should recall that American institutions were still in their formative stage, and Congress itself stood at a turning point. The Hamiltonian experiment had seen strong executive initiative reinforced by congressional support; during Jefferson's Presidency congressional government had been manipulated by presidential management; during the "era of good feelings" congressional government, lacking presidential guidance, degenerated into faction; while Jackson's chief instrument had been the veto rather than positive proposals for legislation. A further turn of the wheel might have seen leaders in Congress determining policy and the President reduced to the faithful execution of the laws. To make this possible Congress would have to develop quicker and more purposeful procedures, but this was already on the way in the House and a little more pressure might have persuaded the Senate. The point may be abstract and hypothetical, but it is not unimportant; the future of the United States might have been very different if legislative conventions had taken a different turn.

A successful two-party system requires a tacit understanding that the majority party will be allowed to legislate after fair discussion. In 1841 this convention was threatened because a new national bank was regarded by Calhoun and most Democrats as so objectionable that it must be resisted beyond the normal limits of free debate and procedural maneuver. In January Calhoun had given fair warning both of his own unyielding opposition and of the dangers involved in pressing forward with a measure on which the country was so divided. The greatest enemies of banks were not, he argued, men like himself but those "who would force them again into union with the Government, against the deep conviction of the injustice, impolicy and unconstitutionality of such union, of a powerful and determined party, not much inferior to their opponents."[14] Democrats were resigned to the loss of the Independent Treasury, but would fight to the last ditch to prevent the incorporation of anything resembling the old Bank of the United States.

In 1841 John C. Calhoun was the same age as Clay, equally ambitious and equally disappointed. He had broken with Jackson, cooperated for a time with the rising Whig opposition, but then, despite his hatred for Van Buren, found himself in close agreement with Democratic policy. Van Buren's defeat opened possibilities that Calhoun

14. *Congressional Globe*, 26.2. Appendix, 21.

could not ignore. The Democrats were shaken and leaderless, but their organization was intact and the man who could restore their morale would have an excellent chance of winning the nomination in 1844. It would be a nice irony if the great Nullifier took over the party alliance created by Andrew Jackson. He was able to secure for himself the chairmanship of the standing committee of Democratic Senators, and from this position directed the strategy of opposition. "Our success was complete," he would claim three years later. "The Whigs were routed in two months,"[15] but this became possible because confrontation in Congress and procedural delays gave way to more subtle attempts to disturb the conscience of a President whose scruples were well known.

John Tyler's nomination as Vice President was a classic example of party folly in choosing a man who belonged to a minority in the party and whose only recommendation was his supposed attraction for men on the periphery. The choice was more extraordinary when the presidential candidate was advanced in years. General Solomon Van Rensselaer of New York, who nominated him at the Whig convention, said that he had had three men in mind—Tyler, Owen of North Carolina, and Bell of Tennessee. Pressed to name one, he had chosen Tyler. "I did it," he said, "for the best. I had served in Congress with him in years gone by, and I then deemed him an honorable man; and as Virginia was nearly balanced, I hoped the nomination of my amiable friend might incline the scale in our favor."[16] Ironically, the calculation failed because the Democrats carried Virginia; and Bell, who won Tennessee for White in 1836, would have been a far better choice. Nevertheless, when Harrison's death brought this little-known man to the White House, most Whigs believed that he would accept or even promote their program.

He was a typical member of the Virginia upper class, had been Governor of his state and a United States Senator. In common with many other upper-class Southerners he disapproved Jackson's demagogic appeal, and regarded Van Buren as the symbol of a decline in public morality and the rise of Loco-Foco radicalism. There was no doubt about his attachment to State Rights. In 1833 he had said, "It is because I owe allegiance to the State of Virginia that I owe obedience to the laws of this [federal] government. My State requires me

15. To Francis Wharton, 4 February 1844. John C. Calhoun, *Correspondence,* ed. J. F. Jameson (American Historical Association Annual Report, 1899), II:565. (Hereafter cited as *Correspondence of Calhoun*).

16. *Niles' Register*, 20 May 1843.

to render such obedience. She has entered into a compact, which, while it continues, is binding on all her people."[17] He compared the federal compact to a treaty with a foreign power, which he would be bound to obey because his state had willed it, but this did not necessarily preclude enlarged national powers if they served the interest of Virginia. Even Clay claimed that his political creed derived from the resolutions of 1798, and John M. Berrien, former leader of the State Rights party in Georgia, was now a strong supporter of protective tariffs and a national bank.

Tyler had been chairman of the Senate committee that had investigated the affairs of the Bank after the failure of re-charter; his report had declared it a safe custodian for public funds, and he strongly opposed Jackson's removal of the deposits in 1833. He was a determined defender of legislative rights in the President's quarrel with Congress, and resigned his seat in the Senate when the legislature of Virginia instructed him to vote for the "expunging"resolution. National financial disorder had persuaded him that some form of central financial institution was necessary. His personal preference might be for some agency that could be clearly distinguished from the old Bank of the United States, but it was thought that he would follow Harrison in respecting the wishes of a congressional majority.

On May 8, 1841, Thomas Ewing, Secretary of the Treasury, reported to Clay that "No man can be better disposed than the President. His former opinions . . . will trouble *him* but *not*, I think, the country. He speaks of you with the utmost kindness, and you may rely upon it his friendship is strong and unabated."[18] Yet some days earlier Tyler had written to his Virginian friend and counsellor, Beverley Tucker:

> I have had too often to deplore the absence of a conciliatory spirit among the members of the Whig party, and my fear is now that nothing short of a National Bank, similar in all its features to that which has recently passed out of existence, will meet the views of prominent men in the Whig party.[19]

In his inaugural address he had said that he would promptly sanction

17. From a speech delivered on 6 February 1833, quoted O. P. Chitwood, *John Tyler* (New York, 1964), 117.
18. Clay Papers, 8 May 1841.
19. Lyon G. Tyler, *Letters and Times of the Tylers* (Richmond, 1884–96), II:32, 25 April 1841.

> Any constitutional measure which, originating in Congress,
> shall have for its first object the restoration of a sound cir-
> culating medium, so essentially necessary to give confidence
> in all the transactions of life, to secure industry its just and
> adequate rewards, and to re-establish the public prosperity.[20]

To anyone reading this sentence through anti-bank eyes it meant that
Tyler might bar a national bank that engaged in commercial business,
but the language did not differ greatly from that of pro-bank Whigs.
To Tucker, Tyler confided that "all that was wanting in order to have a
complete system through the action of the States was a central board,"
though he was puzzled by the proper way to organize it. His private
intention was "to devolve the whole subject on Congress, with a reservation of my constitutional powers to veto should the same be necessary in my view of the subject."[21]

Thus, in the first days of his presidency Tyler displayed that
capacity for confusing the minds of others which was to be disastrous
for himself and his party; he gave one impression to his official advis-
ers, another to his private friends, and used equivocal terms in public.
He would sign "any constitutional measure," but what was "constitutional"? Madison had signed the second Bank Charter Act, and Marshall had spoken for the Supreme Court to declare its constitutionality. Did "constitutional" mean what had been *accepted* or what John
Tyler personally believed? In the event he would neither indicate his
own views nor accept those of a congressional majority. On June 2
Ewing submitted a report to Congress which embodied the main features of a new national bank, but Tyler's determination to leave the
running to others while reserving his right to veto, extended to members of his own cabinet, who might propose measures but could not
rely upon his concurrence.

In all this there was more indecision than guile. "I believe,"
wrote Mangum on June 26, "that the President is probably about the
most miserable man in the Republic, and one could feel a sentiment of
compassion for him, were it not displaced by another sentiment."[22]
He probably wished desperately for a bill that he could sign, but was
nevertheless determined to prevent the Whigs from having the kind
of bank that the great majority of them wanted. So far as the party in
Congress was concerned there would have been a general welcome for

20. *Niles' Register,* 17 April 1841.
21. Tyler, *Letters*, II:32.
22. Mangum, *Papers*, III:128.

a new bank similar in most respects to the second Bank, but with tightened control over the directors. To avoid argument over constitutionality they would agree to charter the bank in the District of Columbia, but a necessary corollary was the power to set up branches in the principal commercial centers. The new bank would deal in foreign and domestic bills of exchange, decide the rate at which the notes of state banks should be accepted (thus regulating the value of paper money), and make advances to merchants by discounting their promissory notes.[23] The most controversial items were the right to establish branches and the power to engage in commercial banking by making loans to individuals.

The leaders of the opposition quickly diagnosed the situation. They made little resistance to the repeal of the Independent Treasury, because it was known that Tyler was with the majority on this issue, but on the bank bill they stressed the points that might touch the President's Virginian conscience without attempting to eliminate the features that he would regard as most objectionable. On distribution they made little attack on the principles involved, because the transference of funds to the states might easily commend itself to a State Rights Whig, but emphasized its effect upon the Compromise Tariff. They encouraged petitions from the states to reinforce the idea that the country was not behind the Whig majority, and made play with the fact that the bank had not been a direct issue in the election. Thus on July 12, James Buchanan said:

> If this bill is to be rushed through Congress when the country is not prepared for it; when the people have not asked for it; when no question has been made before the people on the subject, and in Virginia and North Carolina, even the Whig party, in the Presidential canvass, taking ground against it . . . and that this was the fact generally he would appeal from the Senator from Kentucky to Mr. Tyler, the official head of the party, if the measure was to be adopted under such circumstances, and especially if the gag was to be applied . . . a proper regard to the interests of those we represented would

23. There was considerable confusion over the meaning of the phrase "to discount notes." Bankers dealing in exchange purchased bills at a discount; this power was not controversial, but they might also accept an individual's promise to pay at a future date (a "promissory note"), advance cash at a discount, and perhaps renew the advance at interest when payment became due. In other words "discounting" bills as used in the contemporary argument meant the power to make personal loans to merchants, manufacturers, or farmers.

be prompt as to sound the cry of repeal throughout the land, and that question will be carried, unless the people of this country are willing to be transferred to the government of bank corporations.[24]

The points were skillfully designed to move the man in the White House. There *had* been no clear mandate from the people. Many Whigs in Tyler's own state *had* been against it, and might be expected to oppose him if it passed. The question *would* be carried to the people at the next election, and the President would be held responsible for the measure. A Democratic victory might lead to a repeal of the bank charter, and the President's reputation for consistency would have been sacrificed to no purpose. On August 11, when the bank bill had passed Congress and was awaiting decision by the President, Calhoun rammed home the point by presenting a petition from Isle of Wight County in Virginia, endorsed "by a large and respectable number of the citizens," who declared unanimously "that Congress had no power to create a National Bank," and that "should Congress pass a Bank or Fiscal Agent . . . the charter may be rightfully repealed."[25]

If the situation was exploited by the opposition, supporters of the bank were guilty of peculiar folly in pressing the measure in the way that they did. Some contemporaries suggested that Clay wished to create a breach between Tyler and the party, and deliberately played for the veto to destroy the President's hope of renomination and clear the way for himself in 1844. If Clay did plan in this way he was guilty of a piece of miscalculation which was remarkable in a man who had already suffered one humiliating defeat in 1832 as the champion of the old bank.

Even among some Whigs there was a marked lack of enthusiasm for a restoration of anything like the old bank. On April 22 the *Tribune* explained the Whig consensus editorially.

> All agree that the sub-treasury ought to be repealed, and that an entire specie currency—the natural consequence of carrying out that policy—cannot be tolerated in the country. All agree that a fiscal agent in lieu of the sub-treasury ought to be created for the safety and convenience of the government,

24. *Congressional Globe*, 27. 1. 186.

25. *Ibid.*, 318–19. On 2 August he had also presented a petition from a Democratic meeting in Cumberland County, Virginia (*Senate Docs.* 27. 1. No. 85) claiming that the Whig party in the state had "studiously avoided" making the bank an issue, repelling the idea "with a great show of indignation."

which shall combine banking powers to a greater or less extent, with a view of regulating the paper currency of the country, and for the accommodation of the public, as far as can be done with safety and prudence. But on the question how far this measure of relief can be prudentially carried, there is undoubtedly some diversity among certain portions of the Whig party.[26]

A new bank, which acted as the government banker and regulated the currency by dealing in the notes and drafts of local banks, would be acceptable to all Whigs but beyond this, in the realm of commercial banking, agreement ended. The Chamber of Commerce of the City of New York covered the same ground when it petitioned Congress "that responsibility for regulating the general currency and preserving the specie standard of value should again be assumed by the Federal Administration . . . and entrusted to the care and management of a national institution," but made no mention of other banking functions.[27]

Ewing's proposals went further than the minimum requirements, but stopped short at some significant points. He proposed that the bank should be incorporated in the District of Columbia, with power to establish branches in states which consented. It would be the fiscal agent of the government, and its notes would be accepted as payment for money due to the Treasury. It would have "the ordinary powers and privileges of banking institutions," but would deal only in coin, bullion, promissory notes, and inland bills of exchange, and should not discount promissory notes. The United States Government should subscribe one-fifth of an authorized capital of $30 million, and $10 million of the stock should be allocated to the states in proportion to their population. The remainder of the stock would be offered for public subscription. There would be seven directors of the central bank—two appointed by the president and five elected by the stockholders—and seven for each branch, of whom two would be nominated by the state in which the branch was situated provided that it held stock in the bank. Dividends were limited to 6 percent, note issues to three times the value of the specie held, and suspension of specie payments was forbidden.[28]

Ewing's report went quickly through a Select Committee pre-

26. *New York Tribune*, 22 April 1841.
27. *Senate Documents*, 27. 1. No. 12, 5.
28. *Ibid.*, No. 17.

sided over by Clay, but the real decisions seem to have been made in the Whig caucus, which instructed the Select Committee on each point. The bill that emerged differed from Ewing's proposal in two significant ways: the bank and its branches were allowed to discount promissory notes, and branches could be established without the consent of the states. The Whig caucus was insistent upon unlimited power to establish branches, and Whig opinion in Baltimore, Philadelphia, and New York was said to be unanimous on this point, and in Boston nearly so, because no one would take stock in a bank with branches dependent upon the assent of the states. Mangum told a doubtful correspondent that "a very little analysis will satisfy you that in the affirmation or recognition of this branching power is comprehended the *whole* difference between a Bank strictly local and a National Bank."[29] The report of the Select Committee envisaged that the directors at Washington would become "a board of control, superintending the branches, supplying them with currency, and banking exclusively through the agency of their offices of discount and deposit."[30] What the Whig majority wanted was a national banking organization in which the active elements would be branches in the main commercial centers to set the standard for local paper currency, facilitate trade by dealing in exchange, and finance enterprise by "discounting promissory notes." In this way the flow of public money through the national bank of deposit would provide the base for an enlarged but stable credit structure.

Subsequently, in order to meet the doubts of one or two Whig senators whose votes would decide the fate of the bill, the branching proposal was modified to allow a state to refuse assent, provided that it did so at the first session of its legislature after the passage of the bill. Consent once given, or presumed through lack of dissent, could not be withdrawn and even if refused, the federal government could still, by appropriate legislation, order the directors to set up a branch in that state. This not very satisfactory compromise weighted the law in favor of branches; refusal could be reversed but consent (even tacit consent) could not, and Congress reserved the right to override a Democratic legislature which blocked the establishment of a branch in a commercial city. To refuse assent in a state a bill would have to pass both Houses and obtain consent of the Governor, and failure at any of the points would leave consent presumed.

It is interesting to speculate upon the pressure that persuaded

29. Mangum, *Papers*, III: 184.
30. *Congressional Globe*, 27. 1. 78–80.

Whig Congressmen. Why could they not permit the consent of states to the establishment of branches to be freely and fairly given? An explanation is that several of the principal commercial cities were normally under Democratic state governments, but in 1841 the political situation was unusually favorable. New York was under Whig control and the Whig governor would hold office for another year. In Pennsylvania the legislature and administration were Democratic, but Whigs were present in unaccustomed strength, and some Democrats were pro-bank or susceptible to pressure from Philadelphia merchants. Boston, Baltimore, and Louisville were safely under Whig control but New Orleans, Cincinnati, and Nashville might come under Democratic legislatures at the next election. Once established a branch could not conduct business if its existence depended upon changing fortunes in state politics, and this explained the proposal that consent once given or assumed could not be revoked.

The motive for insisting on the right to discount promissory notes was straightforward. As the most profitable aspect of banking its omission would discourage capitalists from taking shares in the corporation, and Southern and Western Whigs wished to reinforce their own weak banking systems with the resources of a strong national bank holding public deposits and ready to supply capital for expansion.

On August 16, Tyler vetoed the bank bill. His veto message reminded Congress that he had always opposed the constitutionality of incorporating "a National Bank to operate *per se* over the Union."

> Looking to the power of the Government to collect, safely keep, and disburse the public revenue, and incidentally to regulate the commerce and exchanges, I have not been able to satisfy myself that the establishment by the Government of a bank of discount, in the ordinary acceptance of that term, was a necessary means, or one demanded by propriety, to execute those powers. What can the local discounts of the banks have to do with the collecting, safe-keeping, and disbursing of the revenue?[31]

This was the core of Tyler's objection to a bank which conducted commercial business throughout the country under national charter without the consent of individual states. He assailed the compromise on consent in the strongest possible terms, and restated the familiar

31. *Congressional Globe,* 27. 1. 387.

State Rights case. The bill claimed "the power to be in Congress to establish offices of discount in a State, not only without its assent, but against its dissent," and "the right in Congress to prescribe terms to any State, implies a superiority of power and control, deprives the transaction of all pretense to compact between them, and terminates . . . in the total abrogation of freedom of action on the part of the States."

If the Whigs wanted a bank they were now faced with the task of reading between the lines of the veto message to discover what kind of bank bill the President would sign. If the bank were shorn of the power to discount promissory notes, would he regard it as constitutional and not require the assent of the states for the establishment of branches? Or would the power of discounting promissory notes be saved if the unqualified right of the states to consent or dissent were restored? At this stage some anxious consultations took place. A. H. H. Stewart, a representative from Tyler's own state, saw the President, who appeared to sanction a plan that would allow the bank to establish agencies (but not branches) without consent of the states, if the right to discount notes were dropped. After hearing Stewart's report the Whig caucus decided to go ahead, and the bill was placed under the charge of John Sergeant in the House and J. M. Berrien in the Senate. These two saw Tyler twice, and the President again appeared to approve "a fiscal agency divested of the discounting power, and limited to dealing in bills of exchange."[32]

Meanwhile Tyler expressed to his Cabinet a strong and not unreasonable hope that the whole question might be left over to the next session, but he also sowed further confusion. Webster thought that the President wished "in effect, to make a Bank of issues, deposit and exchanges; without the power of discounting promissory notes," and would insist upon state consent for such a bank. Ewing understood this to mean that the bank could establish agencies in the states, receive and disburse public money, and deal in bills of exchange. Webster immediately saw Berrien and Sergeant and arranged for them to meet Ewing. Sergeant's bill, presented to the House on August 20, was therefore drawn up with the expectation that it would be accepted by the President.[33]

32. Chitwood, *John Tyler*, 238–40, 263; "Diary of Thomas Ewing," *American Historical Review* XVIII; Berrien's account is in *Niles' Register*, LXIII: 245.

33. "Diary of Thomas Ewing," *passim*, and especially p. 111. Tyler's early doubts are understandable, but by this time the bank question had been intensively discussed for two months. Ewing claimed that he was unable to extract from the President any precise statement on the conditions he required. (*Ibid.*, 578–86).

The new bill avoided the word "bank" and proposed a "Fiscal Corporation." It would have a smaller capital than the bank previously proposed, was empowered to establish local agencies but not branch banks of discount and deposit, and would confine its dealing to bills of exchange. Under the operation of the "gag" the bill passed the House on Monday, August 23, 125–94; it reached the Senate on August 24 and passed on September 3. On September 9 Tyler returned it with a veto.

Once again the opposition had successfully played upon Tyler's doubts. Four days after the first veto Calhoun had seized upon Tyler's distinction between discounting promissory notes and bills of exchange. "In the former, the banks were restricted by the usury laws of the States where they were situated, while in the latter they were not." He expressed the hope that if a new bill on these lines were introduced, it would be killed by another veto determined by "the same high consideration." He was "opposed to the creation of a bank, or corporation of any form, as the fiscal agent of the government . . . however modified, or wherever located, it would be alike unconstitutional and inexpedient."[34] The doubtful validity of any distinction between different kinds of banking business, was emphasized further in the final Senate debate on the second bill. Senator Benjamin Tappan of Ohio said that in the West there was virtually no difference between making loans to clients by discounting promissory notes or by purchasing bills of exchange from them. The banks preferred a borrower to give a bill, drawn on a distant place where he had no assets, on the understanding that it would not be presented for payment. At the date when the bill was due to be presented the borrower would pay the discount for the time it still had to run and, when making final repayment, would add the rate of exchange. By "dealing in exchange" in this way banks avoided the restrictions on interest imposed by state laws.[35] Tyler may also have been influenced by the report of a committee of stockholders, who had looked into the affairs of the Bank of the United States in Philadelphia and disclosed much unwise speculation. He was sincere in his wish to protect the public against such abuses, but his view of the executive function prevented him from giving a clear lead. He disliked conferences with congressional leaders—even when they were working in close collaboration with the Secretary of

---

34. *Congressional Globe*, 27. 1. 354.

35. Thomas H. Benton, *Abridgment of Congressional Debates* XIV: 366. In his veto message Tyler said that the bill imposed no restraint upon bills drawn in one state and payable in another, and did limit the time that a bill could run or be renewed. A bill might therefore "assume the most objectionable form of accommodation paper."

the Treasury—and his remarks were equivocal, perhaps deliberately so.[36]

The men nearest to the President were eagerly anticipating a breach long before the second veto. As early as June 18—long before the first veto—Henry Wise, who was Tyler's leading adherent in the House of Representatives and a personal friend, told Beverley Tucker that Ewing's report of June 12 was not to be regarded as Tyler's measure.[37] On July 11, after an amendment offering Ewing's proposal as a substitute for Clay's bank bill had failed, Wise wrote with elation that "Tyler is free from it forever now," and being released by Congress from any obligation to his Secretary of the Treasury, would "never look at Ewing's scheme again." He forecast that Clay would force Tyler to a veto, then fall back on Ewing's plan as a substitute, and so appear before the country "as again a great pacificator."[38] Shortly before this Mangum had lamented the condition of the Whig party produced by "a weak and vacillating President surrounded and stimulated by a cabal, contemptible in numbers, not strong in talent, but vaulting in ambition."[39]

There is also evidence that Tyler was planning to change his administration before the second veto. On August 26, when the second bill was under consideration in the Senate, Duff Green, a friend of both Calhoun and Tyler who managed to turn up at most moments of political crisis, wrote to Supreme Court Justice John McLean sounding him about a post in the cabinet. He said "the events of the last few days have been such as to create a belief in quarters *best* informed that there will be an entire re-organization" of the cabinet. He had urged McLean's name for the State or Treasury Department and believed the appointment would be offered to him. McLean replied on September 6 in a long but noncommittal letter. He hoped that the President would not veto because state consent would remove all constitutional difficulties and "in five years after its establishment there would not be five states in the Union that would not apply for a branch bank."[40]

Duff Green had forecast "an entire new organization of parties," and thought that Tyler would take "much the greater part of both

36. Cf. Robert J. Morgan, *A Whig Embattled: the Presidency under John Tyler* (Lincoln, 1954), 27, 35. Chitwood *op. cit.* 258–63 acquits Tyler of deliberate deception but does not explain the confusion of his cabinet or the Whig leaders.

37. Tyler, *Letters*, II: 46.

38. *Ibid.*, 47.

39. Mangum, *Papers*, III: 181–82.

40. McLean Papers, 26 August, 6 September.

parties." McLean, a protegé of James Monroe who thought of himself as an old republican dedicated to the restoration of superior standards in public life, might welcome the prospect of a new era of good feelings under another gentlemanly Virginian. He also thought much about his own prospects for the presidency, and might well wish to assume the mantle of Harrison and displace Clay as the true Western Whig. The hope was made explicit by a friend who told him that "if you desire ever to be President of the United States, now is the time."[41]

By the time McLean's letter reached Washington members of the cabinet, with the exception of Webster, had resigned, but Tyler preferred to offer the Treasury to the comparatively obscure Walter Forward of Pennsylvania. McLean's views on the bank may not have found favor, and some sharp remarks on the Whig use of patronage may have thrown doubt upon his usefulness in the department with the largest number of offices to bestow. The President explained that pending negotiations for a loan made it necessary to appoint someone already in or near Washington, But John Pope suspected the Virginian clique when he said "a certain influence" prevented the Treasury appointment and persuaded Tyler to nominate McLean for the War Office. Daniel Webster urged McLean to accept the lesser office, stressing its importance in the light of troubled relations with England, and added that "there are other subjects of a general nature, which belong rather to another Department—I mean finance, currency, etc., which will nevertheless receive attention from all members of the Administration, and in regard to which your advice will be important." In spite of this, McLean refused.[42]

Tyler wished to place himself at the head of a new national alliance, but the solidarity of the Whigs in Congress narrowed the field for maneuver to minute dimensions. Outside Congress McLean was the only man of national reputation who might counter Clay; his refusal drove Tyler to support Clay's personal enemies in insignificant Kentucky quarrels and he lacked the flexibility or imagination to adopt a bolder strategy.

The New York Whigs of the Seward, Weed, and Greeley school, who had played so large a part in blocking Clay's nomination in 1839, were far from happy at his domination over the congressional party.

41. *Ibid.*, 26 August, 11 September (C. Morris). He was urged to accept by several friends, e.g., T. Newell (11 September). "The whole moral community want your influence."
42. *Ibid.*, 11 September (Webster); McLean's refusal is dated 17 September.

On April 20 the *Tribune* had favored a new bank with "a rigid restriction of its business to the purchase and sale of Bills of Exchange, having not more than sixty days to run, and of Notes of other Banks, to send home for redemption . . . *no notes discounted whatever.*"[43] And on July 23, reporting the defeat of an amendment, which would have restricted the bank to dealing in exchange, the same paper said:

> We profoundly regret this decision. A National Bank restricted to the purchase and sale of Bills of Exchange, the keeping of Deposits, the transaction of the Government business, and the issue of a National Currency, would be infinitely safer, stronger, more popular, more profitable, and more useful than if authorized to discount mere notes of hand.[44]

Nor did the *Tribune* object to a requirement for the consent of states. Thurlow Weed and Seward refrained from joining in the Whig clamor after the first veto, and there was still some doubt whether they would join in the final breach with Tyler. Francis Granger, representative of New York Whigs in the Cabinet, was doubtful about his proper course in September, and consulted Whig congressmen from New York. Driven to decide between Tyler and the main body of the Whig party, they replied, "We state unhesitatingly that in our opinion you ought not to separate from your Whig friends in the Cabinet and in Congress."[45] More adroit management by Tyler might have salvaged some support from this quarter, and an alliance between Virginia and New York was a strong axis for any political grouping. Even after the second veto Weed continued to offer qualified support for Tyler in his Albany *Evening Journal,* and was favored by Tyler in post office patronage, until divided allegiance proved too unrewarding and unconstructive.[46]

There were other reasons why Tyler deserved to fail in his attempt to win a national following. He stood as a barrier between the congressional majority and their objectives, but gave no clear indications of his own preference; he had failed to make clear what bank he would accept (though hinting from time to time that the question was easily soluble), and contrived to appear both ignorant and indecisive.

43. *New York Tribune,* 20 April 1841.
44. *Ibid.,* 23 July.
45. Francis Granger Papers, Library of Congress, Washington, D.C., 11 September 1841.
46. G. G. Van Deusen, *Thurlow Weed* (Boston, 1947), 123–24.

According to one story, circulated by John P. Kennedy, a delegation of congressional Whigs from Ohio had called upon Tyler shortly before the first veto to express their concern, and were asked, "Why did you not send me Ewing's bill?" After the veto one of the Ohio men again visited the White House and saw the President who said, "I am glad to meet you again. I wanted to see one of your delegation. When . . . I told you I would sign Ewing's bill, if it were sent to me, I had not read it. I wish to recall what I said. I could not sign that." It seems barely credible that he had not read the recommendations of his own Secretary of the Treasury, on a measure that had been for six weeks a matter of acute controversy, but the story was not denied.[47]

It is fair to recall Tyler's difficulties. He came unexpectedly to office and had participated in none of the discussions that had prepared the Whig strategy. There was a ring of sincerity in an appeal for harmony contained in his second veto. Observing that Congress had been abnormally busy, and that differences between the majority and himself were, so far, confined to some aspects of one measure, he added "I, too, have been burdened with extraordinary labors of late, and I sincerely desire time for deep and deliberate reflection on this, the greatest difficulty of my administration. May we not now pause until a more favorable time . . . ?"

The plea for delay received support from an unexpected quarter. During the summer Nathan Appleton, the great merchant prince of Boston, had written a short pamphlet on currency and banking.[48] He argued that a bank, acting as a fiscal agent of the government, was the most convenient way of handling the finances of government but did not require a capital of more than $10 million and need not offer more than 6 percent to attract investors who preferred security to risk. He was entirely opposed to a large bank, with capital of $50 to $100 million, with power to regulate the currency, equalize exchanges, and provide a uniform currency. A bank of such magnitude would be "wholly contrary to the spirit of our institutions, which are formulated upon the principle of free competition; of action and reaction among equals." The regulatory functions could be performed more effectively by requiring issuing banks to hold adequate reserves and if this were not done a national bank might increase the evil. Appleton thought that even a small bank with limited functions should be de-

47. John P. Kennedy, *Defence of the Whigs* (New York, 1844), 91, 94.
48. Nathan Appleton, *Remarks on Currency and Banking* (Boston, 1841). Many years later Robert C. Winthrop recalled the strong impression made in Washington by Appleton's argument.

layed until specie payments had been resumed in the great eastern commercial centers. Finally "the details of such a bank will require time to mature," and "its establishment is the last thing to be done in haste—or as a mere party measure." He observed that the British Parliament had had a committee on the subject that had deliberated for many months, heard much evidence and, as yet, had reached no conclusions. This reinforces the argument that a root cause of the failure of government by party in Congress was inadequate preparation for the task.

Tyler promised that he would himself submit a plan at the regular meeting of Congress "with the most anxious hope that the Executive and Congress may cordially unite . . . and some measure of finance may be deliberately adopted." The trouble was that this implicitly claimed the right of the President to initiate policy, against the whole tenor of Whig argument that the President should accept and execute the laws made by Congress. Acquiescence in Tyler's plea would imply that party government was impossible unless the President acted as party leader.

Whigs could find little comfort from the record of the disastrous special session. The Distribution Act was passed, but with a crippling proviso that it could not operate when any tariff duties exceeded 20 percent. Under the Act of 1833 all duties were to be reduced to this maximum by the summer of 1842, but the deficit in the revenue made it improbable that this could be implemented. Before adjournment 205 duties were imposed on some articles hitherto taxed at a lower rate, but hopes that this might provide sufficient revenue were quickly extinguished when Tyler himself recommended that some duties should be raised above 20 percent. This would mean the automatic postponement of distribution, and revenue from the public lands could not be used to prime the economic pump, relieve the indebted states, or provide state funds for internal improvements. In the second session, faced with inadequate revenue and committed to protect industry, the Whig leaders sought to couple a general revision of the tariff with a repeal of the 1841 proviso and distribute land revenues whatever the level of tariff duties. This brought on a second round of acute disagreements between the President and the majority in Congress.

The famous Compromise of 1833 had agreed that duties then in excess of 20 percent should be reduced each year by one-tenth of the excess until January 1840; half of the remaining excess would go on January 1, 1842, and the remainder on July 1 in the same year. For articles that had been heavily taxed before 1833 the final stages were abrupt. Thus in 1834 the tax on rolled iron had been 87 percent; by 1840 it had been reduced to 65 percent; on January 1, 1842, it came down to 42.5 percent, and would fall to 20 percent on July 1. In eighteen months the duty was therefore cut from 65 percent to 20 percent with one short intervening step at 42.5 percent. Iron masters and manufacturers awaited the final sharp reduction with extreme anxiety and expected that depression would be converted into disaster by an inrush of cheap imports. The duties were *ad valorem*, on the importer's invoice, so that their effectiveness fell with prices and foreign suppliers might undervalue in order to reduce payments. The Compromise Act provided that home valuation would be adopted in 1842, and low tariff men made optimistic forecasts of the improvement to the revenue that would result; high tariff men placed more faith in a proposal to replace *ad valorem* by specific duties which would increase the element of protection as prices fell.

Clay read the 1833 Act to mean that protection for the sake of protection was abandoned. In a time of booming economy it had been expected that a maximum of 20 percent would provide adequate revenue, but there was nothing sacrosanct about this figure; indeed a further provision of 1833—that after 1842 the guiding light for tariff policy should be the provision of revenue—implied that 20 percent must be exceeded if duties at that level provided insufficient revenue. From this it was a short step for protectionists to argue that any necessary increase should be borne by imports that competed with American manufactures.

The Compromise of 1833 and the proviso in the Distribution Act of 1841 both depended upon decisions of Congress, and the question was so purely political that Congress might have been allowed to settle it. Tyler thought otherwise. In June 1842 Congress passed a provisional tariff bill which postponed for a month the final reduction in duties due on July 1; at the same time distribution was ordered to proceed. The President vetoed the bill on the ground that distribution violated the Compromise Act and reversed the previous decision of Congress. Congress then passed a permanent tariff bill which included high duties on iron and manufactures and a continuance of distribution. This time a veto was probably expected and quickly delivered. Finally Congress passed, and Tyler signed, a tariff bill which incorporated "incidental" protection while allowing the proviso suspending distribution to stand. Thus Tyler had forced the Whigs to choose between protection for manufactures and the distribution of land revenues; not unexpectedly they abandoned the more imaginative and possibly more productive policy.

Paradoxically a Southern President had forced the Whigs into a measure with decidedly sectional overtones as the sole survivor of what had once been an integrated national program. In the final vote on the tariff Mangum—who had told Clay that the Northern Whigs could have all the protection they wanted provided the South got distribution—cast his vote against the bill; so did Merrick, the Whig Senator from Maryland. Merrick had voted for the tariff bill with distribution, but now described it as "a bill to tax the interests of the agriculturalists for the benefit of the manufacturers." He said that agriculturalists were willing to bear the burden if they had their share of the benefits. "Do not," he said, "cast on them the whole bitter draught, and refuse to share with them the sweets."[49]

Southern anger at the sacrifice of distribution was reflected in votes on the tariff bills. Twenty-eight Whig votes from the upper South were cast in favor of the existing tariff with distribution. There was some complaint when the protective principle was introduced, but not until distribution was abandoned did they reject the tariff.

HOUSE VOTES FROM THE UPPER SOUTH ON THE
THREE TARIFF BILLS OF 1842

| | Vote on the Provisional Tariff Bill (allowing distribution) | | | Vote on the Tariff (with) distribution) | | | Vote on the Final Tariff Bill (without distribution) | | |
|---|---|---|---|---|---|---|---|---|---|
| | 15 JUNE | | | 16 JULY | | | 22 AUGUST | | |
| | For | Agst. | N.V. | For | Agst. | N.V. | For | Agst. | N.V. |
| Virginia | 6 | 11 | 4 | 7 | 12 | 2 | 3 | 16 | 2 |
| Maryland | 5 | 1 | 2 | 5 | 2 | 1 | 4 | 3 | 1 |
| N. Carolina | 4 | 5 | 4 | 3 | 7 | 1 | 0 | 11 | 2 |
| Tennessee | 4 | 5 | 3 | 3 | 9 | 0 | 1 | 11 | 0 |
| Kentucky | 9 | 2 | 2* | 9 | 2 | 2* | 4 | 8 | 1* |
| *Totals:* | 28 | 24 | 15 | 27 | 32 | 6 | 12 | 49 | 6 |

* Includes the Speaker

49. *Congressional Globe*, 27. 2. 953. On 15 June Mangum had written to Clay that "the country most imperatively demands a good tariff," but that a surrender on distribution "or any faltering with the subject puts an end to all hopes for the present passing of any Tariff law at all." (Clay Papers.)

In the Midwest there was also a weakening of support for the tariff when distribution was dropped, though not to the same degree as in the upper South. In Ohio and Indiana there were seventeen votes for the tariff with distribution, twelve without distribution, while four of the members who had previously supported the tariff absented themselves from the final vote.

The final tariff bill (without distribution) passed the House by 105–103; on July 16 it had passed (with distribution) by 116–112. With the substantial swing by Southern Whigs against the tariff without distribution, it may be wondered how it passed at all. The explanation is to be found in the actions of the Pennsylvania Democrats. On July 16, Pennsylvania voted nine to twelve against the tariff, with four not voting; on August 22, fifteen were for the tariff, ten did not vote, and none were against. Eight former opponents of the tariff had changed their votes, and five managed to avoid voting. This, with a few scattered votes picked up in other states (mainly from men who had not voted in the earlier division), and a few abstentions from men who had previously voted against, the tariff bill came home with two votes to spare. Thus the "Whig" tariff of 1842 was made possible by Pennsylvania Democrats against the opposition of a large majority of Southern Whigs.[50]

In the Senate James Buchanan spoke for the Democratic party in Pennsylvania. If no tariff act were passed it might be illegal to collect any duties and though Calhoun and others had maintained that the Act of 1833 warranted executive action, Buchanan sensibly observed that there were sufficient doubts to create great difficulties. The Whigs already claimed that Tyler was acting illegally in collecting duties after July 1 and the veto of the provisional tariff, and further collection might well be challenged in the courts. Buchanan thought that some of the new duties were excessive, but that distribution (which would come into effect if no tariff raised duties above 20 percent) would be the greater evil. He also made it clear that the Pennsylvanians wanted some protection. On manufactured articles he argued that "you must discriminate by imposing a higher duty upon the article produced by the foreign mechanic, or you must deprive our own mechanics of employment." He also maintained that there was a special case for the protection of iron, which produced "a greater amount than the whole value of cotton produced in any State of this Union," and defended the proposed duty by asserting that it would

50. The final roll call is given in *Congressional Globe*, 27. 2. 926.

not be prohibitive, would produce a greater revenue than any other imported article, and that the Pennsylvanians might with justice have asked for still more. Senator Silas Wright of New York also voted for the tariff. He laid special stress on the need to increase revenue and made no plea for special consideration for New York manufactures. Unlike the Pennsylvanians the New York Democrats in the House did not follow the lead of their Senator, and cast their votes against the tariff.[51]

*        *        *

Whig policies had failed. The Bankruptcy Act of 1841 was so badly drafted that it had to be repealed in 1842. No national bank had been established. The one major achievement—the tariff—had been passed with the aid of Northern Democrats and had a strong sectional flavor. The Whigs had failed to maintain the momentum won in 1840, and the Democrats had recovered the initiative. Nor was this disaster entirely the fault of John Tyler. Faced with an unsympathetic President, the Congressional leaders could have pursued a more tactful and eventually more successful course, while the abuse heaped upon Tyler had enabled the Democrats to pose as the guardians of political decency. In the party there was a strong undercurrent of opinion that the leadership had botched the job. In March 1842 Thurlow Weed's Albany *Evening Journal* sounded a note of reproach and pessimism:

> The Whig members of Congress, instead of taking the President "for better or for worse," as wives take their husbands, array themselves against his Administration. This is a source of interminable mischiefs and evils. And what is worse, it's a warfare that will not only bring defeat and disgrace to both parties but is proving destructive to the public interests.[52]

Tyler could also use his martyrdom by slander to score points at the expense of his Whig enemies. When the *Cincinnati Republican* published a letter calling for an end of partisan strife, the President commented in a public letter:

51. *Ibid.*, 950, 953–54.
52. There is a clipping of this passage in the Millard Fillmore Papers.

Personal abuse of myself has entered largely into the discussions in and out of Congress. This any man who has been in office may be ready to expect; but I should be most ready to compromise with my bitter assailants in Congress by conceding to them any portion they may choose of every day, for the display of their unsurpassed eloquence in abuse of me, if the residue of their time could be given for the public good! Is this great end to be sacrificed to gratify a small group of mousing politicians, who think that their petty schemes of hatred or ambition are of more consequence than the consideration of measures designed for general relief?[53]

At the same time Tyler himself lowered the tone of public life by using patronage in an attempt to build up a personal following, which brought meager rewards and much bitterness. The Collector of the Port of Philadelphia wrote to *Niles' Register* to tell how, when first appointed, he had been told to distribute posts among the various Whig factions, and had done so. On April 27, 1842, he was ordered to dismiss thirty-one named employees and appoint other named persons in their places. He sought an interview with Tyler, and gained admittance after a long wait. The President asked him how many of the hundred custom house employees were Clay men. The Collector said that he did not know, as he had obeyed instructions "enjoining silence on political topics." The next step was the arrival in Philadelphia of a man who claimed to be his successor, and subsequently he received a letter of dismissal.[54] Another, among many victims of the purge, was General S. Van Rensselaer, dismissed as postmaster of Albany, who claimed to have chosen Tyler for nomination as Vice President. The Whigs replied in kind by airing the dismissals in Congress, requesting the President (unsuccessfully) to give reasons for removals, and refusing consent in the Senate to various nominations for vacant offices.

These squabbles made worse the demoralization of the party, and local organizations either collapsed or operated inefficiently. The price was paid in the congressional elections of 1842, when the Whigs lost 54 seats in the House, and the Democrats gained 40. The old House

53. *Niles' Register*, 20 May 1843.
54. *Niles' Register*, 1 October 1842. An earlier victim was Calvin Colton, Whig pamphleteer and author of the influential "Junius" tracts; he attributed his dismissal, in September 1841, to an editorial he had contributed anonymously to a Philadelphia newspaper (Mangum, *Papers*, III:237).

had stood at 133 Whigs to 102 Democrats, with 6 Tyler Whigs. In the new House there were 142 Democrats, 79 Whigs, and 1 independent Whig. This outran even the normal expectations of a mid-term swing, for the Democrats recovered their 1840 losses and restored the superiority they had enjoyed in the high days of Jackson's presidency. In the Senate the Whigs held on to their narrow majority. With one party ascendant in the House, the other in the Senate, and a President belonging to neither, there was a complete stalemate in domestic policy. If Tyler wished to leave a record of achievement he would have to turn from domestic problems to foreign policy. His administration had already a major agreement with Great Britain to its credit, but the Webster-Ashburton Treaty owed little to Tyler. There was however one possibility for brilliant achievement, and the President turned his attention to Texas with momentous consequences for the future.

*    *    *

The frustration of the Whigs stirred up deep questions of political theory and practice. Attention focused on the veto but greater principles were at stake. In January 1842 Henry Clay proposed a constitutional amendment which would allow the repassage of vetoed bills by simple majorities in both Houses. He sketched the history of the Republic to demonstrate that there had been "a constant encroachment by the executive upon the legislative department." While Congress assembled intermittently "the executive branch of the government was eternally in action; it was ever awake; it never slept; its action was continuous and unceasing." The most dangerous encroachment had been into the field of legislation. "The executive ought to have no agency in the formation of laws," he declared, but the veto "drew after it the power of initiating laws, and in its effect must ultimately amount to conferring on the executive the entire power of government." In Congress "the will of the nation [was] authoritatively expressed," and "the fundamental axiom of free government" was that the will of the majority should govern. This had been the keystone of Jefferson's political system and not the "doctrine that minorities must govern . . . advanced by gentlemen who professed and called themselves members of the Jeffersonian school."[55]

---

55. In addition to his well-known vetoes Tyler also vetoed an internal improvement bill and a naval construction bill (passed over the veto), and four other bills which came to him at the close of a session without time for consideration. (Morgan, *Whig Embattled*, 54). Yet in June 1842 he signed a bill, to which State Rights Whigs objected, and gave as his reason that

Clay's speech brought a reply from Calhoun which was one of his most luminous though least noticed contributions to political theory.[56] Delivered at a time when he still hoped to create a national constituency to support his presidential aspirations, and before his judgment became clouded by the more virulent stages of sectional controversy, his speech of February 24, 1842, deserves close study by all concerned with the problems of representative government.

Calhoun argued that Clay's doctrine of the ascendant majority threatened not only the Executive but also the Judiciary and the Senate itself, and vigorously attacked the assumptions underlying Clay's appeal to a national will and majority rule. "If . . . the people of these States do really constitute a nation . . . if the nation has a will of its own, and if the numerical majority of the whole is the only appropriate and true organ of that will, we may fairly expect to find that will, pronounced through the absolute majority, pervading every part of that instrument [the Constitution] and stamping its authority on the whole." But there was "not the slightest evidence, trace or vestige of the existence of the facts on which the . . . theory rested; neither of the nation, nor of its will, nor of the numerical majority of the whole, as its organ." On the contrary there had always been "a deep conflict of interests, real or supposed, between the different parts of the community, on the subjects of the first magnitude," and constitutional theory must recognize diversity and not build upon an imaginary national interest. There was an inevitable tendency for powerful interests to seek ascendancy, and it was to prevent this that the makers of the Constitution had labored. They had failed to prevent all abuses of power, and history furnished "proof conclusive that the principle of blunder, so deeply implanted in all governments, has not been eradicated in ours, by all the precautions taken by its framers."

Calhoun went on to argue that two majorities were represented in Congress—that of the people and that of the states. The first was represented by the President and the House. The second was represented directly in the Senate and safeguarded indirectly by the veto

---

"a doubtful opinion of the Chief Magistrate ought not to outweigh the solemnly pronounced opinion of the representatives of the people and the States." *Congressional Globe*, 27. 2. 165–66.

56. John C. Calhoun, *Works*, ed. R. K. Crallé, IV:77–78; also *Congressional Globe*, 27. 2. Appendix, 164–68. Omitted from Benton's *Abridgment of Congressional Debate*—not an uncommon symptom of Benton's contempt for Calhoun.

which could not be overridden by less than two-thirds of each House. The numerical majority was always likely to be the stronger, its views deserved the most weight, but "without subjecting the whole . . . to its unlimited sway." The Constitution provided for "the expression of the voice of each State . . . and as the voice of all by being that of each component part, united and blended into one harmonious whole." The six largest states could not control both houses of Congress without the support of eight others; and the smallest majority that could prevail (calculated from the 1840 census) was 9,788,570 against 6,119,797. If the President used his veto, then it required eighteen states in the Senate and the representatives of 10,600,000 in the House to prevail. The national interest would be distorted, not expressed, by giving unlimited authority to the numerical majority, and limitations on majority rule provided the bedrock upon which the Constitution rested.

In treating the President's powers Calhoun argued that Congress was already the supreme judge of what was "necessary and proper," but used this admission to attack Clay's theory of executive encroachment. If executive power had become a grievance, it was because Congress had erred in "permitting it to be exercised by the President without the sanction of law, and without guarding against the abuses to which it is so liable." However the strength of his argument was weakened by ambiguity in stating the principles that should govern the use of the veto. Its primary purpose was to enable the President to protect his own authority, but he had also a special but undefined duty to safeguard the interest of minorities and "might find it necessary to interpose his veto to maintain his views of the constitution, or the policy of the party of which he is the head, and which elevated him to power." The first purpose would not be denied by Clay or any of his adherents; they might accept the second with the qualification that when a majority had been chosen after a fair contest, minorities had a moral obligation to accept the decision. They would hotly deny that the President had any justification for standing upon his own version of the Constitution against that of other good authorities; while a party that had lost an election—or a faction that had been outvoted—ought not to be protected from the consequences of political failure by presidential action. At this crucial point, therefore, Calhoun did nothing to answer the very real question raised by Tyler's use of the veto.

Calhoun's argument may be compared with Rousseau's (though there is no evidence that he had studied the *Contract Social*). Calhoun would have agreed emphatically that the general will was not the will of a majority, but should be discovered in more subtle ways and by processes which eliminated or neutralized the "particular" wills; but he rejected the idea of a sovereign will, and saw only forces held in equilibrium. Whereas Rousseau's general will was the motive power for improvement, Calhoun's countervailing checks on the numerical majority were essentially conservative. If society did improve it was because the equilibrium of force confined government to an inactive role. Calhoun may have been influenced by Madison's argument, in Federalist X, that the major problem of popular government was presented when a faction comprised a majority, but in his analysis the "numerical majority" always endangered "the permanent or aggregate interests" of society.

A major limitation on Calhoun's thought was his preoccupation with slavery, and though not mentioned in his speech on the veto it was never far from the forefront of his mind. He had been gravely disturbed by the growing possibility that the House would not long retain the 21st Rule or "gag" which forbade debate on anti-slavery petitions, and his argument against the "numerical majority" derived much of its passionate intensity from the thought that a congressional majority might one day pass anti-slavery legislation. This detracted from the subtlety of his argument that constitutional checks were intended to protect the rights of minorities against the majority, and would shortly lead him into a major inconsistency. When the Senate exercised its constitutional right to reject the treaty of annexation with Texas, Calhoun—who deemed annexation to be vital for the protection of slavery—endorsed annexation by the numerical majority in Congress though a very substantial minority in the nation was hotly opposed to this action.

Even if one granted the sociological premise of Calhoun's argument that slavery should not be subject to normal legislative processes, his theory distorted the way in which Southern opinion was formulated. He might argue (as he often did) that the interest of the whole South was opposed to Whig policy but this view was not shared by Southern Whigs. On economic issues majorities and minorities were intermingled throughout the nation, controversy took place in most constituencies, and arguments were put to the test in elections. Except for his somewhat obscure reference to vetoes in defense of party policy, Calhoun conducted his whole argument as though national parties did not exist and ignored the way in which the mechanics of party organization worked to secure the consensus he so much admired. The "numerical majority" as it finally emerged in Congress was not a single consolidated interest, but a blend compounded of many elements through long processes of pressure and adjustment. One can understand why Calhoun—the great outsider—did not choose to bring party into his analysis, but the omission gravely weakened his treatment of the country's constitutional problem. He had provided a masterful examination of the reason why a federal republic could not be treated in the same way as a small unified society, but failed to consider the evolution of parties or explain the added dimension that they gave to political behavior.

In contrast to Clay's essay on constitutional power and Calhoun's reply, the report prepared in the House of Representatives after the veto of the tariff bill was a disappointing document. It was too closely concerned with immediate events, too clouded by personal animosity against Tyler, and too much dominated by the desire to establish a case for impeachment (which was of doubtful constitutional validity and beyond the range of practical politics).[57] Nevertheless the report of the select committee carried weight because its principal author, ex-President John Quincy Adams, spoke with authority on the executive function. He observed that until recently "all reference, in either House of Congress, to the opinions and wishes of the President . . . was regarded as an outrage upon the rights of the deliberative body" which ought, above all, "to spurn the influence of the dispenser of patronage and power." Now the right of Congress "to exact laws essential to the welfare of the people" had been "struck with apoplexy by the Executive hand."

Historical judgment has been weighted against congressional government and has favored the minority report written by Thomas W. Gilmer, a friend of Tyler, who objected to claiming power for Congress that it did not possess "in order to establish a particular system of party policy." It was both unwise and dangerous "to exasperate local or general prejudice against the acknowledged forms of government, and to elicit the spirit of revolution as an ancillary to the spirit of party."

The argument over the veto underlines the fact that the failure of party government was due to institutional causes rather than personal error. A cleverer man than Tyler or a more sensitive man than Clay might have steered the Whig party through its short period of power with less damage, but sooner or later the conflict between executive

57. *Congressional Globe*, 27. 2. 894–96.

authority and party mandate would have become clear. The Whig party did not fail (as is so often said) because it lacked cohesion. On the contrary, from all the confusion and cross-currents of political life it managed to produce a congressional party whose members displayed a high degree of mutual loyalty and scored well for regularity in voting. The Democrats achieved the same solidarity in opposition, and both parties represented broad but contrasting moral, social, and economic attitudes.

Having been brought to the point of confrontation, and then dragged into a frustrating and indecisive conflict, what would be the fate of the two parties which had developed between 1834 and 1840? The positive aims of the Whigs had been frustrated, and the Democrats had achieved a negative triumph. Neither had had the opportunity or stimulus to develop further their social and political philosophies. It was at this moment that they were called upon to deal with questions which embraced the whole character and future of national existence.

*Chapter 4*

# NATIONALISM
# AND THE
# PARTIES

On April 12, 1844, the people of the United States learned through
the press that a treaty had been signed annexing Texas to their country; on April 22 the treaty, still under the ban of secrecy, went to the
Senate, but on April 27 a breach of senatorial confidence led to its
publication in the New York *Evening Post.* The earlier history of relations between the United States, Texas, and Mexico is not the concern
of this chapter, nor are the details of diplomacy that preceded the
secret treaty. What is significant is the way in which the treaty
brought to the fore a series of questions involving national character,
the conduct of a republican nation in international relations, and the
momentous proposition that the protection of slavery was a national
interest. Both parties struggled with these fundamental problems,
and both hoped that their interpretations of national purpose would
steer men away from the obviously divisive issue.

There was political logic in President Tyler's decision to make
the annexation of Texas the major objective of his administration. The
political stalemate made initiative impossible on domestic issues, but
in foreign affairs the executive had more freedom to act. The
Webster-Ashburton Treaty had been acclaimed, and a presidency
combining a long-term settlement of Anglo-American disputes with
the acquisition of a vast new region to the Southwest might win a
place in history. There is indeed an indication that the President intended to include a recommendation that Congress should consider
relations between the United States and Texas in his annual message of
December 1843. After a reference to American interest in ending the

state of war between Texas and Mexico, and the need for Mexico to recognize Texan independence, he passed on somewhat awkwardly to another topic without indicating possible action by the United States. He may have been uncertain of the response from Texas, where President Sam Houston might prefer independence to annexation and the people might resent public discussion of their future without steps to protect their frontiers against Mexican attacks and reprisals. Whatever the reason, Tyler and Abel P. Upshur, the Secretary of State decided to preserve secrecy until a treaty had been signed.

The facts were straightforward, but annexation without public discussion was a hazardous venture. Texas had been recognized as independent by the United States but not by Mexico; annexation might therefore bring on a war and Great Britain's interest in Texan independence might lead to intervention. Generous boundaries were claimed by Texas, and even the most hopeful forecast of Mexican reactions could hardly forecast acquiescence. Texans claimed the Rio Grande to the south and west, though they had never exercised authority south of the Nueces and failed to establish control of Sante Fe in 1843, and a vast region west of the Louisiana Purchase and east of the Rockies. Mexico had abolished slavery in 1829, but the Texans had retained it despite the law. Annexation would mean recognition of slavery in these western lands where it had never existed and its introduction had been illegal under Mexican law. Moreover, from this great region four or five new slave states might eventually be carved.

The earlier approach to Texan annexation, in 1837, had broken down because President Van Buren had preferred to rebuff the Texans rather than risk sectional discord in the United States. Yet President Tyler embarked upon the project with a cabinet that was sectionally lopsided. When Webster resigned, after completing the treaty with Great Britain, he was replaced by the Virginian Upshur. The Secretary of War, William Wilkins, and Walter Forward, Secretary of the Treasury, were Pennsylvanians but neither carried much weight. All the other cabinet members were Southern, and so were the President's few supporters in Congress. Unofficially he relied for advice upon a group of Virginians, among whom Beverley Tucker, Henry A. Wise, and Thomas W. Gilmer were the most prominent. Moreover his quarrel with the regular Whig leaders, meant that his administration represented no more than a segment of Southern opinion. Conspicuous by their absence were any Southerners who had based their policies upon cooperation with Northern interests in political and economic enterprise.

On February 28, 1844, Upshur was killed by an explosion on board the U.S.S. *Princeton,* and was replaced by John C. Calhoun. The new appointment brought a man of known integrity and first-rate ability into the government, but at a particularly unfortunate time. Northern men were already disturbed by rumors of a Texas design and suspicious of Southern intentions, and Calhoun, having abandoned his last hope of winning a national constituency that would raise him to the Presidency, had decided to devote his remaining energies to unyielding defense of Southern interests.[1]

The case for urgent and secret action could be substantiated if it could be proved that Great Britain planned to intervene in Texas, and by accident or design a letter reached Upshur in August 1843 from "a citizen of Maryland" resident in London. The "citizen" was Duff Green, whom Tyler had sent to Europe as an unofficial representative. Duff Green, who liked to have his finger in every kind of political and financial speculation, was a friend of Calhoun and kept him informed of developments. His letter recounted a meeting between Lord Aberdeen, the Foreign Secretary, and an anti-slavery committee, including a delegate from Texas, at which it was said that Aberdeen had promised diplomatic pressure on Mexico to recognize Texas with settled boundaries and a substantial loan to the bankrupt republic, in return for the abolition of slavery. Subsequently Aberdeen vigorously denied any intention of intervening in Texas and Edward Everett, the American minister in London, believed him; nevertheless the Washington government continued to act as though urgent steps were necessary to forestall a British design to make Texas a client state with slavery abolished.[2]

---

1. According to his own account, Henry A. Wise rigged Calhoun's nomination (Burton H. Wise, *The Life of Henry A. Wise* [New York, 1899], 96–101). On 5 March Senator George McDuffie wrote to Calhoun that Tyler was noncommittal (*Correspondence of Calhoun*, ed. J. F. Jameson, Part II, 934–35), but Wise told him subsequently that the nomination would be made. The formal offer was dated the following day, and on the same day Dixon H. Lewis wrote to Calhoun that the offer would be made. The truth is probably that Tyler had decided to strengthen his deplorably weak Cabinet, that Wise acted as an intermediary between the President and Calhoun's friends in Congress, and that their principal concern was to ensure that Calhoun would accept. The incident has some importance in the light of Calhoun's part in identifying annexation with the protection of slavery.

2. The papers submitted with the Texas treaty are in *Senate Documents* 28. 1. V. 341. The correspondence of the British, Texan, and American governments is in G. P. Garrison, ed., *Diplomatic Correspondence of the Republic of Texas* (American Historical Association Annual Report, 1908), II(1), Part II.

Elgin Williams says that Duff Green had offered his services to Nicholas Biddle in 1839 as a propagandist for the sale of Texas bonds (*The Animating Pursuits of Speculation*, New York, 1949, 149). This may or may not be true, but is not supported by the reference to the *Dictionary of*

The men favoring annexation were not content with exerting pressure on Washington. In August 1843 John C. Calhoun, then occupying no official position but regarded as an oracle by a small but influential circle of friends, received a copy of a letter from Ashbel Smith, the Texan chargé d'affaires in London, to his own Secretary of State. The communication of official correspondence of a foreign country to a private person was unusual but calculated to rouse Calhoun to intense activity. Ashbel Smith gave a more authentic report of the meeting between Aberdeen and the abolitionists than Duff Green. He said that Aberdeen had rejected the idea of improper intervention in Texas, professed his concern for good relations with the United States, but stated "the well known policy and wish of the British Government to abolish slavery everywhere," and left open the possibility that the British Government would consent hereafter to make such compensation to Texas as would enable the slaveholders to abolish slavery."[3]

Tyler himself favored annexation for reasons which were economic, strategic, and truly national, but those who were to implement the policy were more and more concerned to protect the Southern flank of slavery against the possibility of Texan abolition. Mexican recognition of Texan independence might be as dangerous as direct British intervention. The Lone Star Republic would be weak, militarily and financially, but with untapped resources and abundant land; there would be a strong temptation to bargain for British economic aid with the abandonment of slavery as a comparatively small price to pay. A former President of Texas, Mirabeau Bonaparte Lamar, warned Southern friends in a public letter that there was "every probability that slavery would be abandoned" if Texas were left alone, and "when slavery gives way in Texas, the ruin of the Southern states is inevitable."[4]

There was more flame beneath the smoke of British designs than the annexationists knew. Late in 1842 Charles Elliot, the British chargé d'affaires in Texas, who was friendly with Sam Houston, had written to his home government that the abolition of slavery might be imminent if Britain promised financial aid, and "money lent to put an end to slavery in a South West direction in America" would be more

---

*American Biography* cited in support. It does however seem to be established that Duff Green had financial interests at stake in annexation (Williams, *op. cit.,* 166).

3. *Correspondence of Calhoun,* Part II, 866ff.
4. M. B. Lamar, *Letter . . . on the subject of Annexation* (Savannah, 1844), 15.

profitable than money spent on troops and fortifications in British North America.[5] Late in 1843 Aberdeen instructed Doyle, the British minister in Mexico, that the abolition of slavery should be a condition for Mexican recognition of Texan independence. In May 1844 he told Elliot that Great Britain and France would offer to mediate between Mexico and Texas "for the equitable settlement of differences and demarcation of boundaries between the two countries," but that if Texas accepted annexation "the policy of Her Majesty's Government will be liable to undergo great modification if not total change." In other words the British would drop their concern for a feasible settlement of boundary disputes and perhaps sustain Mexico against any claims made by the United States.[6]

These British moves were suspected but unproven, and meanwhile Calhoun was propagating a more elaborate explanation of British interest in Texas. "In the advanced state of commerce and the arts," he wrote, "the great point of policy for the older and more advanced nations is to command the trade of the newer and less advanced." Britain could do this by opening a free trade in foodstuffs and raw materials with the less advanced countries, and by relying upon the competitive advantages of her industry to penetrate their markets; but free trade was not yet accepted British policy and the government therefore pursued the alternative, which was a "resort to force to retain her commercial and manufacturing superiority." In this strategy the first British blow must be struck at the slaveholding countries. "The reason is obvious. It is indispensable to give her a monopoly of the trade of the world. The abolition of slavery would transfer the production of cotton, rice, and sugar, etc., to her colonial possessions, and would consummate the system of monopoly, which she has been so long and systematically pursuing." This explained Britain's interest in Texas and abolition. Thus it was imperative to annex Texas to protect the Southern social system and serve the national economic interest.[7]

The lineaments of this elaborate theory of British anti-slavery imperialism (which has not lacked adherents among modern writers) must have been communicated to Upshur for, when he sent W. S. Murphy, the American minister to Texas, a copy of the letter from the "citizen of Maryland" he added that it might be considered "a part of a

5. Clayette Blake, *Charles Elliot R. N. 1801–75: a servant of Britain Overseas* (London, 1960), 73–74, 76.
6. *Senate Documents*, 28. 1. V. No. 341, 18ff.
7. *Correspondence of Calhoun*, Part I, 546.

general plan by which England would seek to abolish domestic slavery throughout the entire continent and islands of America, in order to find or create markets for the products of her home industry, and at the same time to destroy all competition with the industry of her colonies."[8] Murphy discounted the abolitionist plot, but suggested that British diplomatic pressure on Mexico should be countered by "the most prompt and energetic action of the government of the United States." As little as possible should be said about slavery—to avoid offense to "our fanatical brethren of the North"—and the case should rest upon the advancement of civil, political, and religious liberty. This would be "the safest issue to go before the world with."[9]

There was some delay in initiating negotiations for annexation, because Sam Houston was reluctant to commit himself and the Texans wanted an assurance that there would be enough votes in the United States Senate to ratify a treaty.[10] It is difficult to see how Upshur counted the votes to satisfy himself and the Texans, but he may have hoped to play down slavery and give prominence to a letter, written by Andrew Jackson a year previously but held back for publication at an appropriate time, which strongly supported annexation. This might secure solid Democratic support in a Senate that was almost equally divided, while enough Southern Whig support would be won over by evidence of British designs, fears for slavery, and the popularity of annexation among Texans themselves. The weakness of Mexican government rendered serious retaliation against the United States unlikely.

Upshur may also have hoped for a favorable response to a pamphlet, written by Robert J. Walker and published in January, in which the strategic and economic arguments for annexation were laid out with considerable skill and reinforced by an ingenious argument that slavery would be drained away from the old lands of the South— thus accelerating its decline—and would eventually be overtaken by economic pressure in Texas itself. Walker argued that the South could never tolerate a large free black population, and this alone would forever prevent the end of slavery unless outlets for the blacks were found. The diffusion of slavery to the southwest would continue until

---

8. *Senate Documents*, 28. 1. V. No. 341, 19. In London Duff Green tried to enlist the support of prominent free traders, and persuaded James Gordon Bennett, editor of the New York *Herald*, "to co-operate with us most efficiently."

9. *Ibid.*, p. 25.

10. Houston remained doubtful. As late as May 1844 he said that he supported annexation because it was devised by the people but against his better judgment (*Diplomatic Correspondence of Texas*, Part II, 283). In Texas it was thought that 35 to 40 Senators favored annexation (*Niles' Register*, 17 February 1844).

"in the distant future, without a shock, without abolition, without a convulsion, it would disappear into and through Texas, into Mexico and Central and Southern America . . . where nine tenths of the population is of colored race, there, upon that fertile soil, and in that delicious climate, so admirably adapted to the negro race . . . the free black would find a home."[11]

The advocates of expansion also hoped that, in addition to these arguments, popular enthusiasm would be aroused and if the purpose could not be achieved by a duly ratified treaty, it might nevertheless command a majority among the people. Acting upon these assumptions Upshur went forward, the Texans responded, and by the time of his tragic death, the treaty was almost ready for signature, though still unknown to the public. Rumors of the negotiations were not generally believed, even by well-informed men. The treaty might have been ready for submission to the Senate early in March if the *Princeton* tragedy had not caused delay, and when Calhoun arrived to take up his duties at the State Department it required only signature and the selection of supporting papers for presentation to the Senate. On April 12 it was signed and on April 22 went to the Senate. In the interval, Calhoun had added to the accompanying papers an elaborate defense of slavery in a letter addressed to Richard Pakenham, the British minister in Washington. On April 27, as a result of calculated indiscretion by Senator Benjamin Tappan, Democrat of Ohio, the treaty and papers were published in the New York *Evening Post*. On the same day there appeared a letter from Clay, dated April 17 and condemning annexation and, on the following day, a public letter from Martin Van Buren announcing that he too opposed immediate annexation.

In order to understand the motives of Clay and Van Buren it is necessary to assess the information they possessed and what they were trying to do. Both knew that a treaty had been signed. This had been announced in the *National Intelligencer* on April 12—in time to catch the weekly issue of the widely circulated *Niles' National Register*—and was quickly copied by other newspapers. Neither knew whether Texas would come in as a state or territory, or what stipulations were made about boundaries, slavery in the remote northern parts of Texas, the public lands, and debts of Texas. The points to which they addressed themselves were the probability of war with Mexico, executive action

11. Robert J. Walker, *Letter . . . relative to the annexation of Texas* (Washington, D.C., 1844), 15; reprinted in Frederick Merk, *Fruits of Propaganda in the Tyler Administration* (Cambridge, Mass., 1971), 15.

without knowledge of Congress or people, unnecessary haste, and Northern objections to the extension of slavery under the American flag.

Both Clay and Van Buren wrote as party leaders. The Whig convention was due to assemble on May 1, and no one seriously challenged Clay's nomination; the Democratic convention would meet later in the same month and a majority of delegates were already pledged to Van Buren. Both were aware that disputes over slavery could split their parties. A year previously John Quincy Adams, perhaps in response to a public letter by T. W. Gilmer favoring annexation, had persuaded other Whig congressmen from New England to join in a circular letter to their constituents. In it Adams said that "by the admission of a new slave territory . . . the ascendancy of the slaveholding power shall be secured and riveted beyond all redemption." The people would not "become *particeps criminis* in any such subtle contrivance for the irremediable perpetuation of an Institution which the wisest and best of men who formed our federal constitution, as well from the slave as from the free states, regarded as an evil and a curse." Annexation would, declared Adams, be "identical with dissolution" of the Union.[12] Van Buren was equally aware of strong objections to the extension of slavery among the radical Democrats of New York, among whom were his most devoted adherents.

In considering the problem of uniting his party Clay knew that his personal following in the Northeast was uncertain. He was strong among the professional and business elite of the cities, but weak among former Anti-Masons and anti-slavery men. Mutual suspicion existed between Clay and the Seward–Weed group in New York, and his personal relations with John Quincy Adams had never been good. In February 1844 a Whig caucus in Massachusetts accepted a resolution, proposed by Charles Francis Adams and inspired by his father's Texas letter of the previous year, that "the project of the annexation of Texas, unless arrested on the threshold, may tend to drive these States into dissolution of the Union, and will furnish new calumnies against republican governments, by exposing the gross contradiction of a people professing to be free and yet seeking to extend and perpetuate the subjugation of their slaves."[13] Clay also had a friendly but somewhat tense correspondence with Joshua Giddings of Ohio, whom the

12. *Address of J. Q. Adams and others to their Constituents,* 3 March 1843 (*Niles' Register,* 13 May 1843), and also published as a widely circulated pamphlet.

13. Charles Francis Adams, *Texas and the Massachusetts Resolutions* (Boston, 1844). In his Diary

House had censured in 1842 for expressing anti-slavery views but who had won triumphant reelection. Giddings, whose support was essential if Clay were to win Ohio, was implacably opposed to the extension of slavery in any form.[14]

Looking to the South Clay was reasonably certain that he could hold the Whigs in line. Tyler was bitterly unpopular with a majority of Whig leaders, and most of them were gravely suspicious of Calhoun. They believed that progress in the South was advanced by cooperation with Northern interests, and were nervous of moves that emphasized sectional differences. Some believed that their states would be weakened by white migration to Texas, and others were more impressed than Northern anti-slavery men by Walker's argument that annexation would promote the gradual extinction of slavery.

Finally Clay was gravely and honorably disturbed by threats to the Union. On March 16, while the treaty was still no more than a rumor, the staid *National Intelligencer* was roused to unusual emotion when it referred to annexation as "the dark cloud which overhangs the public peace and the national welfare, if not the existence of this Union." Annexation without the consent of Mexico, said the *Intelligencer,* meant a dishonorable breach of international obligations, and opposition from at least a third of the Union.[15] Clay may have inspired the article, for his published letter elaborated the same line of argument, but in seeking a formula to unite the party, and safeguard his own leadership, he produced a not unworthy addition to American political literature.

Clay first raised the constitutional issue of presidential power. Secret executive action might commit the country to untold danger. If Mexico responded to annexation by attacking Texas, the United States would have to fight a war on a distant and largely unknown frontier. If the British interest in Texas was as strong as annexationists claimed, was there not a danger that she would intervene on the side of Mexico? Was it then "competent to the treaty making power to plunge this country into war, not only without the concurrence, but without

(Massachusetts Historical Society) for 14 February 1844, Adams described the Whig caucus and observed that "the opinion was universal that the resistance to Texas must be persisted in at all hazards."

14. On 6 July 1844, Giddings wrote to Clay, "Our people of all political parties regard the great question to be, whether the nation shall assume upon itself the support of slavery in the States. . . . We are therefore rallying upon that issue." (George W. Julian, *Life of Joshua R. Giddings* [Chicago, 1892], 161–62).

15. On 22 March, *The National Intelligencer* also printed several extracts from editorials hostile to annexation.

deigning to consult Congress?" The difficulty might be overcome if the consent of Mexico were obtained, but this would still leave difficult questions unanswered. "True wisdom . . . points to the duty of rendering [the Union's] present members happy, prosperous, and satisfied with each other, rather than an attempt to introduce alien members, against common consent, and with the certainty of deep dissatisfaction." The argument that new slave territory was necessary to maintain the balance of power between the sections was pernicious, because it implied that aggression against neighboring countries was necessary to preserve domestic harmony. It was, in any case, a struggle that the South must lose because land suitable for slavery was limited by climate. Even in Texas the most probable result would be two slave and three free states. Looking to the future he envisaged separate North American republics—the United States, Texas, and Canada —allied by race, harmonious in their interest, but with separate governments.[16]

Van Buren's task was somewhat more difficult. Unlike Clay, his supporters included ardent expansionists, among them no less a person than Andrew Jackson. Followers of Calhoun had abandoned hope of raising their hero to the presidency, but would do all in their power to prevent the nomination of Van Buren whom Calhoun detested. At the same time Van Buren was aware of great dissatisfaction among his most faithful friends. Two years before he had told Francis P. Blair that the Democrats of New York had "suffered so often, and so severely in their advocacy of Southern men, and Southern measures, as to make them more sensitive in respect to complaints of their conduct from that quarter, than I would wish."[17] His closest friend and most distinguished supporter, Senator Silas Wright, who wrote two or three times a week from Washington, left him in no doubt. On March 22 Wright thought that rumors of a treaty were "all hoax," but went on to say that President and Senate had as much right to merge Texas into the United States as to merge the United States into Texas. Even supposing that such a constitutional power existed, Wright continued, "a secret movement of this sort ought not to be sanctioned by the Senate, and would not be by me, until the great outlines of the terms were fully known to and approved by the people of that country."[18]

16. Henry Clay, *Works,* ed. Calvin Colton, 6 vols. (New York, 1855), VIII: 25–31.

17. Blair Papers, Library of Congress, Washington, D. C., 15 April 1842.

18. Van Buren Papers, Library of Congress, 22 March. Wright still believed that the treaty was "all hoax," but on 16 March the *National Intelligencer* reported a strong rumor that it was ready for signature, though up till that time it had thought such reports to be "perfect hum-

On the other hand there was ample evidence that endorsement of annexation might secure Van Buren's position in the South and West, while failure to do so might jeopardize his chances of nomination. Thomas Ritchie, editor of the Richmond *Enquirer* and a great power in Virginia politics passed on to Wright a letter from an unnamed member of Congress asserting that, "the Texan question is destined to succeed. . . . General Jackson is most heartily with us . . . and will *see it through*. . . . Unless there is great imprudence or folly, Van Buren will be re-elected—but if he goes against Texas (which I deem impossible) *all is gone*."[19] Wright rejected this appreciation of the situation, but from Ohio Van Buren was told that the Democrats would "almost to a man go for annexation."[20] On April 6 another New York friend, B. F. Butler, saw several Democratic Congressmen and expressed his doubts about the treaty. Among them was R. J. Walker who "like all of our friends at the South, is full of the idea, that this movement is to prostrate Mr. Clay and to secure you [Van Buren], if you answer favorably, an easy victory"; but Butler had warned Walker that "it would be perfectly easy, by mismanaging this affair, to prostrate, at the North, every man concerned with it or connected with it.,"[21]

Two letters may have been decisive. Jabez B. Hammond, one of Van Buren's leading supporters in the city of New York, wrote,

> I am willing and I feel bound to support the slaveholding States in their right to hold slaves, but so utterly abhorrent is slavery to my principles that I cannot in conscience consent to the further extension of it. . . . I do not wish you to *speak* on that question but I owe it to candor to say that I could not vote for a candidate for the Presidency who I believed would under any circumstances favor annexation.[22]

The other letter was from Wright, written from Washington on April 8, in which he said,

---

bug." On 22 March, Granger told Thurlow Weed that "this nefarious Texas treaty" would be sent to the Senate (Granger Papers, Library of Congress).

19. Van Buren Papers, 22 March.

20. *Ibid.* On April 20 Cave Johnson, an experienced Tennessee politician, warned Van Buren that Southern and Western congressmen were being persuaded to desert him, and Amos Kendall warned him of a plot to replace him by Lewis Cass. It is not certain that Van Buren received these warnings before dispatching his letter, but as they were sent from Washington he probably did so. Joel R. Poinsett, writing from South Carolina, deplored rumors, attributed to Calhoun's friends, that Van Buren intended to withdraw in favor of Cass. (Poinsett to Governor Kemble, 8 March 1844, Poinsett Papers, Historical Society of Pennsylvania, Philadelphia).

21. Van Buren Papers, 6 April.

22. *Ibid.*, 7 April.

I have felt ever since I seriously reflected on the presence of this great question, that it changed the whole case, and made it more noble, more desirable, more important, more patriotic to take boldly the side of truth and principle, though it may be disastrous in a popular sense, than to temporize with a matter which may prove so vital.[23]

Van Buren wrestled with the problem in a series of draft letters, all long and all much corrected. His opposition to annexation by secret treaty was constant but tortuous, and much-amended passages explained his reasons and the extent to which the door might be left open for annexation at a future time and under happier circumstances. The letter was finally pulled into shape and dispatched to Wright who was to send it to the press if he approved it. Wright received the letter on the evening of Friday, April 26. He hurriedly consulted some friends, including Benton, who advised publication. The letter was then sent to the *Globe*, and the proofs were corrected that night; it appeared in print on Sunday, April 28, just twenty-four hours after Clay's letter had appeared in the *Intelligencer*.[24]

Van Buren's virtues as a statesman did not include brevity or forceful statement. As with other such statements of the period the letter was intended for a comparatively narrow circle of political leaders, but even they, in an age of prolix expression, may have found it difficult to follow. It was mature, subtle, balanced, full of fine distinctions, and pervaded by a true sense of the dignity of politics, but did not make its points in clear, lucid, or quotable phrases. Van Buren began by stressing that an American government must be above reproach in international affairs:

We have a character among the nations of the earth to maintain. . . . It has hitherto been our pride and our boast, that whilst the lust of power, with fraud and violence in its train, has led other and differently constituted nations of the earth to aggressive action and conquest, our movements in these respects have always been regulated by reason and justice.

There were, said Van Buren, circumstances which could justify annexation by direct action. If, for instance, there was evidence that

23. *Ibid.*, 8 April.
24. *Ibid.*, Wright to Van Buren, 29 April.

Britain intended to make Texas a colony—but such an idea was incredible. There might be changes in the relationship between Mexico and Texas (either recognition of Texan independence, or an attempt to restore Mexican authority by force) which would "weaken and perhaps obviate entirely the objections to the immediate annexation of Texas." But any action should depend upon recognition by a majority of the American people that "the permanent welfare, if not the absolute safety of all, make it necessary that the proposed annexation should be effected, be the consequence what it may." If he were President, and such an eventuality occurred, he would consult Congress. Moreover the whole question was likely to be discussed fully in the forthcoming election campaign and if the Congress then elected "should express an opinion in favor of annexation, I would hold it to be my duty to employ the executive power to carry into full and fair effect the wishes of a majority of the existing States, thus constitutionally and solemnly expressed."

The trained minds of Wright and Benton could see that Van Buren was pledging himself to abide by the will of the majority in the next Congress, which he would neither anticipate nor direct. The proposition was fair enough: if the Southern and Western expansionists could bring enough Southern Whigs and Northern Democrats over to their side they would carry their point and Van Buren would stick to the principle of majority rule. Annexation would then cease to be a sectional issue, and would represent consensus in all sections. Unfortunately the vital sentences came after some twelve thousand words mainly devoted to the case against annexation in April 1844. There was no doubt, as Wright sadly observed, that the letter was taken as a letter against Texas, and condemned unread. Moreover Van Buren never faced the very real difficulty of what would happen in Texas during the next six months—with annexation the subject of public discussion—and the further six to twelve months that might follow before a new Congress could express its opinion.

The effect of the letter was immediate. In Indiana a Van Buren man confessed that it had had "a dreadful effect." From Washington Silas Wright reported that "the state of things here is as bad as it can be." And on May 5 Thomas Ritchie wrote that it "had produced a condition of political affairs which I did not believe to be possible. . . . I am compelled to come to the conclusion that we cannot carry Virginia for you."[25] Ritchie said that he still supported Van Buren,

25. J. Brown of Indianapolis, 29 April; Wright to Van Buren, 6 May; Ritchie to Van Buren, 5 May. Van Buren Papers.

but was playing a double game. He had already called a meeting of the Shockoe Hill Democratic Association of Richmond, whose members formed a major part of the ruling Democratic caucus in the state, and he himself moved and carried a motion requesting the Democratic Central Committee of Virginia to relieve convention delegates of their obligation to support Van Buren at the national convention and to substitute an instruction to support a man "known and pledged to be in favor of annexation."[26]

A majority of the delegates to the National Democratic Nominating Convention were already pledged to Van Buren, but even before his annexation letter forces were at work to undermine his candidature. Calhoun was doing all in his power to prevent his nomination, and Lewis Cass of Michigan was in the field as an exponent of Western expansionism and Anglophobia. Early in March rumors were circulating in Washington that Van Buren would voluntarily withdraw, and an attempt was made to discredit him at a Democratic Congressional Caucus. Silas Wright was forewarned and ensured that enough "true men" were present to resist the move. The *Globe* gave an enthusiastic account of the harmony at this caucus, but a Whig journalist reported a bitter clash between the supporters and opponents of Van Buren. Colquitt of Georgia was reported to have said that Van Buren had no following in his state and that unless "they came forward and sustained *democratic* principles better than they had done . . . so far from there being enthusiasm, there would be no *union* of the party—it could not even be kept together."[27] In this situation Van Buren's Texas letter provided an obvious rallying point for all malcontents; in spite of pledged delegates, his friends would have to fight all the way at the nominating convention with no more than even chances of success.

Emphatic support from Andrew Jackson might still save or at least improve the situation. On May 22 Alfred Balch, a friend of Van Buren, visited the Hermitage. He found the old man in an agitated state. "Balch," he said, "I have been in much trouble for the last two weeks and I am much jaded. I want to be in peace—I have just prepared an answer to the numerous letters which I have received upon

26. To be fair to Ritchie it should be said that he had already received several letters hostile to Van Buren. On 27 April one correspondent wrote: "The people cannot be excited under the present prospect of V. B. being the candidate." Another writing on 3 May attributed losses in county elections to his candidacy and was endorsed by Ritchie "Written before the Texas letter was received." (Ritchie Papers, William and Mary College, Williamsburg, Va.).

27. *Niles' Register*, 16 March 1844, quoting from Washington *Globe* and "Oliver Oldschool" of the *United States Gazette*.

the question of Texas which I will send to the press. After I write Mr.
Van Buren a letter I shall have done with this business I trust for ever."
His public letter, dated May 13 and widely circulated, reaffirmed his
support for immediate annexation:[28]

> My aim is to give this country the strength to resist foreign
> interference. Without Texas we shall not have this strength.
> She is the key to our safety in the southwest and west. She
> offers this key to us on fair and honorable terms. Let us take
> it, and lock the door against future danger. We can do it
> without giving offense to Mexico.

There are few better testimonies to the power of Jackson's mind
than this letter. Old, troubled, and often in physical pain he could
still produce a statement which was clearer and more cogent than
anything yet written on annexation, and its publication ensured that
an expansionist tide would submerge Van Buren. To Van Buren himself Jackson professed his high and continuing regard, but added the
damning qualification that Van Buren was clearly ignorant of events
which had happened since his presidency and "which manifest the
probability of a dangerous interference with the affairs of Texas by a
foreign power." In Jackson's eyes Van Buren was not merely mistaken
but misunderstood the true national interest.[29]

In seeking to provide formulas that would unite their parties,
Clay and Van Buren had come to similar conclusions. Indeed, before
the close of the campaigns, they would be even closer. For Clay, discovering that he had underestimated expansionist enthusiasm among
rank and file Whigs in the South, pledged himself to give favorable
consideration to annexation if approved by a majority in Congress.
This coincidence gave rise to the improbable accusation of collusion
between the two men in 1842, when Van Buren paid a courtesy call
on Clay during a tour of the western states, but other inferences
can be drawn. The success of a two-party system depends upon the
extent to which both parties share common assumptions, so that the
success of one will not drive the other to extremes of opposition.
Whigs and Democrats represented real differences of attitude and
outlook which ran across the whole field of human affairs, but

28. Balch to Van Buren, 22 May 1844, Van Buren Papers.
29. The version in *Correspondence of Andrew Jackson*, ed. J.S. Bassett, VI, 201, is a draft, more
diffuse than the published letter (*Niles' Register*, LXVI, 70) and does not include the sentence
quoted above.

rival and permanent parties could exist only so long as both agreed on fundamentals and recognized reasonable limits to majority action and minority response. The most important fundamentals were obvious— Union, Constitution, and respect for the Unted States abroad—and unwritten law declared that nothing should damage these three. Issues could be vigorously contested in every state, but not when they endangered the Union by dividing section against section. All the powers sanctioned by the Constitution could be employed, but not to the point that government became oppressive; all constitutional checks could be deployed by the opposition but not to the point that the country became ungovernable. American interests should always be sustained, but a reputation for justice to neighbors was as much a national interest as diplomatic or strategic gains. Both Clay and Van Buren saw these essentials endangered by the way in which annexation had been handled, and strove to repair the damage before it was too late.

Neither Clay nor Van Buren understood that John C. Calhoun had arrived at quite different conclusions. He now insisted that social differences between North and South must not be pushed into the background of politics, but become pivots upon which a new system turned. Traditional diplomacy was no longer enough because the United States faced a world-wide British offensive more insidious and more dangerous than arguments over boundaries or maritime rights, and though Calhoun had no sympathy with the new brand of nationalism, of European rather than American origin, he could use it as a lever to break down the system Clay and Van Buren sought to preserve.

When John C. Calhoun came to the State Department he was sixty-two years old. Since 1811 he had been in the forefront of the national stage; he had been Vice-President for seven years, and before that Secretary of War from 1817 to 1825. He had been a member of the House of Representatives for six years, and a Senator for ten. In November 1842 he had resigned from the Senate to seek nomination for the presidency, and for the next twelve months tried to extend the circle of his supporters, inspire the hard core of his devoted followers, and oust Van Buren from control of the Democratic party. A principal issue in this struggle had been the means by which delegates should be chosen for the national convention. Van Buren's supporters, sure of majority support among the Democratic politicians in many states, wanted the whole state delegation to be chosen in state conventions. The Calhoun men wanted delegates to be elected by districts so that the substantial minorities supporting him might elect some delegates. Calhoun would then emerge as the first choice in some Southern states, the second in others, and demonstrate a broad band of Northern support. These high hopes were dashed in Pennsylvania, when it appeared that Calhoun would not even be the second choice to Buchanan. The fragility of his Northern support became evident and, even if the point over district elections was gained, his hopes of appearing as a vote-getter in the North were meager. Early in January 1844 he decided to abandon the effort, though with characteristic precision he insisted that he had never formally placed his name before the people, and could not therefore withdraw. After reaching this decision he wrote, "I can never consent for my name to go before a convention, after what I have seen. No; our only course is to rally to our own ground, be our number few, or many; or to withdraw and stand aloof from the fraudulent game. The great point for me, is to *preserve my character* in these corrupt and degenerate times." An unkind interpretation would be that Calhoun could not bear the thought that his following should stand up and be counted; a face-saving retreat was better than an open defeat.[30]

The intense light of Calhoun's intellect shed a narrow beam. Geographically he was the most limited of American statesmen; since his student days at Yale, he had hardly strayed from the line between South Carolina and Washington. Clay had traveled in most parts of the Union, and had visited Europe. Webster had visited England and was at home with the intellectual culture of Boston and the quasi-cosmopolitan atmosphere of New York. Buchanan had been Minister to Russia, Van Buren Minister to England, and Benton had traveled all over the West; but it was not until 1846 that Calhoun crossed the Appalachians for the first time. His intellectual horizons were equally limited: on the literature of politics, he was well-read, but his correspondence reveals little knowledge that was not derived from the debates of Congress, the diplomatic correspondence of the United States, or his own experience. He was the most egocentric of men and, in his own eyes, stood as an unchanging rock amid the swirling malevolence of the times. Calhoun could abandon economic nationalism, turn against John Quincy Adams, quarrel with Jackson, join with the Whigs, support Van Buren and finally move all things to prevent his renomination; yet in his own estimation he remained a paragon of consistency with a duty to confront those who had been

30. To James Edward Calhoun, 7 February 1844, *Correspondence of Calhoun*, Part I, 567.

tempted into devious courses. He was now convinced of Van Buren's infamy. Van Buren's friend Silas Wright voted for the tariff of 1842, and in 1844 the New York Democrats had voted against the 21st Rule of the House of Representatives which barred the consideration of abolitionist petitions. Though the motion to rescind the Rule had been laid on the table of the House, this was not enough. "I regard with surprise," wrote Calhoun, "that the deceptive vote of laying on the table by one vote, should be regarded as a triumph by some of our Southern friends. It is obvious that it is but a trick, in the infamous scheme of endeavoring to catch the abolitionist votes, without offending the South, and ought to be so treated. . . . It would be better by far to bring the question at once to the issue, than that we should be made the dupes and victims of a fraudulent game."[31]

In modern societies, moving through economic and social changes of unpredictable magnitude, good fortune has attended conservatives who have learned to yield gracefully while retaining much of their former influence. It was Calhoun's conviction that no one should ever yield anything, and this disastrous wisdom he eventually imparted to the South. It is a recurrent theme in his letters that he and his friends should "take the high ground," which meant first discovering a point at which one should yield nothing, adhering to this at whatever cost, and finally condemning more flexible seekers after compromise.

As his hopes of the presidency dimmed, Calhoun determined to become the spokesman of a united South. "Things cannot go on in the direction they are taking much longer. A split between us and the northern Democracy is inevitable, unless we should prove [to] be the most base and submissive people on earth, or they should reverse their course on the Tariff and slave questions, which I do not expect." Yet these facts, which to him seemed self-evident, failed to convince even his fellow Southerners. "We must show as fixed a determination to defend our property and our safety, as the friends of the tariff and the abolitionists do to assail them. If I thought that the South would sustain me in taking the course, which the occasion demands, I would make the sacrifice and brave the hazard, as great as they might be, to repel the attack on their property [and] safety. But I see no prospect of that at present. . . ." Indeed, from Calhoun's point of view, the South was in a lamentable condition, and solidarity seemed as remote in 1844 as it had been in 1832 when so few had rallied to the standard of

31. *Ibid.*, to Armistead Burt, 9 March 1844, 573.

nullification. Somehow a remedy must be found and it was in this mood that Calhoun reached Washington early in April to find the Treaty of Annexation almost ready for signature.[32]

As he looked over the papers in the State Department, Calhoun's logical mind must have been worried. From the attitude of the *Intelligencer* it seemed that Southern Whigs would oppose the treaty, and without their support it could not pass the Senate. If Northern Democrats supported annexation most Whigs would probably refuse to do so; if they opposed, nothing could save it. How and where had the optimistic Upshur found the two-thirds majority to ratify with which he expected to pass the treaty? If the papers supporting the treaty had demonstrated the existence of a British threat the case for secrecy and for urgency might be sustained, but this was not so. The diplomatic exchanges had extracted explicit denials from the British Government, and there was no evidence, save the doubtful gossip of the "citizen of Maryland," to substantiate the existence of an Anglo-abolitionist conspiracy. There was a further danger. The treaty might be lost because of objections to its secret execution, but the articulate opposition was likely to come from the opponents of slavery, and its defeat would be regarded as their victory. Three months before, Calhoun had made up his mind how to meet such an opposition, when he wrote to T. W. Gilmer that "the objection that it would extend our domestic institution of the South, must be met as a direct attack on the compromise of the Constitution, and the highest ground ought to be taken in opposition to it on our part."[33]

Win or lose, the case for annexation should thus be based firmly upon the need to protect slavery. If the treaty was to be attacked as a pro-slavery conspiracy, it must be defended as a pro-slavery instrument. The Southern Whigs must be persuaded to see it in that light, and the good faith of Northern Democrats must be put to the test in an unequivocal way. In particular Van Buren must be forced off the fence which he had so often occupied; if he opposed the treaty Southern Democrats would know what to do about his candidature for renomination, and with luck Western expansionists might be carried by their zeal for annexation into Southern alliance and pro-slavery commitment. But here again the papers relating to the treaty were defective. Upshur had stated the case for slavery in a letter to Everett, but

32. *Ibid.*, to James E. Calhoun, 7 February 1844, 567; to James H. Hammond, 5 March 1844, 572.
33. *Ibid.*, 25 December 1843, 560.

on grounds of expediency rather than principle. Something more was necessary, and in Calhoun's analysis it was essential to shift the ground for annexation from an unverified abolitionist plot to a clear statement that the United States was committed to the general support of slavery. Anti-slavery was an international movement and must be presented as a world-wide threat to American interests; its demonstrable effects in particular circumstances might be slight, but even a token victory would inflict irreparable harm on the United States.

Looking over the correspondence in search of "high ground" Calhoun observed that in one official letter Aberdeen, while repudiating interference with the internal concerns of other countries, had said that the British government would welcome emancipation wherever it occurred. This presented Calhoun with the opportunity he sought of making the protection of slavery the central issue of annexation, and on April 18, six days after the signature of the treaty, he addressed his letter to Pakenham, ostensibly to notify the British government of the treaty's existence but in fact to present a defense of slavery as a permanent and beneficial institution which the United States government would protect wherever it was in their power to do so. This letter was attached to the other treaty documents and sent with them to the Senate.

Francis Blair, editor of the *Globe*, believed that Calhoun had inferred from a *Globe* article that Van Buren intended to support annexation but not the treaty. On May 2 he wrote to Andrew Jackson that "the moment that Calhoun saw from the *Globe*, that Mr. Van Buren would go for bringing Texas in by a vote in Congress as soon as practicable, he immediately addressed his letter to Packenham [*sic*], putting it on the ground to drive off every northern man from support of the measure." In Blair's view Calhoun intended to sacrifice the treaty in order to break Van Buren's support in the South.

> He goes for renewing the war in the midst of the Armistice between Mexico and Texas upon the sole ground that Texas must be taken to support slavery, without regard to any Northern interest, principle or prejudice, being perfectly conscious that this would be taking a stand which Mr. Van Buren could not take, that it would drive off every Northern man from reannexation, that the treaty would thus be defeated by an overwhelming vote in the Senate and that he would be furnished with a pretext to unite the whole South

upon himself as the champion of its cause and give him the pretext of urging the slaveholding States into his scheme of dissolution of the Union and a Southern Confederacy.[34]

Blair was desperately anxious to prevent Jackson from saying or writing anything that might prejudice Van Buren's chances, and he played upon memories of nullification in hope of persuading the Old Hero to disavow the treaty in favor of Van Buren's more cautious approach to annexation.

Calhoun himself saw his letter in the same light: as a test of Northern intentions. He wrote that if the documents did not prove the case for annexation to Northern Democrats,

> It is owing to the fact, that that portion of the Union has not duly weighed the damage to which the movements and avowed policy of Great Britain . . . would expose the southern and western States, and the obligation which this Government is under to defend them. . . . If our safety and the great interest we have in maintaining the existing relation between the two races in the south, are of no estimation in the eyes of our northern friends . . . it is time that we should know it.[35]

The arguments presented by R. J. Walker and others were forced into the background, and the price of Union was commitment to slavery —as abolitionists had long maintained.[36]

Calhoun had high hopes that his strategy would succeed. In the West there was strong support for expansionist policies, and even a suspicion of British opposition might bring a surge of popular support once the project of annexation became known. Anti-slavery opposition would be outflanked and his own brand of sectionalism would be recognized as truly national policy. If the issue was presented as a

34. Blair Papers, 2 May 1844. On 7 July Blair wrote to Jackson that "Nobody knew better than Calhoun the effect of thus making reannexation a sectional instead of a national question as you say it should be. Yet he wantonly made it sectional to defeat the measure and make it ground of collision between the north and south after he had reason to believe from the *Globe's* article that Van Buren and his friends would go for annexation by Congress."

35. To Francis Wharton, 28 May 1844. *Correspondence of Calhoun*, Part I, 593.

36. Charles M. Wiltse in *John C. Calhoun*, 3 vols. (New York, 1944–51) observes that the Pakenham letter "was an error, and undoubtedly one that he would never have committed had he realized the letter would be published. He was impelled to say what he did by his own innate honesty" (III, 169). But papers sent with a treaty were likely to be published sooner or later, and Northern senators were not going to conceal the reason for their opposition. All the evidence suggests that Calhoun knew what he was doing and calculated the odds.

choice between gaining and losing Texas, there might be many Easterners who would go for expansion and condemn opposition whatever
the grounds. In the words of Calhoun's leading supporter, Dixon H.
Lewis of Alabama, annexation "will unite the hitherto divided South,
while it will make Abolition and Treason synonymous and thus destroy it in the North."[37] Given these prospects, the failure of the
treaty in the Senate would be an advantage because this would open
the way for a majority commitment to the proposition that slavery
followed the flag. Calhoun's own advocacy of expansionism was limited; he wanted Texas urgently not the acquisition of territory for
its own sake. Later he was to oppose war with Mexico because he
anticipated correctly that further acquisition would do nothing to
strengthen slavery where it existed.

   Defeat of the treaty was inevitable. Clay and Van Buren had
timed their letters so that their friends in the Senate would be left in
no doubt, and it went down by 35 against 16 with two abstentions.
Over two-thirds of those present and voting were opposed, with 20
against 5 from north and 15 against 11 from south of the Mason Dixon
line. The most telling attack came from the formidable John M. Berrien of Georgia who had once been Jackson's Attorney General but was
now a pillar of the Southern Whig party.[38] He took up Clay's warning
that a struggle for new slave territory could do no good to the South.
He accepted the right to acquire land by treaty "as a necessary incident
of sovereignty," argued that it must be treated as a national not sectional question, and that if a paramount national interest were involved a secret treaty might be justified; but no such interest had been
proved and support was urged mainly on sectional grounds to preserve
slavery. The continued ascendancy of the free states was certain—
either by the occupation of new lands by free settlers or by the abandonment of slavery in states where it was not legal—and this was a
tide that could not be resisted. Southerners should rely upon existing
law and the Constitution—which provided adequate safeguards—
and not chase after an illusory balance of power. Nor would the Southern states win economic advantage from Texas for, under present circumstances, few masters would sell their slaves and move to Texas,
but if, in the future, they did so, the old South would be weakened.

   37. Letter to S. P. Chase published in several newspapers, quoted in Eugene I. McCormac,
*James K. Polk* (New York, 1922), 615.
   38. *Congressional Globe*, 28. 1. Appendix, 701ff. Benton also attacked the treaty vigorously. In
Jackson's opinion "ever since the explosion of the big gun Benton has not been in his right
mind." Quoted in McCormac, *Polk*, 257n.

What the Southern states needed most were immigrants and profitable enterprise; Texas would attract both at the expense of the older states. As for the abolitionists, who so much alarmed some of his colleagues, "their only real coadjutors were those southern men who agitate this question for party purposes, and seek to make political capital by the exaggerated descriptions of their power, and the consequent danger to which the South is opposed." In this Berrien spoke with the authentic voice of Southern Whiggery; deeply committed to slavery but pleading with Southerners to concentrate on economic development within a national framework, ignore the friends and enemies of slavery who wished to place it at the forefront of politics, and rely upon the goodwill of the great majoriy of Northern men to secure the mutual benefits which all enjoyed under the Constitution. It was better to divide the nation into two parties than two sections; the first could foster constructive action, the second nothing but bitterness and disappointed hopes.

*      *      *

When the Democratic Convention assembled, between 148 and 154 delegates were pledged to vote for Van Buren's nomination, but James Buchanan of Pennsylvania—an experienced observer with presidential ambitions—believed that he would not be nominated because too many delegates were looking for an excuse to desert him.[39] Their opportunity came as soon as the convention assembled and proceeded to debate whether two-thirds or a simple majority should be necessary for nomination. The two-thirds rule had been adopted in 1836 with the intention (which became ironic in 1844) of demonstrating massive support for Van Buren. There had been no opposition to his renomination in 1840, so opportunity to argue the principle came for the first time in 1844. While many delegates looked to the two-thirds rule to ease their consciences—by allowing them to cast a vote on the first ballot for Van Buren and shift when he failed to obtain two-thirds— some Southerners took a longer view. If nomination by convention had come to stay, and if a permanent Northern and Western majority were certain, then it was important to ensure that Southern interests should be protected by allowing a nomination to be vetoed by a third plus one of the delegates.

George Bancroft, who attended the convention as manager of the

39. James Buchanan, *Works*, ed. J.B. Moore, 12 vols. (New York, 1908–11), VI:2.

Van Buren delegates, wrote that "the disorganizers want two-thirds, and on this the battle will turn."[40] B. F. Butler, another Van Buren-ite, made a vigorous defense in the convention of "the good old doc-trine of democracy that the majority should rule," but after hours of bitter debate a motion requiring two-thirds was carried by 148 to 118.[41] Sixty delegates pledged to Van Buren voted for two-thirds, and so did 17 Virginians who had been pledged but released before the convention. Of 77 delegates originally pledged to Van Buren, who voted for two-thirds, 25 came from New England and Pennsylvania, 14 from Illinois and Michigan, and 38 from Virginia, Alabama, Mississippi, and Louisiana. If all the pledged delegates from the free states had voted against the two-thirds rule it would not have carried, but what struck the mind was the massive defection in four Southern states. "Where," exclaimed Bancroft in a letter to Van Buren, "is the boasted honor of the South?"[42] Silas Wright thought that the true culprit was Calhoun; the Texas treaty had "from the beginning been made up to make it impossible that any Northern man could go for it," and Calhoun "wrote his dispatch to Pakenham to make the point perfectly secure."[43] Calhoun's private comment was that the conven-tion had "done much by freeing the country of the dangerous control of what may be called the New York dynasty," and deserved congratu-lation because "a more heartless and selfish body of politicians have rarely ever been associated together."[44] Against this a leading Demo-crat from Massachusetts later asserted that the wounds inflicted "will not soon heal, and may prove fatal." By giving control to a minority "we did violence to the fundamental principles which the people will not soon forget or forgive."[45]

Having disposed of Van Buren's chances, the majority of the convention was in doubt over the alternative. Lewis Cass of Michigan seemed to be gaining ground, and of all possibilities the Van Buren-ites regarded him as the most unsuitable.[46] The moment was there-fore ripe for the astute friends of James K. Polk, who had hoped for the Vice-Presidency on a Van Buren ticket, to bring forward his name.

40. Van Buren Papers, 23 May.

41. *Ibid.*

42. *Ibid.*, 25 May.

43. *Ibid.*, 6 May.

44. *Correspondence of Calhoun*, Part I, 601.

45. Marcus Morton to Tappan, 25 January 1845, Benjamin Tappan Papers, Library of Con-gress, Washington, D.C.

46. Cass announced his support for immediate annexation in a public letter dated 10 May. This was seen as a deliberate attempt to steal Van Buren delegates.

VOTES CAST FOR THE TWO-THIRDS RULE AT THE
DEMOCRATIC NATIONAL CONVENTION 1844

| | For<br>the Rule | Against<br>the Rule |
|---|---|---|
| Massachusetts | 5* | 7 |
| Vermont | 3* | 3 |
| Maine | — | 9 |
| New Hampshire | — | 6 |
| Connecticut | 3* | 3 |
| Rhode Island | 2* | 2 |
| New York | — | 38 |
| New Jersey | 7 | — |
| Pennsylvania | 12* | 13 |
| Ohio | — | 23 |
| Indiana | 12 | — |
| Illinois | 9* | — |
| Michigan | 5* | — |
| Missouri | — | 7 |
| Delaware | 3 | — |
| Tennessee | 13 | — |
| Kentucky | 12 | — |
| Arkansas | 3 | — |
| Maryland | 6 | 2 |
| Virginia | 17† | — |
| North Carolina | 5 | 5 |
| South Carolina | (Did not vote) | — |
| Georgia | 10 | — |
| Alabama | 9* | — |
| Mississippi | 6* | — |
| Louisiana | 6* | — |

* Delegates pledged to Van Buren.
† Delegates previously pledged to Van Buren but released from the pledge before the convention.
SUMMARY: *For the Rule*: 148
          *Against the Rule*: 118
    Van Buren pledged delegates voting for the rule: 60
    Virginia delegates released from their pledge to Van Buren voting for the rule: 17
SOURCE: *Niles' Register,* 1 June 1844.

Though little known in the country he was personally acquainted with many delegates as a former Speaker of the House, was presented as "the bosom friend of Jackson, and a pure whole-hogged Democrat, the known enemy of banks and distribution," and, though favoring annexation, was in no way associated with Calhoun. Within a remarkably short space of time he won support from all parts of the convention, and the climax came when the South Carolinians, who had hitherto abstained on all votes, announced their support. With the vote nearing unanimity, the only discordant note was struck by an obscure and angry delegate from Missouri, who claimed that he had been denied a hearing earlier and seized a final opportunity to shout that he accepted no responsibility for "a gross fraud—a fraud upon the democratic party—a fraud upon the country."[47]

\*    \*    \*

Cave Johnson, a Tennessee politician, writing to Silas Wright on April 13, had hoped that Van Buren would endorse annexation and added "if the treaty is not ratified, which is probable, it will control the destinies of our public men for years to come."[48] The prophecy was true, but why did the Texas treaty start a train of events with such momentous consequences? An easy answer is that it first brought to the fore the extension of slavery over which men would argue until secession and war. But this does not explain why they attached such importance to hypothetical possibilities which could inflict no material damage upon anyone. A more penetrating answer is that annexation was intimately connected with the nature and purpose of national existence. American nationalism was different from European nationalism. It did not have to contend with alien rule, was not the product of comparatively small but cohesive ethnic groups, and focused upon just and successful political institutions rather than upon visions of the future independence. Nevertheless the impulse to explain and justify national character and destiny was felt with increasing urgency. Slavery was caught up in the ensuing controversy, but the essential point of debate was the relation of slavery to national character rather than the nature of slavery itself.

Any discussion of nationalism must begin with a warning that the term is a comparatively recent invention to describe earlier movements which had substance but no generic name.[49] The word "nation" is of great antiquity, but in the early nineteenth century the

47. As reported in *Niles' Register*, 1 June 1844.
48. Johnson to Wright, 13 April, Van Buren Papers.
49. Cf. Hans Kohn, *Nationalism: its meaning and history*, revised ed. (Princeton, N. J., 1965), 9. "Nationalism is a state of mind. . . . Formerly, man's loyalty was due not to the nation state, but to differing other forms of social authority, political ideology and ideological cohesion"; also Elie Kedouri, *Nationalism* (London, 1960), 9. "Nationalism is a doctrine invented in Europe at the beginning of the nineteenth century."

idea that a nation possessed a collective personality, with character and will, was still a novel concept. It will be recalled that Henry Clay, when speaking on the veto, referred to the "national will," and was rebuked by Calhoun who asserted that there was no evidence that such a thing existed.

In Europe the new idea that nations were the "natural" political units—as distinct from empires or dynastic states which grouped many races under one ruler—was first advanced by small countries protesting against alien domination. The inference that a nation had an inalienable right to self-government was an article of faith not yet tested by experience. It was equally novel to suggest that the "will" of a nation could be found out by democratic processes, and Calhoun correctly questioned the premise that a majority in Congress could claim to represent the will of the people. A congressman was the choice of a majority in a single district, at a particular time, when specific issues or persons were presented for approval. Majority decision was a matter of convenience, did not create a collective will, and the "numerical majority," obtained at a single election, must recognize the rights of other elected persons and bodies to represent the interests of the people in other legitimate ways.

Nevertheless since the Revolution, Americans had been conscious of their reputation in the world. They knew that their political experiment had no precedent in history, expected admiration, and were acutely sensitive to criticism. Individual Americans felt themselves affected by national reputation, and foreigners assumed that all were represented by the conduct of a few. To a considerable extent the American character had been negatively defined. Americans were not monarchists, had no hereditary aristocracy, and were not subject to the constraints of Europeans. The Old World, and especially England, was a "negative reference point" which helped Americans to define their own positive qualities. In this process there was also an implicit idea that Americans had accepted some values while rejecting others, but less agreement on which European features deserved approbation.

A good deal of American perplexity can be understood as a response to conflicting views of England. That country was best able to inflict material and moral damage on the United States, but was also the parent of America's most treasured traditions. Was it America's mission to preserve this English heritage in the present and propagate it in the future? England was the source—and still poured forth the living stream—of a culture that all admired; yet indigenous

American culture had always to resist British influences or risk being smothered at birth. Most American literary men aspired to an English reputation and would go far to win it, but English criticism of American manners was indignantly rejected. One often feels, as one reads contemporary American explanations of their history, traditions, and prospects that the unseen audience is composed of Harriet Martineau, Charles Dickens, Sidney Smith, and Edinburgh reviewers. Thus Americans of this era were already familiar with the task of justifying their collective national character. If they made little use of the word "nation," and would not have understood what "nationalism" meant, they were familiar with the idea that traditional, religious, and ethnic differences could be discounted, leaving a quality defined as "American."

This had deeper roots than contemporary sensitivity to British criticism. It was commonplace that the original colonists had settled in America with a purpose, and even when that purpose was purely material they nevertheless established institutions to preserve political and religious freedom. For two centuries the quest for *novus ordo seclorum*, in which people were masters of their own destiny, had been the guiding spirit of American history. This was, above all, the lesson Americans learned from George Bancroft's history, even if many of them rejected his political conclusions. This had produced a society superior to all others, but imposed great responsibilities. Steeped in the Bible most Americans knew the punishment that awaited people chosen by God who sinned against the light. As Martin Van Buren said, in his letter on Texas, "We have a character among the nations of the earth to maintain." Other nations were "differently constituted" and might resort to aggression and conquest, but Americans lived under a moral injunction to be above reproach.

All countries seek to justify themselves in the language of self-righteousness, but for Americans it was of practical as well as sentimental significance. If ideas of moral purpose were dissolved, what then remained? The core of national existence was Divine Truth expressed in a political philosophy, and to deny this, to stand before the world and admit that America was as other nations, would be moral treason.

John C. Calhoun often appeared to discount every motive but that of self-interest. His explanation of British anti-slavery in terms of economic power policy allowed no room for humanitarian influence except as delusion and hypocrisy. He judged the Northern majority in Congress by the same criteria, but in explaining his own conduct no one appealed more readily to moral principles or the need to "take the high ground." So though Calhoun, in some of his utterances, seems to present a startling departure from the general tendency to explain national character in moral terms, he is a variant rather than a departure from the normal rule. It was however a dangerous variant for it claimed exclusively for a novel political entity—the South—the moral values that others hoped to preserve in the nation as a whole.

A typical representative of the "moral nationalism" of the North was Charles Francis Adams. In 1843 he was invited to give the Fourth of July Oration in Faneuil Hall, and, with Texas in mind, delivered a speech which he described as "somewhat unusual."[50] Aware of the claims of romantic nationalists in Europe, and perhaps aware of contemporary echoes in America, he dismissed them as wholly irrelevant to the United States. Schemes for expansion and aggrandizement were not the fulfillment of American purpose, but would be destructive of it. He said that the "three great pillars of the political system" were equality of social condition, moral qualities founded upon religious faith, and devotion to the public interest." The Declaration of Independence laid down basic requirements for freedom, among which the most important was the consent of the governed. The author of the Declaration had himself ignored this precept when he added Louisiana to the United States without seeking the consent of the inhabitants, and though possibly justified by paramount national interest, the precedent ought not to be followed. There was a present danger. "Are not the same arguments, which have once availed to stretch our territory at the expense of our principles, likely to be pressed again?" The danger would not be avoided by inaction for "a new era must take place and questions must again arise. . . ." Charles Francis Adams, like his father, could be a robust defender of national interests, but on this occasion he stressed the temptations of power. "The age is full of gigantic systems, the country is full of exaggerated sympathies. Within as well as without the elements of commotion are working to produce fearful agitation." The clearest threat to American principles came from men who claimed the right "to spread our own system over the territories of neighboring nations."

Two years later, before the same audience, Charles Sumner lectured on false notions of "national honor." Among individuals a pernicious code, to which men attached the name of "honor," sanctioned duelling, undermined law, and excused moral depravity. Among nations it provided the motive and the justification for needless wars;

---

50. *An Oration delivered before the City Council and Citizens of Boston . . . on July 4, 1843.*

and war was the ultimate political evil, leading inevitably to persecution and the suppression of rights. Nations like men must learn to
distinguish between the just and unjust use of the capacity God had
given them.[51] The existence of power was not a justification for its use
and in 1843 Charles Francis Adams concluded that "our highest duty
as a people is self-restraint."

These austere notions of national character were challenged by a
rival theory of national destiny. John O'Sullivan, editor of the *Democratic Review* was a principal exponent of party ideas and a major prophet of the new nationalism. He was an immigrant from Ireland and
heir to a fiercely nationalist tradition evolved in protest against alien
rule, but when the nationalism of a small, oppressed race was placed
in the context of a half-empty continent, the arguments became
paradoxically similar to those employed by apologists for British rule
in Ireland. Geographical necessity, superior civilization, and historic
destiny justified American expansion. The map of North America
showed an enormous inland valley, flanked by mountain ranges and
fertile coastal plains; surely this symmetry indicated Divine purpose
to place the whole under the domination of a single people? The vigor
and republican institutions of the Americans were proof that they
must be that people, for they alone could secure liberty and progress
for all who came under their rule or for the millions who would come
to occupy the empty lands. All this "left no doubt of the manifest
design of Providence."[52]

These romantic visions could hardly have had the success they
did if they had not echoed older American traditions. If one strand of
the Puritan heritage led to preoccupation with the need to stand before the world as a redeemed people, another told of communities
built by a God-fearing race called to settle in a Promised Land. It did
not require a large step to move from Exodus to expansion, and the
seed of new nationalism fell on good ground.

Expansionists could also appeal to the technological revolution
which was changing the world. In his influential pamphlet advocating the annexation of Texas, Robert J. Walker referred to men who
believed that it was too large or too remote to govern and scornfully

51. *An Oration before the City Council and Citizens of Boston* (Boston, 1845); also in Charles
Sumner, *Complete Works,* 15 vols. (New York, 1900; reprint ed. 1969), I: 5ff. Samuel Gridley
Howe wrote to congratulate Sumner. "You have struck a blow at the false Gods which people
worship; you have proved them to be of wood, hay, and stubble (Howe to Sumner, July 1845,
Houghton Library).
52. *U. S. Magazine and Democratic Review* VI (April 1844): 424 ff. and VII (July 1845): 7.
Cited hereafter as *Democratic Review.*

observed that they "must have been sleeping since the application of steam to locomotion." O'Sullivan believed that California would seek independence from Mexico and union with the United States, if a transcontinental railroad were built in the near future. Science was the handmaid of Providence in spreading American civilization across the continent, and extending the Union far beyond the limits imagined by men of narrow vision. In 1845, with annexation almost complete, O'Sullivan declared that it was "the inevitable fulfilment of the general law which is pressing our population westward." So far from endangering the Union it would gather strength for, as Walker had asserted without resort to proof, "as you augment the number of States, the bond of union is stronger."

The new style "design of Providence" implied a duty to rebuke those who obstructed its fulfillment. When advocating annexation, Robert J.Walker wrote scathingly of anti-slavery men who "hold conventions in the capital of England, and there . . . brood over schemes of abolition, in association with British societies . . . join in denunciations of their countrymen, until their hearts are filled with treason, and . . . return home Americans in name but Englishmen in feelings and principles."[53] O'Sullivan condemned the writers in American newspapers and journals whose attacks on their own government were eagerly copied in the foreign press. "The honor of their country should be no less dear to each of her sons not wholly unworthy of that parentage." This "traitorous Anti-Americanism" had, in O'Sullivan's opinion, been treated too leniently; the expression of opinion might be a sacred right but universal condemnation should silence "the scoffer and slanderer of his own country."[54]

The new view of national character was at variance with old Republican theory, and annexation prompted a revered voice from the Jeffersonian past to break silence. "I am highly gratified," proclaimed Albert Gallatin, "that the last act of a long life should be that of bearing testimony against this outrageous attempt; that the last accents of an almost extinguished voice should have been heard in defense of Justice, of Liberty, and of the Constitution." The great hope, which was America, had been "checked by a measure in which treaties are violated, and unjust war undertaken."[55] The treaty had been engineered by two Virginians and one South Carolinian, who claimed to

53. Walker, *Letter* in Merk, *Fruits of Propaganda*, 11.
54. *Democratic Review*, XVI (May 1845), 421–22.
55. *Proceedings of a meeting to consider the annexation of Texas* (New York, 1844).

make strict construction a way of life, but Charles Francis Adams observed that Southern reverence for the principles of Jefferson went "no further than they happened to coincide with the immediate policy which they had in view."[56]

Inevitably abandonment of principles was attributed to slavery. Theodore Sedgwick, a New York Democrat, pointed out that his party's uniform opposition to abolitionist agitation did not imply uncritical adherence to slavery. "We are gravely informed that slavery, if left to itself, will work its own cure. I quite agree to the proposition; but when shall we begin the experiment?" He criticized Walker's argument and pointed out that the mechancial function of a safety valve was to keep the engine working efficiently. "The annexation of Texas is but another name for the perpetuity of slavery."[57] Another New York Democrat, Jabez Delano Hammond, elaborated the point in his *Letter to the Hon. John C. Calhoun:*

> Does not everyone know that slavery, from the redundancy of slave population, would long before this time have been abolished in Virginia and the Carolinas, had it not been for the "safety valve" spoken of by Mr. Walker, furnished by the market for slaves in Louisiana, Alabama and the other new States.[58]

Mirabeau Buonaparte Lamar, ex-President of Texas, in an address to the citizens of Macon, Georgia, unwittingly supported these arguments. "The system of servitude is the best relation which has ever been established between the laboring and governing portion of mankind," but without Texas "the slaves shall so accumulate in the South, and the lands so decline in fertility, that this species of property will not only cease to be profitable, but will become a burden to its owners."[59] Further evidence was found in a Democratic campaign pamphlet—intended for circulation in the South alone, but given wide circulation in the North by the Whigs—which took up "the balance of power" argument, and concluded that "The only hope of the South is the annexation of Texas, which would give the South a

56. *Diary of C.F. Adams,* Massachusetts Historical Society, Boston, Mass.

57. Veto [pseudonym for Theodore Sedgwick], *Thoughts on the Proposed Annexation of Texas* (New York, 1844).

58. Hamden [pseudonym for Jabez D. Hammond], *Letter to the Hon. John C. Calhoun* (Cooperstown, N.Y., 1844), 12.

59. *Address to the Citizens of Macon, Georgia* (Macon, 1844).

majority in the Senate." Clay's opposition to annexation made him the ally of abolitionism; a vote for him was a vote against slavery.

Charles Francis Adams wrote that "some of the leading presses of the north have lately attempted to keep studiously out of view the subject that is at the bottom of it all," but others joined him in seeing slavery as the fundamental issue.[60] If annexation succeeded in the manner proposed, said Theodore Sedgwick, "we who now enjoy the rights and hold the soul of the Union, must bid farewell for ever to the hope of relieving ourselves from the danger, the odium and the disgrace inseparable from this pernicious institution." On many matters, he said, especially those connected with commercial policy, he would as soon be governed by the South as by the East or the West, "but the northern man must be false to his education, and blind to his interests, who does not, inch by inch, and hand to hand, resist the extension of the slave-holding power."[61] In this way, wrote Charles Francis Adams, the great issue "between the Constitution and slavery, between the rights of the many freemen and the privileges of the few, must be met."[62] In Congress Joshua Giddings put clearly the consequences of national commitment. "The real issue has been made up. It has been placed upon the records of Government, and will remain there in all coming time." Annexation meant "that this nation shall take upon itself the support and perpetuation of slavery."[63]

For fifty years there had been a tacit agreement that the Union was more important than slavery, and on this assumption the discussion of slavery had been kept out of Congress. Reactions to the occasional breaches of this unwritten rule—such as the attempted censure of Adams and the successful censure of Giddings—had indicated a Southern readiness to exploit the advantages derived from Northern acquiesence in the convention of silence; but until the Texas question forced the issue, majorities in both parties assumed that no one's interest could be served by opening the slave controversy at a national level. The way in which annexation was handled changed all that, and even O'Sullivan's enthusiasm for expansion did not extend to endorsement of the treaty. In the *Democratic Review* of January 1845 he put the question forcibly:

60. Adams, *Texas and the Massachusetts Resolutions*.

61. Veto, *Thoughts on the Proposed Annexation*.

62. Adams, *op. cit.*

63. *Congressional Globe*, 28.1. Appendix, 704. There is a slightly different version in J. R. Giddings, *Speeches in Congress* (Boston, 1853), 97.

What has become of the Southern doctrine—what, of the Northern Democratic position—that the institution of slavery, whether good or evil, was a local and not a federal institution—with which the Free States had nothing to do—for which they were in no wise responsible, either to their own conscience or to the judgment of the world, even though it existed on the common ground of the District of Columbia.

This State Rights doctrine had suffered a shattering blow when slavery was justified, "through the peculiar organ of our collective nationality, for which if anything, the Union is emphatically responsible— in public diplomatic papers, addressed to England, to France, to the whole civilized world." Annexation nationalized slavery and it could no longer be kept out of politics. "There can be no doubt that a more vehement and powerful agitation of Abolitionism will take place than has yet been known . . . in consequence of that collective, national responsibility for the institution, in the eyes of the whole world."[64]

The *Democratic Review* was gravely concerned by the apparent blindness of some Southerners to the implications of Calhoun's Pakenham letter, and asked them "to imagine a *Northern* Secretary of State possessed with the opposite fanaticism on the subject of slavery, volunteering the discussion of the merits of that institution, on a slight pretext afforded by a letter of a foreign minister and strongly urging, in the name of the nation, all those views of that subject which are most obnoxious to the feelings and opinions of the South."[65] Nor were reproaches confined to the North. Willie P. Mangum, anticipating further attempts after the failure of the treaty, wrote that it would "produce deep and dangerous excitement in portions of the North and East. Beside the outrage upon the Constitution and past precedents, it will stir deeply anti-slavery feelings, and shake profoundly the confidence of higher and better men in the perpetuity of our system."[66]

In all the controversy over annexation the word "nation" ap-

64. *Democratic Review* XVI (January 1845), 8–9.
65. *Ibid.* (February 1845), 108. An editorial article asserted that "a great wrong was done to the North . . . and a doubly great wrong to the Democratic Party . . . which has so long and so well stood by its Southern friends and brethren, at great peril and injury to its own proper interests."
66. Willie P. Mangum, *Papers,* ed. Henry T. Shanks (Chapel Hill, 1950), IV: 271. To W. A. Graham, 21 February 1845.

peared with greater frequency than ever before. "It is not a question of national politics but of national identity," declared Rufus Choate, the brilliant orator and lawyer of Boston.[67] This sudden alarm came at a time when other problems raised penetrating questions about the character and prospects of the United States. The incoming tide of immigrants who were neither Anglo-Saxon nor Protestant had provoked some violent popular reactions, local political activity, and more temperate but equally disturbing thought about the preservation of American political and cultural traditions. These alarms were to grow with the great Irish immigration after 1845. The economic growth of the United States gave rise to serious debate—with the advocates of national growth behind protective tariff walls ranged against free trade theorists—and both profoundly aware of the need to avoid domination by the overwhelming economic power of Great Britain. On top of these problems of policy Americans were well aware of and generally sympathetic to European nationalist movements, and even men who reacted most sharply against Irish immigrants could deplore the state of things which forced them from their own country. Many Americans also watched with hopeful enthusiasm the rise of nationalist movements in Italy, Hungary, and Poland. George Bancroft's *History* taught a sophisticated but romantic view of America's past and awareness of a national mission created the determination that it should not be betrayed.

There was plenty of room for debate within the existing party system. There were traditional arguments over the role of the federal government which could be continued in the new context. Rapidly increasing population, the coming of the railroad, the growth of cities, the invention of the telegraph, and the return of economic prosperity after the depression years combined to prompt speculation and argument over the shape of things to come. The debate would range widely over the whole field of religion, education, and literature, but parties provided the means by which the political problems of the changing world could be discussed and decided. Agreement on detail was unlikely but the process of debate might gradually narrow the area of disagreement. In this way the parties would play their part in political education as well as provide the machinery for dealing with immediate issues. This was the kind of dialectic instinctively welcomed by such men as Henry Clay, Martin Van Buren, Thomas

67. Rufus Choate, *Works,* ed. Samuel G. Brown (Boston, 1862). "Speech to the Young Men's Whig Club of Boston, Aug. 19, 1844."

Hart Benton, and James Buchanan; they might appear irreconcilable, but shared common assumptions about the subjects that should be discussed and the way in which conflicts should be resolved. So indeed did James K. Polk—the new man with an expansionist vision—hope for nationwide support for the fundamentals of his policy. From other points of the political spectrum William H. Seward, Thurlow Weed, Willie P. Mangum, John M. Berrien, and a rising star of the West, Stephen A. Douglas, could agree that beyond party conflict there was a national interest which all men would recognize and serve. If some rejected the version of national character sketched by Charles Francis Adams, and others the fervent expansionism of John O'Sullivan, they could agree that both expressed views which deserved attention. By listening to both, the United States might grow while retaining "a decent regard for the opinions of mankind."

The evolution of American nationalism in the South was distorted by the Texas question. It was not so much the proposal to annex, for that could have been amicably settled with patience and a little goodwill, but the way in which it was handled and the arguments used to support it. In May 1844 Calhoun wrote privately, "I regard annexation to be the vital question. If lost now, it will be forever lost; and, if that, the South will be lost, if some prompt and decisive measure be not adopted to save us." At the same time he himself received a letter from a fellow South Carolinian that "the very existence of . . . Southern institutions depended upon annexation" and if Southerners did not rally to the cause they must be "content to be Hewers of Wood and Drawers of water for our Northern brethren." James Hammond was shocked to find that some of his slaves were "aware of the opinion of Presidential candidates on the subject of slavery and doubtless much of what the abolitionists are doing." There was a growing spirit of insubordination among the slaves, and some house had recently been burnt. "This is fearful—horrible. A *quick* and *potent* remedy must be applied. *Disunion* if *needs* be."[68]

Serious talk to disunion was still unlikely except among a very small minority of Southerners, but the way in which Calhoun and his friends put the argument ensured that the satisfaction of their demands must lie outside the limits of any possible consensus on national character and policy. They presented propositions which could not be compromised within the normal framework of party politics, and

68. *Correspondence of Calhoun,* Part I, to Mrs. G. Clemens, 10 May 1844, 585. Part II, from J. Gadsden, 3 May 1844, 952–53; from James Hammond, 10 May 1844, 955.

their alarm at the consequences—which might have been regarded as exaggerated and false if directed to other controversial questions— proved to be true prophecies of the future.

Without the distraction of slavery it is probable that the two parties would have met the challenge of nationalism by adapting their different views of America's past and future promise, but this became impossible once expansion became entangled with controversy over national responsibility for slavery. The leaders in both parties had to fall back on ambiguous statements. The Democrats might have patched up an agreement to support annexation provided that it was supported by the people and desired by the Texans. The Whigs might have agreed that expansion was not worth a war, pressed for strict observation of constitutional forms, expressed reservations about the wisdom of acquiring any territory, but ended by taking what opportunity offered. Whatever the precise nature of the consensus between the two parties, it could have been produced by the normal processes of argument and adjustment. The slavery issued changed all this, and the most perceptive comment is found in a private letter in September 1844 from William Henry Seward to an anti-slavery friend:

> The reckless folly of the Administration in regard to Texas, and the unprincipled adoption of it by our opponents have loosened our tongue strings. Slavery is now henceforth and forever among the elements of political action in the Republic. Let Mr. Clay treat it as he may, and be the result of this canvass what it may, the ground the public mind has traveled cannot be retraced.[69]

69. To E.A. Stansbury, Seward Papers, University of Rochester, Rochester, N. Y. Quoted in Glyndon G. Van Deusen, *William Henry Seward* (New York, 1967), 103, but reads "tongue stays" for "tongue strings."

*Chapter 5*

# TWO
# CRITICAL
# YEARS

The period that began with the presidential campaign of 1844 and closed with the presentation of the Wilmot proviso on the night of August 8, 1846, was critical in American history. In 1844 two parties fought as national institutions; by the close of 1846 sectionalism had become a political force which could not be ignored. In 1844 Texas was not a part of the United States, the future of Oregon was doubtful, and though war with Mexico had been predicted, the acquisition of California was no more than a dream in a few minds. In 1844 the Whig program of economic nationalism seemed to have a fighting chance; by August 1846 it was dead beyond hope of recovery; the principles of Jacksonian democracy were entrenched in an Independent Treasury, a low tariff had become law, and a decided check had been given to federal aid for internal improvements. The achievement of these objectives had placed a severe strain on the internal cohesion of the Democratic party, and the principle of "regularity" had been pressed almost beyond the limit of minority acquiescence.

In the fall of 1846 critical elections began to go against the Administration, and the party that had seemed so triumphant a year before lost control of the House. Whigs looked hopefully for a candidate to win the presidency in 1848; but whatever their electoral prospects the disappointments of preceding years had eroded the enthusiasm of 1840 and left them intellectually barren. Democrats might lose elections, but Whigs had nothing new or constructive to offer the people.

There were other movements of great significance for the future.

In 1846 the great tide of Irish migration flowed westward with a force and dimension never before experienced. This in turn led to a resurgence of nativism, and serious concern among conservative Americans. The population was rising even more rapidly than contemporary observers believed; during the two years under consideration it is estimated to have increased by over 1,200,000. Economic life was marked by dramatic change and growth. In the wake of depression and with rising optimism, railroad building forged ahead and plans were laid which resulted in the addition of over 3,000 miles of railroad track in operation between 1848 and 1850. The total mileage doubled between 1844 and 1850, reaching 9,021 in the latter year. This revolution in transportation affected life in countless ways and offered the prospect of economic integration at the very moment when politicians were becoming obsessed by sectional disputes. Ship-building, which had fallen to a low point in 1843, reached a peak in 1848 (stimulated by wartime demand) and again climbed upward after a temporary check in 1849. The big leap from low to high ship production occurred in 1844 and 1845. From somewhat uncertain figures it appears that the value added by manufacturing doubled between 1839 and 1849 and almost doubled again in the next decade. Cotton exports fluctuated in quantity but with an upward trend; following a short recovery in 1844 their value fell and was particularly low in 1846 (which may have had political implications) but from 1847 to 1851 it moved steadily upward.

With a few qualifications the figures show the years 1844 to 1846 standing at the threshold of a great period of growth; optimism was already evident and reflected in greater willingness—perhaps enthusiasm—for investment in long-term production. Whig policies were an inevitable casualty when the economy flourished without their adoption and prophecies of doom went unfulfilled. In 1844 their arguments were still credible and by 1846 not wholly discredited, but there was a lamentable failure to shift from remedies for distress to precepts for prosperity. This was evident in the states as well as in Congress, and can be explained by ageing leadership and lack of interest in theoretical analyses of economic data. Henry Carey was an economic thinker of some originality but he was too prolix and too inconsistent to provide the party with an updated version of "the American system." The Democrats were equally sterile in economic thought, but fortunate in that the adoption of their favorite policies coincided with economic growth which they had done little to promote.

The lack of new economic theory is but one aspect of the general failure of parties during the period. The lively intellectual controversies of 1830 to 1840 had had many repercussions, the urge to reform appeared in many different guises, and much goodwill had sought embodiment in political action. Some of this energy had borne fruit in state and municipal affairs, but there was little to show on the national stage. In its formative period the new party system had appeared to offer two broad channels through which might flow the creative forces of the age, but by 1848 it was clear to most thinking and humane men that they contained little but stagnant water. Intense activity continued among politicians, but the gulf widened between professional politics and the whole army of reform with permanent divorce rather than temporary separation as the outcome.

Annexation and war convinced some articulate and high-principled Americans that their government was acting immorally. Generations had been bred to believe that the last and best hope of the world depended upon unique Republican institutions; now the faith became dim. A few years before, anti-party rhetoric had developed from the belief that parties were corrupting the purity of politics and introducing dissension where nothing but harmony should exist; then, for a short period, the organized conflict of parties was seen as the best means by which political objectives might be advanced, but the subsequent failure of parties to play an educative or constructive role generated deeper doubts about the future of the system. Men of ideas and ideals were left without a political home. They did not, however, turn back to the rhetoric of anti-party, but sought rather to identify other forces which perverted the political system and prevented it from serving the true purpose of the American nation. For Northern Americans a ready explanation was at hand, for abolitionists had already defined the corrupting role of slavery. In response, Southerners quickly learned to identify and condemn Northern "aggressions." Both concepts were welcome to men who had been bred to expect much but had received little from political action.

It is this failure—which proved to be of devastating significance —that can be detected from the summer of 1844 to the fall of 1846. It is this rather than the particular events which make this short period the pivot upon which so much was to turn. There are indeed deeper causes, but historians are concerned with the event as much as with the analysis, and for this reason it is necessary to examine in detail some aspects of controversy during these two years.

\* \* \*

Clay lost New York by 6,000 votes out of 486,000. If he had secured the 36 votes of the state he would have been President, but with a minority of the popular vote. The national figures were 1,338,000 against 1,300,000 with 60,000 going to the Liberty party. He would certainly have faced a hostile Congress as the Whigs recovered none of their 1842 lossses, the Democrats had a healthy majority of almost two to one (143–77) in the House, and the Whigs lost control of the Senate.

Congressional elections were spread out over a long period, the earliest being held in July 1844 and the latest in November 1845. The earlier states to poll were more favorable to the Whigs than the later, and when Polk was inaugurated it looked as though the Democratic majority would be cut in the House and that the Whigs would hold their narrow lead in the Senate; but all states polling after March 1845 returned Democratic majorities. As most late elections were in the South doubt is thrown on the assumption that there was stronger pro-Texas feeling in that section. The Texas question was virtually settled by March 1845.

All three parties increased their presidential vote, but the Democrats were up by 206,000, the Liberty party by over 54,300, and the Whigs by only 22,250. The voter participation was slightly lower than 1840, but the Democrats had clearly attracted the bulk of new voters. In Massachusetts, Vermont, North Carolina, and Tennessee the Whigs won with fewer votes than they had gained in 1840, and in New Jersey, Delaware, Maryland, Ohio, and Kentucky with an increased vote but a narrower margin. Only in New England were abstentions significant and only in New York did the Liberty party hold the balance of power. In New England as a whole the Democratic total dropped, probably because many anti-Texas Democrats stayed at home, and in Connecticut abstentions gave Whigs their only gain. Outside New England the Democratic vote increased everywhere: by over 25,000 in New York, by nearly 24,000 in Pennsylvania, by over 5,500 in Virginia, and by massive numbers in all states west of the Appalachians. In the lower South they won Georgia, Mississippi, and Louisiana—which Harrison had carried easily in 1840—with considerably increased votes.

There is no evidence that Texas alone explains Democratic success, and Whigs believed it was exploited to divert attention from other issues. "At this moment," said John M. Clayton, "you see the foes of the American system, conscious of their approaching defeat, if two issues (Protection and currency) shall be submitted to the country, and everywhere endeavoring to direct public attention . . . to other subjects presented for the purpose of exciting popular feeling."[1] Democrats were aware of their danger in Pennsylvania and New York where the Tariff of 1842 was popular. Whatever low tariff gestures Democrats might make, fifty-four of them had voted in 1843 with fifty-eight Whigs against a resolution that all duties should be progressively reduced to 20 percent, and thirty-seven of them against a more vaguely worded resolution for a reduction of duties and a tariff for revenue only. Polk was known for low tariff views and many Democrats in the vital middle states might decide that the price of manufactures was nearer to their hearts than distant Texas. This threat was successfully countered when Polk wrote what James Buchanan called a "discreet and well-advised" letter to a Mr. Kane in which he said that duties should be levied "to defray the expenses of a Government economically administered" but with "such moderate discriminating duties as would . . . afford reasonable incidental protection for our home industries," and though a tariff should not be imposed for protection only it was the duty of government, "by its revenue laws and all other means within its power to give fair and just protection to all the great interests of the Union." The carefully chosen phrases delighted Buchanan who wrote, "Let him stand upon that; and I think that he may rely with confidence on the vote of Pennsylvania." The Kane letter may well have prevented the 3,500 swing which would have given the state to Clay, and may have had a similar effect in New York.[2]

Polk's commitment to the "re-occupation" of "all Oregon" had little influence on the election, but served to disassociate him from the doctrine of Calhoun's Pakenham letter (which he regarded as mistaken and irrelevant), and by making clear his commitment to territorial expansion rather than the defense of slavery. Comparatively few voters can have regarded Oregon as anything but an emotional issue, but many Northern and Western Democrats could reassure their constituents that expansion was not merely a pretext to add more slave territory to the Union.

How far the Democrats were helped by corrupt practices cannot

1. *Speech of the Hon. J. M. Clayton at the Delaware Whig Convention,* 15 June 1844.
2. Eugene I. McCormac, *James K. Polk,* 261 (New York, 1922); Charles G. Sellers, *James K. Polk: Continentalist 1843–1846* (Princeton, 1966), 119–21; James Buchanan, *Works,* ed. J.B. Moore, VI:70–71.

be known, but many Whigs nourished the conviction that vice had triumphed over virtue. Henry Clay wrote to John M. Berrien that "in Georgia, as elsewhere, I observe that you were defrauded. What will we come to, if there can be no prevention or corrective of these alarming frauds?"[3] A flagrant case in Plaquemines Parish, Louisiana, attracted nationwide attention. It had always been a Democratic county, but in 1844 the majority suddenly jumped from about 270 to 970—a significant number as Polk carried the state by 690. It was said that boatloads of Democrats had been brought from New Orleans to "vote early and vote often," and that the organizer of the operation was John M. Slidell. Whether honest or dishonest it is clear that Democrats owed much to their superior organization.

\*     \*     \*

If anyone had a mandate for the annexation of Texas it was the President-elect and the Congress which would probably assemble for the first time in December 1845. Nevertheless President Tyler, in his annual message dated December 3, 1844, claimed that "the decision of the people, and the States, on this great and interesting subject has been decisively manifested," and "a controlling majority of the people, and a large majority of the States, have declared in favor of immediate annexation. . . . It is the will of both the people and the States that Texas shall be annexed to the Union promptly and immediately."[4]

Some Whigs and a few Democrats clung to the view that the only constitutional way to annex Texas would be by treaty and preferably by one to which Mexico was a party. The constitutional procedure for ratification was expressly designed to prevent a substantial minority from being overruled, and in a treaty the Senate would expect precision on terms, debts, public lands, boundaries, and the rights of

3. Berrien Papers, Southern Historical Collection, University of North Carolina, Chapel Hill, N.C., 14 January 1845. In New York it was alleged that 2,500 were naturalized in the two weeks preceding the election (*National Intelligencer,* 13 November 1844). Other extracts printed by the *Intelligencer* blamed the naturalization of Irish laborers working on the canals. These allegations were more common than attacks on the abolitionists. In August Horace Greeley accurately forecast 15,000 Liberty votes, but counted 240,000 for Clay and 220,000 for Polk (actuals 232,000 and 238,000). Seward and Weed blamed an ill-judged fusion between Whigs and Native Americans in New York City for the loss of some Catholic support and a surge of Democratic support among recent immigrants. This would be sufficient to explain Clay's defeat, even though bogus naturalization may have increased Polk's total by a small amount. Greeley's estimate is in a private letter to Schuyler Colfax in the New York Public Library.

4. *Congressional Globe,* 28.2. 4–5.

new citizens. Thus preference for annexation by treaty was not a constitutional quibble but touched fundamental questions on the balance of power and the process of decision in a federal republic. Yet, whatever the outcome of the election, a Senate that had once rejected a treaty was unlikely to reverse itself, and the Texans would hardly commit themselves to so uncertain a prospect. It was therefore decided to circumvent the two-thirds requirement and to convert the treaty into a bill or to use the normal procedure for the admission of a new state by joint resolution of the two houses of Congress. Calhoun as a theorist had argued against decision by a numerical majority, but as Secretary of State he was prepared to accept the barest of majorities provided annexation was achieved.

Tyler wished to avoid argument by making the conditions imprecise; there would be no decision on boundaries and "future legislation can best decide as to the number of States which should be formed out of the territory, when the time has arrived for deciding that question." He proposed that the United States should assume the debt of Texas, to a maximum figure of $10 million and pledge the sales of Texan public lands for its redemption. Administration strategists must have decided to move first to the House, where a majority was probable, and on January 3 C. J. Ingersoll, from the Committee on Foreign Affairs, introduced a resolution which was almost identical with the rejected treaty and proposed annexation as a territory, assumption of the Texan debt, and establishment of a commission to investigate the claims of creditors and other liabilities. Slavery was guaranteed indirectly by the provision that "the citizens of Texas shall be . . . protected in the free enjoyment of their liberty and property," and that "until future provision shall be made, the laws of Texas, as now existing, shall remain in force." It would require an act of Congress to abolish slavery in the annexed territory (which was as unlikely as a positive act to establish it) and the institution would expand in default of action by Congress.[5]

In introducing the resolution Ingersoll tried to have it both ways. "Southern interests, Southern frontiers, Southern institutions— . . . slavery and all—are to be primarily regarded in settling the restoration of Texas," but if two Southern secretaries had displayed "partialities which many of us deem not quite national" this should not prevent a great national measure from being decided on national considerations." In the Senate a different approach was advocated by

5. *Ibid.*, pp. 26, 85–86.

Thomas Hart Benton, who now regarded annexation as inevitable, but wished to provide assurance for those who feared the advance of slavery northward across the great plains and the admission of four or five slave states to the Union.[6] Benton proposed giving authority to the President to negotiate with Mexico and Texas, though Congress might dispense with the assent of Mexico if this could not be obtained. The annexed territory would have its frontier well to the north and east of the Rio Grande but extend northward to the center of modern Nebraska. Within this area the people of Texas could apply for admission as a state, with boundaries fixed by themselves, but not exceeding in size the largest existing state. Slavery would be forever prohibited in the northern part of the territory west of $100°$. Benton, who believed that speculation in bonds and land was a mainspring of the annexation movement, made no mention of the Texan debt. This plan had great merits. It ensured that a treaty would be brought back to the Senate, but that a majority in both Houses could dispense with Mexican consent; it proposed a definite limit to slavery, while permitting the establishment of slavery in the Southwest. While Benton was always an individualist, his plan, or a modified version of it, was likely to attract enough support to kill the administration measure in the Senate.

Southern Whigs were now in some difficulty. They felt obliged to stand by Clay's condemnation of immediate and unilateral action, but believed that annexation could not now be defeated. Northern Whigs and Van Buren Democrats might oppose annexation in the first instance, but would then fight for the prohibition of slavery over as wide an area as possible. Southern Whigs hoped to maintain party unity, but could not vote for congressional prohibition of slavery. They were therefore anxious to ward off this possibility, and two Tennessee Whigs, Senator Ephraim Foster and Representative Milton Brown, after consultation with Alexander H. Stephens of Georgia, brought forward a compromise proposal generally known as the Milton Brown plan. The whole of Texas would be admitted as a state, the United States would accept responsibility for settling the frontiers, the Texan debt would not be assumed, and the new state would retain possession of its public lands. New states (the number was subsequently fixed at four) could be admitted with the consent of Texas "and such States as may be formed of that portion of said territory lying south of $36° 30'$ north latitude, shall be admitted into the

6. *Ibid.*, p. 19.

Union with or without slavery, as the people of each State asking permission may desire." A later amendment prohibited slavery in states formed north of 36° 30'.[7]

The compromise proposal included or implied most of the issues which provided a focus for controversy for the next fifteen years. It incorporated the principle of "popular sovereignty" and guaranteed admission of states south of 36° 30', slave or free as their people should decide. It accepted the westward extension of the Missouri Compromise line, and admitted the right of Congress to prohibit slavery north of it. Yet it was clouded with extraordinary looseness of thought. There was no method known to the Constitution by which a state could be compelled to agree to the formation of new states within its boundaries; Congress could prohibit slavery neither in the northern section so long as it remained part of Texas nor in a new state after admission. These evasions meant that the compromise heavily favored slavery. Under Texan law it would extend over the whole area and, while the northwestern section might be settled by non-slaveholders they could not form a separate state without the consent of a slaveholding state legislature. In effect Texas would become the guardian of sectional balance with the right to decide if and when new slave or free states should be admitted to the Union.

The Milton Brown plan disarmed anti-slavery men, whose principal objective was to establish the right of Congress to prevent the extension of slavery, and commended itself to Southern Whigs because it promised to remove this dangerous question from Congress without sacrificing party unity. Others, who took a moderate line on slavery or believed that it could not be abolished but ought not to expand, found consolation in the argument that the issue would ultimately be decided by the great westward tides of migration. Social forces rather than political argument would settle the fate of slavery in the nation.

The Milton Brown plan passed the House by a small but safe majority (120–98), but the Senate Committee on Foreign Relations, with a Whig majority and Archer of Virginia as chairman, reported against it on the ground that annexation by joint resolution was unconstitutional. Benton now reentered the field, dropped his requirement for prior negotiation with Mexico, gave the President a free hand to negotiate annexation, proposed that a state "with suitable extent and boundaries" should be formed from Texas as soon as the

7. *Ibid.*, pp. 129–30, 193.

negotiations were complete, while safeguarding the right of Congress
to review the terms. The major point to be gained was that the President would negotiate to form a state *from* Texas. "Gentlemen suppose
that Texas will voluntarily reduce herself; it is a supposition contrary
to all human experience." He dropped the proposal to prohibit slavery
in the northern part of Texas, but expected that the President would
bear this point in mind. When Benton proposed to hand over these
extensive powers to the President he believed that they would be exercised by James K. Polk, not John Tyler. [8]

Some Southern Whigs liked the Milton Brown plan because they
believed that it would take slavery out of politics. For different reasons
Calhoun instructed his friends to oppose Benton because he believed
that delay might be dangerous and that Texas might be lost without
an immediate and unequivocal offer. The position was therefore that
most Whig senators opposed both the Milton Brown plan and the
Benton bill on constitutional grounds; most Democrats and three or
four Southern Whigs would vote for the Milton Brown plan; but
Benton and three or four Northern Democrats would not. It looked
like defeat for annexation or a tied vote, with Willie P. Mangum in the
chair as president *pro tempore* and known to be opposed. The month of
February was drawing to a close and Congress would adjourn on
March 3. The President-elect had arrived in Washington and was
known to be extremely anxious for the passage of some annexation
measure before his inauguration. This prompted Robert J. Walker, an
ardent supporter of annexation who believed that slavery would be
extinguished by economic forces, to propose that Congress should
accept both the Milton Brown and the Benton measures and leave the
president to choose between them. He assumed that Tyler would leave
the choice to Polk. [9]

Even now success was uncertain. Ephraim Foster believed that
the plan he had sponsored with Milton Brown would take slavery out
of politics while the Benton plan would invite continued dispute, but
despite his impassioned plea the twin-headed bill passed by 27 to 25
with the support of all the Democrats and two Southern Whigs. In the
House Milton Brown joined other Whigs in opposition, but a number
of Northern Democrats joined their Southern brethren to pass the bill

8. *Ibid.*, pp. 244–45.
9. *Ibid.*, p. 359. In a letter to the *New York Tribune*, 31 July 1845, Benjamin Tappan, Democratic senator from Ohio, explained that he had voted against the treaty but for the joint resolution as amended. He said that Senator Haywood of North Carolina had obtained from Polk an
assurance that he would use the Benton procedure and that Senator McDuffie had said that
Calhoun "would not have the audacity to act before March 4."

by 132 to 76. It is a curious reflection that, after all the ingenious compromises, backstairs negotiations, and changed votes the final result closely followed party lines. In the Senate two Whig votes held the balance, but all other Whigs opposed and all Democrats were in support. In the House, with few exceptions, Whigs from both sections opposed and Democrats (with some abstentions) were in support. The broad issue, at the end of the day, was whether annexation by simple majorities in both houses was constitutional or whether one-third plus one of the Senate could block the addition of new land to the United States. Southern Whigs voted for what they believed was the constitutional mode, even though it recognized the right of Northern Senators to block Southern expansion; Southern Democrats voted as they did in the belief that immediate annexation was more important than strict construction. Reflection may suggest that Whigs were correct in their constitutional view and Democrats ill advised to abandon their normal doctrine.

In the event several calculations went astray. President Tyler did not leave the choice to his successor, acted upon the Milton Brown plan, and dispatched a messenger, in the last hours of his presidency, offering statehood to all Texas. The elaborate provisions for the admission of new states never came into operation, because none were formed from Texas, but the unsettled boundaries remained to plague debate in 1850, and so, behind the scenes, did disappointed holders of Texan bonds and land scrip.[10] Finally President Polk did not choose to recall his predecessor's message to Texas, though some believed that his prior conversations with Benton and others had placed him under a moral obligation to do so. It seems probable that, sooner or later, greater or smaller, Texas would have joined the United States, but the manner of annexation sowed seeds of disquiet and disillusion in a fertile soil. A new factor in politics was a growing conviction among many Northern men that a malign force which they named "the slave power" threatened the moral character of the nation.

\*     \*     \*

Some prophetic utterances were made during the closing stages of the annexation debate. Senator Archer believed that a government of bal-

10. The interests of the bondholders has been investigated by Elgin Williams in *The Animating Pursuits of Speculation* (New York, 1949). Nicholas Biddle was deeply involved and supplied information for Henry S. Foote's *Texas and the Texans,* and in 1843 Biddle sent a copy of this book to Tyler with a letter supporting annexation; T. W. Gilmer was an agent for Texan bonds; Duff Green was interested in Texas lands, canals and railroads.

ances and checks, destined to extend over large areas of the continent and to represent a great variety of interests, could not accept the proposition that measures must be undertaken to sustain particular interests. This was "in direct opposition to the very principle of confederation upon which this government was founded, and entirely at variance with the intention and object of its framers." Similar arguments could justify the annexation of Cuba, Haiti, and other West Indian islands, and in response the Northern people would bid for New Brunswick, Newfoundland, and Canada. "After acquiring these immense territories north and south, then comes the question of the rights of man!" What was at stake was not merely the overthrow of checks and balances, but "a question to be settled on the battlefield."[11]

Senator Ephraim Foster was concerned for the fate of slavery if it remained in the forefront of political controversy. He wanted "no further Missouri compromises" or further agitation of the slavery question when it could be settled at a stroke. The vital point in his plan was the commitment to admit new states with or without slavery; otherwise the addition of every territory or admission of every new state would become an occasion for controversy. He had "no confidence in the North on this subject; it would crush the South if it could," and an unequivocal undertaking had been destroyed by the addition of an alternative "placed there to qualify a great act—placed there by opponents of the institutions under which we live."[12]

George W. Julian, a young protegé of Joshua Giddings and himself destined for a distinguished career, left a retrospective comment on annexation which deserves quotation as an example of the way in which it affected so many idealistic young men of the North.

The barbarous war, the bloodshed, the devastation, the corruption, the civil war which resulted from the triumph of the slave power, were at no subsequent period more vividly before his mind than they were that evening while alone in his rooms, contemplating the results which would naturally follow the action of Congress on that sad day.[13]

---

11. So reported in *Congressional Globe*, 28.2. 359 (also in Benton, *Abridgment of Congressional Debates*): an amplified version of the speech (*Ibid.*, Appendix, 326–30) expresses the same sentiment but in less dramatic form (it is also incorrectly dated at 28 February). The last sentence quoted is in the Appendix version but not in Benton.

12. *Ibid.*, pp. 359–60.

13. George W. Julian, *Life of Joshua R. Giddings* (Chicago, 1892), 183.

Hyperbole informed by hindsight may not provide unimpeachable historical evidence, but for men bred in the belief that republicanism guaranteed virtuous government the shock was profound. For Senator Archer, a conservative Virginian, "the result would be the disappearance of our political Eden as complete as that of which tradition only remains, that had its position on the Euphrates. So of ours that had its place on the Potomac."[14]

The final act was delayed until January 1846 when the formal application from Texas for admission came before Congress. Most critics had been prepared to accept the inevitable, but in Massachusetts an Anti-Texas Committee had been active. It included such men of the future as Charles Francis Adams, Henry Wilson, Charles Sumner, and John G. Palfrey. William Lloyd Garrison was consulted, and Elizur Wright, the prominent abolitionist, edited their newspaper. Their immediate aim was to ensure that the admission of Texas did not pass without protest, but the result was to provide the experience of organization and an armory of ideas for men who believed that "the slave power" was massing its forces for further aggression.

In Congress Julius Rockwell of Massachusetts expressed the view of the Anti-Texas committee. He went over familiar ground in attacking the acquisition of foreign territory by congressional action, but then enlarged his argument to speculate on the future. He believed that the country stood at the threshold of events which would "connect the territories of this entire continent into one consolidated body, and constitute them the United States of North America," but at the very outset came the question of extending and protecting slavery. The hollowness of compromise was shown when Congress agreed to prohibit slavery in states formed from Texas north of 36° 30' while the constitution of the new state prohibited emancipation without the consent of owners. Could slavery be eradicated at some future time when it had for years been protected by state law? This, said Rockwell, was a momentous question for America and "darkened that national character which she ought to hold up to all nations and ages of the world."[15] The New York *Tribune* had made the same point in December: annexation was "a National question which must fix the character of the Nation in the eyes of the civilized world, and render its pretense of zeal for Universal Freedom the scoff of despots and an offense in the sight of God."[16]

14. *Congressional Globe*, 28.2. Appendix, 330.
15. *Ibid.*, 29.1. 62–64.
16. *New York Tribune*, 2 December 1845. In his *Rise and Fall of the Slave Power* (Boston, 1876), II, 1, Henry Wilson wrote, "In the acquisition of Texas the Slave Power had compelled the

*     *     *

For the purpose of this study the policies of James K. Polk will be discussed only so far as they influenced basic political attitudes. The Oregon settlement, the causes of the war with Mexico, and the details of domestic measures will be dealt with cursorily, but the character of the President himself requires more extended treatment. From one point of view he was the right man at the right time and deserved success but his Presidency did much to accelerate the deterioration of political life which had begun with Tyler's administration. Thanks to his diary we know far more about the austere, self-righteous, secretive and strong-willed President than ever his contemporaries did. We know that he set definite objectives, exercised a tight mastery over his Cabinet, and kept Democratic leaders in Congress up to the mark. He achieved a sensible settlement of the Oregon question and initiated the war which added California, New Mexico, and Arizona to the nation. Under his guidance Congress restored the Independent Treasury and—against considerable opposition in his own party— adopted the low tariff of 1846. Relentless pressure from behind the scenes by the President was largely responsible for these achievements. In true Jacksonian spirit he struck down an attempt to introduce federal aid for internal improvements by the back door, and his veto message lectured Congress severely on the impropriety of all such measures. Finally his last message to Congress warned of the dangers which would follow in the wake of war, if victory led to economic nationalism and political consolidation.

The record is that of a man whose vision was sometimes limited but always clear, but he remained little known to contemporaries. Even tributes from his Tennessee associates were formal rather than revealing. No Washington gossips recorded familiar stories, and ceaseless attention to duty allowed little time for travel or public appearances. He prided himself on acquiring enough knowledge of government to conduct the affairs of any department if called upon to do so, but the effort made him a desk-bound President, with little energy at the end of the day to enjoy social duties, which he performed manfully though with distaste. Gideon Welles, who headed a Bureau in the Navy Department and was already influential in Connecticut poli-

---

nation to adopt and proclaim the principle that slavery had become a national interest, to be cherished by national legislation, cared for by national diplomacy, and defended by national arms."

tics, kept a diary during his years in office but recorded no first-hand impression of the President.[17] The omission is testimony to the remoteness of the President and to his lack of political tact in failing to show personal courtesy to a devoted supporter in a marginal state. If Clay had been in the White House, administration might have been less efficient, but everyone would have been aware of the President's personal charm.

Thus the chosen instrument of romantic nationalism, who successfully accomplished all that he planned, communicated neither enthusiasm nor idealism to the nation. Of no leader could it be more truly said that he lacked charisma. He was blamed for having brought on the war, but received no credit for victories in the field. Democrats who were prepared to praise another Jackson found themselves defending the policy of a man who gave them no rhetorical slogans, made little personal impression, and offended important sections of the party.

George M. Dallas, the urbane Pennsylvanian who became Vice President, had frequent opportunities for observing James K. Polk at close quarters, and recorded acid comments in letters to his wife and in his diary.[18] In June 1846 he was summoned to the White House for "a most important communication" and commented that "the President . . . has the faculty of making mountains out of mole-hills," and the interview itself "altho' somewhat interesting was, compared with its pompous and mysterious prologue, another illustration of the mountain and the mouse." He added, "I am heartily sick of factitious importance." Toward the end of his term Dallas was reading Macaulay's *History of England,* observed that two passages on the character of Charles I were directly applicable to President Polk, and proceeded to transcribe them into his diary. The key sentences were:

Faithlessness was the chief cause of his disasters. . . . In every promise which he made, there was an implied reservation that such promise might be broken in case of necessity, and

17. The Welles Diary for these years is in the Huntington Library, San Marino, California. In old age George Bancroft dictated some observations on Polk's character, and these are now in the New York Public Library. His verdict was favorable but his comments were confined to superficial remarks on the President's political views, physical appearance, and style of speaking. The result is disappointing, coming as it does from a man of high intelligence who served in the cabinet and was, for a period of two years, in almost daily contact with the President.

18. George M. Dallas, "Diary and Letters," ed. Roy F. Nichols. *Pennsylvania Magazine* LXXIII, no. 3 (July 1949): 349ff. and no. 4 (October 1949): 475ff. The originals are in the Historical Society of Pennsylvania, Philadelphia, Pa.

that of the necessity he was the sole judge. . . . Cunning is the natural defence of the weak. . . . To such an extent, indeed had insincerity now tainted [his] whole nature, that his most devoted friends could not refrain from complaining to each other, with bitter grief and shame, of his crooked politics. His defeats, they said, gave them less pain than his intrigues.

Political strategy indicated the need to conciliate the followers of Van Buren. For good or ill they held the key positions in Northern Democracy, and Polk possibly owed the presidency to Silas Wright who won the governorship of New York by a wide margin and may have persuaded many reluctant Democrats to support the national ticket. Polk made some half-hearted attempts at conciliation, but appointed William M. Marcy, an opponent of Van Buren, to the War Department; and though George Bancroft got the Navy, the Treasury went to Robert J. Walker whose advocacy of annexation had helped to undermine Van Buren's position in the party. C. C. Cambreleng, one of Van Buren's friends, wrote that while Polk had "professed every desire to please Mr. Van Buren and Gov. Wright, and did in the beginning most anxiously consult them," he had not appointed anyone whom they recommended. "On the contrary he has selected conservatives only for every important appointment." He concluded that "the little man thinks he can operate for *himself,* in our State, most successfully through the conservative wing of our party."[19] Calhounites, who had first feared that Polk would concede too much to Van Buren, were delighted. As early as June 1845 Calhoun could write that there were "no hostile feelings" towards him on the part of the President.[20]

A year after his inauguration Polk led a party that was outwardly united but weakened by feuds beneath the surface. When he abandoned the extreme claims to 54° 40′ in Oregon he was reproached by Western expansionists for betraying a bargain which had won united party support for his nomination, and exposed him to the accusation that he intended to benefit the South while compromising Northern aims. However, defeat of the 54° 40′ owed more to the weakness of their case than to the President. They had been outmaneuvered in

19. Cambreleng to J. R. Poinsett, 25 November 1845, Poinsett Papers, Historical Society of Pennsylvania, Philadelphia, Pa.

20. *Correspondence of Calhoun.* Part I, 663. To Thomas G. Clemson, 7 June 1845. Reassuring news from Washington had come in a letter from John S. Barbour, who had had informal talks with the President and members of the Cabinet (*Ibid.*, Part II, 1036. 2 May 1845).

Congress and reduced to a small and angry minority against a clear majority wanting no war with Great Britain. Though Oregon left some Democrats resentful, it would not in itself have caused a rift in the party or a desire to embarrass the Administration and there is no clear link between the disappointment of the expansionists and later support for the Wilmot proviso. Indeed the Oregon settlement was the most successful and widely welcomed achievement of Polk's administration.

Before the Oregon settlement was complete Americans learned suddenly on May 11, 1846, that they were at war with Mexico. The causes of the conflict lay deep in the history of relations between the two countries. The United States had legitimate grievances against Mexico over the non-payment of claims due to American citizens and vexatious border incidents. Mexico had good reason to complain of the way in which the annexation of Texas had been handled, but obstinate refusal to give *de jure* recognition to an accomplished fact was unwise, and more skillful diplomacy might have secured reasonable compensation for the "loss" of Texas. Refusal to negotiate provided justification for Polk's decision to order an army under Zachary Taylor to move south from the Nueces to take up positions on the Rio Grande; but his true motive was to further the achievement of his major objective—the acquisition of California. The Nueces might mark the southern limit of effective Texan government, but the Rio Grande was the key to western expansion.[21]

Polk would have preferred to purchase rather than fight, but early in May 1846 he knew that Mexico would neither sell California nor negotiate on boundaries, and decided to use the unpaid debts and refusal to accept an American mission as justification for war. He won majority assent from a reluctant Cabinet, but before acting learned that a small Mexican force had crossed the Rio Grande, clashed with a detachment of Taylor's troops, and inflicted American casualties. In a less tense situation this might have been accepted as a border incident, caused by the indiscretion of local commanders and open for settlement by apology and compensation, but for the President it confirmed his decision to fight with the added advantage that responsibility for firing the first shot could be firmly nailed on the Mexicans. In fairness to the President it should be added that the news related to

21. Polk's early determination to acquire California, recorded in his own diary, is confirmed by George Bancroft's recollections (New York Public Library). Bancroft was present when Polk declared this intention.

events which had taken place two weeks before, and that, for all anyone knew, Taylor might be now engaged in full-scale hostilities defending American positions north of the Rio Grande. Nevertheless,
after all allowances and explanations have been made, it is hard to
avoid the conclusion that President Polk took the United States into a
war of aggression.

When news of the clash on the Rio Grande reached the press, the
*Tribune* cried out against the iniquity of "our Army of Occupation—
insanely and wickedly pushed across the well-known boundary of
Texas into the heart of a province of Mexico of unshaken loyalty." The
President's War Message was anticipated in an editorial which sounds
more like twentieth-century radical protest than the measured conventions of nineteenth-century political debate:

> People of the United States! Your Rulers are precipitating
> you into a fathomless abyss of crime and calamity! Why sleep
> you thoughtless on its verge, as though this was not your
> business, or Murder would be hid from the sight of God by a
> few flimsy rags called banners? Awake and arrest the work of
> butchery ere it shall be too late to preserve your souls from the
> guilt of wholesale slaughter! Hold meetings! Speak out!
> Act![22]

From the Democratic press came a very different reaction, and
the President's War Message, sent to Congress on May 11, was welcomed as a just and unavoidable response to Mexican intransigence.
For Democrats the superior qualities of American institutions and
character conferred the moral right to possess and occupy the continent, but in Whig eyes war was the sequel to sustained Democratic
attempts "to inflame the excitable imaginations of an impulsive
people, by continually presenting the thrilling image of vast and easy
acquisitions; familiarizing them with visions of boundless empire—
of extraordinary and sudden wealth, until now they have come to look
upon these profitable dreams as actualities in the future, and to demand their realization."[23]

Confronted with the War Message the Whigs in Congress found
themselves in a dilemma. If Taylor's army was really in danger, and if
the Mexicans were indeed advancing into Texas, no one could refuse to

22. *New York Tribune,* 11 and 12 May 1846.
23. *American Whig Review* II (September 1845): 226.

vote money for defense; but it was one thing to defend a frontier (however dubious) and another to concur in the President's assertion that "hostilities have commenced, and that the two nations are now at war," and that "war exists, and, notwithstanding all our efforts to avoid it, exists by the act of Mexico herself." Some Democrats were at first disposed to accept the suggestion that the two issues should be separated. Senator Benton proposed, and Senator Allen agreed, that the question of appropriations should be referred to the Committee on Military Affairs and the question of peace or war to the Committee on Foreign Relations. One could expect a quick report from the Military Committee recommending an appropriation, and a lengthier consideration of the case for war from the other committee. Senator Cass, most bellicose of Western Democrats, argued that a defensive posture would leave the initiative in the hands of Mexico. "There is but one course for us to take. Push an expedition into Mexico, till we compel her . . . to make such a peace as we have a right to demand."[24]

The most acute diagnosis of the constitutional issue was presented by John C. Calhoun, and his case against commitment to war by executive action was of permanent significance.

> The President has announced that there is war; but according to my interpretation there is no war according to the sense of our constitution. I distinguish between hostilities and war, and, God forbid that, acting under the constitution, we should ever confound one with the other. There may be invasion without war, and the President is authorized to repel invasion without war. But it is *our* sacred duty to make war, and it is for *us* to determine whether war exists or not. If we have declared war, a state of war exists, and not till then.

On the following day (May 12), with an appropriation bill for $10 million before the Senate, Calhoun renewed his plea for a separation of the two issues; he would vote at any time for the military appropriation but not for the preamble to the bill which endorsed the President's assertion that war already existed. "It was just as impossible for him to vote for the preamble as it was for him to plunge a dagger into his own heart, and more so. . . . War must be made by the sovereign authorities, which in this case, were the Mexican Congress on one side, and the American Congress on the other." There was no evidence

24. *Congressional Globe*, 29. 1. 30.

that the Mexican Congress had declared war, and the American Congress lacked sufficient information upon which to act.[25] Despite this powerful argument Benton, who had first suggested separating the two issues and privately expressed to the President the same view as Calhoun, was not prepared to stand out against a majority of his Democratic colleagues.[26] The crucial vote came on a motion to strike out the preamble, which was lost 20–25. Most of the Whig Senators then decided to support the bill, though five with protests against the preamble. Daniel Webster was a conspicuous absentee, Calhoun even more conspicuously refused to vote.

The declaration of war against Mexico was the most severe shock so far delivered to the American political system. There had been sharp differences in 1812; but these had been concerned with expediency and calculation rather than moral principles. The new war was begun "without authority of law, and without being in the right," said a member of the House. "It came upon the country like a clap of thunder in a clear sky."[27] For the first time the government of the United States was engaged upon an enterprise which many believed to be both inexpedient and immoral, and they would have been even more disturbed if they could have penetrated the secrets of the Cabinet. On May 13, James Buchanan, as Secretary of State, had prepared a draft dispatch for American ministers in London, Paris, and other foreign courts which stated that the American object "was not to dismember Mexico or to make conquests . . . that in going to war we did not do so with a view to acquiring either California or New Mexico or any other portion of Mexican territory." This was flatly rejected by the President who said "it was clear that in making peace we would be sufficient to indemnify our claimants on Mexico and to defray the expense of the war which that power by her long continued wrongs and injuries had forced us to wage."[28] However veiled the motive, it was from the outset a war to acquire California and as much else as a beaten and bankrupt Mexico could be forced to yield as "indemnity."

Nevertheless there is little doubt that the President would have been sustained by a majority of the people. Dilating upon the theme of manifest destiny, the *Democratic Review* proclaimed that "the task of the American people for the present century, is clearly to take and

25. *Ibid.*, p. 784.
26. James K. Polk, *Diary*, ed. Milo M. Quaife, 4 vols. (1910) I: 390; *Polk: Diary of a President*, ed. Allan Nevins (New York, 1929), 86.
27. Columbus Delano of Ohio. *Congressional Globe*, 29.1. 815 (13 May).
28. Polk, *Diary*, ed. Nevins, 86; ed. Quaife, I: 390.

occupy the northern continent of America. Its plains and valleys, its rivers and mountains, with their great agricultural wealth are spread out before them." The opposition was attributed to the supposed Whig aim of securing the ascendancy of wealth over people.[29] Yet once more the expansionist ideal, manifest in aggressive war, was incompatible with an older tradition of American nationalism. In 1846 as in 1844 Albert Gallatin—old, wealthy, yet still an orthodox Jeffersonian—voiced his opposition:

> The Mission of the United States . . . is to improve the state of the world, to be the "Model Republic," to show that men are capable of governing themselves, and that this simple and natural form of government is that also which confers most happiness on all, is productive of the greatest development of the intellectual faculties, above all, that which is attended with the highest standard of private and political virtue and morality. . . . In their external relations the United States, before this unfortunate war, had, whilst sustaining their just rights, ever acted in strict conformity with the dictates of justice, and displayed the utmost moderation.[30]

Far more than the annexation of Texas, the war with Mexico seemed to be a betrayal of this ideal, for while the joint resolution had been exhaustively debated before a decision had been taken, and no Mexican had suffered deprivation or death as a consequence, now a neighboring republic was to be invaded and her people assaulted. It was the moral aspect of the war rather than its connection with slavery that first assailed the American conscience and shook the assumption that though Americans might differ on material questions, they stood together on the firm ground of "republican virtue."

The most eloquent and renowned critic of the war as a moral failure was Tom Corwin of Ohio. His speech denouncing the war was widely circulated in pamphlet form, and in a public letter of April 1847 he justified voting against war appropriations on the grounds that they were being asked to extend a war "for conquest alone." Corwin also invoked the idea of America as "the model republic" not

29. *Democratic Review* XIX (August 1846): 85.
30. Albert Gallatin, *Writings*, ed. Henry Adams (Philadelphia, 1879), III: 551–52; also published as a pamphlet (New York, 1847).

now engaged in helping a struggling nation to adopt similar government but grasping her territory and driving her leaders "to beg the aid
of Kings."[31]

Could one absolve the people from blame and attribute all to
demagogues? Strong anti-slavery men, equally conscious of unpopularity and moral rectitude, were certain to raise the question. In February 1848 Lewis Tappan was appalled by the "blood-guiltiness" of
the nation. Politicians waged war to sustain their party, he said, but
succeeded because "the heart of the people is in favor of war, conquest
and oppression." The Americans had become "a wicked people."[32]
Most public men declined to judge "the people" and preferred the
course of a Massachusetts Whig Convention in casting the blame exclusively on the "illegal and unjustifiable act of the President of the
United States," but an essayist in the cautious *Whig Review* wondered
whether the fault did not lie deeper in the character of the political
system. "Radical tendencies assume no more fearful form than that of
the overshadowing, paralyzing despotism of 'Public Opinion' which
threatens to banish all free and manly thought." In characteristic
Whig style the writer professed faith in the people "if questions could
be got fairly before the minds of a community generally so intelligent
and virtuous as ours." Unfortunately people were "fallible and gulli-
ble," and there were "sharp-witted men enough who know how to
make their account of it."[33]

Thus the Mexican War raised deep questions about the past traditions and future policy of the United States. If the war was popular
it was not what the people ought to want; if unjust, the character of
the nation had been tarnished. Republican institutions had produced
a collision between national aims and the moral instincts of mankind,
and once raised these issues could not be evaded.

\*     \*     \*

Most Democrats rallied behind the President in support of the war,
but the domestic policies of his administration caused dissension. Van
Buren's supporters applauded the restoration of the Independent

31. *National Intelligencer*, 14 January 1848.
32. Tappan to Rev. J. S. Green, 13 February 1848. Tappan Papers, Library of Congress,
Washington, D. C.
33. *Whig Review* IV (July 1846). The article is called "Civilization: American and European."

Treasury, but the repeal of the 1842 Tariff was another matter. Polk had won Pennsylvania by implying that a revenue tariff could be combined with incidental protection for American manufactures, and elsewhere many Northeastern Democrats supported modest protection and claimed, with some reason, that it was not large manufacturers but men who practiced skilled crafts who would benefit. Immediately after the election Buchanan, who suspected that the President-elect would be under pressure to abandon protection, wrote that "the violence of the Southern papers, & some of the Southern statesmen" indicated that they clung "with great tenacity to the horizontal ad valorem duty of the Compromise Act." This would ruin "the Democracy of the Middle and Northern States in a single year," and "prostrate mechanics who work up foreign materials." A 20 percent ad valorem duty on cloth, readymade clothing, hats and shoes meant that "we should have no use for tailors in our large towns and cities; so of shoemakers, hatters, etc., etc."[34] Despite the warning, Polk gave full support to Robert J. Walker when he proposed to cut duties until none should be above the minimum level necessary for revenue, replace specific by ad valorem duties, and abandon the principle of incidental protection.

The President interested himself keenly in the progress of a bill on Walker's lines, had several interviews with James J. McKay, chairman of the House Ways and Means Committee, and turned a deaf ear to Buchanan's pleas that Pennsylvania could not be held in future elections without some concession. In the House there was a safe majority for the bill, despite the opposition or abstention of several Northern Democrats, but in the Senate two influential Democratic Senators, Cameron of Pennsylvania and Niles of Connecticut, were actively opposed and the outcome was doubtful. Much depended on Spencer Jarnigan, a Tennessee Whig who had been instructed by his state legislature to support the bill but followed Whig practice in disregarding instructions. Having cast the deciding vote to refer the bill to the Committee on Finance with instructions which would have had the effect of raising some duties while lowering others, he then voted to discharge the committee from this task, and finally abstained with the deliberate intention of forcing the Vice-President, George M. Dallas, a Pennsylvanian and protectionist, to use his casting vote. Dallas gave his vote for the bill on the ground that, whatever his personal views, he was bound, as Vice-President, to give effect to the

34. James Buchanan Papers, Historical Society of Pennsylvania, Philadelphia, Pa.

views of a majority in the country.[35] Jarnigan then voted against a motion to postpone, and "aye" on the final vote, with an explanation that it would be best for the country to try low tariffs and experience their depressing effects. In this unsatisfactory manner the tariff of 1846 became law. It was noted that the principal agents were a President from Tennessee, a Secretary of the Treasury from Mississippi, a chairman of Ways and Means from North Carolina, and a chairman of the Senate Finance Committee (Dixon Lewis) from Alabama. Senator Niles demanded rhetorically whether "Southern gentlemen . . . will press a measure upon the North so unjust and so unequal," and Gideon Welles, a close friend of Niles, recorded his private indignation at the way in which the bill had been forced through Congress against the express wishes of an important segment of the Northern party.[36] One Southern Senator, William Haywood of North Carolina, resigned rather than vote for the bill, and Northern Democrats joined Whigs to defend him against attacks by the Administration press.

While the Whigs had been ruined in 1841 by lack of legislative achievement and deadlock between President and Congress, the Democrats were damaged by the success of executive leadership. In a major speech against the tariff bill Senator Cameron complained that "now the representatives of the people are saved the trouble of reflecting upon the difficult subject of revenue." The Secretary of the Treasury made a bill, and the chairman of Ways and Means was instructed to see it through; "cabinet ministers bring all their influence to bear, and, by the aid of the previous question, force the bill through." In the Senate "some mysterious influence" prevents the bill from "taking the ordinary course of all measures of this kind."[37] Everyone seems to have believed that the President could have lifted the pressure and relieved Northern Democrats from considerable embarrassment, but characteristically Polk believed that opposition was the work of monied interests, armed with bribes and influence, and was determined to yield nothing.

The summer of 1846 saw another shock to the normal process of legislative maneuver by which congressmen expected to serve their

35. Dallas was aware that however he cast his vote he would be "exalted to the skies by one side, and sent heartily to the opposite place by the other." (*Pennsylvania Magazine* LXXIII, no. 3: 385–86). His brief explanatory speech was a minor but dignified exposition of constitutional doctrine.

36. *Congressional Globe*, 29.1. Appendix, 1118; Welles Diary, Huntington Library, San Marino, Calif.

37. *Congressional Globe*, 29.1. 1184.

constituents. Though Democrats were formally opposed to a general system of subsidy for internal improvements, many Westerners believed that the Great Lakes and the navigable rivers of the Mississippi valley should be treated (in a phrase popularized by Calhoun) as an "inland sea" and benefit from the constitutional power of Congress to regulate foreign commerce by ensuring safe navigation. The Rivers and Harbors Bill of 1846 proposed federal aid for a large number of improvements in western waters, but was vetoed by Polk with a lengthy message which treated it merely as a scheme to resurrect the Whig policy of subsidized internal improvements. This angered Western Democrats and their most vigorous spokesman was Stephen A. Douglas, the rising star from Illinois. While admitting the validity of Polk's argument against the constitutionality of federal aid for internal improvements, Douglas distinguished it from the principles embodied in the bill. It was necessary, he said, "to meet the broad question boldly, whether Congress has the right, under the Constitution, to protect commerce on our navigable waters." If so, the principle must be applied to all alike. "The West," he said, "would never submit to an odious and unjust discrimination, which lavishes millions on the seaboard and excludes the lakes and rivers from all participation."[38] The bill was passed again, but failed to obtain the necessary two-thirds. Though the vote of 96-91 was not sectional it was noted that nearly all Southern Democrats had sustained the veto, and Western resentment was a more important factor in weakening party cohesion than the decision to abandon "54° 40' or Fight."

The President could not be blamed for another aspect of sectional feeling when Southern fears were aroused by Northern attitudes on the well-worn subject of abolitionist petitions. In 1844 the 21st or "gag" rule, which forbade debate on petitions touching slavery, was dropped, and at the beginning of the 1845–46 session an attempt to restore it failed. No more than eleven votes from the free states were cast for the rule, and only seven from the slave states against it. All the affirmative Northern votes were cast by Democrats and included two men destined for future fame, Stephen A. Douglas and (surprisingly) David Wilmot; all the negative Southern votes came from Whigs. Across the nation Democrats voted 67–57 for the "gag" and Whigs 63–17 against. Negative Southern votes came from Delware, Kentucky, Tennessee, and Louisiana—all states with strong commercial

---

38. *Ibid.*, 28.1. 1184. In the light of future events it is interesting that David Wilmot supported the veto, and thought that "the democracy of the country" would approve it.

ties with the North—and Illinois was the only free state with a majority for the gag.

*    *    *

The loosely organized American government depended more than most upon unwritten rules. Within parties established conventions governed the behavior of factions, and especially the extent to which they should persist in their claims or accept the views of the majority; equally, majorities should realize when concession was justified and respect the limits to which minorities could be forced while preserving party unity. At one extreme a party would fail if no internal controversy were allowed and no concession ever given; at the other extreme a majority which always conceded to a vocal minority would abandon majority decision for minority veto. The conventional understandings ensured that the balance of advantage lay with the majority, and, though tenuous and indefinable, had to be observed if the party was to serve a majority of its supporters, but the door by which minorities might reenter the fold should be left open. The delicate balance between what the majority wanted and what the minority would accept, formed the central task of party management. Posts, patronage, and support at the local level were the major counters in the elaborate task of balancing interests and retaining the allegiance of disappointed friends or defeated factions.

Between two parties there were other important conventions to observe. Recognition of the rights of minorities implied the opportunity to obstruct. In practice the scales were normally weighted in favor of free discussion. Debate could be prolonged until all the issues had been considered, and when argument was exhausted there remained a range of procedural points to be exploited. The House had been forced to discipline itself by limiting speeches to an hour, using the device of the Previous Question to bring a bill to an immediate vote, or deciding in advance to close the debate at a specified time. At the beginning of the 29th Congress in December 1845 the House refused to relax the hour rule, so that control over the length of debate was retained, but there remained many procedural devices by which a determined minority could delay decision. The Previous Question, which cut off debate, had to be used sparingly, and could usually be applied only when a party was united, the issue at stake was already familiar, and the motion not unexpected. Even when used discreetly the curtailment of debate might occasion unfavorable comment or

even be met by retaliatory obstruction when other essential business
came before the House.

In the Senate there was no limitation on debate, and it is sometimes a puzzle to discover how any save non-controversial measures
could be brought to the vote. Every Senator had the right to be heard,
nothing could stop him once in possession of the floor, and he alone
could decide whether to yield. In the House the Speaker exercised
considerable power by nominating committees, recognizing members who wished to speak, and ruling on procedural points. He was
expected to ensure that while the minority had a fair hearing, his own
party passed its legislation. In the Senate the Vice-President carried
nothing like the same weight; often he lacked legislative experience,
owed his position to the vagaries of interfactional battles, and exercised an authority which was nominal rather than real especially when
his political rivals were in a majority. Since the early days of the Union
Senators had ignored or resisted attempts by Vice-Presidents to impose their authority, and the most influential man in the Senate was
usually the president *pro tempore,* elected by the majority party, who
was mainly responsible (after consultation) for arranging the business
of the Senate. Then as now real power lay with the committees,
though they had less independent power than their modern succes-
sors.

In the Senate the principal sanction behind the conduct of business was the members' sense of their own importance and dignity. On
the one hand they must have their say if they wished, but a reputation
for constructive statesmenship could not be won merely by verbosity
or skill in obstruction. The simplest convention was therefore that the
majority must normally be allowed to bring their proposals to a vote.
Anarchy was avoided by the knowledge that no one was served by a
stalemate. The preservation of a balance between the right to delay
and the need to obtain a decision, often resulted in a frantic rush
during the closing hours of a session when dozens of major and minor
measures had to be brought to the vote if they were to beat the clock.

In both houses the majority had therefore the right to organize
Congress, set up the committees, decide the order of business and,
after full debate, pass those measures on which they were agreed. In
the House of Representatives these conventions were reinforced by the
hour rule, the previous question, votes to terminate debate at specified times, and the authority of the Speaker; in the Senate they depended upon mutual understandings between political rivals who had
often known each other for many years. If these conventions were in

good working order, Congress could operate effectively, though the way in which things got done might appear to outsiders as time-wasting, confusing, and inefficient.

While Congress depended upon an accumulated body of written and unwritten rules, the relationship between it and the Executive varied from presidency to presidency. Each new man in the White House imposed his own pattern upon the crucial but perplexing links between the two branches of government. Moreover, there had been little experience of harmony between them. Looking back from 1846 over twenty years, there were perhaps six in which President and Congress had worked closely together, but these had been branded as periods of "Executive tyranny" by the Whigs. Even though Democrats had adopted the Jacksonian thesis that the President represented all the people, they were not happy when he appeared to exert too much pressure on the legislature. His claim to represent the popular will looked shallow when majorities had been narrow and his nomination opposed by influential factions in his own party. The President had no fund of precedents to govern his relationship with Congress. Was he a party leader who should give close support to the men at the head of his party in Congress, or was he to initiate policy and expect support from the party? President James K. Polk adopted the latter course, but his methods of management placed the system under severe strain.

The President consulted members of Congress at important junctures but his diary gives little evidence of attempts to work out political strategy. Members of Congress who sought him out at the White House seldom went away satisfied. The contempt for congressmen, which appears so frequently in his diary, could not have been entirely concealed in conversation, while his public messages were often didactic, moralistic, and assumed a righteous superiority which others were loath to concede. He was hardly to blame for pressing measures in which he believed, and historians have credited him with courage and honesty; but when he left office the relationship between Executive and Congress had deteriorated to the point that the capacity to govern had become gravely weakened.

The final component in American government was the President's relations with his own administration. Here President Polk scores: he was master of his Cabinet, and managed to drive an ill-assorted and sometimes reluctant team without open dissension. We know little of the details of the lower federal administration, yet silence is itself a tribute when scandals and complaints have disfigured most other presidencies. At least we know that Polk set himself the highest standard in public ethics, and dealt firmly with the few cases of corruption or incompetence that came to his notice; but his use of patronage was not skilled in the political sense, and left a trail of grievances among those who thought that they had been treated ungenerously. The supporters of Van Buren were particularly resentful, and nothing was done to heal the rift of 1844. At the highest level the Cabinet, though generally united, was clearly not content. The pages of Polk's diary convey something of the tension, uncomfortable silences, tentative criticisms, and the President's sharp reaction when someone was out of line. The President usually opened proceedings in a formal way, allowed discussion to go on for some time, and then abruptly announced his decision. He was impatient with objections, particularly when advanced by James Buchanan. The Secretary of State could see all the difficulties, the President could see plainly the main objective; perhaps in this way they complemented each other during a decisive period in American policy, yet for neither was the association happy. "When I differ from you," wrote Buchanan to Polk in February 1846, "it is always with reluctance and regret. I do not like to urge arguments in opposition before the whole Cabinet. I appear then to be occupying a position which is always painful to me. A little previous consultation with me on important questions of public policy relating to foreign affairs would always obviate this difficulty, because if I failed to convince you there would be no appearance of dissent." This mild complaint from the principal member of his Cabinet is a revealing comment on the statesmanship of James K. Polk. [39]

In all its aspects the delicate balance of forces in government had therefore been disturbed during the first two years of President Polk's administration. Many Whigs were convinced that he had gone beyond the limits of executive power in launching war with Mexico; Whigs and dissident Democrats were shocked when a measure so controversial as the tariff was forced through the Senate with the slenderest margin of votes; Western Democrats were annoyed by a veto which deprived their constituents and districts of benefits which they believed to be constitutional and which had been won by fair but intricate congressional maneuver. Some Democrats resented the way in which Oregon had been compromised, and this contributed to a

---

39. Samuel F. Bemis, ed., *American Secretaries of State,* 17 vols. (New York, 1927–67), "James Buchanan" by Sr. George L. Siossat, V: 334.

willingness to detect, in all measures of the administration, a Southern influence which had passed beyond the reasonable limits of political pressure. It is against this background that the famous Wilmot proviso, and the support it received, must be judged. It is idle to attribute to any one measure or disappointed hope a move that was rather the symptom of a condition in which normal loyalties had been strained and conventions that made the system workable were no longer observed.

\*     \*     \*

Congress was due to adjourn at noon on August 8, and on the last full day of the session McKay, from the Ways and Means Commitee, moved for an appropriation of $2 million with a request that debate be limited to two hours and each speaker to ten minutes. The President wanted cash in hand in case the Mexicans agreed to negotiate during the recess and were prepared to sell their western lands. During dinner David Wilmot of Pennsylvania and Jacob Brinkerhoff of Ohio consulted with other Northern Democrats, and it was agreed that Wilmot should move an amendment to the bill in the form of a proviso that slavery should be prohibited in any territory acquired as a result of the appropriation. Wilmot would later explain that, so far as he was able to discover, "northern Democrats were unanimous in favor of the movement," though Robert Dale Owen doubted the propriety of tacking the proviso on to an appropriation. Wilmot also said— perhaps with less accuracy—that he "never heard the suggestion made that it would embarrass the Administration."[40] Urgency was explained by the fear that if territories were acquired during the recess slavery might be permitted by executive action before Congress had an opportunity of debating the question, but the proviso was more than a plea for delay. Following the wording of the Northwest Ordinance it declared that "as an express and fundamental condition to the acquisition of any territory from the Republic of Mexico . . . neither slavery nor involuntary servitude shall ever exist in any part of said territory."

Wilmot was a Democrat in good standing who had supported annexation and the war, and though opposed to the Oregon settlement had not embarrassed the administration by speaking against it.

40. *Speech at the Convention of the Democratic Party of New York held at Herkimer* (New York, 1847).

He was the sole Democrat from Pennsylvania to support the tariff of 1846 and one of the few Northern representatives to vote for the "gag." He had also praised the President's veto of the Rivers and Harbors Bill as "Jacksonian in character." It would have been hard to find a man who fitted more precisely the definition of a "regular" Democrat, and he was one of the few politicians to earn a morsel of praise in the President's private diary. Why should a man who stood so well with the Administration and might be marked out for political advancement choose to encumber an appropriation requested by the President with a controversial proviso?

Ingenious explanations have been advanced to avoid the conclusion that Wilmot was genuinely alarmed by the prospect of slavery in the new territories. There is no doubt that he and his friends believed that the proviso would be popular with their constituents, and they were anxious to rebut the Northern Whig allegation that they were supporting a war to extend slavery. It has been suggested that Wilmot's personal motive was to secure himself against unpopularity earned by his low tariff views,[41] but he did not exploit the proviso in his 1846 campaign for reelection which he fought and won with the tariff as a major issue. Nor did he contemplate any break with his party; despite his difference with Pennsylvanian colleagues over the tariff, he was in a strong position with Vice-President Dallas as a firm friend and had expectations of administration favor.[42] He was a representative Northern Democrat who had imbibed the heady stimulant of manifest destiny, but shared the common assumption that the republican blessings to be carried across the continent should not include slavery. He had good reason to regard himself as a faithful Jacksonian, but felt it time to remind the President that Northern sentiment deserved a full and fair hearing.

41. The tariff explanation was advanced by R. Stenberg, in "The Motivation of the Wilmot Proviso" *Mississippi Valley Historical Review,* XVIII, 533–41. Another argument, of little merit, links the proviso with Western dissatisfaction over the Oregon settlement (C. E. Persinger, "The Bargain of 1844 and the Wilmot Proviso," American Historical Association Report, I [1911], 189). It is, however, correct to set the proviso in the general context of dissatisfaction and confusion which has been sketched in the preceding papers. Another controversy centers on the authorship of the proviso. Its later celebrity made several anxious to claim the honor, and particularly Jacob Brinkerhoff. In his speech at Herkimer Wilmot said that "after various drafts had been drawn and uttered, the language in which the amendment was drawn was the result of our united efforts."

42. Seth Salisbury to Dallas, 14 September 1846. Dallas Papers, Historical Society of Pennsylvania. Philadelphia, Pa. Salisbury was working actively for Wilmot. "His victory is your victory here, and I will say that his triumph is your triumph." A further letter on 10 October said the tariff was the main issue.

The proviso passed in the House with a large majority, though a significant number of non-voters indicates doubt or early departure under the impression that the remaining business was formal. Members from free states east of the Appalachians voted 66 to 6 in favor, with 18 not voting; from west, the tally was 18 to 7 and 17 not voting. It reached the Senate in the last hour of the session.

John Davis of Massachusetts got the floor in the Senate, and it soon became apparent that he intended to continue speaking. Later he would be praised by Northern conservatives for avoiding a sectional clash, but he himself explained that an amendment had been moved to strike out the proviso (of which he approved), that he judged that this would succeed, and that the House would then pass the bill, shorn of the proviso. He probably hoped to hold on until the motion to strike out the proviso was withdrawn, and leave Senators the choice between accepting the House bill or refusing the President his appropriation. "I was not answerable for springing such a question upon us in the last moments of a long session . . ." he said, "but great as were my objections to other provisions of the bill, if the mover had withdrawn his motion to strike out, the question might have been taken." Davis was one of the two Senators who had voted against war supplies, so he was certainly not trying to defend the Administration against the consequences of its policy. He was still speaking, despite frequent interruptions, when a message arrived that the House had adjourned. The Senate clock, which Davis may have been watching, was eight minutes slow.[43]

The strong support in the North for the proviso can be attributed to many motives—from abolitionist sympathy to dislike of blacks, slave or free—but there was an unmistakable consensus that slave society ought not to expand. Even Senator Lewis Cass, who very much wanted to be President and would later turn against congressional power to prohibit slavery in the territories, was reported as saying that he would have supported the proviso if the bill had come to a vote. Later he would say that the issue was presented prematurely, but still indicated that he would support it if raised again. The House vote was a warning rather than a revolt, and was intended to guide, not cripple, the Democratic party, but once raised the question could not be forgotten and compromise would be difficult. Thus the confused events of August 8, 1846, mark the dividing of sectional ways.

In subsequent argument Northern Democrats insisted that their

43. Davis explained his actions during the next session. *Congressional Globe*, 29.2. 509.

concern was with the damage done by slavery to white society. Wilmot believed that soil exhaustion and increasing slave population would undermine slavery and that "these causes, if permitted to exert their legitimate influence, and not retarded in their operation by an extension of slave territory, will, at no distant day, put an end to slavery and all its concomitant evils." When Southerners argued that they had a constitutional right to carry their property into all the territories of the United States, John A. Dix of New York refused to accept the argument that the Constitution was "armed with full power to bring slave territory into the Union, but void of all power to bring in free territory and maintain it free."[44] The point was a telling one, and Southern doctrine constantly foundered on the precedents set in 1787 and 1820.

The real weakness of the proviso lay not in constitutional theory but in refusal to face the social realities of race or accept national responsibility for the problems it presented.[45] The causes that Wilmot hoped would "exert their legitimate influence" would subject the slave states of the Union to the twin evils of diminishing returns and rising populations for years to come. Falling standards of life would affect both races and relations between them were not likely to improve. In the process the largest slaveowners, with ample assets, reserves, and alternative opportunities would suffer least, while thousands of small slaveowners would face a grim struggle for economic survival and the severest consequences were likely to fall upon the slaves. There was a perpetual fear in the South of what might happen if large numbers of blacks, turned free because it was too expensive to keep them, roamed the country, formed marauding bands, or squatted on unoccupied lands. Above all, Southerners resented the implied condemnation of societies where slavery already existed. They could live with the abolitionist allegation that slavery was sinful, but could not reconcile themselves to the fact that a Northern majority regarded them as inferior.

44. *Ibid.*, 29.2. 543, 1 March 1847.
45. With the single exception of Massachusetts no Northern state gave equal political rights to blacks. In New York they could vote only if they owned substantial property, and an attempt to put equal suffrage into a revised Constitution was decisively defeated by popular vote in the fall of 1846. The *New York Tribune* campaigned vigorously for the measure, but privately Greeley expressed his belief that it would fail. "I have fought the battle for justice and democracy to the best of my ability." (Greeley-Colfax letters, New York Public Library, 22 April 1846).

## Chapter 6

# RESPONSE IN THE NORTH: WHIGS AND CONSCIENCE WHIGS

The Mexican War and the Wilmot Proviso came upon a society which was already in ferment, but for many Americans the leading issue of the day was not slavery in the West but Catholics in the cities. In 1844 a newly formed American Republican party ran James Harper, a well-known publisher and prominent Methodist, as candidate for Mayor of New York. The election address broadened the party's appeal by promising to "reform all the numerous orders of misadministration and political malpractice which exist in every department of our State govenment." If their immediate aim was to extend the time required for naturalization, prevent illegal voting, and counter Catholic influence, they also attacked "the million monied robber" who swindled the community under the cover of corporate privilege, and demanded a revision of the legal code.[1] With Whig support, given in return for an undertaking (not always honored) to support Clay in the presidential race, Harper won with a substantial majority.

In the same year the American Republican party also won the mayoralty of Philadelphia, and of Boston in 1845. In Massachusetts they disclaimed religious bigotry, repudiated both major parties, and claimed "to protect our institutions from all enemies, both Foreign and Domestic."[2] Their success in the three principal cities of the nation promised further triumphs, and a New York manifesto pro-

1. *Address . . . of the American Republican Party of the City of New York* (New York, 1844), 6–7.
2. *Address of the Executive Committee of the American Republicans of Boston to the People of Massachusetts* (Boston, 1845), 9, 15.

claimed that "the people have caught the electric fire," and would "by one concentration of principle and action, form one of the mightiest parties—truly American—that has ever ruled the destinies of this Republic."[3]

Whig leaders were alarmed by the local threat and feared a national movement. They might welcome allies against the Catholic rank and file of the urban Democracy, but were not prepared to endorse violence that would alienate high-minded easterners and midwestern Germans. In June 1844 Thurlow Weed deplored the "rivalry, jealousy, etc., among our friends. The School Question, Native Americanism, Naturalization, etc., are mixing themselves up with religious prejudice and create much feeling."[4] Disgraceful anti-Catholic violence in Philadelphia during the summer of 1844, in the so-called "Kensington riots," brought the dangers into the open, and after Clay's defeat the *New York Tribune* observed that the alliance between city Whigs and nativism had thrown the whole naturalized vote to the Democrats. Clay himself would later blame "the influence of the Native American question, uniting against the Whigs all the new Catholic immigrants,"[5] and Weed and Seward ordered an end to deals with the American Republicans.

The American Republican successes demonstrated the existence of popular disquiet at real or imagined threats to American institutions. Judge John McLean, who always watched for an opportunity to win popular support in the East, was asked about naturalization and fraudulent voting. He came out strongly for a national registration law. "Unless the ballot box shall be purified and kept pure corruption will increase as the right of suffrage shall be increased." No man who loved his country could be satisfied "until this great work shall be accomplished."[6]

Voters who were honestly attracted to the Americans might be won over if the Whigs could find the right candidate for 1848, and the chances would improve still more if the movement appeared to originate with the people themselves. The candidate must embody all those American characteristics that commanded popular respect: he

3. *Address of the American Republican Party of the City of New York,* 9.

4. Quoted in Glyndon G. Van Deusen, *Thurlow Weed: Wizard of the Lobby* (Boston, 1947), 134.

5. *New York Tribune,* 9 November 1844; Clay to Epes Sargent, 15 February 1847, Epes Sargent Collection, Boston Public Library, Boston, Mass. On 13 November 1844 *The National Intelligencer* printed a number of editorials from New York newspapers on why the Whigs lost; all blamed illegal naturalization of voters; only one mentioned the abolitionists.

6. Draft reply to an interrogatory, 29 January 1845. McLean Papers, Library of Congress, Washington, D. C.

must be honest, straightforward, resolute, and patriotic. In the early months of 1847 it occurred to a great many people that the man to fit the bill was General Zachary Taylor whose victories in Mexico had caught the public imagination. In April 1847 he was nominated by a meeting of "democratic Whigs" in Philadelphia[7] and a friend told Judge McLean that "the intense enthusiasm" in the Whig rank and file extended also to Democrats and Native Americans; while an experienced politician in Washington told him that Taylor was the man of the hour, for every effort of the Administration "to disparage him or place him in the background, has, in ways wholly unexpectedly and it seems by the hand of Providence, contributed to his military achievments and his popularity."[8] From South Carolina it was reported that "the movement in favor of Taylor has penetrated every section." Southern politicians were determined to have a popular candidate "without regard to creeds or principles."[9]

By summer the Taylor movement had burst upon New York, and crudely drawn portraits, with the caption "Rough and Ready" appeared everywhere on the streets. It was painted on the tailboards of ice carts and other vehicles. "It is on the butcher's stall, it is in the market places. It is on the fish stands. It is on cigar boxes and divers other places. Such are the impulses of our people."[10] Subsequently Nathan Appleton, the leading merchant prince and Whig of Boston, described the Taylor movement as "the most spontaneous outburst of general popular feeling" within his recollection.[11] Spontaneity did not shake the allegiance of New York to Clay or of Massachusetts to Webster, but Thurlow Weed was no friend of Clay and may have promoted the General's candidacy to demonstrate that he could win at the polls if not in the state convention.

As Taylor's stock rose Clay's fell. In October 1847, the Whigs lost the governorship of Ohio after a campaign in which they had endorsed Clay's protectionist policy and opposition to war, and "argued to ignorant German masses precise points of policy—to masses who for the last two years have been receiving enormous prices for their produce and who care nothing about the tariff or its repeal so that

7. H. Mueller, *The Whigs in Pennsylvania* (New York, 1922), 146. Scott and Clay were more popular in the western part of the state.

8. L. C. Levin, 17 April 1847; Elisha Whittlesey, 6 May 1847, McLean Papers.

9. W. P. Mangum, *Papers,* ed. H. T. Shanks, 5 vols (1950–56) V: 66; McLean Papers, 23 June 1847.

10. McLean Papers, 16 August 1847.

11. Transcript of correspondence between Appleton and Charles Sumner. Boston Public Library.

these prices can be maintained."[12] In New York City, the great mass of the people cared "no more about a Bank, or the Tariff . . . than do Hindoos."[13] In October one of McLean's friends reported a significant conversation with J. J. Crittenden, Senator from Kentucky and a lifelong Clay supporter, but now "a decided Taylor man and entirely averse to taking up Mr. Clay, deeming his election too uncertain and equivocal." Crittenden also expressed strong disapproval of Horace Greeley—still a Clay supporter—who had attempted to get anti-war resolutions adopted by a Whig meeting in New York. "While I disapprove of this miserable war," said Crittenden, "and of the miserable men who brought it on, I was glad to see this anti-American faction put down in the empire city of the Empire State. It will do good to the Whig cause."[14]

In the South, the Wilmot proviso boosted Taylor's popularity. It was confidently asserted that a Southern man and a large slaveowner would never permit the proviso to pass and would use executive influence to open the territories to all without discrimination. In the North it was asserted with equal emphasis that Taylor would stand by "Whig principles" and accept the will of Congress if a majority approved the proviso. In April 1848 Taylor described the veto as a "high conservative power" which should not be exercised except when the Constitution had been clearly violated or if Congress had acted in haste and without adequate consideration. The personal opinions of a President, he wrote, "ought not to control the action of Congress upon questions of domestic policy."[15] Some Northern Whigs may have found greater assurance in the doctrine publicized by Judge McLean, that inaction could prevent the extension of slavery. "Without the sanction of law," he wrote, "slavery can no more exist in a Territory than a man can breathe without air." A Territory could not legalize slavery without authority from Congress, and everyone knew that a majority could never be found to give slavery national recognition.[16]

Nevertheless, the Taylor movement left a train of discontent. John Minor Botts, a faithful Clay Whig, wrote passionately that the issue to be decided was as important for Whigs as their twelve-year struggle against the Democrats. Should "all party lines and distinc-

12. R. J. Arundel, 15 October 1847, McLean Papers.

13. *Ibid*.

14. To Dowling, 30 October 1847, McLean Papers.

15. This statement was known as the "Alison Letter"; Taylor was probably advised by John M. Clayton. The phrase "high conservative power" may have been borrowed from Calhoun.

16. *National Intelligencer,* 23 August 1848 (reprinted from *Cleveland True Democrat* of 28 July).

tions" be obliterated by the selection of a candidate who recognizes no party principles?"[17] Horace Greeley complained that "great fundamental principles" which had been "gradually elaborated and assimilated" were being wantonly abandoned, and Taylor's apparent popularity was really the work of "active, managing, leading politicians." The press campaign had been pervasive, and not more than four journals with more than local circulation had favored Clay, while most Whig members of Congress had used their influence to support Taylor.[18]

There was more force in these criticisms than mere disappointed ambition. If the Whigs were wise in dropping the bank and keeping the tariff in the background they were at fault in devising no policies for the future. There was an opportunity but nothing was done. The country was prosperous, and little political capital could be made out of attacks on the Independent Treasury or the tariff of 1846. There was real dissatisfaction with Polk's attitude toward river and lake improvement, but the Whigs enunciated no general policies to meet this need. Immigration, public lands, railroads, and foreign relations were important issues, but on these questions the Whigs had nothing to say. Perhaps one simple fact was that the men who had given the party such momentum before 1840 were growing old, and wanted nothing more than a comfortable period in office to end their days.

Leadership and national organization are perennial problems for American parties, but the Taylor movement left the Whigs more than usually incoherent. A little noticed aspect of Clay's service to the party had been the assiduous correspondence he carried on with political friends in all parts of the country. Who else could exchange equally friendly letters with Joshua Giddings of Ohio and John M. Berrien of Georgia? Taylor had neither the taste nor tact to perform this task, and when he reached the White House the Whigs became a party without a head. Senator John M. Clayton of Delaware aspired to manage the party, and tried to obtain a compromise on the territorial question which would unite the Whigs before the campaign; but Clayton was little known outside Congress and not much respected in it. As some prophets of doom realized, the heady stimulant of Taylor's popularity would leave the party too weak for survival.

Despite the momentum of the Taylor movement his nomination proved to be less convincing than might have been expected. On the first ballot he was only just ahead of Clay, with Winfield Scott a good

17. HM 15865, dated 6 April 1848, Huntington Library, San Marino, Calif.
18. *New York Tribune*, 10 June 1848.

third and Webster trailing behind. Two-thirds of Taylor's support came from the South; two-thirds of Clay's vote and all cast for Scott and Webster came from the North making an overwhelming northern majority against Taylor. In the next two ballots Pennsylvania switched to Taylor, Clay's support began to crumble, and Webster weakened outside Massachusetts, but Scott was the principal beneficiary and finished with as many Northern votes as Taylor. In the South it was a different story, with Taylor gathering in every vote but six, and this Southern sweep gave him the nomination. Despite his popularity in Northern cities, his victory could be interpreted as a sign that Southern domination now extended to both parties. This view was to prove curiously mistaken, but in the hot summer days of 1848 it seemed ominously true to many anxious Northerners.

The exertions previously made to promote Taylor's candidacy in the North were not without fruit. He was stronger with the voters than with the politicians, and alone among the Whig candidates could take the American vote and cut into Democratic support. Moreover Taylor's views on the veto encouraged some Northern Whigs to think that they could hold the anti-slavery vote. With these calculations in mind the natural response of most Whigs was to close ranks behind the nominee and fight as a united party, whatever their private views of his fitness for the presidency. However, times were not normal. Scattered throughout the Northern states were men convinced that a great moral crisis was at hand and a considerable number of them, concentrated in and around Boston, had already earned the name of "conscience Whig." A minority in the party, and even in the city where they flourished, these dissenters were of great significance for the future. They would provide a tap root for the future Republican party and generate its most distinctive beliefs. It is therefore important to understand the political and intellectual climate in which they flourished.

*       *       *

The wide consequences of the conscience Whig movement derived in part from the unique situation of Boston in American life. Wealth, learning, and literary achievement were brought together as in no other city; religious thought was dominated by Unitarianism which was, of all churches, the most influenced by rationalism and most responsive to calls for social reform; immigration and urban congestion had made Bostonians more conscious than most of the problems in the new age, and nativism had administered a shock to the political system. From nearby Concord the influence of Transcendentalism was felt by most men who were active in the religious and cultural life. It was also in Boston that William Lloyd Garrison published the *Liberator,* and from Boston the oratory of Wendell Phillips carried the Garrisonian message far and wide. From the same city some of the most powerful businessmen in the United States controlled commercial empires which embraced worldwide trade, textile factories, and cotton plantations. Boston was an epitome of Northern American problems, and nowhere else were they discussed with such intensity.

The belated attempt to prevent the annexation of Texas gave idealistic men of the rising generation the opportunity of working together, and from that time onward the fight against the extension of slavery absorbed most of their energies.[19] Anti-slavery dragged them into the morass of local and later of national politics, and this preoccupation drained the life out of many other movements for social betterment. It was not that other things ceased to be important, but that the "slave power" seemed to block all the paths to the future. Few were prepared to travel the whole way to immediate abolition, but most of them would have endorsed the views of James Russell Lowell, poet and abolitionist pamphleteer, who asked, "Shall we ever be Republican?" Slavery made true republicanism impossible. There were a great many things to be done in America, but so long as slavery remained "all outward prosperity was a cheat and a delusion."[20]

To men who had fought the annexation of Texas, the outbreak of war with Mexico came as an anticipated sequel which proved the wisdom of their course. If the morality of annexation was dubious, war was outrageous. It was naked aggression, palpably unjust, and positive proof that American promise was debased by association with slavery. Conscience Whigs were not alone in this reaction, but they were the most sensitive to war's impact on the moving currents of the nineteenth-century thought. The outbreak of war was not merely a political event but a shocking proof that the nation could act immorally, and in defiance of all hope for the betterment of mankind.

The key to the thought of conscience Whigs was found in liberal Unitarianism with William Ellery Channing, the wisest and most widely cultured man of his generation in America, as its prophet. When he died in 1842 no one could take his place as the exponent of

19. For a detailed account see Kinley J. Brauer, *Cotton versus Conscience: Massachusetts Whig Politics and Southwestern Expansion, 1843–1848* (Lexington, 1967).

20. James Russell Lowell, *Anti-Slavery Papers* (New York, 1902; reprint ed., 1969, Negro Universities Press, 1969) I: 58–59.

the "calm, stable, universal good-will to all" which he had learned from the Scottish moral philosophers of the eighteenth century.[21] Theodore Parker, who became the leading exponent of Christian reform, was more radical in temperament, more impetuous, and less disposed to extend charity to those who sinned against the light.

Nor did Parker's association with the Transcendentalists commend him theologically to conservative Unitarians, and despite his eminence as a scholar he was unable to obtain a Boston pulpit until 1845, when a group of lay friends rented the Melodeon Theater on Sundays and invited him to preach. In 1852 his popularity as a preacher caused him to seek larger and still more incongruous accommodation in the Music Hall. The congregation included William Lloyd Garrison, Charles Sumner, Samuel Gridley Howe and his wife Julia. Anti-slavery politicians such as John P. Hale, Salmon P. Chase, and Joshua Giddings attended when they visited Boston and the atmosphere was often as much political as religious. Parker was a man of wide learning, enormous industry, and impulsive judgment. His circle of friends reached far into the cultural life of Boston and his academic achievement commanded respect at Harvard. The Mexican War, coming shortly after his removal to Boston, provided him with a theme for eloquence and righteous indignation.

"We are waging a most iniquitous war," Parker declared. American institutions might be superior to Mexican, but "in this issue, and this particular war . . . we are wholly in the wrong." Who was responsible? It was not enough to blame slaveowners and Democrats, for the burden of guilt must be shared by men nearer home. "The eyes of the North are full of cotton; they see nothing else, for a web is before them; their ears are full of cotton, and they hear nothing but the buzz of their mills; their mouth is full of cotton, and they can speak audibly but two words—Tariff, Tariff, Dividends, Dividends." Northern capitalists had done as much as slavery—with which they were allied—to betray America, "its great ideas, its real grandeur, its hopes, and the memory of its fathers." In a speech in Faneuil Hall Parker met the accusation that criticism in time of war was disloyal. "If it be treason to speak against war, what was it to make war? . . . If my country is in the wrong, and I know it and hold my peace, then I am guilty of treason, moral treason."[22]

Was it even sufficient to blame cotton planters and merchants?

21. See Chapter 2, pp. 48–49.
22. Theodore Parker, *Collected Works*, ed. Frances Power Cobbe (London, 1863), 23, 38–39. There is a good brief study of Parker in Robert C. Albrecht, *Theodore Parker* (New York, 1971) with a bibliography giving a critical estimate of the printed collections of Parker's works.

Parker, who never claimed to be a systematic political thinker, could mix attacks on individuals or groups with accusations of collective guilt. "The nation is traitor to its great idea—that all men were born equal, each with the same inalienable rights." At other times false leaders were responsible. "It was not the people who made this war. They have often done a foolish thing. But it was not they who did this wrong. It was they who led the people; it was the demogogues that did it."[23] This betrays the classic confusion of moral reformers in a democratic society, and was characteristic of the conscience Whigs. Socially and intellectually they belonged to an elite; yet republican thought demanded respect for the judgment of the people.

There were other philosophic weaknesses. Despite their array of talents the liberal Unitarians included no one with knowledge of economics. So far as they deemed this a valuable branch of knowledge they depended upon Francis Bowen, who taught classical political theory at Harvard. Henry Carey, the one American economist with a streak of originality, wrote of Bowen that "he knew nothing of political economy and was therefore totally incompetent to teach history."[24] They were also weak in social theory and their political science did not get beyond the familiar aphorisms of the revolutionary tradition. While rejecting the rigors of Calvinist theology, they substituted for it nothing save a somewhat vague Christian ethic. They paid little attention to Lysander Spooner (of whom more hereafter) when he tried to construct a rational theory of society on a foundation of natural law, especially when his arguments advanced toward atheism. They knew little of Richard Hildreth, the historian, who knew some economics and was influenced by Benthamism.

Liberal Unitarians had more in common with romantics than rationalists. Transcendentalism, which affected all of them directly or indirectly, attempted to express romantic verities in philosophic form and, with men who lacked philosophic discipline, became a confused belief that intuitive ideas were universal truths. Precise statements were avoided, and the liberal Unitarians pictured themselves as romantic heroes who would defend the truth against all its enemies and particularly, as events turned out, against the wealth of Boston and the false chivalry of the South. James Freeman Clarke caught the mood precisely when he preached in 1847 at the ordination

23. Parker, *Collected Works*, 74.

24. Carey to Nathan Appleton, 10 February 1851, Appleton Papers, Massachusetts Historical Society, Boston, Mass.

of Thomas Wentworth Higginson who was young, impressionable, idealistic, and destined to rescue fugitive slaves, command black troops, and live on to become a revered patriarch of the anti-slavery movement. At the outset of his career Clarke charged him to live up to the professions of his faith.

> Be a reformer of the Church, of Society, of the State; for un-christian institutions, manners, and ideas nestle like reptiles in all of these. . . . While the nation, in the name of liberty, plants its feet on the necks of three million slaves, God forgive the minister of Christ who neglects to show the people the blackness of this sin.[25]

This was strong meat for a conservative Newburyport congregation but typical of the spirit that moved among the young liberal Unitarians. It was an injunction to attack evil, to cry aloud and spare not, to battle with the hosts of Armageddon be they ever so numerous and well armed.

In 1847 the students at the Harvard Divinity School elected Samuel J. May to give their graduating address. It was a bold choice, for May was known as an abolitionist, and since Emerson's radical address in 1838 caution had prevailed. There was nothing revolutionary in the theology of May's address, but his practical advice was radical. The distinctive vices of every age were "entrenched behind the example, are sustained by the influence, of the wise, the prudent, the professedly pious, the men of property and standing." To be "instrumental in carrying forward the work of the Lord" men must have the courage to assail wrongdoing in high places. The righteous minister should assail the men of the North who upheld their Southern brethren in iniquity, and expounded the Constitution to protect slavery. "They . . . should be held up before our country and the world as responsible for this system of tremendous wickedness."[26]

Thus the movement of the conscience Whigs was a revolt against the domination of Boston by respectable merchant families. It was also a protest against the intellectual establishment, including the more conservative elements in their own Unitarian Church. Samuel May's exhortation may be compared with Orville Dewey's plea for

25. James Freeman Clarke, *Charge at the Ordination of T. W. Higginson* (printed copy in the Houghton Library, Harvard University, Cambridge, Mass.).
26. Samuel J. May, *Jesus the Best Teacher of Religion* (printed copy in the Houghton Library, Harvard University).

moderation "commonly considered a very tame quality," but properly understood a "complete harmony of opposite qualities," and impossible without the example of Jesus in whom "there was nothing in excess . . . no conflict, no clashing in the qualities of his perfect character."[27] In the eyes of ardent reformers this comforting belief that everyone could work his own salvation provided he lived in love and charity with his neighbors, seemed too much like a cloak for the complacency epitomized by "moderate" preachers with prosperous congregations and cautious literary gentlemen disseminating platitudes through the press.

From his detached viewpoint in Concord Emerson observed that "the puny race of Scholars in this country have no counsel to give, and are not felt." Politicians made furious contests "but the voice of the intelligent and the honest, of the unconnected and independent, the voice of truth and equality is suppressed." In England the journals and newspapers always expressed "a better and a best sense as well as the low coarse party cries"; but in New England this was not so.[28] In 1847 Theodore Parker tried to persuade Emerson to edit a new journal to redeem the reputation of New England. "The incubus of the Unitarian Church," had strangled what little life was left in the *Examiner*. "Dyspeptic Tutor Bowen rides the lean and limping *North American* carrying its double load of bigotry and Ultra Whiggism"; only the New England *Quarterly* made some show of "liberality," but "the ghost of Calvinism hovers about even that."[29]

The revolt against the establishment became politically manifest in November 1845 when the Anti-Texas Committee sent copies of their petition to Nathan Appleton and Abbott Lawrence, who were leaders of the Whig party in Massachusetts and principal exponents of cooperation between Northern and Southern Whigs. If they endorsed the petition they would offend their Southern allies, if they refused to do so they might lose control of the Massachusetts party. Lawrence replied briefly that it was too late to stop annexation, and further agitation would harm the party; Appleton's carefully composed reply observed that the signatories of the petition included many

27. Orville Dewey, *Discourses and Discussions in Explanation and Defence of Unitarianism* (Boston, 1840), 297.

28. Ralph Waldo Emerson, *Journals and Miscellaneous Notebooks*, ed. Ralph H. Orth and Alfred R. Ferguson (Cambridge, Mass., 1971) IX: 194. Undated but written during 1845.

29. Parker to Emerson, 14 March 1847, Emerson Papers, Houghton Library, Harvard University, Cambridge, Mass. Emerson refused. It was the year of his visit to England and he had other things on his mind. He found editorial duties uncongenial, and was not yet ready to take a public stand on issues affecting slavery.

abolitionists whose aims were probably unconstitutional and had "produced nothing but evil." The committee decided to publish Appleton's letter without his consent. This caused deep resentment, but in August 1846 the quarrel became acrimonious when Charles Sumner told Appleton that his letter had done "much to encourage the esprit de corps among slaveholders," and implied that it had helped to bring on the Mexican War. Appleton replied that he had not wished to make public a letter written "with a legitimate and virtuous purpose . . . in the hope to win back if possible a young friend from the gulf of abolitionism into which he was plunging,"[30] and bitterly resented the accusation that his action had anything to do with the Mexican War. Henceforth the breach between "conscience" and "cotton" was complete.

Charles Francis Adams, chairman of the Texas Committee, did not intend to break the Whig party but to control it. The attack on Appleton was intended to drive him from his position in the state party, and discredit his friends who defended the national party against disruption threatened by the conscience Whigs. The wisdom of this deliberate challenge to conservative leadership is questionable. Nathan Appleton was certainly conservative but he was also enlightened. He could claim to be a model manufacturer, with a genuine interest in the welfare of his employees. He had written authoritatively on the bank question in 1841, and sensibly on labor problems in *Hunt's Merchants' Magazine*. He was one of the founders of the Boston Atheneum, an active member of the Massachusetts Historical Society, and Longfellow's father-in-law. He also had an abiding interest in theology. In their attack on this eminent Bostonian the conscience Whigs did not merely aim to discredit an individual, but also to cut adrift from the tradition of liberal conservatism which had for so long dominated Massachusetts. It might have been wiser to work from within, wait upon events, and exert influence through a united party.

The bid to win control of the state party inspired a group of wealthy conscience Whigs to purchase *The Boston Whig*, a small paper with limited circulation and shaky finances, and install Charles Francis Adams as editor. In his first editorial, appearing on June 1, 1846, Adams wrote,

---

30. Appleton's draft reply, much corrected, is among his papers in the Massachusetts Historical Society. Charles Sumner's letter is dated 11 August 1846. Appleton's letter to Sumner is in a transcript of correspondence between them in the Boston Public Library.

> The aspect of public affairs is troubled, and people know not
> what a day may bring forth. There is an earnest looking back
> in many quarters to first principles to find some landmarks by
> which their course may be guided.[31]

The people, he believed, were confused rather than apathetic. They
wanted guidance, which it was the duty of leaders to give. This did
not mean the abandonment of the Whig party, for there could "never
be more than two parties, between which control of public policy
must rest," but its conversion. Some Whigs were conservative only in
their eagerness to protect the right of property, but others strove "to
attain a nobler position." The great error of false conservatism was "to
sustain property which is held on no principle of justice or right,"
while true conservatives should concentrate upon opposing "the prosecution of schemes subversive of the political balance of the Union."

In the second issue of *The Boston Whig* Adams accused the conservatives of dividing the party by abandoning their opposition to annexation, "for never since the organization of government did Whigs
enjoy so strong a position." On June 27 he repeated his opposition to
third parties, but called for cooperation among men opposed to the
extension of slavery so that it would be "impracticable for the Whig or
Democratic party, but especially the former, to enter into any general
election hereafter without a distinct and unequivocal declaration of its
policy respecting slavery." In other words the parties should be preserved, but a bipartisan anti-slavery alliance should seek to direct the
policy of both. Given this approach it was logical to support the Wilmot Proviso, even though it originated with staunch Democrats.
Wilmot had "knocked the nail right on the head," declared *The Boston
Whig*, and on August 18 held up to opprobrium the free state representatives who had voted against him.

By this time the prospect of uniting Massachusetts Whigs behind the proviso had become remote. *The Boston Whig* had printed
a series of attacks on Abbot Lawrence over the signature "Sagitta,"
written by Charles Sumner. Lawrence had written a public letter
to W. C. Rives of Virginia, about the promotion of manufactures in
that state, without mentioning slavery as a major obstacle. Surely,
said "Sagitta," it was time to speak out, and "break up this miserable
system of truckling to expediencey in everything, for the sake of better filling our pockets with slave-holding gold." The idea that the

31. Files of *The Boston Whig* are rare; there is a set in the Massachusetts Historical Society.

Free States should have nothing to do with slavery was now "nearly obsolete." Of greater significance were a series of letters, also published in *The Boston Whig*, and then in October as a pamphlet, by John Gorham Palfrey. The title was *The Slave Power* and the argument was to have a powerful effect and survive as one of the mainstays of Republican rhetoric.

Palfrey was a Unitarian minister with some reputation as a scholar, and an apparently secure position in the Massachusetts establishment. He had been editor of the *North American Review* at a time when it was singularly unadventurous, a member of the state legislature, and latterly secretary of the Commonwealth. In 1846 he was running for Congress, and while firmly aligned with the "conscience" group was anxious to establish his credentials as a Whig. Some anti-slavery men saw him as a potential leader, and Samuel Gridley Howe urged him "to be among the foremost in crossing the Rubicon which environs slavery."[32] But a leader without troops could achieve nothing and Palfrey was anxious to elaborate Adams's argument that conservatives had abandoned the party line while the conscience Whigs had adhered to it. "The departure of a portion of the Whig party in Boston, while the annexation of Texas was still pending, from the ground steadfastly held by that party . . . was a great public wrong, the consequences of which may not pass away in our day." The true Whig position could not be alliance with the "slave power" which he defined as "that control in and over the government of the United States which is exercised by a comparatively small number of persons, distinguished from the other twenty millions of free citizens, and bound together in a common interest, by being owners of slaves."[33] The true Southern Whig party was not composed of 100,000 slaveowners but of non-slaveowners whose real interest coincided with that of Northern Whigs. Southern Whites paid dearly for domination by slaveowners in low living standards, few churches, and no schools. As soon as the power of the slave-holding oligarchy was challenged there would spring up in the South "a large, brave, honest, available Whig party. . . . The Southern non-slaveholders belong of right to our party—the party of the free." The true interests of Northern Whigs were not served by subservience to supposed Southern leaders. Indeed Mr. Appleton's concern, in 1845, to save the tariff of 1842

32. Palfrey Papers, Houghton Library, Harvard University, Cambridge, Mass., 23 September 1846.
33. This definition occurs in the second edition of *The Slave Power* published in 1851.

had been a sad miscalculation; it had been lost by the vote of two Senators from Texas thereby stripping "thousands of freemen in the North of their means to an honest livelihood." In any case, Appleton's economic theory began and ended with cotton which accounted for less than one-sixth of the industrial output of Massachusetts and was outstripped by the manufacture of leather goods.[34]

Thus Palfrey's papers on the "Slave Power" attempted to explain why a popular government had become perverted, how the nation could be rescued from injustice, and what policies would save the national party without concessions to slavery. This argument that slaveowners could be isolated in the South, and attacked without endorsing abolitionism, was to have a powerful influence on the future. Palfrey was not an original thinker, but he provided the intellectual core for Free Soil and later Republican parties. His legacy was apparent in the Republican attitude to secession in 1861 and traces can be observed in the theory and practice of Reconstruction.

As a would-be political leader of the anti-slavery Whigs Palfrey was less successful. In 1846 he failed to obtain the absolute majority in his district, which Massachusetts law required for election, and won by only a handful of votes, with conservative support, at the run-off election in December. Nevertheless for a moment he seemed to be a man of the hour, and at his first appearance in Congress attracted national attention by his part in the drama which may be described as "Winthrop's Vote and Palfrey's Vote."

Robert C. Winthrop was the most active politician among the younger conservative Whigs. He was intimate with Appleton, Abbot Lawrence, and Edward Everett who had recently returned from the Ministry in London to become president of Harvard. He was a temperate man who disliked slavery, distrusted agitators, believed devoutly in the Union, and was convinced that the national Whig party enjoyed divine approbation. In May 1846, when President Polk sprang the announcement of war on Congress, Winthrop was a member of the House of Representatives and like other Whigs distrusted the President, believed him guilty of unnecessary provocation against Mexico, and suspected inexcusable double-dealing. But American troops had been attacked and might, for all he knew, be already engaged in full-scale warfare, and maneuver by the Democrats forced the Whigs to choose between refusing appropriation for defence and accepting a preamble which asserted that the Mexicans were

34. *The Slave Power* (Boston, 1846), 33–34, 54.

responsible for hostilities. In common wcth many other Whigs Winthrop chose to vote for supplies and swallow the preamble; but he was the only Massachusetts Whig to do so, and for this was exposed to the full fury of attack in anonymous articles written by Charles Sumner. Privately Charles Sumner acknowledged his authorship to Winthrop and to Appleton (from whom, inexplicably, he seems to have expected sympathy). To Appleton he expressed his former friendship and respect for Winthrop but wrote—and heavily underlined— that *"he has done the worst act that was ever done by a Boston representative."* Winthrop had approved an unjust war, implied hope for its success ("in other words for the triumph of *injustice*"), joined in a "national lie," and connived at an attempt to extend and fortify slavery. "His choice was not difficult. . . . Of two caskets before him he chose the blazing one of the majority filled with a death's head." Winthrop's guilt was intensified by the report that he had cast his vote to dispel the notion that all Boston was committed to abolitionism.[35] In the congressional elections of 1846 Samuel Gridley Howe, the well-known philanthropist and humanitarian, was persuaded to oppose Winthrop in his own district and suffered a humiliating defeat, but honor was not satisfied and the conscience Whigs remained implacably opposed to a man who might have helped them much.

In December 1847 the Whig congressional caucus selected Winthrop as their candidate for Speaker. Palfrey conferred with Joshua Giddings, the veteran anti-slavery Whig from Ohio, and then addressed a number of questions to Winthrop: would he constitute the committees of the House so that war would be brought to a speedy conclusion, slavery excluded from acquired territories, and jury trial guaranteed for alleged fugitive slaves? Winthrop refused to give pledges, and on the first ballot Palfrey cast his vote for Charles Hudson of Massachusetts, while Giddings and Tuck of New Hampshire voted for another anti-slavery Whig. This left Winthrop three short of the required total: on the second ballot he gained two votes from minor candidates, and on the third an independent South Carolinian, Isaac Holmes, ostentatiously left the House to give Winthrop a majority of those present and voting.

When the news reached Boston Theodore Parker was entertaining Samuel Gridley Howe, H. L. Bowditch, William H. Channing, and Charles Sumner at dinner, and the five men immediately dashed off a letter to Palfrey expressing their grateful thanks that he had "so

35. Appleton Papers, 11 August 1841.

firmly yet courteously, temperately while uncompromisingly asserted
—on the first occasion that offered—the rights of a freeman of the
Republic. We feel that in that good deed you have helped to lay the
cornerstone for a new temple of our liberties."[36] Others thought differently. It was a matter of pride for a state to secure the Speakership,
and generally expected that a man would vote with his party on this
important occasion. Appleton, who had already crossed swords with
Palfrey in a pamphlet exchange arising from remarks in the *Slave
Power*, later expressed his private opinion of "a gentleman who left the
pulpit for the arena of politics—who was smuggled into Congress as a
Whig, whilst holding the especial purpose of acting in opposition to
that party, who dishonored himself by making a most dishonorable
proposition to Mr. Winthrop at the time of his vote for speaker."[37]
Commenting on attacks in the press Parker wrote to Palfrey that a
man "as much in advance of the moral sentiment of the times" must
expect his path to be "a little steep and thorny." Winthrop was "an
unworthy son of most worthy sires," and despite newspaper attacks
Parker assured Palfrey that he had received the warmest praise from
those whose opinion he would value most highly, and was "glad it falls
to the lot of a man constitutionally courageous to stand up in the
Bear-Garden of American Politics and show that a man may be in
Politics and not out of Morals."[38]

The limitations of Charles Francis Adams and the conscience
Whigs was well understood by his son and first biographer who wrote:

> What Mr. Adams and his associates did then see and all they
> clearly saw, was the immediate work cut out for them to do.
> It was for them to arouse the country to a consciousness of the
> danger of the situation, and the consequences involved if
> events went unchecked.[39]

There was the assumption that if the "danger" could be removed a
condition of health would be restored; hence the fury with which they

36. Palfrey Papers, 10 December 1847. On the same evening S. G. Howe wrote independently
that his "heroic vote has proved (if proof were wanting) that the opinions of men do not weigh as
much as the small dust of the balance when any high principle is in the opposite scale."

37. The comment occurs in an anonymous letter which Appleton sent to *The Christian Register*, a Unitarian journal, complaining that it was "changing its character and giving itself up to
the political discussion of slavery." The veteran H. G. Otis approved of Appleton's course in the
controversy with Palfrey: he could not recall "a more waspish and unmerited outbreak" than
Palfrey's published letter. Appleton also received a letter of support from Andrews Norton.

38. Palfrey Papers, 19 January 1848.

39. Charles Francis Adams, Jr., *Charles Francis Adams* (Boston, 1900), 54–55.

attacked the "slave power" and sought to discredit its supposed Northern allies. The issue must not be allowed to rest, because all the evil of the times was the consequence of acquiescence and false hope. In the light of these limitations it is instructive to turn to other more fully developed arguments which would, in course of time, affect the mainstream of anti-slavery thought.

\*     \*     \*

In 1840 Richard Hildreth, the future historian, published a small book called *Despotism in America* which attracted little attention at the time, but was republished in 1854.[40] Hildreth had a conventional New England Federalist upbringing, but came under the influence of the English Benthamites and classical economists. His book focused on the economic consequences of slavery, but also applied utilitarian principles to the Union. The Founding Fathers had rightly seen the Union as the defense of liberty, but "suppose this same Union to be made the pretext for a violent interference with our dearest rights?" When a thing changed its nature, its name became a delusion. "Though it be called a Union, What is it but a base subjection, a miserable servitude?"[41] The target of Hildreth's criticism was romantic nationalism which substituted devotion to the Union for the pursuit of happiness.

> An idea seems to prevail, that excellent a thing as the Union is, the people, ignorant and short-sighted, may sometimes take it into their heads to think otherwise; and therefore it is necessary to erect a *prejudice* in favor of the Union—a sort of feeling like that of loyalty, which has often upheld a throne in spite of the vices and the tyranny of him who sat on it.

This substitution of emotion for a rational examination of results was the harbinger of conflict, not harmony.[42]

The greater part of Hildreth's book was devoted to a demonstra-

40. Hildreth had written a moderately successful anti-slavery novel called *Archy Moore : the white slave*. *Despotism in America* was originally attributed to "the author of *Archy Moore*"; the 1854 edition was published under his own name. The quotations that follow come from the second edition.

41. *Despotism in America*, 28.

42. *Ibid.*, 27.

tion that slavery was not and could not advance the greatest happiness of the greatest number. It failed the test of utility, and should be treated as other relics of the past preserved to buttress the power of privileged classes. Refusal to face these facts could only worsen and prolong the conflict. "The struggle that impends is of a nature to shake the country to the center, and to end, if we believe the prophecies of our Southern friends in civil commotion, infuriated hostilities, and savage war." The sane way to preserve the Union as a blessing to all the people was to institute "an Inquiry into the Feasibility, Expedience, and Necessity of the Abolition of Slavery in the United States of America, with Outlines of a Practical Plan for its Accomplishment—a second treatise to which the present one is intended as an introduction."[43] This second treatise was, unfortunately, never written.

Lysander Spooner, who was born in 1808 at Athol, Massachusetts, practiced irregularly and unsuccessfully as a lawyer, speculated —with equal lack of success—in Western lands, operated a private mail service between Boston and Baltimore until Congress drove him out of business in 1845 by halving the regular postal rates, and published wide-ranging but little-read books on banking, credit, and poverty. Spooner became involved in anti-slavery controversy and, though his major work on "The Unconstitutionality of Slavery" published in 1845 was financed by Gerrit Smith of the Liberty party, Spooner belonged with Hildreth and Nathaniel P. Rogers in a small group which might be named "rationalists against slavery."[44]

Lysander Spooner was a self-taught disciple of eighteenth-century rationalists, and expressed natural law theory in its most dogmatic form. In a work on *Poverty,* published in 1846, he wrote that "Natural law, in regard to human rights, is capable of being ascertained with nearly absolute certainty," and was or ought to be the sole standard by which man-made laws and institutions should be judged.[45] If the natural law foundation was abandoned, nothing remained but force and numbers. "If the arbitrary commands of legislative bodies are better standards of right, than the everlasting principles of justice and natural law, why are not the former substituted for the latter in all cases whatsoever?" This was a shrewd hit at much

43. *Ibid.,* 9, 303.
44. There is a modern edition of Spooner's works in 6 vols., edited by Charles Shively (Weston, Mass., 1971). The introduction includes a biography of Spooner. Quotations that follow are from the 1845 edition.
45. Lysander Spooner, *Poverty* (Boston, 1846), 63–64.

constitutional theorizing which claimed to respect self-evident truths but treated the letter of the law as sacrosanct.

According to Spooner the definition of law was "the natural, permanent, unalterable principle which governs any particular thing or class of things," and the law of civil rights was "the rule, principle, obligation or requirement of natural justice." Either the Constitution embodied this principle or it did not. There was a presumption that the framers of the Constitution intended to build on natural law and to secure natural justice in all its forms.[46] After a lengthy and often tedious examination of the Constitution Spooner concluded that this assumption was valid, and that slavery, being a denial of natural justice, was "inconsistent with nearly everything that is either expressed or legally implied in the constitution."[47] If the Constitution were not a pro-slavery document it must be an anti-slavery document, and therefore conferred upon the national government ample power to legislate against slavery and no power to protect it.

In an interesting passage Spooner tackled the problem raised by Parker and Palfrey of the conflict between consent as the moral basis for authority and the injustice of acts sanctioned by popular majorities. "Natural law" was "paramount law" and legislative action that denied natural justice had no moral validity, but this did not conflict with the supreme power of "the people" because they had, in practice, no part in legislation. Their consent had "no existence in fact," and government was in reality established by the few who "assume the consent of the rest, without any such consent being actually given."[48] Spooner might have been helped, at this point, by some distinction between what the people appeared to want and what they would really want if the principles of natural justice were put fairly to them; but the differentiation between real and particular wills would have been too metaphysical a concept for so stout a believer in the power of pure reason.

Lysander Spooner was attacked by Wendell Phillips in a long pamphlet which sought to prove, with ample documentation from the Madison papers, that the Constitution was a pro-slavery instrument. This was important to the Garrisonians in their quarrel with the Liberty party, but misunderstood Spooner's major contention that all laws and institutions must conform to common standards of jus-

46. Lysander Spooner, *The Unconstitutionality of Slavery* (Boston, 1845), 153.
47. *Ibid.*, 166.
48. *Ibid.*, 270.

tice, and were defective if they did not do so. If laws were unjust, or had become corrupt, then they must be amended to conform with the principles of natural justice. It was irrational to tolerate injustice because it claimed the protection of the law. Spooner believed that the Constitution was not defective but had been misinterpreted, and this brought his argument close to that of Palfrey. Indeed, in an Appendix, he anticipated an essential link in the argument of the *Slave Power* when he wrote that slaveowners were few in number, that their power depended upon the supposed constitutionality of slavery, and that if this were seriously questioned a blow would be struck "at their influence and wealth and power." This would separate the non-slaveholders from slaveowners for "it is idle to suppose that the non-slaveholders of the South are going to sacrifice the Union for the sake of slavery."[49]

James Russell Lowell was drawn into the campaign against slavery and in 1845 began to publish occasional papers, first in the *Pennsylvania Freeman* and then in the *Anti-Slavery Standard*.[50] His best known contributions to the controversy were, of course, the *Bigelow Papers,* but his prose works deserve more attention than they have received. At thirty Lowell looked, in appearance and dress, everything that the age expected of a romantic poet. It was probably his young wife who stirred him to engage in abolitionist propaganda, but his cast of mind owed more to his father, a minister in Cambridge, who epitomized the spirit of rational and benevolent Unitarianism. In the internecine struggle among abolitionists Lowell ranged himself with Garrison against the Liberty party and political involvement, but his ideas were more subtle and expressed with greater elegance.

In his first paper he defended Garrison's American Antislavery Society because it had "refused to fling away its impenetrable moral buckler, or to fight the enemy with their own clumsy weapons of politics and guile, in which it has no skill, and with which it would surely be defeated." Anti-slavery men should seek no aid of existing institutions, for, "if a man leans upon the church or state, these crutches will sooner or later break under him." If anti-slavery became political, its success would be delayed, and "when it comes will produce results as unstable as those of political victory."

49. *Unconstitutionality of Slavery,* 295.
50. For a modern study of Lowell see Martin Duberman, *James Russell Lowell* (Boston, 1964). His *Anti-Slavery Papers* (New York, 1902) have been reprinted by the Negro Universities Press, 1969. The quotations in this and the following paragraphs are all drawn from the first five Anti-Slavery Papers published in 1845.

So far from enlarging anti-slavery aims, politics would limit them. "No tall moral beacon fire will be kindled, flinging its light into the unwilling recesses and hideous caverns of other oppressions." Experience over annexation proved the point, because, in both parties, opposition had been manufactured in response to Northern abolitionism—"not to meet the moral but political demand"—and the controversy had then degenerated into procedural and constitutional disputes. So it would always be "till the utter worthlessness of that piece of parchment had been demonstrated," and politicians learned not to ask "Is it constitutional?" but "Is it right?"

Lowell believed that opposition to slavery must retain its broad base and not be maneuvered into concentrating its force on limited objectives which would yield no strategic advantage. An attractive aspect of his argument was a straightforward approach to race relations. He believed that abolitionists could perform no more useful service than to elevate the condition of the colored race in the free states. "While our moral atmosphere is so dense and heavy with prejudice, it will be impossible for the colored man to stand erect or breathe freely," and it was as necessary to struggle against "the slave system of the North as against the South." This implied that the thrust must not be against the slave power—a small number of men who had inherited a system which many disliked—but against racial oppression everywhere.

Lowell paid particular attention to the condition of the churches. If the Church were "only a part of our civilized machinery for *getting along*," its views could command no more respect than those of "any other of the thousand shapes into which policy has divided our social organization." The American Church claimed divine authority, but might be compared to the buried churches of German legend, from which mysterious bells could sometimes be heard or the ghostly strains of monks chanting forgotten ritual; the great majority of American churches were equally remote from reality and the seeker after truth could hear only an obsolete language teaching "a vague reverence for what is ancient, a mysterious awe for what is past." Divine wisdom must always be in advance of public opinion and, when a church did no more than echo the views of its congregation, it "degraded the moral sense of the nation which it was its duty to elevate." Americans had ceased to expect moral leadership, and gave praise to those who justified timidity with sententious rhetoric. New England had given unstinted praise to Daniel Webster, but what had he done to deserve it; what man among God's hungry poor lived better because Daniel Webster had lived? At the gate of judgment he would be found wanting, and "What voice of one enfranchised man, what saving testimony of a single truth made clearer, of a single human sorrow made lighter, shall plead for a reversal of the decree?"[51]

Lowell enjoyed a comfortable private income, lived most of his life in the house now occupied by the president of Harvard, won an enviable literary reputation, and did not greatly distinguish himself in later life as a crusader for social justice. Nevertheless his excursion into anti-slavery radicalism deserves notice, because of its telling comment on the perennial problem of moral authority in a democratic society. He made no claim to be an exact philosopher, but his insistence that institutions and authority must be judged by their moral consequences derived from an ancient and honored tradition. In the immediate context his questions might have been taken to heart by the conscience Whigs. Could they make any real impact on slavery by using conventional political means? Could they achieve anything by limiting their objectives, even if these included curbs on the "slave power"?

These questions became relevant as the Taylor movement gathered momentum, and a note of desperation began to sound among the conscience Whigs as their hope of influencing the party diminished. "A great crisis is at hand," wrote Samuel Gridley Howe at the end of April, "the North cannot, must not be longer *particeps crimines* in this infernal business. It is looking now for leaders and champions."[52] Yet what was to be done when Taylor was nominated? "The Slaveholders are once more victorious," declared *The Boston Whig* on June 10, and added, "There is no longer any Whig party." A week later it gave prominence to a letter from "A Whig" which said that "the Whig party in great convention assembled, have deliberately and voluntarily, in the eyes of this great people, signed and sealed the death warrant to the principles, by which they have strongly and long professed to be governed." In the same issue it reported a "People's Convention" at Worcester, Massachusetts, at which the first version of a famous slogan was heard: "Free Soil—Free Labor—Free Speech."[53]

Reports of a similar movement were received from Ohio, at which resolutions were passed that the Whig party of that state would

51. This attack was published in July 1846. Webster had failed to oppose the war (though condemning the way in which it had been started) and his son had been recruiting volunteers in Boston.
52. To Horace Mann, 23 April 1848. Howe Papers, Houghton Library.
53. *Boston Whig*, 28 and 30 June 1848.

never consent to the further extension of slavery. Yet a speaker at this meeting expressed the conscience Whig dilemma. "I have never been anything but a Whig. I don't know how to be anything else but a Whig, and when I found that the Convention would not declare for Whig principles, I felt like asking, Where, oh! where shall I go?"

Threats of a bolt from the national party not only alienated conservatives but also divided men who had been strong against the extension of slavery. Julius Rockwell, who had made an eloquent last stand in Congress against annexation, wrote to Appleton that "the most sensible thing the Northern Whigs can do, is to support General Taylor,"[54] but Joshua Giddings, on a visit from Ohio to Lowell, spoke against the nomination while "the lords of the loom attempted to interfere" and urged support for Taylor. This was received with groans and cheers, and though Giddings thought that "the groans were stronger,"[55] it was soon clear that the Taylor men controlled the party. What, then, could a minority, however indignant or articulate, hope to accomplish? What could men who had so often argued against third parties, and the folly of voting for Liberty candidates, do when they had committed themselves in opposition to the party nominee? The answer came from an unexpected quarter, from men who had been variously regarded as keepers of the Democratic faith or the vanguard of political corruption, from the radical followers of Martin Van Buren.

54. Appleton Papers, 15 July 1848.
55. Giddings to his daughter, 20 June 1848, Julian-Giddings Papers, Library of Congress, Washington, D.C.

## Chapter 7

# RESPONSE IN THE NORTH: DEMOCRATS AND FREE SOILERS

The events of 1846 presented more threats to Democrats than to Whigs. Though united in support of the war, the conflict between romantic nationalism and the territorial extension of slavery was demonstrated by Northern support for the Wilmot Proviso. Nor could Democrats heal their differences by patriotic appeals to the country, for too many men believed that the war was unnecessary, had been launched unconstitutionally and—as hopes of quick victory receded—was not being conducted efficiently. Moreover there was strong support for the argument that territorial gains should be limited to what was strategically necessary for the defense of the existing United States.

Apart from war and the Wilmot proviso, there were other strains on Democratic loyalty which have already been discussed. The tariff of 1846 was unpopular in the Northeast, the Rivers and Harbors veto in the Northwest, and the Oregon settlement with the more ardent expansionists. To make matters worse, Polk's preference for conservatives in federal appointments had alienated many old Jacksonians. All these discontents were likely to fasten on the President's refusal to endorse the principle of the Wilmot Proviso, or even to recognize that it has a rational basis. In his diary the President expressed his incomprehension: slavery had nothing to do with the acquisition of California, and those who argued that it had could not be inspired by worthy motives.[1]

1. "The slavery question is assuming a fearful and most important aspect. . . . Slavery was one

On March 1, 1847, John A. Dix, radical Democrat from New York, delivered a carefully prepared speech which served notice on the administration and the party that support for the proviso must be taken seriously. It was nonsense, he argued, to say that prohibition of slavery in the few territories would mean "an entire exclusion of the Slaveholding States" from their share in the gains of war. Men from the Southern states had freedom to migrate provided that they did not take slavery with them, and "the free laborer of the South was surely not injured in his condition"; it was the free laborer of the North who would be wronged if he had "to toil side by side with the slave." The annexation of Texas, the acquisition of Florida, and the admission of Arkansas and Missouri had added to the Union all the territory where slavery existed, and now it was claimed that land where it had been abolished or never existed was "by virtue of the compromises of the Constitution, open to slavery." At what point then would the rights of free labor be recognized?[2]

A man who wished to win the Democratic nomination in 1848 would have to reckon with this sentiment, and the implication of the speech by Dix (and of others with similar intent) was that the Van Buren Democrats could play the two-thirds rule as well as anyone else. In the light of Southern opposition it might be too much to expect an outright endorsement of the proviso from the nominee, but at least he must promise not to veto majority decisions in Congress. The man who wished most earnestly for the nomination was Lewis Cass of Michigan who was particularly disliked by Van Buren's friends. In 1844 the delegates pledged to Cass had voted to sustain the two-thirds rule, and later refused Van Buren the votes that would have given him the nomination. Cass was therefore regarded as the natural ally of the conservative Democrats in the East, and his nomination might consolidate the victory that Polk's appointments had placed within their grasp. Nevertheless the support for Cass in the West made him a contender who could not be ignored and if it came to the test he might be preferred to Buchanan or a Southern Democrat. It therefore became important to discover his views on the proviso.

John Van Buren, the ex-President's son and not an entirely reli-

---

of the questions adjusted in the compromises of the Constitution. It has, and can have no legitimate connection with the war with Mexico, or the terms of a peace which may be concluded with that country. . . . Such an agitation is not only unwise but wicked." (Polk's *Diary*, ed. Milo M. Quaife, Monday, 4 January 1847).

2. *Congressional Globe*, 29. 2. 543.

able witness, would later claim that immediately after the events of August 8 Cass had expressed regret that the proviso had not come to the vote in the Senate for he, and every other Northern Democrat, had agreed to vote for it. Some months later (the date is not clear) John Van Buren and Jacob Brinkerhoff paid him a visit and questioned him further. In Van Buren's words,

> We found him somewhat bustling and busy in his prepara-
> tion to go out. Mr. B. led off in some casual remarks about
> the Proviso and its prospects—the bustle increased a little.
> The Senator "thought it premature,—better give it the go
> by this session—nothing to be gained by pressing it now—
> sufficient for the day is the evil thereof."

Cass then claimed that he was still for the proviso on general grounds, but John Van Buren concluded that he was looking for a way to wreck it as the price of Southern support. He had told a Southern friend that Cass was certain to vote against the proviso and if pressed would "throw in the hanging of a few northern men in addition."[3]

Sometime during 1847 Cass came to an understanding with Senator Daniel Dickinson of New York, the most prominent Democratic opponent of Van Buren in the state, and decided that the only way to outflank the proviso Democrats and secure Southern support was to make a bold denial of congressional power to prohibit slavery, while safeguarding the right of free settlers to reject it. On December 14, 1847, Dickinson introduced a resolution in the Senate that "in organizing a territorial government . . . the principle of self-government . . . and the true meaning of the Constitution ought to be observed . . . by leaving all questions concerning the domestic policy therein to the Legislatures chosen by the people thereof."[4] This was followed by a letter, written by Cass to A. O. Nicholson of Tennessee, dated December 24, 1847, and published in all the leading newspapers. He first observed that in the eighteen months since the introduction of the proviso "a great change has been going on in the public mind upon this subject—in my own as well as others; and that doubts are resolving themselves into convictions that the principle it involves should be kept out of the national legislature, and left to the people of the confederacy in their respective local governments."

3. Speech by John Van Buren at the New York Democratic Convention at Utica, February 1848. A slightly different version was given in a speech by George Rathburn.
4. *Congressional Globe,* 30. 1. 21.

The language of the Nicholson letter was equivocal. Was Cass denying the power of Congress to prohibit slavery or arguing that expediency made such action unwise? He said "I am opposed to the exercise of any jurisdiction by Congress over this matter"; but this could be read either way. It was, of course, always convenient for a presidential candidate to mean one thing in the South and another in the North, but the point was of more than theoretical significance. If Cass meant that it was unconstitutional for Congress to prohibit slavery in the territories, and if this doctrine was endorsed by the party, the door was closed upon future action. Even if the majority in the South eventually turned against the extension of slavery, it would still be impossible to prohibit it when sustained by a local majority.

Perhaps Cass wished to preserve the ambiguity, but his ally took the question further. On January 12, 1848, Dickinson, in an important speech on his resolutions, argued that strict construction of the Constitution meant that Congress could not legislate for the territories without the consent of the people. The Northwest Ordinance had been of doubtful validity, and preceded the adoption of the Constitution. The Missouri Compromise could not be taken as a precedent, because it had been "rather in the nature of a compact," and without "binding force upon any State beyond that of moral obligation." In annexing Texas Congress had agreed to prohibit slavery north of 36° 30', but this had been ignored by the new state and could not be enforced.[5] It followed that there was no true precedent for the prohibition of slavery, and one must take the question back to the Constitution, which conferred no such power upon Congress. This was startling constitutional doctrine, which denied a right that generations had believed to exist. Could one stop at that point? Senator Yulee of Alabama took the logic a step further when he moved a resolution that neither the federal government nor a territorial government had "any inherent right to exercise any legislative power . . . by which the equal right of all the citizens of the United States to acquire and enjoy any part of the common property, may be impaired or embarrassed." The resolution was not put to the vote, but the implications were clear. If Congress could not prohibit slavery, it could not delegate the power to a territorial legislature.[6]

The issue now became deeply involved in the complex politics of New York. A conservative majority controlled the state Democratic convention, but the radicals refused to accept their authority, seceded

5. *Ibid.*, 157.
6. *Ibid.*, 160.

to hold their own meeting at Herkimer, adopted a platform (written by John Van Buren) which opposed the extension of slavery, and chose a delegation to attend the National Democratic Convention. This followed the advice of the elder Van Buren who sent them an address, phrased in characteristically oblique terms but concluding that the further expansion of slavery should be opposed, that the delegation should press for recognition at the national convention, and withdraw if this was refused. They should then "disavow all connection with the nomination and recommend the selection of a State candidate . . . then take up General Taylor if he is in a state to be taken up by you, or some other person."[7] This was momentous advice from the man who had built up the most successful party organization in the country on the principle of regularity and acceptance of majority decisions. It was at this time that the radicals became known as "Barnburners" who would destroy the party edifice in order to get rid of the opposing faction.

The Democratic Convention at Baltimore tried to settle the dispute by seating both delegations and giving a half vote to each member; but this did not satisfy the Barnburners who withdrew. The convention then proceeded to nominate Cass and endorse the principles of his Nicholson letter. Everyone now looked to ex-President Van Buren and bombarded him with conflicting advice. Thomas H. Benton thought that everyone recognized that the Barnburners had been the true representatives of New York, "but separate action would brand them as schismatics." He claimed (incorrectly) to speak for Francis Blair and John A. Dix. B. F. Butler advised Van Buren not to accept nomination, but strongly favored separate action. Gideon Welles thought that the states which had remained in convention at Baltimore were bound to support the nomination, but expected New York to act alone. Francis P. Blair thought that "a general revolt" was possible, and might end "the everlasting dominion of the South in the presidency."[8]

On June 20 Martin Van Buren wrote a carefully phrased letter to the Democratic committee of New York City. He believed that it had been the intention of the makers of the Constitution to give the states exclusive control over slavery where it already existed, but "to prevent by united efforts its extension to Territories of the United States in which it did not in fact exist." The Northwest Ordinance had been as

7. Martin to John Van Buren, 3 May 1848, Van Buren Papers, Library of Congress, Washington, D. C.
8. Benton, 29 May; Butler, 29 May; Welles, 30 May; Blair, 16 June, Van Buren Papers.

much a Southern as a Northern measure; the Democratic nomination meant the denial of a power "most clearly and fully granted to Congress by the Constitution." In May he had said that he would be a candidate only if his name were "brought forward by the South in good faith." In June he did not say that he would accept nomination, but pointedly omitted all reference to refusal and the letter was read to mean that he was now available. The Radical Democratic Convention, called into session once more, read it in this light and nominated the elder Van Buren for the Presidency.

What was the nature of the revolt that had occurred? It might be seen as a desperate bid by Van Buren's followers to recover their former position in the party. It was certainly a protest against the supposed Southern assumption that others would always yield. As Francis Blair wrote in his letter of June 5, "We know what course South Carolinians or Virginians, with all their love of patronage, would take were either of *their* States excluded." It was also a reaction against conservative attempts to take over leadership in the Northern states with help from the national administration. Could it then be argued that resistance to the extension of slavery was a pretext rather than a cause? Or did the radical Democrats believe that vital principles were at stake, which could be maintained only by breaking with the party that had nurtured them?

It is possible to give affirmative answers to all these questions without becoming inconsistent. The Barnburners were a faction, and from the moment of Polk's nomination they had been a disappointed faction. Like the conscience Whigs they had not wished to disrupt their party but to control it and had failed to do so; but they were also a faction with a distinct tradition and a fixed belief that the conservatives had never represented the true interests of the party which they had always been ready to betray. As C. C. Cambreleng told Joel R. Poinsett in November 1845, "In this state . . . we have our differences—the Conservatives who betrayed us and became Bank men in 1837 and the staunch Democracy."[9] Not all the Barnburners had been Loco-Focos, but most of them were ready to acknowledge belief in equal rights. They could trace their origins as a self-conscious political group to the crises of Jackson's second administration, and their view of politics formed a coherent whole.

At the Herkimer Convention in October 1847 John Van Buren had outlined the essential points. "What is the great feature of the age in which we live? It is freedom and progress. The shackles in which

9. Poinsett Papers, Historical Society of Pennsylvania, Philadelphia, Pa., 25 November 1845.

commerce has been bound are falling before the enlightened reason of the day. . . . Freedom of trade, of thought, of action, and of mind were stamped in characters of living light upon the face of the civilized globe." Opposition to the extension of slavery fitted with ease into this syndrome; so did the conviction that the dominance of Southern slaveowners was detrimental to the true interests of the party. "We have followed these Southern lights to the verge of the Constitution," said John Van Buren. "If we pursue these Will o' Wisps further we are in danger of being mired and irrecoverably lost. It would be better to be guided by the light of civilization, by the light of humanity, the light of freedom; in a word . . . by the Northern lights."[10]

The address of the Barnburner Utica Convention in February 1848 took further this claim to represent the true tradition of the Democratic party. "By a fortunate accident, or a special providence, the assumption by the slaveholders of a new and indefensible position on the subject of slavery, has enabled Democrats to stand forth in their natural and true attitude, as the champions of human freedom." The conservative Democrats had abandoned the party and "the Democratic party of New York moves on without the fetters upon its actions that selfish and sinister influences have hitherto imposed." The "just and virtuous and true" were invited to rally round a standard on which was inscribed "Free Trade, Free Labor, Free Speech, and Free Men."

In their own view the radical Democrats took up the best traditions of the party, and saw themselves not as a faction but as the architects of a new movement which drew strength from rediscovered principles. In private letters to Martin Van Buren, Benjamin F. Butler argued in similar vein. There was no hope of immediate success, but "if we *start* right in this forlorn hope, we shall form a nucleus for the organization of a northern *Democratic* party which, within the next four years, will control the votes of the Northern States, and bring the despots and ingrates of the South and their obsequious satellites of the North, to their senses, and thus render a great and lasting service to the country and the world." The prohibition of slavery in free territories was "the greatest question of the day." As soon as the war ended, it would be the only question. "It will eventually carry or revolutionize the country, and fifty years hence those who took a firm stand for the prohibition will be regarded as the greatest of public benefactors."[11]

10. Oliver Cromwell Gardiner, *The Great Issues* (New York, 1848), 63.
11. Van Buren Papers, 29 and 30 May 1848.

\* \* \*

Meanwhile there had been stirrings in Ohio where both parties divided into complex factions. The Liberty party was strong in some districts, and had in Salmon P. Chase a leader of outstanding ability and ambition. Chase was by upbringing a Democrat, and careful to keep on good terms with men prominent in that party, while the most widely known anti-slavery leader, Joshua Giddings, was a lifelong Whig. John McLean, associate justice of the Supreme Court, with his political base at Cincinnati, might unite the various factions opposed to the extension of slavery by pursuing his claim that slavery could not exist in the territories without positive national law to establish it.

If the Western Reserve, dominated by Giddings, was strongly anti-slavery, and if Chase led a sizeable Liberty party around Cincinnati, there was also intense dislike of Negroes in the state. For years the state had had "Black Laws" on its statute book. These laws required black residents to lodge bonds for good conduct, excluded them from public schools, and made it illegal for them to act as witnesses in cases where whites were a party. Indirectly, however, anti-Negro sentiment tended to strengthen Free Soil in unexpected ways. If whites in Ohio disliked the presence of blacks, they would not welcome the prospect of filling the West with slaves. On the other hand, the black laws gave anti-slavery men a limited yet attainable object; they did not have to battle against slavery in the abstract but against injustice on their doorstep.

There survives an extended correspondence between Salmon P. Chase and Joshua Giddings on the strategy of anti-slavery politics.[12] Giddings clung for years to the belief that the Northern Whigs would unite in opposition to slavery. In 1842 he wrote that he entertained "no doubt that the Whigs of the North will stand, indeed they must stand upon the protection of Northern rights." In October 1845 he wrote to Chase that the difference between them was that he thought it far easier "to bring the present parties to support anti-slavery measures, than it will be to form a new party on that ground." Of the two parties the Whig had shown itself more receptive to anti-slavery arguments and was able to cooperate with abolitionists; but Democrats would not "permit their partisans to act for liberty."[13]

The outbreak of the Mexican War brought Giddings a step

12. Chase Papers, Historical Society of Pennsylvania, Philadelphia, Pa.

13. *Ibid.*, 19 February 1845. Morris, an anti-slavery Democrat, had been refused renomination, but Giddings himself had been thrice reelected. In 1842 the censure on Giddings had been supported by almost all Democrats but by only a minority of Whigs.

nearer separate action. He wrote to Chase that the people were in advance of the politicians, and a "large portion of all parties was ready to throw off the Slave Power." He proposed that Chase and himself, with an equal number of friends from their respective parties, should meet "for the purpose of consulting upon the best manner of uniting the whole anti-slavery strength of Ohio." But Giddings was not yet willing to make a break with his party and suggested that the conference should exclude the tariff, bank, or other measures on which parties divided, while concentrating on repeal of the black laws in the state, the maintenance of state rights against Virginia and Kentucky, and a law making it a penal offence to assist in the recovery of fugitive slaves. Nationally the alliance would demand the repeal of all federal laws upholding slavery, including its recognition in the District of Columbia and the Fugitive Slave law of 1793, the prohibition of the internal slave trade, and a "solemn determination to unite with no further slave holding territory or State." Finally they would pledge themselves to support no one for office who did not accept these proposals.

On September 18 Giddings still clung to the idea that a united front against slavery could be achieved without commitment on other issues, and favored a National Convention; but on October 30 he wrote that nothing separated Whig and Liberty men "except the name and spirit of party." In recent speeches he had made a point of complimenting Wilmot and John P. Hale (the anti-slavery Democrat from New Hampshire). "The time has come," he declared, "when party claims must sit loosely upon us." In reply to an argument by Chase that neither old party could act against slavery because both contained slaveowners, Giddings pointed out that the Wilmot proviso had been carried in the House by men of both parties. "As the anti-slavery sentiment increases, northern men of both parties will unite in support of our rights and the rights of mankind." In other words Giddings believed that a Northern union against slavery was still compatible with national party organizations to support other traditional policies. But events were beginning to overtake him, and on November 23, 1846, he wrote, "Now is the time to form a Union when no great political excitement prevails." Long-standing controversies over banks and tariffs had been made irrelevant by the war and prosperity.

In February 1848 Giddings cut through his dual loyalty. In an important speech in Congress he announced that the tariff, internal improvements, banks, and public land were no longer thought of. "The members here are divided into the propagandists of slavery and the advocates of freedom. The old party lines are indistinct and uncertain. . . . New political associations are forming, and have been for years, and the trammels of party are often broken and their influence disregarded." He had been ready to accept Clay's proposition that Congress had no power either to abolish or establish slavery, and that it depended exclusively upon state law; but this was no longer the doctrine of leading Whigs who dominated the congressional party.[14]

In April Giddings still refused to believe that the Whigs could nominate a man not opposed to the extension of slavery. For himself he could support no other, and stood "pledged before the world on that point." If Taylor were nominated, he would not himself take the step of calling a convention because such a move "should be of the people and emanate from them."[15] As someone would have to take the initiative, this meant that Giddings would, for the moment, take a back seat and allow others to make the running; but the knowledge that he would support a separate movement must have influenced events. Immediately after Taylor's nomination the Ohio delegation forced the issue in the convention. First Tilden of Ohio moved a resolution declaring that Congress had power to prohibit slavery in the territories and should use it; when this was laid on the table, John A. Bingham of Ohio moved that the nomination of Taylor should be supported on condition that he adhered to Whig principles, defined as no extension of slavery, no acquisition of foreign territory by conquest, protection for industry, and opposition to executive patronage. This was ruled out of order.[16]

Delegates from Massachusetts now took up the challenge. Charles Allen declared that the free states would not submit, and that the Whig party was "here and this day dissolved." Henry Wilson announced that he would not be bound by the convention proceedings, and added "We have nominated a candidate who has said to the nation that he will not be bound by the principles of any party. Sir, I will go home; and, so help me God, I will do all that I can to defeat the election of that candidate."[17] In the evening, after the convention had disbanded, Wilson called a meeting of those opposed to the nomination. There were tactical doubts, because some present wished for immediate action to form a new party, while others wished first to hold meetings in their states. The difficulty was resolved when it

14. *Congressional Globe,* 30. 1. 394, 28 February 1848.
15. Chase Papers, 7 April.
16. Henry Wilson, *Rise and Fall of the Slave Power in America* (Boston, 1876), II: 135.
17. *Ibid.*, 136.

became known that a meeting was already called in Ohio. On Wilson's motion a committee of three was appointed to make preparations for a national convention at Buffalo early in August, but one of its members, John C. Vaughan, was to attend the Ohio meeting and persuade it to issue the convention call.[18]

The Ohio meeting was held on June 20 and 21. Opposition to the extension of slavery married easily with other grievances, and a resolution declared that "an adequate system of River and Harbor improvements" had been thwarted because of "the ascendancy of the slave power in the National Councils." The principal business was to issue a call for a national convention of all opposed to both Cass and Taylor to meet at Buffalo on August 9. The address proclaimed that, "A great crisis has arrived in the history of our country. The events of the next few months must decide whether the American people are in truth a Free People, or the voluntary bondsmen of the slaveholding oligarchy."[19]

News of the call had been anticipated in Massachusetts by antislavery Whigs, with a meeting already summoned to meet at Worcester on June 28. When it assembled the conscience Whigs of Boston were strongly represented. Charles Francis Adams spoke and so, with great effect, did Charles Sumner. There were also two visitors from Ohio: Lewis D. Campbell and Joshua Giddings, who was now everywhere active in the new cause. The convention hoped to hear from Daniel Webster, but could get no more than an authorized statement from one of his friends that the great man was not committed to support Taylor and was opposed in principle to the extension of slavery. Nevertheless the conscience Whigs had now found allies among men of both parties in the country districts and small towns and in the key state of Ohio. They no longer battled alone against the Boston conservatives, and Charles Francis Adams agreed to head a state committee of fourteen to attend the Buffalo convention with a delegation of two Whigs, two Democrats, and two from the Liberty party.

*     *     *

On July 16 Charles Francis Adams wrote a letter to Martin Van Buren which was to be of high significance for the future. He said that he was

18. *Ibid.*, 142–43.
19. *Address of the Free Territory Convention of Ohio* (Columbus, 1848).

convinced that "nothing but union among those who dread the effect of the policy prevailing in both parties at Washington can now avail to counteract it." How was such a union to be achieved? He thought that Van Buren's arguments against immediate annexation in 1844 and against the extension of slavery in 1848 provided "the best point of union in the country."[20]

On what assumptions did men of different parties rest the case for joint action? They had been brought up to believe that their differences were based on a fundamental conflict of ideas and interests; now a single issue brought them together. Though some had long records of anti-slavery utterance, the majority had accepted the conventional wisdom that slavery ought to be kept out of politics. Both Whigs and Democrats had denounced third parties and deplored division on sectional lines. An important clue to their thinking is found in a speech in Congress by John Gorham Palfrey before separate action had become a reality. Thomas Clingman of North Carolina was a moderate Whig, one of the few Southerners to vote against the gag, and a speech, in which he warned against making slavery a political issue and dividing parties on sectional lines, had attracted considerable attention. Late in January 1848 Palfrey had his first opportunity to make a major speech, and chose to present it as a reply to Clingman. Slavery could not be kept out of politics, he declared: "It is the great political question of the country, and has been since the beginning of this century. . . . It is the question which underlies all other great questions and determines their solution." If slavery could not be excluded from controversy, and if it had this fundamental character, opposition to its extension provided a large enough platform for men of widely differing views on other questions. The danger to the Union was illusory because the issue was not between North and South, "but between many millions of non-slaveholding Americans . . . and the very few thousand of their fellow citizens who hold slaves." Slaveowners talked of disunion, but they would be wise not to air these views among their neighbors at home. "If they insist that the Union and Slavery cannot live together they must be taken at their word, but it is THE UNION THAT MUST STAND."[21]

It followed that the Free Soil movement was necessary, need not be sectional, would soon command a majority in the South, and need

---

20. Van Buren Papers, 16 July 1848.
21. For Clingman's speech see *Congressional Globe*, 30. 1. Appendix 41ff.; Palfrey's speech (delivered 26 January) is also in the Appendix (133ff.).

not endanger the Union. It was not a temporary revolt against party leaders but a long-term movement against the slave power. The men who cooperated now would find that their other differences could be resolved, since it was the political power of slavery which had set class against class and section against section. On these assumptions the Free Soilers based their plea for action.

\*        \*        \*

The emergence of Free Soil posed difficult questions for anti-slavery Whigs. Before the nomination Horace Greeley had supported Clay, but after an interval and with bad grace announced his support for Taylor. He may have been persuaded by Seward and Thurlow Weed, though he was no longer in close alliance with them. Seward's views are of particular interest in the light of his subsequent career. His commitment against slavery was real, but he clung to the belief that, in a united Whig party, the Northern majority could gradually lead Southern colleagues to accept the end of slavery as inevitable. A few days after the first appearance of the Wilmot proviso he wrote to John McLean that he hoped to persuade the Whig party "to adopt the noble and true principles of Emancipation to be carried into effect in a conservative and just, not fanatical or violent, manner." He thought that anti-slavery gestures among the Northern Democrats were intended to divide the Whigs rather than to achieve results, and in all his policies his principal aim was to destroy "the very roots, trunk and branches of the New York demagogues." He had already "won the support of nearly the whole Whig party in the State, and yet no ultraism on any subject marks its progress."[22]

The Barnburner revolt had to be taken more seriously, but Seward held firmly to his belief that Free Soil would damage the anti-slavery cause. He also had a personal interest because Whig victory would probably bring him election to the Senate. On August 26, 1848, soon after the Buffalo convention, when many Whigs were dismayed by Taylor's apparent lack of understanding of Northern views, Seward agreed that the question of slavery had "underlaid all national politics," and said that for more than ten years he had looked "to the day of ripening of Conscience on the subject of that evil." He would have preferred to see a Whig candidate "representing the prin-

22. Seward Papers, Rush-Rhees Library, University of Rochester, Rochester, N. Y., 12 August 1846.

ciple of Emancipation," but there were two things he could never do: the first was to share responsibility for any concession to slavery, and the second "to oppose a candidate of the National Whig party."[23]

Seward campaigned actively for Taylor in New York and Ohio, and in his own state there were few defections from the Whigs. In Kentucky an ardent anti-slavery man, Cassius M. Clay, approved Seward's course. "Whatever General Taylor may do the battle among Northern Whigs was fought on anti-slavery ground. As the fountain of power is there—there is meaning in it for the future." Another correspondent, writing from St. Louis, thought that in a future contest, with slavery as a major issue, Missouri and Kentucky would "go with the North."[24]

Horace Greeley also left a record of his doubts and eventual decision to stand by the party ticket. In April 1848 he told his friend Schuyler Colfax that "we cannot with any decency support General Taylor."[25] He remained faithful to Henry Clay until his chance of nomination finally disappeared, and then withheld endorsement of Taylor. When conscience Whigs joined Free Soil Greeley was sorely tempted, not only because his heart was with the new movement but also because he believed that the support of his influential newspaper might have been decisive in the North. Free Soil was "the only live party around us," and the *Tribune* might have been its oracle. After much hesitation he announced grudging support for Taylor because he came to believe that without it Cass would carry New York and perhaps the national election. To Colfax he explained that,

> Party fidelity—or rather fidelity to men I love who still cling to the putrid corpse of the party butchered at Philadelphia —has withheld me. . . . I could shake down the whole rotten fabric by a bugle blast, yet will not sound it, because some good men I love would be crushed beneath its ruins.

A distinguished Whig who had difficulty in choosing his course of action was Horace Mann of Massachusetts. In 1848 he had already established a national reputation as an educational reformer, and when John Quincy Adams died Mann was invited to accept nomination from Whigs in his district. He had some doubts about embarking on a

23. To Edward J. Fowle. Seward Papers.
24. *Ibid.*, 22 December 1848; 15 November 1848.
25. All quotations in this paragraph from Greeley-Colfax Letters, New York Public Library.

political career and his friend Samuel Gridley Howe told Palfrey that Mann was "in great tribulation lest he should be elected, and be obliged to give up the cause of little children for the cause of 'children of a larger growth.'" Mann promised to follow in his distinguished predecessor's footsteps as a resolute opponent of the slave power, and was urged by Howe to place himself at the head of the movement against slavery. "You can be the man, the leader, the hero of this coming struggle for freedom and the right."[26]

In Congress Mann was appalled by the tone and fury of Southern oratory. "We have had threats, insults, the invocation of mob-rule and lynch law."[27] Nevertheless he still acted with caution. His final report as educational commissioner had yet to be received by the Massachusetts legislature, and he was extremely anxious that it should not fall a victim to conservative vengeance against conscience Whigs. By the end of June the report was through the legislature, and he felt free to speak, and with telling rhetoric pointed out that Southerners had long blamed the British for bringing slavery to America, but now insisted upon their right to carry slavery into lands yet free. "Here is the test. Let not southern men, who would now force slavery upon new regions, ever deny that their slavery at home is a chosen, voluntary, beloved crime."[28]

Yet Horace Mann could not align himself with Free Soil. He was a Whig from a strong Whig district—elected with conservative support—and judged it neither honorable nor expedient to cut adrift from his party. In Congress he attended the Whig caucus, and even cast his vote for Robert C. Winthrop in the speakership election of December 1849.

In Congress a group of Senators, mostly upper South Whigs and Western Democrats, were desperately anxious to get the territorial issue settled before the campaign began. This attempt at compromise carries the name of John M. Clayton of Delaware, prominent among the Taylor forces, but owed as much to Jesse Bright, Democrat of Indiana. The Senate was at a deadlock over a bill to organize Oregon Territory. The House bill recognized the prohibition of slavery by an unauthorized local legislature, while Southern Senators led by Calhoun maintained that there must be no restriction. Clayton moved for the appointment of a committee, four from the North and four from

26. Howe to Mann, 28 April 1848, Palfrey Papers, Houghton Library, Harvard University.
27. Mann to Howe, 21 April 1848 (quoted in Jonathan Messoli, *Horace Mann* [New York, 1972], 462). Massachusetts Historical Society, Boston, Mass.
28. 30 June 1848, quoted in Messoli, *Horace Mann,* 462.

the South, to be chosen by ballot, and on a motion by Bright its terms of reference were enlarged to include California and New Mexico.[29]

The committee proposed the organization of Oregon with a temporary prohibition of slavery until a duly constituted legislature could act. California and New Mexico would be organized without power to act on slavery, leaving the courts to decide whether the Constitution did or did not protect slave property. The practical consequence would be that "the country would be slave-holding only where, by the laws of Nature, slave labor was effective, and free labor could not maintain itself." Clayton claimed that this resolved "the *whole* question between North and South into a constitutional and judicial question."

The proposed compromise was exceedingly unpopular with Northern Whigs. Thurlow Weed believed that Taylor would lose New York if it passed.[30] Nevertheless it passed the Senate on July 27 after a session lasting twenty-one hours, was promptly laid on the table in the House, and only a two-thirds vote could revive it. An Oregon Bill passed the House, with prohibition of slavery, 129–71, and was accepted by the Senate with the addition of a clause stating that prohibition was justified because all the territory lay north of 36°30′. This was unacceptable to the House majority because it implied that slavery might be legal south of that line, and the amendment was struck out. In this form it finally passed the Senate at 9 A.M. on Sunday, August 13. It was signed by Polk with an explanation that he did so because the territory lay far north of 36°30′, thus giving the last word to proponents of this view.

Northern Democrats could take comfort from this result, because it demonstrated that the Cass doctrine worked and slavery could be excluded by the men on the spot. Northern Whigs were gratified by the failure of the compromise because it left intact the theory that slavery could not be established without positive federal legislation to sustain it. Free Soilers were deprived of an issue, as slavery had not yet been legalized in any of the newly acquired lands. Nevertheless the Clayton measure had attracted sufficient support from North and South to encourage the belief that it might be easier to find a compromise formula than to face the troublesome question of slavery's future in the nation.

Despite the schism which rent the Northern Democrats it was

29. *Congressional Globe*, 30. 1, 927, 950, 12 July 1848. The committee members were Clayton (Del.), Bright (Ind.), Calhoun (S. C.), Clarke (R. I.), Atchison (Mo.), Phelps (Vt.), Dickinson (N. Y.), and Underwood (Ky.).

30. Weed to Seward, 29 July 1840, Seward Papers.

the national Whig party which suffered most in the crisis. Communication between Whigs at the center was now sadly impaired, and cooperation became increasingly difficult. The qualified agreement, which had been apparent as late as the annexation debates, was now at an end and the harmony of 1841 was entirely a thing of the past. The disarray was not the result of temporary difficulties but of profound differences over the future character of the nation.

*    *    *

The Liberty party had nominated John P. Hale, the anti-slavery Senator from New Hampshire, but in a year of political fragmentation the ranks of even so small a party were broken. The major question was whether it should remain a party of one aim and one idea or broaden its appeal. Lewis Tappan explained to John Scobie, secretary of the British Anti-Slavery Society that,

> Although efforts were made by Mr. Gerritt Smith and those especially sympathising with him and his peculiar views, to engraft upon the Liberty party other branches of political and moral reform yet a very large majority decided to adhere to the original principle of Association and adopt no new text.[31]

In June 1848 the followers of Gerritt Smith, styling themselves the true National Liberty party, met in convention at Buffalo, denounced the nomination of Hale "who holds not a single one of the distinctive principles of that party," and condemned his willingness to combine with others on the Wilmot proviso basis. Colored citizens were urged to leave pro-slavery churches, and an address to the people of the United States repudiated "a mere Wilmot Proviso party" and adopted the most radical economic and social program ever yet published.[32] They attacked taxes on articles of common consumption, land monopoly, protective tariffs, federal construction of roads and canals, advocated a ten-hour labor law and a direct graduated tax as the principal source of government revenue. Their program for tax reform was based on "the novel and startling doctrine that . . . taxes should be imposed upon . . . subjects in proportion to their ability to pay, . . . [and] either they, who have barely the means of subsistence should

---

31. Letter dated 14 November 1848. Abel and Frank Klingberg, eds., *A Sidelight on Anglo-American Relations, 1839–1858 . . . the Correspondence of Lewis Tappan and others with the British and Foreign Anti-Slavery Society* (Lancaster, Pa., 1927), 228.

32. *Proceedings of the National Liberty Convention, at Buffalo, June 14 and 15, 1848* (Utica, 1848).

be exempted from taxation, or they, who have more, should be assessed with a higher rate of taxation." These planks in the National Liberty party platform may be merely of academic interest (for there was no hope that any major party would adopt them), but they were prophetic in linking abolition with a wide range of domestic reforms. Anti-slavery would no longer stand in isolation, but become the nucleus for a cluster of proposals for improvement. Anti-slavery had ceased to be a lonely crusade and was becoming an ideology.

The constitutional theory of the National Liberty party owed something to Lysander Spooner, but diluted his rationalism with Christian philosophy. Civil government had been "a conspiracy of the few against the many." Its true funciton was to protect rights given by God, and it had no authority to destroy some rights while protecting others. Slavery was the most glaring example of this fallacy, and its abolition was a natural consequence of the duty to protect all rights. The United States Constitution imposed obligation on both federal and state governments, and if the latter failed to act, the former must do so. This theory was likely to attract few converts in 1848, but contained the seed of the Fourteenth Amendment, and therefore deserves its place in history.

\*       \*       \*

Not all the Free Soil allies were happy with the prospect of Van Buren as their nominee. In Ohio many considered that Supreme Court justice John McLean would be the ideal candidate, and in June the judge received a letter from "some citizens of Cleveland" which stated that

> The recent triumph of the slave power at the Baltimore and Philadelphia conventions has produced great dissatisfaction, and disaffection in the two great political parties of the day. . . . Under these circumstances enquiry is made all over the land for some candidate for President who can unite the full strength of the opposition and concentrate the votes of those who are opposed to the further extension of slavery and of the slave power.[33]

Joshua Giddings (who may have inspired this letter) assured McLean that the new movement "will not vanish after a short display. The

33. McLean Papers, Library of Congress, Washington, D.C., undated but probably late June 1848.

feeling in favor of free territory has taken a strong hold of the public mind. The feelings of the masses in all the free states are enlisted." If they did not succeed in this election they would surely do so at the next, but the fairest start would be made with nominees who could rally the diverse elements opposed to slavery in the various states. Giddings then asked if he could, at his discretion, nominate McLean for President or Vice-President.[34]

McLean was in a dilemma. He had wanted to be President for several years, but he would not take the vice-presidency. Moreover, the debates in Congress indicated that the question of slavery in the territories might reach the Supreme Court, of which he was a member. Could he therefore commit himself publicly to the Free Soil platform, particularly when he believed that the extension of slavery could be prevented without legislation? The most that he would say to his supporters was that if Van Buren withdrew, and if the nomination for President were made unanimously, he might feel obliged to accept. Under no circumstances would he accept nomination for the vice-presidency. He adhered to this despite an earnest plea from Salmon P. Chase that "if any man can save the Union, settle the national policy as to slavery, upon the basis of Jefferson and the Fathers of the Republic, without alienating any part of the Union, you can do it."

McLean was respected and widely regarded as the ablest member of the Supreme Court.[35] He had a personal following in the West, especially among Whigs who had never been satisfied with Clay's leadership. He might have been the Whig candidate if the Clay and Taylor forces had deadlocked, and if Ohio had given him solid support. All this made him attractive to men who were beginning to think seriously of a permanent Free Soil organization. There were already firm bases in New York and the Western Reserve; Massachusetts, Vermont, and perhaps New Hampshire were hopeful. McLean would bring in many from southern Ohio and everywhere a top dressing of more conservative Whigs. Five or six states, with a strong showing in some others, would indeed be a dramatic success for a brand-new party fighting on an issue which both major parties were trying to evade.[36] In 1841 Tyler's hope of wresting the Whig party away from Clay had been thwarted by McLean's refusal to serve in his

34. *Ibid.*, 13 July.

35. In an article on the influence of the West, published in the *U.S. Magazine and Democratic Review* in May 1848 (XXII: 405), the writer observed that though there were nine judges of the Supreme Court, one dwarfed the others; between McLean and the others "there is such a contrast that he seems to be the only judge." Admirers of Chief Justice Taney did not comment.

36. One observer believed that his nomination "would have changed the complexion of the

cabinet; in 1848 the caution of this distinguished judge (who has left little positive impression on history) did something to retard the growth of the new national alliance which would eventually blossom as the Republican party. In another light, however, the pressure on him was the measure of Free Soil weakness. The new party was a genuine response to popular feeling but lacked organization, had no ready-made alliance of interests and no firm commitments (outside New York) from professional politicians. If these essentials had existed there would have been no lack of aspirants and no necessity to press a reluctant candidate to stand for a nomination that he did not want.

As it was Van Buren was the only available candidate, for he alone could detach enough Democratic votes to prevent the success of Cass. Moreover, he would bring with him a number of skilled political leaders, and some mass support in key states. Even a strong anti-slavery man, H. B. Stanton, thought that whatever judgment one might make on Van Buren's past, his nomination would be the shrewdest blow against slavery. "The main prop of the slave power has been the Northern Democracy and he is *the* man to shiver that in pieces and forever."[37]

Like other and later movements of protest Free Soil was stronger in oratory, literary outpouring, and appeal to a highly educated minority than among the voters. The middle-class and intellectual character of the movement assured an impressive representation at Buffalo on August 9; The convention was said to be the largest gathering ever assembled on American soil, included representatives from all the free states, and covered a spectrum of opinion from old Clay Whigs—who could not accept Taylor—to abolitionists of the purest breed—who had never before entered into any political association. Martin Van Buren was nominated, and with him Charles Francis Adams of Massachusetts. The Liberty party withdrew Hale's name and agreed to support the Free Soil nominees. Van Buren's letter of acceptance was typically prolix and hedged with qualifications, but encased in a paragraph on the sixth page was the crucial sentence: "We are threatened with a subversion of the spirit and character of our government through the successful encroachments of the slave power."

---

canvass very materially. It would have settled New York, Ohio, and three of the New England States, and thus thrown the election into the House. What would have happened there it is useless now to speculate upon." (James E. Harvey, McLean Papers, 30 August 1848).

37. McLean Papers, 28 July.

*        *        *

The Free Soil party carried no states; and New York and Massachusetts accounted for over half its votes. Understandable disappointment was felt by those who had been so enthusiastic in August, yet an analysis of the votes could do something to restore confidence in the future. In seven states the Free Soil vote exceeded the margin by which the state was won.

|  | Winning Party | Majority (Nearest 1,000) | Free Soil Vote |
|---|---|---|---|
| *Massachusetts* | Whig | 26,000 | 38,000 |
| *New York* | Whig | 74,000 | 120,519 |
| *Vermont* | Whig | 12,000 | 13,857 |
| *Ohio* | Democrat | 16,000 | 35,494 |
| *Indiana* | Democrat | 5,000 | 8,100 |
| *Illinois* | Democrat | 3,000 | 15,157 |
| *Maine* | Democrat | 5,000 | 12,157 |

There were many abstentions but it is impossible to decide how many were deliberate gestures of disapproval or were caused by confusion or apathy. In Pennsylvania there was a high turnout, with the Whigs increasing their 1844 vote by over 24,000 and the Democrats by little more than 5,000. Free Soil got 11,000 which was 8,000 more than the Liberty party in 1844. A fair guess is that the Democrats lost heavily to Free Soil (it was Wilmot's home state), but even more to the Whigs who gained from the unpopularity of the 1846 tariff. In the whole of the Northeast and Mid-Atlantic region the Democrats had 12,000 more votes than the Whigs in 1844, but even if the whole Free Soil vote had gone to the Democrats they would still have been short of the Whig total. In this region the Whig victory was comparable to that of 1840.

In Ohio the Free Soil intervention seems to have damaged the Whigs more than the Democrats. "We are beaten by our friends, and not by our old enemies," wrote an Ohio Whig, but he hoped that Taylor's victory would open a new chapter in Whig ascendancy. "We shall have no annexations, no slavery extensions, no wars or rumors of wars, and no experiments upon the currency or the labor of the country excepting to put its rights in *status quo*."[38] Yet the Whigs had most reason to be apprehensive, for the loss of Ohio showed how vulnerable they were to the Free Soil attack. Indeed, Seward's Ohio correspondents believed that only his speaking tour in the state, expressing his opposition to the extension of slavery, had headed off more spectacular Free Soil advances. As it was, the Whigs had lost counties of the Northeast to Free Soil which they never regained.

Despite the difficulties of political analysis, many experienced observers believed that something positive had been achieved. This belief was summarized by Francis P. Blair when he wrote to Martin Van Buren:

> Our forlorn hope has accomplished all that was wished and more than we had any right to expect for the Free Soil party. Every Cass and Taylor man in the North were [*sic*] compelled to give an adhesion for their chiefs, to the principle of no new Territory to be annexed to our Africa.[39]

The Taylor headquarters in New York were illuminated with a collossal figure of the general bearing the watchword "No extension of slavery," and Whig leaflets distributed to voters bore the same slogan. It was said that Cass supporters were equally ready to proclaim "No more slave States." Blair believed that if these commitments were now repudiated, the Free Soil party would immediately increase in strength to "shake from their lofty pedestals those who gained them by hollow professions."[40]

Another of Van Buren's correspondents noted the absence of recriminations after the election and attributed this to a general confidence that there would be no more slave territory.

> The territorial question—so far as regards the extension of slavery—is certainly settled. . . . There will be no compromise either legislative or through the medium of the Judiciary, by which slavery will be permitted to put its foot there.[41]

Cassius Marcellus Clay, the flamboyant Kentucky Whig turned abolitionist, wrote that "whatever General Taylor may do, the battle

38. John W. Allen to Seward, 13 November 1848, Seward Papers.
39. Van Buren Papers, 30 November 1848.
40. *Ibid*.
41. *Ibid.*, 30 December. H. D. Gilpin.

among Northern Whigs was fought on anti-slavery *ground*," and drew the conclusion that "as the fountain of power is there—there is meaning in it for the future."[42] Two months later the veteran abolitionist Lewis Tappan wrote to Joseph Sturge in England,

> Were you here you would be astonished to see the prevalence of anti-slavery principles. Although the number of those who think slavery is, under all circumstances, wrong, does not rapidly increase, yet . . . hundreds and thousands of newspapers, throughout the country, now contain facts, arguments etc. against the extension of slavery, and very many of them against slavery itself. The moment *extension* is stopped the questions whether slavery shall *exist* will be discussed with new vigor.[43]

Cassius M. Clay wrote that even in Kentucky the cause of emancipation was advancing, and "nearly all the presses are open to discussion." He contrasted the situation with that three years earlier when his own anti-slavery newspaper had been attacked by a mob with the connivance of authority. "If we do not win now, we will know and feel our own strength and enter anew on the great battlefield for life or victory. . . . I trust that we shall year by year form 'a more perfect Union' in which there is strength and that without a sacrifice of independence and individuality on the part of any—all may pull more and more together."[44]

When men are convinced that they have embarked upon a great moral cause and that victory is at hand, there are dangers ahead if their drive is suddenly checked. With all its political fumbling the Free Soil movement had roused hope, enthusiasm, and confidence; moreover protest against the expansion of slavery was on the way to becoming a symbol for the aspirations of a dynamic and developing society. From the chair of the Buffalo convention Charles Francis Adams had proclaimed "I regard the Wilmot Proviso as covering a great deal more ground than you may at first imagine. I regard the Wilmot Proviso as, in substance, struggle between right and wrong."[45] Behind this conviction, shared by so many throughout the North, lay the Puritan

---

42. Seward Papers, 22 December 1848.
43. To J. Sturge, 20 February 1849, Tappan Papers, Library of Congress, Washington, D.C.
44. Clay to Seward, 22 December 1848, Seward Papers.
45. Oliver Dyer, *Phonographic Report of the Proceedings of the National Free Soil Convention* (Buffalo, 1848).

heritage and the great tide of intellectual and romantic revolt which had already caused much stirring in Europe.

Thus the events of 1848 mark a turning point in the political status of slavery. The controversies of the year had revealed the extent to which Northernmen were agreed that slavery was sick and should not be revived by the promise of new land. Even the *Democratic Review*, now bitterly opposed to Van Buren, affirmed that slavery was "an evil whose lamentable effects are to blight and wither everything with which it comes in contact," and argued that slaveowners would themselves yield to intellectual and economic forces without the intervention of Congress. A significant article in the same magazine declared that ninety-nine out of every hundred thinking men in the Union were anxious to get rid of slavery, and that "the landholders and citizens of the South are doubly anxious to discover some means by which the evil may be removed from their doors, because it is felt to be an annually increasing burden upon their resources."[46]

The *Democratic Review* estimated that the annual product of a slave on a cotton plantation was four bales of 400 lbs. each and the cost of his food, clothing, housing, and medical care about $30. The average price in New York was $22.50 a bale, and out of this the planter had to find bagging, rope, machinery, and overseer's wages. So though a return of over $90 on an outlay of $30 might look high, the overhead could not be less than $50, and freight, insurance, and commission had still to be paid. Many slaves had been bought on borrowed money at 8 percent, and planters had to carry the cost of the old and infirm. There was thus no economic incentive to keep slavery, let alone extend it, and many planters were driven to dispose of old and infirm slaves by nominal sales to a trader, who then took them to free states and set them at liberty. The real cause for the expansion of slavery had been cheap money in the early 'thirties when large sums had been borrowed at low rates in London and the North. States had guaranteed bonds at 6 percent and with this capital banks had advanced large mortgages to planters. Something like $200 million of foreign capital had financed the expansion of slavery, and Southerners had been laboring under the burden of debt ever since. Where alternatives offered, as in the upper South, they had escaped from the chains of unprofitable agriculture and reduced the slave population of Delaware, Maryland, Virginia, and the District of Columbia by over 26,000. From this it might follow that prosperity and emancipation

46. *Democratic Review* XXXIII (September 1848): 219.

went hand in hand, and that as planters paid off their debts (secured by land and slaves) they would abandon an unprofitable labor system.[47] The econometrics were dubious but helped to convince Northern Democrats that the Wilmot proviso was unnecessary, and might even prolong bondage by weakening demand for redundant slaves and depriving them of the chance of freedom by the action of the people in the territories. "The remedy for the evils which now threaten us is for the Democratic party as one man to resist any attempt of Congress to interfere with the local laws of any community . . . whether situated in territories or in states."

Between the two old parties in the North there was therefore a difference over means rather than ends. Both hoped to see slavery gradually decline. Both agreed not to press the prohibition of slavery in the territories as a means to this end, but differed on whether the settlers could establish it by local law. Both proclaimed that they had no right to interfere with slavery where it existed in states, but both believed that sooner or later, despite this constitutional barrier, the future of slavery must be settled by the national majority. In a sense, therefore, the real issue between the parties in the North in 1848 was how best to persuade the South that slavery was a dying institution.

47. Ibid.

## Chapter 8

# SOUTHERN RESPONSE AND THE PARALYSIS OF GOVERNMENT

In 1846 the "slave power" was represented at Washington by 30 Senators and 92 Representatives. Northern states mustered the same number of Senators and 135 Representatives. The Northern numerical majority haunted the political imagination of the South, but Southern Representatives divided on party lines on most issues, and even on questions with a strong sectional flavor twenty-two Northern votes added to those of a solid South gave a majority. The relative strength of the South Atlantic states, with the exception of Georgia, had steadily declined, but the Southwestern states had grown dramatically and settlement in Texas promised to add more Representatives. With this strength the South united could block unwelcome measures, exert a powerful influence within the parties, and obtain a large share of national offices.

The apportionment of Southern representation was based on all free and three-fifths of the slave population, and in 1844 John Quincy Adams attributed Southern power to "that fatal drop of Prussic acid in the Constitution, the human chattel representation." This was "an element of organized *power*" and every member representing slaves was "bound in League offensive and defensive with all the rest." The other portion of the House was divided by diverse interests and conflicting opinions and, faced with the solid phalanx of Southern votes, invariably surrendered "the cause of freedom to the congregated representatives of slaves." This consolidated power was driving on to "the dissolution of the Union and an imperial race of Caesars under the name of Democracy."[1]

1. Seward Papers, Rush-Rhees Library, University of Rochester, Rochester, N.Y., 10 May 1844.

This analysis reflected experience with the "gag" rule, but in December 1844 Adams won his long battle against the denial of the right of petition. This was regarded as ominous proof of Northern treachery by Calhoun, but no flood of abolitionist petitions descended on Congress and most Southern representatives tacitly agreed to let the contentious question die a natural death. On the great questions of Texas, Oregon, and Mexico Southerners were divided and, while Adams may have been correct in his diagnosis of the long-term consequences of the three-fifths rule, there had been few occasions on which every slave-state member was bound in "league defensive and offensive with all the rest."

In March 1843 Henry Clay found Southern and Southwestern support for "the combined principle of revenue and protection" far stronger than he had expected, and the Whigs appeared to be "nearly, if not quite, unanimous."[2] Clay often stated as fact what he hoped was true, but his evidence cannot be disregarded. Many Southerners were disturbed by the slow progress of Southern manufactures, and still hoped for protection to foster them. The difficulty was that while the tariff of 1842 had had an immediate effect upon manufacturers and iron production in the North, it had been in operation for too short a time to produce long-term benefits for struggling Southern industries. Low-tariff Democrats had been able to argue that protection increased the competitive advantages of Northern industry, and associated returning prosperity with the low tariff of 1846. Moreover, in 1842, Southern Whigs had failed to obtain the distribution of land revenues on which they had placed great store.

Tariffs and distribution belonged to that area of political controversy in which there was room for maneuver and negotiation. There was no "irrepressible conflict," and Southern Whigs who gave such enthusiastic support for Taylor in 1848 expected to use their influence to secure the best possible deal for their states. Anyone who thinks that Southern Senators and Representatives were reluctant to seek federal aid need only consult the list of improvement bills presented to Congress. Southern majority support for Polk's veto of the Rivers and Harbors Bill had been based on the belief that Western interests had won more than their fair share by devious means rather than on consistent opposition to internal improvements. Calhoun himself had endorsed the principle that federal money could legiti-

2. Berrien Papers, Southern Historical Collection, University of North Carolina, Chapel Hill, N. C., 23 March 1843.

mately be used to improve navigation in the "inland sea" of the Mississippi valley.

Many Southerners were disturbed by slow progress in railroad building and by the decline of direct trade with Europe from the South Atlantic ports. J. B. D. De Bow launched his *Review* to express this disquiet, explore the many possibilities for Southern development, and stir Southern men into activity. Manufactures, railroads, and shipping received much attention in his pages, but De Bow found himself caught in a familiar trap. Operating within a great free-trade area, available capital and accumulated experience gave Northern interests a competitive advantage. Comparative costs drew trade away from Charleston and Savannah to New York, Philadelphia,and Boston. At the two extremes of the Southern coastal arc, New Orleans and Baltimore were thriving, but international commerce languished in the South Atlantic ports, manufactures faltered, railroad plans were unfulfilled, and there was every incentive to put more and more effort into the one activity at which the South could beat the world—cotton planting. From this it was a short step to insist that the South could not flourish without cotton, and cotton depended on slavery. After 1846 more and more space in *De Bow's Review* was devoted to pro-slavery articles. Some were devoted to philosophic justification, many to problems of plantation management and medicine, and a few to arguments that slaves could be profitably used in manufactures.

Southerners did not speak with one voice on the complexities of economic policy. A somewhat unusual example of support for national initiative was provided by Nathaniel Ware, whose book, written under the pseudonym "Southern Planter," was bolder and more original in its ideas than the Old Republican philosophy still popular in Southern colleges. His views had little influence but provide evidence, in an extreme form, of Whig thought in the South.[3] Ware observed that two hundred millions of federal stock, issued at 3½ percent would pay off all the state debts and restore credit with little burden on the revenue. "Our politicians ought to wake up to this disgrace, and labor to overcome the actions of that party that does not feel the dishonor or the necessity of having a government free from reproach on charges of fraud, and a want of high and honorable sentiments." At the same time he strongly approved of "deficit financing" for useful purposes. "Many objects of national improvement require

3. A Southern Planter (Nathaniel Ware), *Notes on Political Economy* (New York, 1844). Quotations (in order as in the text) from pp. 291, 225–26, 239.

some debts to be incurred, and the nation is greatly the gainer by them, even at the expense of some taxation." A national school fund would justify running up a debt, and so would investment in useful manufactures. Over-production and the harmful diversion of capital could be checked by taxes on excess commodities or manufactures, but great dangers arose when industries were starved of capital. "The country had better risk something in banks . . . government credits and loans, or even debase the coin, than stand back so many years and be utterly impoverished." As a firm believer in economic growth he favored protection for manufactures. Finally Ware condemned un-planned and scattered settlement, for "when mankind live more concentrated they act beneficially upon each other; a dense settlement has in its bosom a thousand facilities for improvements, and the effecting and carrying out any project or plan that promises well."

Southern leaders were as ready as anyone to play an opportunist game in persuading the national government to promote the general welfare in their interest, but welfare meant more than profits, liquidation of debts, promotion of manufactures, or improved communications. Implicitly or explicitly most Southerners were concerned with the problem of social stability and acutely aware of the difficulties peculiar to a society of two races. The idea of a large free black population haunted Southern imagination, and provided a reason for non-slaveowners to accept the privilege and power exercised by those who provided police and economic security for the black race without charge to the community. The possibility of social disorder gave the word "conservative" compelling attraction for Southerners.

The Southern upper class was not a closed caste, and the absence of hereditary privilege went far toward reconciling the "plain people" to class rule. Frederick Law Olmsted observed that while a few planters of old family clung "with some pertinacity, although with too evident an effort, to the traditional manners and customs of an established gentry," this was not true of the majority of wealthy planters who were "not only distinguished for all those qualities which our satirists and dramatists are accustomed to assume to be the special property of the newly rich of Fifth Avenue, but . . . are far more generally and ridiculously so than would-be fashionable people of New York, or any other part of the United States."[4] In any society the presence of self-made men is evidence of social mobility. Class distinctions were clear but not insurmountable, and there were oppor-

4. A. M. Schlesinger, ed., *The Cotton Kingdom* (New York, 1962), 563.

tunities for the enterprising poor. The traditional means by which a Southern farmer could better himself was by moving to new land and acquiring slave labor for its development, and it is in this context that Southern reactions to the Wilmot proviso must be understood. The large planters had little economic incentive to move, and if they wished to do so there was abundant land in Texas and Florida; but the argument for geographical mobility as the condition for social mobility was very strong. The Wilmot proviso transformed Southern sectionalism from the self-conscious preoccupation of a minority of the upper class into a broad-based popular movement. The abstractions which Calhoun was so often accused of uttering became clothed with reality as the plain people realized that the proviso would close the familiar road to self-improvement. With this was combined the fear of a large free black population as old land became unprofitable, and the psychological impact of a proposal that condemned by implication their whole way of life.

The immediate reaction to the proviso was to treat it as an aberration engineered by dissatisfied politicians who wished to embarrass the President. It was in the next session, when the proviso was again moved as an amendment to an appropriation bill, that Southerners realized the full seriousness of the situation. Their reaction was sharp. A challenge had been laid down which many would wish to take up, but predictably it was John C. Calhoun who saw the danger most clearly and first moved to meet it.

On February 19, 1847, Calhoun moved a set of resolutions intended to rally the South and warn conservative men of the North.[5] He declared that the territories were "the property of the states united, held jointly for their common use," that Congress had no right to discriminate between states, that a law which prevented citizens from migrating with their property would be discriminatory, and that no conditions could be imposed upon states when admitted save that their governments should be republican. Despite an indignant comment from Benton that he was not going "to lay aside the necessary business of the session to vote on such a string of abstractions," Calhoun persisted. Though it would have been poor tactics to force a vote, he wanted an opportunity of declaring the principles involved. While claiming to uphold conservative ideas he introduced a new principle of "equilibrium" on which he would insist until his death

5. John C. Calhoun, *Works*, ed. Richard K. Crallé, 6 vols. (New York, 1853–55; reprint ed. 1968), IV: 332 ff. The wording differs slightly from that in the *Congressional Globe*.

three years later. "The day that the balance—between the slaveholding States and the non-slaveholding States—is destroyed, is a day that
will not be far removed from political revolution, anarchy, civil war,
and widespread disaster." The promised admission of Iowa and the
expectation that Wisconsin would soon follow meant that the slave
states would become a minority in the Senate, while the proviso implied that no new slave states would be admitted. In this situation the
slave states would be "at the entire mercy of the non-slaveholding
States."

Calhoun argued that Northern conservatives should recognize
this as a threat to themselves and the Union. The slave states were "the
conservative portion—always have been the conservative portion—
always will be the conservative portion; and with a due balance on
their part may, for generations to come, uphold this glorious Union of
ours." But if the balance were destroyed then, "Woe, woe, I say to this
Union." Southern men could not—would not sacrifice their equality.

> What! Acknowledged inferiority! The surrender of life is
> nothing to sinking down into acknowledged inferiority.

In this speech, as on other occasions, Calhoun confused the
rights of states and the rights of individuals, implied that the freedom
of states to deal with their domestic institutions would be abridged if
former citizens were prevented from holding slaves beyond their borders, assumed that a free state majority would act unjustly, and demanded innovation under the guise of conservatism.

Nevertheless Calhoun's warning, if not its logic, had effect
when, on the last day of the session, the House rejected the Wilmot
proviso by 102 against 97. The issue was decided by 17 from the free
states who voted against and 23 who did not vote. Other influences
helped to obtain this result. It was known that the President wanted
an appropriation without the proviso, and influential Democrats including James Buchanan and Lewis Cass, with eyes on the presidency,
were trimming their sails. Nevertheless Calhoun's speech may have
been decisive in persuading some conservatives to oppose or abstain. If
the non-voters from any one of five states—New York, Pennsylvania,
Ohio, Indiana, or Illinois—had voted in favor the proviso would have
passed the House for a third time. It is therefore a possible hypothesis
that Calhoun intended to prevent the House from making this commitment, and succeeded in doing so. This would allow him time to
rally and stiffen Southern opposition while appealing to the caution of
Northern conservatives.

The issues at stake were momentous. The first and major point was whether the national majority, given time and due opportunity for argument and counterargument, could settle the future of slavery. The second and almost equally important issue was whether this question could be argued in the normal way, using accepted methods of give and take, demanding majority respect for minority rights, but expecting minority acquiescence in majority decisions. Calhoun had clearly stated the issue could not be settled by the normal processes of debate and legislative adjustment. The real heart of his speech lay in the passage in which he rejected solution by congressional government.

I see my way in the constitution. I cannot in a compromise. A compromise is but an act of Congress. It may be overruled at any time. It gives us no security. But the constitution is stable. It is a rock. On it we can stand. It is firm and stable ground, on which we can better stand in opposition to fanaticism, than on the shifting sands of compromise. Let us be done with compromises. Let us go back and stand upon the constitution![6]

The doctrine might have been unexceptionable if there had been a precise understanding of what the Constitution meant, but what Calhoun was asking was that a new interpretation of the Constitution—devised largely by himself—must now be invoked to limit the processes of democratic politics. If he was right in demanding that the issue must be faced and could not be evaded, he also avowed that the patterns of political behavior, developed since 1789, were no longer adequate. The politics of adjustment must be replaced by the recognition of a fundamental conflict in American society.[7]

Calhoun carried his argument a step further in the summer of 1848 when confronted with the Oregon Bill and the proposal to recognize laws framed by the settlers, including one prohibiting slavery. He was joined by several Southern Senators, including Jefferson

6. Calhoun, *Works,* IV: 347.
7. Thomas Hart Benton later pointed out that abolitionism and Calhounism were two sides of the same coin. The abolitionists declared that "the admission of slavery in any part of the Union is a violation of the Constitution and a dissolution of the Union; the new resolutions declare that the prohibition of slavery in any Territory of the Union is a violation of the Constitution and the rights of States and subversion of the Union!" The consequence would be the dissolution of parties, and a new Southern party "founded on the sole principle of slavery propagandism." Speech at St. Louis, 5 June 1847, reprinted *Niles' Register,* Vol. 72: 223.

Davis, John M. Berrien of Georgia, and many others. Berrien's stand was ominous, for he was a long-time supporter of Clay who had consistently maintained that slavery must not be planted by law in places where it had not previously existed. Calhoun argued that Congress could not prevent citizens of slave states from migrating with their property, could not prohibit slavery when they settled in a territory, could not delegate this power to a territorial legislature, and that the people of a territory had no inherent right to act on their own. In other words there was no legal way in which the extension of slavery could be prevented until such time as a territory became a state and by then, as everyone knew, it might be as firmly established as it was in Missouri. Jefferson Davis made it clear that the cardinal point was that slaves were property. "On the acquisition of territory, the condition of slavery was not changed. The Government acquired no new power over it, but stood merely in the position of an agent for its protection."[8]

When the House majority finally forced the Senate to recognize the settlers' law prohibiting slavery, Calhoun saw it as a watershed in sectional relations.[9]

> The great strife between the North and South is ended. The North is determined to exclude the property of the slaveholder, and of course the slaveholder himself, from its territory. . . . The effect of this determination is to convert all the Southern population into slaves; and he would never consent to entail that disgrace on his posterity. . . . The separation between the North and South is completed.

Southerners must now consider their course of action, and there were no alternatives worth consideration. "This is not a question of territorial government, but a question involving the continuance of the Union." The North had rejected compromise and "at the next session the South will demand all and will not be satisfied with anything else."

Characteristically, Calhoun claimed to speak for "the South" and John Bell, the Whig stalwart from Tennessee, was immediately on his feet to point out that Calhoun did not speak for him.[10] It was quite wrong to say that the die was cast and "the issue must now be

8. *Congressional Globe*, 30. 1. 927, 12 July 1847.
9. *Ibid.*, 1074, 12 August 1847.
10. *Ibid.*, 1074–75.

made which involved the dissolution of the Union." He thought it nonsense to say that even if the whole country, North and South, were opposed to the extension of slavery, Congress had no power to legislate upon the subject; nor did he believe that the North would insist upon conditions so intolerable to the South that disunion would be the only possible remedy. But even Bell's temperate speech carried a warning note. "When the whole question as to the Territories of California and New Mexico should come up, it would be time enough to make the issue."

*       *       *

Of all the assumptions upon which the political system depended the simplest and most essential was that it would work. This platitude carries more meaning than may be apparent. A system of checks and balances, separate powers and divided sovereignty, can be so precise in its equation of forces that nothing at all can happen. Yet the most rigid formulation of limited government did not call for complete inaction, and in practice men wanted a good deal that only Congress could deliver. If obstruction were carried to its logical limits the men who were determined to talk could bring the legislative process to a halt, and paralysis would affect not only major issues but all the measures of local importance which Congressmen hoped to secure for their constituents. The assumption was that this would not happen, or occur infrequently and for short periods; but by 1849 it seemed that sectionalism had produced a chronic stalemate that the parties were unable to resolve.

In 1841 the Whig experiment had failed; in 1846 the Democrats had succeeded at the cost of much ill-feeling; in 1849 both parties became ineffective. The Whigs had a slender majority in the House, but thanks to the defection of Palfrey and his friends had depended upon the intentional absence of one Democrat to elect Winthrop Speaker by the narrowest of margins. In the Senate the Democrats had a majority, but this included Calhounites who could not be depended upon to follow any party line. Whatever tolerance Calhoun might have extended to erring Northern friends had been destroyed by passage of the Oregon bill, and he now devoted himself without reserve to the cause of Southern union.

The major challenge before the second session was to provide territorial government for California and New Mexico. By now the outlines of controversy were clear. The Northern readiness to prohibit slavery was weakening, but no majority would be found to give it positive protection even south of 36°30', particularly when it had been abolished by Mexican law. Nor would a majority accept the thesis that slavery was automatically extended as soon as the new lands came under the Constitution; to do so would have proved Garrison's point that the Constitution was a pro-slavery document. The issue was further complicated by the Texan claim to most of the settled portion of New Mexico—which would bring it under the jurisdiction of a slave state—and doubt whether Mexican law continued in force until repealed by Congress. All this created a complex problem which could only be solved with common sense and goodwill; both were conspicuous by their absence in the second session of the Thirtieth Congress.

No one hoped more ardently for a solution than President Polk. In his last message on the State of the Union he argued that the question was more abstract than practical, that statehood for California and New Mexico could not be long delayed, and that the fate of slavery would then be settled by their people. There was, he said, no practical obligation on Congress to legislate against slavery and its right to do so had been seriously questioned "by many of the soundest expounders of" the Constitution. Expediency and constitutional doubts both argued against action; but if Congress would not leave the matter alone, then the President believed that the best solution would be to extend the Missouri Compromise line to the Pacific; or if agreement on this was impossible, the Clayton Compromise would be acceptable.[11]

In this passage Polk gave Congress a broad hint that he could not accept the Wilmot proviso, and the point was emphasized by his inclusion, later in the message, of a long defense of the presidential veto. He went over familiar ground in arguing that "the Constitution interposes checks upon all branches of the Government, in order to give time for error to be corrected, and delusion to pass away," and that "the President represents . . . the whole people of the United States, as each member of the legislative department represents portions of them." This could be read primarily as a defense of the Rivers and Harbors veto, but the argument that followed looked more directly to the Wilmot proviso.

The objection to the exercise of the veto power is founded upon an idea respecting the popular will, which, if carried

11. *Congressional Globe*, 30. 2. 5–6.

out, would annihilate State sovereignty, and substitute for
the present Federal Government a consolidation, directed by
a supposed numerical majority. A revolution in Government
would be silently effected, and the States would be subjected
to laws to which they had never given their constitutional
assent.[12]

Calhoun himself could hardly have said more, though the master logi-
cian would have foreseen the difficulty in suggesting "constitutional
assent" by the states when no such process was known to the Constitution except when ratifying amendments.

Privately the President had little faith in admonitions. On December 12 he told his cabinet he feared that no action would be taken
on California and New Mexico, and based this view on conversations
with several members of Congress. A few days earlier he had seen
samples of gold from California, and knew that the rush to the Pacific
coast had begun. "Among the emigrants would be men of enterprise
and adventure, men of talents and capital: and that finding themselves
without a government or protection of law, they would probably organize an independent government, calling it the California or Pacific
Republic, and might endeavor to induce Oregon to join them."[13]
Under the incoming administration the "leading Federalists (alias
Whigs) would be glad to avail themselves of the opportunity to give
up the country" to rid themselves of the Wilmot proviso because their
party had always been opposed to the acquisition of new territory.
Since Congress was not likely to act, the President asked the administration to agree on a plan of settlement and use whatever influence
they possessed to carry it through. It was, he concluded "a question
rising above ordinary party considerations."

The plan the President was now prepared to back was a clumsy
proposal, made by Stephen A. Douglas on December 11, for immediate admission of all the acquisitions as one state, though reserving the right of Congress to form other states from it east of the Sierra
Nevada. He saw the President on the same night, and his plan was
discussed and approved on the following day by the Cabinet, with the
suggestion that Douglas might introduce a separate bill for New
Mexico. On December 13 Polk wrote in his diary that he was "more

12. *Ibid.*, 11. He also argued that many Representatives had been chosen by pluralities and
could not speak for a majority of their constituents. This was an invidious argument from a
President who had secured less than a majority of the popular vote.
13. James K. Polk, *Diary*, ed. Milo M. Quaife, 4 vols. (1910) IV: 252; *Polk: Diary of a
President*, ed. Allan Nevins (New York, 1929), 360.

than satisfied that unless Senator Douglas's bill is accepted, no adjustment of the territorial questions can be effected at the present session."[14]

This was the first major contribution to the territorial question by the young Senator from Illinois. His reputation and career would be inextricably and tragically interwoven with the interminable controversy, but of all his plans and proposals this was perhaps the most statesmanlike. His original bill contained geographical absurdities, for the two main centers of population—San Francisco and Santa Fé—were a thousand miles apart with no regular communication between them, and it was difficult to imagine a state government operating over such a vast area or where its capital would be located. In his opinion these would be minor blemishes if statehood took controversy out of Congress, and held the pro-slavery and anti-slavery men apart. It was obviously a second-best but there could be no agreement on westward extension of the compromise line, and the Douglas plan might save California for the nation when fruitless controversy might throw away the results of two years' war and effort.

Unfortunately tempers were rising in Congress. Benton and Clayton presented a petition from New Mexico asking for civil government, stating that "we do not desire to have domestic slavery within our borders" and asking to be protected by Congress against its introduction.[15] This brought Calhoun to his feet with a furious speech made with less than his normal deliberation. The petition was "insolent"; a conquered people had no right to address their conquerors in this way; the convention from which it purported to originate was irregular and unauthorized; it had been a hastily contrived meeting of abolitionists and a few Mexicans. Senators should not introduce a petition from such a disreputable source demanding action that was highly improper; for "our right to go there with our property is unquestionable, and guaranteed and supported by the Constitution."[16] A long and bitter debate followed on a motion to print the petition (finally carried by 33–14), while the chance for calm discussion of the Douglas plan receded. Moreover, the Douglas plan at first

14. *Ibid.* (Nevins, 357; Quaife, IV: 235). He observed that in the Cabinet "all were agreed that this was the most feasible plan of settling the slavery question, by leaving it to the inhabitants of the new state to decide for themselves, and at the same time avoid the danger of losing California." Douglas did not adopt the suggestion of introducing a separate bill for New Mexico.
15. *Congressional Globe,* 30. 2. 33, 12 December.
16. *Ibid.*

made no specific reference to the Texas boundary, and the petition
—making clear the intention of New Mexicans to exclude slavery—
determined many Southerners to support Texan claims to the limit.
Meanwhile the House was considering a bill to organize territorial
government and had, by a majority, approved the principle of the
Wilmot proviso.

The Senate debated the Douglas bill at length with the committee to which it should be referred as the first main issue.[17] The Committee on Territories consisted of Douglas as chairman, Bright of Indiana, Clayton of Delaware, Butler of South Carolina, and Davis of
Massachusetts. Davis might stand out for the Wilmot proviso, and
Butler would oppose any arrangement that did not open the territories
to slavery, but this would leave a probable majority in favor of the
Douglas bill. The Committee on Judiciary, to which the constitution
of a state seeking admission would normally be referred, consisted of
Butler, Berrien of Georgia, Westcott of Florida, Dayton of New Jersey, and Downs of Louisiana, and a majority would certainly insist
on a bill that safeguarded the rights of slaveholders. Bright of Indiana warned that no bill framed by the Committee on Judiciary could
pass Congress, but the Senate agreed by 25–24 to refer the Douglas
bill to it. The vote was purely sectional, with nine Senators absent,
and two from Iowa not yet formally seated. If the Senate had been
full, the bill would have gone to the Committee on Territories, a
majority might then have carried it on report from the committee
and sent it to the House with a fair wind. Hypothesis can go no
further, and even if the statehood proposal had got so far, ugly storms
were brewing.

On December 21 the House passed a resolution instructing the
Committee on the District of Columbia to present a bill abolishing
the slave trade in the federal capital. This came after the House had
rejected a more drastic move to abolish slavery in the District, but
even so was enough to create great alarm among the Southerners. On
the following night seventy Southern members of both Houses met in
the Senate chamber and agreed unanimously to set up a committee of
one from each slave-holding state to prepare an address for consideration. Senator Foote of Mississippi, who had acted as Calhoun's principal lieutenant in summoning the meeting,[18] told the President that,

17. *Ibid.*, 46ff.
18. Foote's account of his own part was given to the Senate on 23 February. *Ibid.*, Appendix,
264.

There was no violence, but a calm and firm purpose on the part of those present to assert and maintain the constitutional rights of the Southern States if the majority in Congress should attempt to carry out the purpose indicated by the late votes in the House of Representatives on the subject of slavery in the District.[19]

\*    \*    \*

If such harmony reigned in December it was dissipated by mid-January. On January 13 Senator Westcott of Florida told Vice-President Dallas that the Southern members were much divided and in his own state some even favored the proviso because it would persuade planters to try Florida rather than the West. Dallas could hear "the loud and exasperated discussion" from his room in the Capitol. On January 14 James M. Mason of Virginia, taking tea with the Vice-President, was "extremely excited"—apprehended a breach among the Southern members, and threatened "the dissentients with immolation by their constituents." He was "resolved . . . on separating from the Union, should any such law as the Wilmot Proviso be adopted."[20]

On January 15 the Southern members received the address from their committee. It had been prepared by Calhoun, and described by one historian as "one of his ablest state papers, destined like nearly everything he wrote to take a powerful hold upon the Southern mind."[21] Calhoun addressed himself to the basic question of race in the South, where white and black could not be separated and could not "live together in peace or harmony, or to their mutual advantage, except in their present relation."[22] Abolition decreed by a majority in Congress could never be accepted in the South, and would irrevocably divide the white people of the two sections. The blacks in the South would, however, regard the Northern emancipators as "friends, guardians, and patrons," and in words prophetic of Reconstruction he outlined a future in which

The people of the North would not fail to reciprocate and to favor them, instead of the whites. Another step would be

19. Polk, *Diary* (Nevins, 360; Quaife, IV: 252).
20. George M. Dallas, "Diary and Letters," ed. Roy F. Nichols, *Pennsylvania Magazine* LXXIII, no. 4 (October 1949): 492.
21. Allan Nevins, *Ordeal of the Union*, 2 vols. (New York, 1947), I: 221.
22. *Address of the Southern Delegates* (Washington, 1849), 13; Calhoun, *Works*, VI: 309.

taken—to raise them to a political and social equality with
their former owners, by giving them the right of voting and
holding public offices under the Federal Government. . . .
But when once raised to an equality, they would become first
the political associates of the North, acting and voting with
them on all questions, and by this political union between
them, holding the white race of the South in complete subjection.[23]

This would lead to a degradation of the white race "greater than has
ever yet fallen to the lot of a free and enlightened people." There could
be no escape if emancipation came, "which it certainly will if not
prevented," and "our country [would] become the permanent abode
of disorder, anarchy, poverty, misery, and wretchedness." This appeal
for Southern unity won a majority of Southern congressmen and was
signed by forty-eight, but twenty-four Whigs and seventeen Democrats refused to sign. The signers were nearly all Democrats, and the
Address appeared as a party manifesto rather than a demonstration of Southern solidarity. On January 27 a more moderate
address to the Union, written by Berrien, was also adopted. Yet if
Calhoun failed in his major objective (as he did on most crises during
his career), he succeeded in marking out the position to which a majority of Southerners would eventually move.[24] He had linked limitation
on the extension of slavery with eventual abolition, forecast the im-
position of civil and political equality, and predicted the dire consequences of political alliance between Northern whites and Southern
blacks. In the South only a minority were prepared to accept these
hypotheses as credible prophecy, and outside the South they appeared
as forced conclusions drawn from imagined premises; yet for good or
ill the argument once launched could not be stopped in its tracks.

The true significance of Calhoun's address was its attempt to
discredit party leadership in the South. The planter gentry might
detect the specious reasoning, and they at least were unlikely to be
frightened by the specter of black supremacy and Northern oppression. Southern Whigs who were working for Northern support for the
nomination of a Southern president, and moderate Democrats who
knew the extent of negrophobia among the constituents of their
Northern allies, refused to contemplate the "abstractions" of emanci-

23. Calhoun, *Works*, VI: 310.
24. Vice-President Dallas noted in his Diary Calhoun's "utter failure in the great project of
disunion on which his whole soul has been long and inflexibly set."

pation, racial equality, and political subjugation. In a longer view Calhoun's wisdom may also be questioned; if he seemed to display some prophetic insight into the consequences of emancipation, he foresaw neither the catastrophic war that would intervene nor the ruin of the South, which would not flow from abolition but from attempts to put his precepts into practice. His Southern critics had their feet more firmly on the ground, were not prepared to accept the logic which demanded immediate action to ward off remote dangers, and put their reliance on their continuing influence in party and nation. It was among the plain people of the South, whose knowledge of the world was meager and fear of the Negro intense, that Calhoun's argument represented reality, and the *Address of the Southern Delegates* laid foundations for popular support of Southern separatism by purporting to prove that racial equality was the inevitable consequence of majority sentiment in the North. In Calhoun's analysis promises to respect the rights of states should be ignored, for even if sincere, they would be broken by the logic of events; Northern discrimination against Negroes was irrelevant, for they would cross racial barriers when it became necessary to subdue the South; the benefits of economic association were illusory, for they concealed an intention to impoverish the South. The plain people of the South were ready to accept this explanation of their economic backwardness and the hypothesis that malignant forces might reduce them to the level of slaves.

\*      \*      \*

On January 9 the Committee on Judiciary presented its report on the Douglas bill. As expected it was unfavorable though concerned principally with technicalities: the Constitution empowered Congress to *admit* states, the bill proposed to *create* one, and if passed would leave the new state and Texas at odds over the boundary. Douglas replied that there was no constitutional requirement that Congress should consider the constitution of a state before admission, and therefore no implication that the establishment of new states required the initiative to come from the territories. Congress was therefore free to reverse the normal procedure, declare that a state existed, and require its people to establish a republican constitution. This was a realistic but weak argument with which to counter the strict construction of the committee, but one of its members, Solomon Downs of Louisiana, was prepared to meet Douglas more than halfway. At least, he said, his colleagues should have proposed some positive step toward statehood when everyone knew that an attempt to organize two territories would plunge Congress into a dangerous morass of controversy. "I have," he added, "strong forebodings of evil, that are every day increasing. I see the cloud coming. I see the danger afar off. I see the position that any section of the country must take when that event shall come. But I believe that we should use every means and put forth every exertion to avert the crisis."[25]

Thanks to the fears expressed by Downs and shared by some other Southerners, the Douglas bill was saved from instant death, came up again on January 24, and was then referred to a select committee with an even sectional balance and weighted slightly in favor of the bill.[26] Its chances of winning some Southern support were improved by an amendment that nothing in the bill should prejudge the just claims of Texas. Indeed Douglas was now prepared to give the whole of inhabited New Mexico to Texas and settle for a state of California west of the mountains.[27] The improved prospects of the bill, after its rough passage with the Southern-dominated Judiciary Committee, may have been due to the influence of the President. On Saturday, January 20 he again discussed the question at length with his Cabinet, stressed the impending rush of migrants to California and the anarchy that would prevail. He recorded his reasoning in his Diary.

> I had become perfectly satisfied that no bill to establish territorial government could be passed through the House of Representatives without having the Wilmot proviso attached to it as a condition, that with this provision the bill would probably be rejected by the Senate, and that if it was not, and the provision was made to apply to territory South of 36°30' I must veto it, and in either event the people of California would be left without a government.[28]

25. *Congressional Globe,* 30. 2. 190–98. The remark by Downs is on p. 194.

26. Douglas (Chairman), Reverdy Johnson of Maryland (moderate Whig), Jones of Iowa (newly elected), Clayton of Delaware (Whig author of abortive compromise, to be Taylor's Secretary of State), Jefferson Davis of Mississippi (State Rights Democrat), Badger of North Carolina (conservative Whig), Niles of Connecticut (Democrat with Free Soil sympathies). It would have been difficult to select a stronger or more representative committee though it included no Northern Whig with professed anti-slavery views. It was asserted later that three from the slaveholding and two from the non-slaveholding states supported the bill in committee, which suggests a majority composed of Douglas, Johnson, Clayton, Badger, and either Jones or Niles; with Davis and Jones or Niles opposed.

27. Polk, *Diary* (Nevins, 367; Quaife, IV: 287).

28. *Ibid.* (Nevins, 370; Quaife, IV: 397–98).

The President concluded that the only way out was to admit California as a state as proposed by Douglas and Downs. That same night he sent for Douglas to say that he and the whole Cabinet supported the statehood bill. Douglas "expressed himself as much gratified, and thought there was a fair prospect for passing the bill."[29]

The gathering support behind the Douglas proposal can also be explained by the proceedings of the Southern members in their adjourned meeting. The danger of going too far—perhaps reinforced by the unwelcome prospect of having to rally behind Calhoun—alarmed some Southern Whigs, especially Alexander H. Stephens of Georgia, the frail gaunt man who was to play so significant a role in years to come. The President may also have used his influence with some Southern Democrats. These pressures undermined the show of Southern unity that Calhoun so ardently desired, though the vote for the address made an impressive show of strength and an impact where most desired. If moderate Southerners of both parties cast about for compromise, Calhoun's initiative found a wide audience in the South for his theory of Northern aggression.

The evening after the Southern meeting Calhoun called on the President. "He was very earnest in the expression of his opinion that the South should no longer delay resisting the aggressions of the North upon their rights." Polk urged the merits of the Douglas proposal, and went on to explain that a further adjustment proposed by Douglas would give Texas all of New Mexico south of 36°30′, including the entire inhabited portion, in return for the cession by Texas to the United States of the barren wilderness north of that line. In this way "the whole difficulty would be settled, . . . the Free Soil agitators or Abolitionists of the North would be prostrate and powerless, . . . the country would be quieted, and the Union preserved." Calhoun seemed impervious to argument, and "proposed no plan of adjusting the difficulty but insisted that the aggressions of the North upon the South should be resisted and that the time had come for action."[30]

Would the Southern determination to resist lead to any relaxation of Northern pressure? It might persuade some Northern Whigs and regular Democrats to unite behind the Douglas proposal but not to adopt a Southern plan (particularly when none had been proposed). It might swing three or four Northern Senators against a bill abolishing slavery in the District of Columbia if it ever reached the Senate,

29. *Ibid*. (Nevins, 371; Quaife, IV: 302–3).
30. *Ibid*. (Nevins, 367; Quaife, IV: 288).

but even without this its passage was doubtful. For Northern opinion as a whole the talk of "aggression" was both incomprehensible and offensive. The obscure Representative Ephraim Smart of Maine spoke for many when he said, on January 24,

> It is said that to oppose the extension of slavery will lead to a dissolution of the Union. It comes then to this: if certain gentlemen cannot extend slavery they will go for a dissolution. . . . The northern man who will catch up the cry, and ring it through all its changes, endeavoring to alarm the people of the north who love the Union, into an acquiescence in the propagation of slavery, is scarcely worthy to be free himself.[31]

The main difficulty now lay in the House, where the principles of the Douglas bill were freely discussed in a debate on the bill organizing two territories. On February 23 there was a powerful speech by James McDowell of Virginia supporting the original Douglas proposal to admit all the acquisitions as a single state. He argued that it made the Wilmot proviso out of date, for it required no one to abandon his principles and allowed both proviso and anti-proviso men to maintain "perfect consistency with what each of them had said of his own opinions, and what each has said against the opinions of the other."[32] From New York Dickinson warned that "this attempt to create sectional parties is the evil tendency of the age."[33]

As usual the forces against the extension of slavery combined men of very different views on racial questions. While there was much genuine condemnation of slavery as an iniquity, John A. Dix— recently one of Van Buren's New York supporters—opposed the extension of slavery, because it would reverse Mexican abolition, damage American society as a whole "by promoting the multiplication of a race which adds neither to the intellectual nor physical power of the body politic, and which excludes free labor as far as it extends the labor of slaves," and inflict injustice on the people of New Mexico and California who neither possessed nor wanted slaves. For Dix the great object of national policy should be "the extension of free labor and the most effectual [method] is to devote the unoccupied spaces of the

---

31. *Congressional Globe,* 30. 2. 355.
32. *Ibid.,* Appendix, 215.
33. *Ibid.,* Appendix, 298.

West to the white race"; there was no economic need for the African race in developing the West, but this did not excuse inaction, for experience had proved that men would take slaves (upon whatever false calculation of advantage) wherever they were allowed to do so.[34]

With the end of the session but a few days away, the Senate still arguing about the Douglas bill, the House majority resolved to insist upon the Wilmot proviso, and practically no business transacted during the session, there was need for urgent action. It was left to Senator Isaac Walker from the recently admitted state of Wisconsin to suggest a compromise, and his opportunity came when the normal Civil and Diplomatic Appropriations Bill reached the Senate on February 21. Walker's original intention was to add a simple amendment to the Appropriations Bill authorizing the President to execute the revenue laws and maintain order in all the territories acquired from Mexico west of the Rio Grande. He was persuaded by Senator Foote (who knew a good deal more about the intricacies of the question) to include a phrase extending the Constitution to the territories and voiding Mexican law when inconsistent with the laws of the United States. This brought on a high-powered debate (with Calhoun and Webster participating) on the application of the Constitution to territories. Webster argued that the Constitution applied to states and that all it said of territories was that Congress had sovereign power over them. To this Calhoun might have replied that a United States citizen had rights, guaranteed by the first eight amendments, that were inalienable wherever the American flag flew, but instead he continued to assert in general terms that the Constitution applied to the territories and carried slavery with it.

Calhoun's reason for this calculated vagueness is obvious. In a wide-ranging congressional debate someone might well seize upon the point that the amendments guaranteed many other rights, and did not speak of "citizens" but of "people" and "persons." The fifth amendment said that no *person* should be deprived of life, liberty, or property without due process of law. The seventh amendment guaranteed jury trial in suits at common law where the value in controversy exceeded twenty dollars (which could mean that a slaveholder might be challenged before a local jury to prove his right to possess slaves). Calhoun had savagely attacked the petition from New Mexico, but the first amendment guaranteed the right of "the people" to petition the government for a redress of grievances. Article IV of the Constitu-

34. *Ibid.*, Appendix, 293.

tion itself guaranteed the return of fugitive slaves and criminals who escaped from one state to another, but said nothing about territories. There were many provisions in the Constitution that could not apply to territories, because there were neither laws nor rights until Congress exercised its power to make "all needful rules and regulations." Americans were endowed with certain "inalienable rights" including "Life, Liberty and the pursuit of Happiness" but these rights, however defined, could not be safeguarded until Congress had passed laws and established courts. From then on the judges might interpret the Constitution, but what they said would depend very much upon their political and regional loyalties and ultimately on the right of the President to appoint and the Senate to confirm. Thus argument about the Consitution could be a two-edged weapon and it was better to be imprecise than accurate.

An amendment by John Bell of Tennessee to admit all the territory west of the Rio Grande as a state was rejected by a large majority, and with it went all hope for the original Douglas bill. An attempt by Dayton of New Jersey to confine the operation of the Walker amendment to revenue laws and extend it to all the acquired territories was voted down, and it became clear that a majority of the Senate from both slave and free states was resolved to pass the Walker amendment which would at least give California law (and perhaps order), leave the President discretion to apply what laws he saw fit, and cast around individuals the protection of whatever meaning the legal profession might discover in the Constitution. Finally the Appropriations Bill so amended passed the Senate by 25–18. It was now February 28, and as March 4 fell on a Sunday, the third day of March would be the last of the ill-fated Thirtieth Congress.

On March 2 the House rejected the Walker amendment (or as it now came to be styled, the 53rd amendment) 115–101. A committee of conference failed to agree, and on March 3 Charles S. Morehead, a representative from Kentucky, moved to strike out the phrase "west of the Rio Grande" from the 53rd amendment and add the proviso "that nothing in this act shall affect in any way the question of the boundary of the State of Texas." This was passed 187–19, but Representative Richard W. Thompson of Indiana next moved a further amendment that "unless Congress shall sooner provide for the government of said Territories, the existing laws thereof shall be retained and observed." This passed 111–105, and the Wilmot proviso men had scored a notable tactical victory; while accepting the Senate formula that the Constitution covered the acquired territories, and endorsing the authority of the President to apply the laws of the United States to the area claimed by Texas, the majority had agreed that the Mexican abolition law remained in force until superseded by congressional act. On present showing the House would not vote to repeal the Mexican prohibition of slavery. Whether or not there had been any master mind behind the moves in the House, the Calhounites had been outflanked and the men seeking a compromise had been disarmed. By amending an amendment to an Appropriations Act, the majority of the House had virtually enacted the Wilmot proviso: slavery would remain prohibited in all the territories acquired from Mexico, the Texas boundary would become an issue between the state and the federal government, and the operation of the whole scheme would be at the discretion of a Whig president.

Meanwhile the Senate had rejected the House bill establishing territorial government in California, and hurriedly turned back to the Appropriations Bill with the Walker amendment amended. The dilemma of the Senate was revealed when Senator Mason of Virginia moved to strike out the phrase "the existing laws . . . shall be retained and observed." Several Senators who would go along with equivocal phrases about the Constitution were not prepared to cast votes explicitly recognizing slavery in the territories, and Mason's resolution was rejected 27–21.

Both houses were now in turmoil and the hour was approaching at which Congress must expire and all pending bills lapse. President Polk had arrived at the Capitol, as was the custom, to be on hand to sign bills passed in the final hour of Congress. He learned that the Senate was considering the House amendment and many of the Southern members of Congress in both Houses came into his room in a great excitement. Members of the cabinet were present and gave their views. Buchanan, Walker, Marcy, and Toucey advised him to sign the bill if it came in this form. In his diary Polk wrote that "they drew a distinction, which I did not perceive, between the amendment in this form and the Wilmot proviso."[35] Other Southern members came crowding in and Senator Houston told him that Southern members were signing an address urging him to veto.

> I at once told him to return to the House and stop signatures to the paper, for the President could not perform a high constitutional duty of this kind upon a petition. I then told him

35. Polk, *Diary* (Nevins, 383; Quaife, IV: 365).

he might rest easy, that I was prepared with a veto message in my pocket, and that I should veto the bill if it came to me.[36]

It was, he added, "a moment of high responsibility, perhaps the highest of my official career." Despite his belief that failure to provide law for California would lead to the independence of that province, Polk was prepared to throw away the greatest prize of his administration rather than sign. This would also leave the country without revenue, and thus make certain that the next Congress must be called immediately into special session.

It was now past midnight. Some believed that the Thirtieth Congress had no longer any legal existence, but the Vice-President refused to accept motions to adjourn and the Senate continued talking through the night. The President retired to Willard's Hotel, but still the Senators continued their debate, perhaps in the hope that by a miracle someone would be convinced, or that the need to provide for the expenses of government would prevail over the question of slavery on the Rio Grande. Finally a motion was moved and carried 38–7 that the Senate should abandon the Walker amendment, and thus consigned to oblivion the House amendments to the amendment. At about 6 A.M. the President was called from his bed to sign enrolled bills; observing that the Appropriations Bill was not encumbered with the 53rd amendment, he signed it. At 7 A.M. on March 4, Congress rose and ended its term of office, having left California and New Mexico without government, demonstrated the impossibility of doing so, and exhibited to all the paralysis of the American political system.

A few days before, Horace Greeley, the volatile editor of the *New York Tribune* and a Representative from New York, got the floor in the House. He was a frustrated and angry man, for he had been waiting since December for an opportunity to speak and his head was full of schemes in which he wished to interest the House. Yet nothing had been done.

> From the day I entered this Hall to this moment—no matter what the bill before us—we have had discussions of slavery and nothing else. Slavery in its nature—slavery in its effects —slavery in the District—slavery in the Territories—has been the one perpetual theme.[37]

36. *Ibid.* (Nevins, 384; Quaife, IV: 366).
37. *Congressional Globe*, 30. 2. Appendix, 247, 26 February 1849.

The introduction of slavery into every question was mainly at the instance of Southern members who, but a short while before, had maintained that it should not be discussed at all; but once battle was joined, Northern members had to retort. Even a Post Office Bill had been the occasion for a debate on slavery, and the House sustained the Speaker's ruling that it was in order.

Congress almost failed to pass the civil appropriation bill, and only in its final days could find a few minutes to pass the laws necessary for the 1850 Census. Major legislation was not usual during the lame-duck session, but normally a host of private and local bills were carried so that congressmen could report advantages won for their constituents. The Senate Journal shows that thirty-nine bills of this character were introduced or received from the House; many more were introduced in the House but got no further than committee. Of the bills awaiting action by the Senate only three became law; one gave a right of way through public lands to an Illinois railroad, and the other two performed similar services for the Atlantic and Gulf and Mobile and Ohio railroads. Two other railroad bills were lost, and there was great havoc among bills for rivers and harbor improvements with no fewer than twenty-one frustrated. Several bills granting public land to states were lost, and so was a bill to make new grants in place of school sections which had proved to be worthless.

The one major achievement was the establishment of the Department of the Interior, but the first great department to be added since 1800—and one that would be responsible for the vast public domain and for Indian affairs—was dealt with in a brief debate. It was fortunate that the bill was not killed by amendments requiring the new secretary to protect or prohibit slavery, but the bankruptcy of the political system was made clear when Senators preferred to make three-hour speeches on the Walker amendment rather than spend one evening discussing the responsibilities and administration of the new department. For most practical purposes the government of the United States had ceased to govern. This, more than threats of disunion, was the true nature of the crisis that confronted the country when a politically inept President and an undistinguished Cabinet took up the reins of office.

*Chapter 9*

# DECISION
# IN THE
# SOUTH

Five weeks after the passage of the Southern Address Senator Foote claimed that

> The South is roused up to a circumspect and scrutinizing survey of all the dangers which threaten her present peace and future safety. Our enemies stand paralysed by the moral energy so suddenly and so imposingly displayed by Southern Senators and Representatives and the contemporaneous legislative resolves of nearly all the Southern States of the Confederacy.[1]

Calhoun was determined to seize this favorable moment to achieve Southern unity, and this meant doing all in his power to break down the old parties in the South. In February 1849 he wrote to James H. Hammond of South Carolina that the first step was to "put an end to old party divisions, which might be effected by an understanding between a few prominent leaders on both sides and short well written Articles through the leading presses of both parties, showing the folly and danger of continuing our party warfare when our existence is at stake."[2]

Calhoun put the two great parties in the South on the defensive, placed upon them the onus of defending their Northern allies, and

1. *Congressional Globe*, 30. 2. Appendix, 264.
2. *Correspondence of Calhoun*, Part I, 762. To J. H. Hammond.

required them to justify their policy in purely sectional terms. The great weakness of the Whigs in the South was their inability to offer their constituents a record of achievement in the national sphere, and their failure to extract from their Northern allies any satisfactory statement of future policy. There were, indeed, conservative Northern Whigs who would subscribe to any declaration short of a positive approval of slavery, but their voices were no longer of commanding influence in the party. In 1848 the followers of Clay went down to defeat in the great centers of Northern Whiggery—in New York, in New England, and in Ohio—and conservatives were at odds with Whigs opposed to slavery. The Southern Democrats were stronger because they could point to genuine allies in the North. The party as a whole had endorsed the doctrine of the Nicholson letter in 1848, which, if not satisfactory to all Southerners, offered a hope of meeting Southern difficulties over the Wilmot proviso. Yet Southern Democrats were apprehensive because the Free Soil defection left doubts which were not easily laid at rest. As one Georgia Democrat asked,

> Can the Hunker democracy of the North be now depended upon by the democracy of the South? . . . Old associations, old pledges, old hopes, perhaps convictions, may for a while keep a few of the old leaders of the Northern democracy in their old position on the slavery questions; but the body and the present leaders are gone, gone forever.[3]

A well-informed newspaper editor was even more positive when he wrote that the Northern Democrats had fought their last battle for the constitutional rights of the South: "They are but *men*, noble specimens I grant you, and must yield to the storm."[4]

For those who followed Calhoun's lead the Wilmot proviso had offered a welcome demonstration of hostile Northern intentions. Elwood Fisher inquired rhetorically how the Northern states would respond if a Southern majority "were to announce its determination to arrest the further progress of commerce and manufactures in consequence of . . . poverty, pauperism, crime and mortality.[5] The number of pro-slavery articles and attacks on the North increased in

---

3. Hopkins Holsey to Cobb, 24 February 1849, *Correspondence of Robert Toombs, Alexander H. Stephens, and Howell Cobb*, ed. Ulrich B. Phillips (American Historical Association Annual Report, 1911), II: 153 (hereafter cited as *Toombs, Stephens, and Cobb*).

4. Henry L. Benning to Cobb, *ibid.*, 169.

5. Elwood Fisher, *Lecture on the North and the South* (Washington, 1849), 28. This publication was widely noticed. The *Southern Quarterly Review,* 2 July 1849, printed a long and highly favorable review which was attributed to James B. Hammond.

both major Southern periodicals, the *Southern Quarterly* and *De Bow's Review*, and increasing stress was laid on the damage that would be done to Southern society. Early in 1849 Hopkins Holsey, a Georgia editor, believed that among the slaveholders and those connected with them there was "an ultra feeling roused up in their bosoms which they did not feel before."[6] The Wilmot proviso, with its implied condemnation of all societies in which slavery existed, helped to spread the "ultra feeling" beyond the ranks of slaveowners. The specters of abolition and free Negro hoards could be called up to demonstrate the logical consequences of Northern policy.

Nevertheless the cause of Southern union did not move forward unchecked, and there was lack of confidence among Southern politicians. In January 1849, while the Southern Address was in preparation, Calhoun received a letter from H. W. Conner of Charleston recording impressions received during a tour of the lower South. In Georgia both parties were "sound" and ready to act, but "owing to their northern population" Savannah and Augusta were more doubtful than the country. In Alabama the people would be with Calhoun, but the politicians would make difficulties. In Louisiana "the country was sound . . . altho they would not make any noise by resolutions or otherwise," but New Orleans was "almost Free Soil." Even where determination should be strongest, doubt was expressed.

> Our own people many of them are desponding. They begin to think that the Institution of slavery is doomed. That all the world is opposed to it, and that we ourselves will not or cannot do anything to avert it. . . . Here to my mind is the *only danger* of the South.[7]

Equally significant was the reluctance of many Southern political leaders to abandon national parties. As Thomas Clingman of North Carolina said (in the speech that prompted John G. Palfrey's elaborate reply), "The abolitionists of the North and the ultras at the South have united in lamenting the existence of political parties, which they say prevents men from making a direct issue of slavery. . . . Whenever . . . you see political parties divided by strict geographical lines, the Union is virtually at an end."[8] Robert Toombs, a leading Whig from Georgia, was prepared to settle for a shadow rather than embarrass General Taylor's administration. The

6. Holsey to Cobb, 13 February 1849, *Toombs, Stephens, and Cobb,* 149.
7. *Correspondence of Calhoun*, Part II, 1189, 12 January 1849.
8. *Congressional Globe*, 30. 1. Appendix, 47.

disputed territory could not, he said, be a slave country. "We have only the point of honour to save"; sensible compromise would save it "and rescue the country from all the danger from agitation." Toombs thought that "the Union of the South was neither possible nor desirable until we are ready to dissolve the Union," and people should not be advised "to look anywhere else than their own government for the prevention of apprehended evils."[9]

In the summer Herschel V. Johnson, of the Georgia Democratic party, had to explain to Calhoun that "for the sake of harmony" the subject of the Southern Address was not touched upon in the state convention. Howell Cobb had been a leading non-signer, and any attempt to make approval a party test "would have torn us in atoms, without giving us any strength."[10] Cobb himself criticized Democrats who were "blindly following the erratic call of the madcap Carolinian." One of his friends, a member of the influential Lumkin family, hoped for the day "when the Democratic party of the South will become purged of Calhoun, Calhoun men, and Calhounism." When James Buchanan, operating from the shelter of the State Department, was inclined to favor resolute Southern action, he was sharply reminded by Cobb that Calhoun's purpose was to organize "a Southern sectional party to supplant the democratic party." Acceptance of the Address would mean "the disruption of the democratic party as a *national* party, which would be the accomplishment of Calhoun's schemes ever since I have been in public life." In August Calhoun's followers were "most gloriously rebuked" in the Alabama elections when all those who had refused to sign the address were re-elected.[11]

It was at this time that Howell Cobb made his important speech in defence of party to which reference was made in the first chapter. He argued that party was "not only right and proper, but absolutely necessary for the preservation of our free institutions." Though the ostensible target of his attack was Zachary Taylor's short-lived dalliance with the idea of running as a "no-party" candidate, Cobb must also have had in mind the situation in the South. He was deeply involved in the effort to head off Calhoun's designs, and to preserve the national Democratic party.[12]

9. Toombs to Crittenden, 22 January 1849, *Toombs, Stephens, and Cobb*, 141.
10. *Correspondence of Calhoun*, Part II, 1198, 20 July 1849.
11. *Toombs, Stephens and Cobb*, 145 (Cobb to Mrs. Cobb, 1 February 1849); 157 (Lumkin to Cobb, 12 March 1849); 164 (Cobb to Buchanan, 17 June 1849); 173 (George S. Houston to Cobb, 10 August 1849).
12. *Congressional Globe*, 30. 1, Appendix, 775.

A Southern politician could not be indifferent to the implications of the threat to break down parties. If old rivalries were to be forgotten, there could be no further use for the two party organizations, and fusion in a single Southern party would mean that many aspiring politicians would find the results of years of careful planning swept away. A hierarchy of politicians, from the top to the bottom of each party, would be rendered redundant. One-party rule would mean that office and patronage would be concentrated in the hands of single dominant groups, and there would be no hope of displacing them at the next election. Moreover, in most states, this would mean handing over power to a Calhounite minority consisting of men whose claims had been rejected and defeated in the regular parties.

Nor could a man such as Howell Cobb ignore the consequences for his own career on the national stage. He was able and ambitious, and though the time was not yet ripe, had every reason to hope that fortune might one day make him the presidential nominee of the national Democratic party. The prospect was more attractive than commitment to the exclusive defence of Southern rights. Nor should one forget the wide range of issues upon which Northern and Southern Democrats had cooperated in the past. Surely if Northern Democrats could no longer find Southern allies, they would look elsewhere? The emergence of Free Soil spelled out the obvious lesson; the interests of the South were best protected by national parties, and might be irretrievably ruined once parties became sectional.

These considerations suggest that the politicians were pressed from below toward Southern union, or at least to the point of agreeing that party was irrelevant when slavery was at stake. Whatever arguments had been presented against the Calhoun movement, and whatever success his opponents claimed, party lines in the South seemed to have almost disappeared when the 31st Congress assembled for the first time in December 1849. The immediate cause of this solidarity was the news that California sought admission to the Union with a constitution prohibiting slavery; but the real causes lay deep in Southern institutions and ideas. A brief review of these forces is therefore necessary.

The paradoxes of Southern society are familiar. The economy was retarded or in decline, yet produced much wealth and the country's principal export crop. Railroads lagged and manufactures had hardly begun on any considerable scale; yet cotton on new lands was very profitable and despite sensitivity to world-wide business fluctuations the trend in production was generally upward. In this respect the South shared fully in the prosperity that returned after 1844. The economic paradox was that of an expanding society which failed to provide a majority of its people with more than subsistence, ignorance and isolation. The political paradox was the combination of hierarchy and democracy. Public office was reserved for the upper class of planters and their lawyer allies, yet power could be exercised only with the consent of numerous white adult males who owned small farms and few or no slaves. Nor could upper class leadership rely upon the unruffled calm of convention, for territorial and economic expansion constantly threw new regions and new interests into the political scales. Parties had developed because multiple interests could no longer be contained within the framework of élite rule, but the upper class itself had grown so that new families joined in the struggle for power. The combination between real conflicts of interest and upper class factionalism produced a further paradox. The parties offered a real choice and distinctive rhetoric, but both were led by men of the same class.

A further consequence is that despite the bitterness of party warfare, both Whig and Democratic leaders observed an unwritten agreement that neither must disturb the hegemony of the planter class. Yet this objective could be achieved only by convincing the white voters of the South that existing leadership deserved respect, and this necessarily involved a defense of slavery as an economic and social institution. The revered fathers of the Southern tradition had agreed that slavery was an evil that would decline as civilization advanced; but by 1850 there seemed to be no alternative labor force capable of supporting great landowners and commercial farmers, and no other way of providing the service that made civilized leisure possible. Slavery had been challenged in the South in earlier years, and one could not tell what mute or latent anti-slavery sentiment was still nourished in Southern homes (especially among the plain people upon whose votes political authority was based). Uncertainty is a surer spur to rhetoric than confidence, and the flowering of pro-slavery argument was not a response to William Lloyd Garrison or the Liberty party but an anticipation of Southern criticism of traditional leadership. It would have been possible to ignore what was said in Boston or New York, or even in Washington, if silence had not been a possible prelude to defeat at home, and Southern leaders were impelled to answer every real or imagined criticism. They could not rest content with the knowledge that a large majority of Northerners were prepared to leave slavery alone, but must have positive assurances that it deserved preservation. Though abolitionists were in an unpopular minority, every man who said that slavery was an evil must be classed with them, for the only truly dangerous thing was moderate criticism which might win friends. What hurt most was not condemnation of slavery but of slaveowners, and especially that species of criticism which aimed to separate slaveowners from the society which they controlled. The rise of Free Soil added to anti-slavery rhetoric a condemnation of the society that slaveowners had created.

In reply a Southern chorus proclaimed that slavery was a benevolent institution, but the real purpose was to clear the good name of slaveowners. In the past Southerners had sometimes apologized, professed their dislike of an institution they had inherited, and deplored their inability to change it, but this was becoming rare. In 1852 George Fitzhugh observed that he had never met a Southern men in recent years who "did not think slavery a blessing to the negro race." Slaves formed "the only laboring and serving class on this earth, between whom and his master there is any love, any friendship; and it is the only class of day-laborers or slaves on the face of the earth which is improving."[13] This positive attitude was the product of experience that slaveowners were now eager to share with the world.

An Alabama planter was typical of the Southern chorus when he wrote, "If you could hear the songs, and witness the dances which enliven their evenings, you would never believe one word of the vile abuse which has been heaped upon us for badly treating our slaves."[14] John M. Berrien, the respected Senator from Georgia, protested against the belief that planters bred slaves to profit from their sale, and asserted that "anyone capable of appreciating the feelings of a southern man toward those untutored beings, who, in the Providence of God have been not merely subjected to his control, but also committed to his protection . . . would know that few slaveholders, and that few only under the pressure of stern necessity, would profit by the sale of slaves."[15] Though these words were spoken almost within earshot of the well-stocked slave markets of Washington, many conservative Northerners probably came to believe that slave-trading was morally no more offensive than the decision of an employer to dismiss workpeople. Whatever misfortune befell him, the slave in an auction did

13. George Fitzhugh, *Sociology for the South* (Richmond, 1854). Reprinted in Harvey Wish, ed., *Ante Bellum* (New York, 1960), 43–95.

14. From an anonymous article in *Niles' Register*, 16 December 1843. In a widely noticed address (*Lecture on the North and South delivered before the Young Men's Mercantile Library Association of Cincinnati, Ohio, January 16, 1849*) Elwood Fisher observed: "The people of the South prefer slavery to the evils of a dense manufacturing and commercial population . . . and the black man may prefer the slavery of the South to the want, the crime, the barbarism and blood which attend his race in all other countries."

15. *Congressional Globe*, 28. 1, Appendix, 702.

not starve. Francis Lieber, who worked in South Carolina and was acutely uneasy about slavery, nevertheless assured a Northern friend that no Southerner of any reputation would pursue a runaway into free territory, and repeated the story that John C. Calhoun received regular letters from a former slave in the North whom he had never attempted to recover.[16]

In the South slaveowners succeeded in harnessing one of the dynamic forces of the age—evangelical Protestantism—which elsewhere enlisted in the anti-slavery crusade. The South contained many sincere Christians who conceived it their duty to introduce slaves to the faith, but how was a religion with revolutionary origins and contemporary radical manifestations to be harnessed to the need for social order? The resolution of this contradiction was exemplified in the life and influential writings of Charles Colcock Jones, slaveowner, Presbyterian minister and Professor of Ecclesiastical History at the Columbia Theological Seminary of South Carolina.

There is no reason to doubt the sincerity of Colcock Jones, and his *The Religious Instruction of Negroes*, published in 1842, was based on his own experiences as an active evangelist to the slaves. He insisted emphatically that Christian slaves were more industrious and more amenable to discipline, but that "as ministers or missionaries to the Negroes . . . we should have nothing to do with their civil conditions."[17] These arguments were typical of those that pressed for religious instruction among the slaves. Thousands of black people were inspired by the promise of a religon which blessed the humble and weak and sent the rich empty away, but the majority also learned the duty of obedience.[18] So far from being a disruptive force Christianity reinforced the authority of masters and "all at the South were aware of the difference between religious and irreligious Negroes."[19] In 1853 a British observer thought there was clear evidence of the improvements wrought by religion in the housing, clothing, and food provided for slaves, that Sunday was generally treated as a day of rest

16. To G. S. Hillard, 28 April 1850. Lieber Papers, Huntington Library, San Marino, Calif.

17. Charles Colcock Jones, *The Religious Instruction of Negroes in the United States* (Savannah, 1842), 270.

18. In 1845, twenty-four South Carolinian planters issued a circular requesting information about the effect of religion on slaves. Among the many replies a typical one was that "plantations under religious instruction were more easily governed than those which are not." One Southern writer asserted that since "all our negroes have grown up under religious instruction . . . we scarcely hear of depredations upon stock, etc. They are more obedient and more to be depended upon. We have few or no runaways, and corporal punishment is but seldom resorted to." Iveson L. Brookes, *A Defence of the South* (Hamburg, S.C., 1850).

19. Matthew Estes, *A Defence of Negro Slavery* (Montgomery, 1846), 96.

"especially in those parts of the South where Christianity was most prevalent, and that whatever the law might permit much had been done to respect slave marriages and to prevent the separation of families by sale."[20]

Clergymen and pious laymen joined the controversy to prove that slavery was sanctioned by religion in a host of speeches, sermons, debates at local or national church meetings, and laboriously argued pamphlets. The neutrality of the Church on all matters affecting slavery was demanded. "The legislation of the Bible on the subject of slavery . . . is full and explicit, varied and multiform, in its notices and instructions," and it was therefore unnecessary and presumptuous for churches to supplement or supplant the word of God.[21] The Bible was the source of all morality; it recognized slavery, and behind scriptural authority lay "the stern but wholesome truth that the existence, as well as the universality of slavery, is to be attributed to the labor required in the infancy of man to subdue the earth. . . . It is only when we have lost sight of this sublime truth, that we proclaim our absurd system of equality in a state of nature."[22] Men were not created equal and it was evident that it was "the design of God, and necessary for the aggregate happiness of the human race, that there should be different degrees and dependencies among men."[23] Denials of this truth were associated with eighteenth-century Deism, and even the patriarchs of the South had fallen into dangerous error when "Mr Jefferson . . . by his mistaken and strange notions of universal liberty and equality, led to the adoption of the worst sort of infidelity."[24]

Biblical authority was advanced against rationalist heresy or sentimental deception, and with this moral sanction it was possible to discover empirically the real blessings of slavery. "Lawful dependence of our fellow creatures upon us . . . is one of the greatest aids to the advancement of piety in our hearts."[25] It was an advantage to Negroes who were happier, healthier, and better cared for than any free laborers. For the masters it increased intelligence and inculcated a spirit of "lofty and generous patriotism" while "an acknowledged inferior is

20. Robert Baird, *Christianity in the United States* (London and Glasgow, 1853), 33.

21. H. B. Basom, A. L. P. Greene and C. B. Parsons, *A Brief Appeal to Public Opinion against . . . the course of the Methodist Episcopal Church from 1844 to 1848* (Louisville, 1848), 26.

22. Edward B. Bryan, *The Rightful Remedy: Addressed to slaveholders of the South* (Charleston, 1850), 37.

23. *Slavery: a Treatise showing that Slavery is neither a moral nor political evil* (Penfield, Georgia, 1844), 21.

24. Brookes, *A Defence of the South,* 8.

25. *Slavery: a Treatise . . . ,* 21.

always treated with more respect and kindness in his subordinate, dependent position, than when he aspires to an equality."[26] At the same time slavery made possible mutual respect among all whites whatever their wealth or station; honest labor was not despised, but Calhoun hoped "that the time would never come when the white man of the South would brush a coat or clean a pair of boots."[27] Harmony and order were the Christian virtues of the South and "the existence of slavery *radiates* a proper spirit of discipline throughout the entire community of those States in which we find it."[28]

Christian consciences might be troubled by the number of mulatto witnesses to a breach of the seventh commandment, but one writer pointed out how unfair it was to judge the South in this way when no mingling of colors betrayed Northern immorality. "Who, on entering any large Northern city, is not made painfully aware of the low state of moral feeling? . . . What visitor to New York City has not failed to notice with what unblushing effrontery prostitutes of both sexes make Broadway their place of assignation." No system was without cruelty, abuse of rights and injustice, but the scale of iniquity was far greater in the North where "society is the great slave-holder, and millions are crushed and victimized beneath the weight and cruelty of its Juggernaut oppression, without appeal or remedy of any kind."[29] The South was said to be ignorant, but education was not necessarily beneficial; on the one hand were the slaves "whose happiness obviously depends on their ignorance, and whose discontent, under the presence of their bonds, must keep pace with the progressive illumination of their minds,"[30] and on the other hand there were illiterate whites who "like the Athenians can discriminate and judge as well as any others of the age we live in."[31]

It has been argued that the triumph of slavery over Christian criticism can be explained by the fragmentation of American Protestantism, and that a united and authoritarian Church could have humanized and ameliorated slavery. The denominations that were small, weak, and organized on the congregational principle, became

26. Estes, *A Defence of Negro Slavery*, 148.

27. *Congressional Globe*, 31. 1. 876, 28 June 1848.

28. Bryan, *The Rightful Remedy*, 71.

29. Basom, Greene & Parsons, *A Brief Appeal . . .*, 30.

30. Quoted in Asa E. Martin, *Anti-Slavery in Kentucky prior to 1850* (Louisville, 1915), from the presentment, by the Grand Jury, of a school for slaves as "an evil of the most serious and portentous character."

31. *Southern Quarterly* XV (July 1849): 292. "We yield to none in the desire for a spread of *knowledge* far and wide among the people—but we are persuaded that there is a great deal of charlatanry in all schemes for teaching them to read and write and nothing more."

tools rather than critics of the slaveowners.[32] There are a number of assumptions in this argument which do not bear close examination. Humanitarian reform in Britain would have been long delayed if it had had to wait upon the official leaders of established churches, and dissenters and evangelical factions within the Church provided the mainspring for anti-slavery and social reform. Indeed, fragmentation was a more prolific parent of religious interest in social questions than unity. The resources of American Protestantism were not weak if anyone wished to employ them, and observers were impressed by the strength and multiplicity of the voluntary associations which promoted so much religious and social activity. The answer in the South lay not in the intrinsic weakness of the churches, but in the absence of an active, pious, urban middle class which elsewhere provided leadership and funds for missionary effort and humanitarian reform.

Up to a point, Southern apologists were remarkably effective. They convinced themselves, reassured slaveowners, and won guarded assent in the North. Was slavery the greatest evil with which men had to contend? A majority of Northern Americans agreed that it was not, and deplored activity which placed abolition ahead of peace, harmony, and union. Typical sentiments were voiced by a critic of William Ellery Channing's book on slavery, who asked "What possible benefit is to be gained by repeating, in every inflection of taste and style, and with all the gorgeousness of rhetoric, long-established truisms which nobody denies?"[33] If discussion of slavery excited Northern Americans against their Southern brethren, "the bonds of our political union may remain indeed undivorced, but we have prepared for ourselves a condition of wretchedness, to which their actual dissolution would be infinitely preferable."[34] In 1835, the *Baptist Banner* of Louisville admitted that slavery was an evil but condemned as "irreligious and as tending to the worst consequences the course pursued by the abolitionists. . . . It is not to the master but to the slave that they speak . . . when we see men whose acts are calculated to excite the slaves to the worst and most horrid deeds of rapine and bloodshed we can not call them misguided philanthropists of enthusiastic Christians; but revolutionists and assassins."[35]

32. Stanley M. Elkins, *Slavery*, 3rd ed. (Chicago, 1976), chapter II *passim*. For a criticism of other aspects of Elkins's book see David Brion Davis, *The Problem of Slavery in Western Culture* (Ithaca, 1966), 224–26, 238.
33. James T. Austin, *Remarks on Dr. Channing's "Slavery"* (Boston, 1835), 5.
34. *Ibid.*, 23.
35. Quoted in Martin, *Anti-Slavery in Kentucky*, 76–77.

These themes became commonplace among Northerners who abhorred dissension and sought to justify their tacit acceptance of slavery. Each American had two political characters, as a citizen of a state and a citizen of the United States, reflecting in each individual the dualism of the federal system. As citizens of the United States they could discuss and ask for decisions on all questions that came under the authority of Congress, but as citizens of a state they had no right to discuss the domestic affairs of a sister state. Even if it were right to discuss the morality of slavery as an abstract proposition, it would be wrong to condemn others for thinking differently. It was doubly wrong to condemn slavery when one could offer to the slave states no practicable alternative to their present system of race relations.[36]

Northern conscience was further comforted by the belief that while unseen forces were moving to improve the condition of the black race, servitude was itself evidence of present inferiority. "No intelligent and virtuous people has ever been long held in bondage, and no ignorant and vicious community has long enjoyed even the appearance of freedom."[37] Given these uncertainties the American Constitution provided the *modus vivendi* by leaving responsibility to those best able to assess the needs of both races. Perfection was not a condition of human society, but "it has been wisely left to each political community to decide for itself what form of government—or in other words, what degree of bondage—is best adapted to its peculiar circumstances." A community might act unwisely but that was "exclusively its own business."[38] Views such as these were expressed with varying degrees of prejudice, complacency, and self-deception, but errors of the present age suggest that no one should rush to judgment.

\*     \*     \*

Strongly entrenched in politics, buttressed by social, religious, and scientific argument, and assured on every side that no one intended to interfere with slavery where it existed by law, one may wonder what slaveowners had to fear? Was their controlling sentiment, as some

36. This paragraph paraphrases the argument of William Henry Harrison during the 1840 campaign (*Niles' Register* LIX: 42–43).

37. James Shannon, *The Philosophy of Slavery as identified with the Philosophy of Human Happiness* (Frankfort, Ky., 1849), 29. Shannon was president of Bacon College, Harrodsburg, Ky., and his *Philosophy of Slavery* was delivered as an address in June 1844. It drew a reply from Cassius M. Clay.

38. *Ibid.*, 30.

critics of the "slave power" implied, not fear but ambition to control the nation? To answer these questions it is necessary to consider further the character of Southern society. It will become apparent that contradictory forces were at work to persuade the Southern upper class that the Wilmot proviso must be voted down, disavowed by party leaders, and publicly repudiated.

In the lower South the great number of large slaveowners formed a compact group, trained to judge every event by its long-term consequences for their own position, and from them issued most of the abstract, hypothetical, and constitutional arguments. In the upper South slaveowning was far more middle class in character; there were large slaveowners, but the great majority were farmers, small planters, and townspeople for whom the issues were not abstract but real. Large numbers of Western migrants had come from these states, and many wished to go; for them the right to take slaves into new lands would be an enormous asset in a society where hired labor was scarce. When fugitive slaves became an issue, the small slaveowners of the upper South knew what it was to see a part of their life-savings taking to his heels on the road to the North. It was these pressures within Southern society that forced Southern spokesmen of conciliatory disposition to take up extreme positions when confronted by the condemnation of Southern society and the threat to close the West to slavery.

The census of 1850 enumerated 347,525 slaveowners. Some were elderly or single persons, but the majority were heads of families and in a prolific society it is safe to assume that, on the average, four persons were directly dependent on each slaveowner. This adds 1,390,100 to the total. In addition there were overseers, bookkeepers, and other whites employed on plantations so that slaveowners, dependents, and white employees may account for two million out of a total of six million white persons. The upper class slaveowners at Washington belonged to a minority indeed, but spoke for a far larger proportion of population than a crude numerical comparison between slaveowners and total population might suggest.[39]

The political strength of slaveowners was significant. If one assumes that 10 percent of the slaveowners were women or minors, there were about 318,000 adult male slaveowners out of a total of approxi-

---

39. Cf. Otto H. Olsen, "Historians and the Extent of Slave Ownership in the Southern United States" (*Civil War History* 18, 2, 1972, 101–16). In 1860, 31 percent of the white families in the Confederate states owned slaves, and in South Carolina as many as 48.7 percent.

mately 1,200,000 potential voters. In some counties the proportion of slaveowning voters would be much higher; in others it would be much lower or negligible but these were usually in the poorer and more remote regions. The political impact of the slave-owning vote becomes more apparent if one considers the states separately. In Alabama the estimated number of slave-owning voters was a little under one-third; in Florida, Georgia, and Louisiana over a third; and in South Carolina nearly one-half. At the other end of the scale there were only 809 slaveowners out of 14,000 white males in Delaware. Virginia had the largest number of slaveowners in the South but they cast only about 50,000 votes out of a total of 177,000. In North Carolina fewer than a quarter of the voters owned slaves; in Tennessee and Kentucky about a quarter; in Maryland and Arkansas less than one-fifth. The slave-owning constituency was therefore much larger in the lower than in the upper South.

There is another significant difference. In the upper South over two-thirds of the slaveowners possessed fewer than 10 slaves, and over half less than 5. In the lower South over half owned more than 10, while only 3,439 out of 77,608 owned less than 5. In the upper South only 264 were very large slaveowners, with more than 100 slaves, and Virginia and North Carolina accounted for 207 of them. In the lower South 1,463 came into this category, with no fewer than 484 in South Carolina and 320 in Louisiana. The difference is equally striking in the category of slaveowners with 50 to 100 slaves: 1,660 in the upper and 4,698 in the lower South. In gross numbers they begin to even out in the 20–49 slaves range—12,490 in the upper, 16,867 in the lower South—but the ratio of slaveowners in this category to white population is striking: in the upper South one in about 330, in the lower South one in 108. From these figures one can conclude that the slaveowning constituency was predominantly middle class in the upper South and predominantly upper class in the lower South. In both sections wealthy slaveowners provided the leaders, but in the upper South they operated from a much broader popular base than in the lower South where slave power represented concentrated wealth and large plantations.

The most vulnerable point in the slave power's armor was the possibility of a movement against slavery in the South itself. The "white counties" of western Virginia had taken the lead in pressing for emancipation in the famous debates of 1831, and the spirit though subdued was not dead. There was an active anti-slavery movement in Kentucky, and much sympathy for gradual emancipation. Delaware was already regarded as lost, because the number of slaves was small and the state had little economic incentive to cling to the institution. Voluntary emancipation was making headway in Maryland. In Missouri events might easily turn the large minority of non-slaveowners against the slave-owning elite. Many of the areas where slavery was weak were poor and backward, but some were relatively prosperous and produced educated leaders to voice their complaints. Such men were likely to link the economic or social grievances of their region with slavery, which provided wealth and status for the men who dominated state governments.

A contemporary historian of Virginia probably exaggerated when he wrote that "the people . . . hold slavery to be an enormous evil, bearing with fatal power upon their prosperity," but it was nevertheless significant that such a statement could be published in 1848.[40] In 1847 Henry Ruffner, president of Washington College at Lexington in Virginia, published an *Address to the People of West Virginia . . . showing that Slavery is injurious to the public welfare, and that it may be gradually abolished without detriment to the Rights of Slaveholders.* Ruffner was a remarkable man whose published works included two volumes of Calvinist theology, a history of the early Christian fathers, and a romantic novel. He produced figures to show that Virginia had lost more people by migration than the total of all the old free states, and concluded that,

> It is a truth, a certain truth, that slavery drives free laborers — farmers, mechanics, and all, and some of the best of them too—out of the country and fills their places with ne-groes.[41]

Adherence to slavery had given a preponderance to the East, and all "just and enlightened policy" had been sacrificed. The dominant slaveowners had refused to make roads and thus impoverished the West.

Cassius M. Clay, the flamboyant Kentucky abolitionist, who

40. R. R. Howison, *History of Virginia* (1848), II: 519. Quoted in Beverley B. Munford, *Virginia's Attitude toward Slavery and Secession* (New York, 1909), 99.

41. Ruffner believed that slavery would increase in western Virginia. The price of cotton would fall and with the demand for slaves from the lower South, the situation would then be that "the headspring in East Virginia cannot contain itself; it must find a vent: it will shed its black streams through every gap of the Blue Ridge and pour over the Alleghany, till it is checked by abolitionism on the borders." In the next stage Eastern slaveholders would move to new lands, and cheap slaves would be offered in thousands.

came himself from the Southern upper class, saw deference to slave-owners as a major obstacle to progress.

> To this insignificant minority we have sacrificed common schools—we cannot maintain them; the national and state constitutions—they have been trampled underfoot; liberty of speech and the press—there is not a despotism in Europe that has less than we; . . . manufactures, they are impossible with slave labor; all the arts and sciences, the useful and ornamental—they perish here.[42]

In 1849, at a Constitutional Convention held in Kentucky, one speaker emphasized that political advance had also been thwarted by slavery.

> The ballot system is called for . . . we are told that it will prove injurious to the slave interests; constitutional reform would endanger slave property; driven in at all points, we ask that representation shall be equal and uniform. . . . Even at this point they meet us, and say that we must yield. They tell us the dearest rights of Kentucky freemen must yield to the slave . . . where is this matter to stop?[43]

This was the substance behind James G. Palfrey's hope that "the Southern non-slaveholders belong of right to our party—the party of the free," but anti-slavery men in the South knew what cards were stacked against them. Ruffner recalled that in 1831 "strong hopes were entertained that in a few years, a decided majority of the legislature would be for ridding us of this deleterious institution," but when he wrote in 1847 any discussion was unwelcome. The inability of those who favored the removal of free Negroes and slaves to suggest any place save Liberia to which they could be sent, and the abolitionist assertion that the freed slave must take his place as an equal citizen, combined to increase fear of the consequences of emancipation. The large slaveowners might not provide very good government, but they kept the blacks under control in areas where their labor was valued. This feeling intensified an argument over the extension of slavery and monopolized political thought in the South.

42. C. M. Clay, *Writings*, ed. Horace Greeley (New York, 1848), 41.
43. Quoted in Martin, *Anti-Slavery in Kentucky*, 135–36.

\*     \*     \*

To the rural middle class of the South the Southern Address was more potent than appeals to the past or to abstract interest. Should men who held slaves, or wished to hold slaves, "be disenfranchised of a privilege possessed by all others, citizens and foreigners, without discrimination as to character, profession, or color." The drastic verdict on Southern character would not be ignored when "all, whether savage, barbarian, or civilized, may freely enter and remain, we only being excluded." Beyond that horizon abolition lurked just out of sight and with it a tidal wave of free blacks, in alliance with the Northern majority, who would hold "the white race at the South in complete subjection."[44] The extent to which this was permeating the conscience of the plain people of the South was illustrated dramatically in Kentucky.

A plan for gradual emancipation was submitted in 1849 to the Kentucky Constitutional Convention and sponsored by Henry Clay. All slaves born in or after a year to be decided (1855 was suggested with 1860 as an alternative) would become free at the age of twenty-five, but would be required to work for a further three years. Wages earned would not be paid in cash but accumulated to pay the cost of transportation to a colony (which was not named). The offspring of this emancipated class would first be apprenticed without wages, and then be hired out for three years to earn the cost of their transportation. Thus no slave would be free before 1880 (or 1885 if the later date were adopted), those born before 1855 (or 1860) would remain enslaved, and as late as 1945 there might still have been nonagerian slaves in Kentucky. Gradualism could hardly have been more gradual.

Nevertheless when the Kentucky convention met, the pro-slavery men won a resounding triumph. All existing slave laws were retained; voluntary emancipation was made more difficult; the immigration of free blacks was forbidden; and a clause in the new constitution declared:

> The right of property is before and higher than any constitutional sanction; and the right of the owner of a slave, and its increase, is the same and is as inviolable as the right of the owner to any property whatever.[45]

44. John C. Calhoun, *Works,* ed. Richard K. Crallé, 6 vols. (New York, 1853–55; reprint ed. 1968), VI: The Southern Address, 303, 310–11.
45. Martin, *Anti-Slavery in Kentucky,* 137.

This triumph of slavery in its most exposed bastion was received with delight in the Southern press. The *Banner* of Augusta, Georgia, expressed immense relief, because if the Kentucky plan had been adopted abolition would have followed everywhere. The *Richmond Enquirer* proclaimed that Henry Clay's character was now revealed. "The man is an abolitionist."

There were further aspects of this defeat for emancipation. Of the hundred counties in Kentucky, forty-four had fewer than one thousand slaves, and only nine had more than five thousand, and in one of these (Jefferson) the white population was over forty-seven thousand. In 1847 the legislature had voted by a large majority to call a constitutional convention, though it was known that emancipation would be an issue. By the later months of 1848 the situation had changed dramatically. It was noted that avowed supporters of slavery were everywhere successful, and that even in the more populous "white" counties opponents of slavery went down to defeat.

The remarkable victory of slavery in Kentucky illustrates an aspect of Southern society which Northern critics persistently ignored. The forgotten man of anti-slavery discourse was not the "poor white" but small farmers who formed the vast majority of the Southern electorate. For them the Wilmot proviso was not an abstract argument about Southern rights, but a real issue which affected their immediate prospects. In Southern settlement the successful men had broken new land with slave labor and much of the pioneer work had been done by small slaveowners. Large slaveowners had little incentive to move to the West, and Texas and Florida still had enormous areas of vacant land suitable for large-scale planting or farming; but for small slaveowners, or men who hoped to rise in the world, the denial of "Southern rights" meant that in the competitive struggle for new land they would be unable to use the labor to which they were accustomed. Or, as many of them bought slaves as an investment, they would be deprived of would-be purchasers.

Thus the reaction in the South to the Wilmot proviso grew from two powerful roots, the alarms of an establishment and the aspirations of a rural middle class. To this was added the fear of what might follow if slaves were released from the discipline of their owners. Their natural inclination to flee from the place of bondage would be reinforced by economic imperatives which would drive them into competition with whites for land. More remote, but still very real, were fears that a relatively stable society would become disorganized, social life be debased, and the races become hybrid.

When Southern politicians returned to Washington in December 1849, to renew the fight which had been adjourned in March, they did so in the knowledge that on vital issues they spoke for a united society. There were still strongly partisan Democrats and Whigs in the South—and a vast number of devoted Unionists—but there was a growing conviction that the two-party system could not meet their needs. In this mood they were sure that duty called them to meet any new "aggressions" from the North, and that if they failed to do so, an aroused electorate might drive them from public life. Ironically their popular support owed much to the class which John Gorham Palfrey had presented as the ready-made constituency for a national anti-slavery Whig party.

# Chapter 10

# COMPROMISE

During the fall of 1849 news came from California that the inhabitants, recently joined by thousands of gold-seekers and unwilling to wait longer for organized government, had called a convention, drawn up a constitution, prohibited slavery, and would apply for immediate admission as a state. The procedure was irregular but not illegal. It had become customary for territories to await enabling acts before proceeding to draw up state constitutions, and the territory of California had not even been organized; but direct action was not forbidden and the Californians had been encouraged by a personal emissary from the President, T. Butler King of Georgia.

If California was admitted with the proposed constitution slavery would be prohibited on the whole Pacific coast from Canada to Mexico. If an enabling bill had come before Congress the Southerners would certainly have pressed for a division between northern and southern California, and some Northern Democrats might have joined them to organize southern California as a separate territory. This would not have averted a crisis—for the Wilmot proviso would have been proposed while some Southerners would have pressed for federal protection of slavery—but it would have taken a different form.

In California there had been some doubt over eastern boundaries, but no suggestion that Californians should voluntarily lop off their southern portion. Only an act of Congress could now force them to do so, and there was not the slightest chance that the House of Representatives would pass such a law, and though some Southerners continued to talk of extending the Missouri Compromise line, the main thrust of their demands shifted to different ground.

If California was admitted it was claimed that the South would be so adversely affected that compensation must be given. The exclusion of slavery from the only part of the West that offered scope for large-scale commercial farming, a free state majority in the Senate, the probable prohibition of slavery in all the remaining territories, and its possible abolition in the District of Columbia would combine to create a situation that demanded radical remedies.

President Taylor was resolutely opposed to the principle of compensation. He took the reasonable view that the Union could not endure if terms of alliance had to be negotiated every time a new state applied for admission, while common sense suggested that if the Californians were kept waiting much longer they would lose patience and declare their independence. For the rest of the vast area he had the advantage, enjoyed by few politicians, of knowing the country and its climate, and decided that it was folly to quarrel over an area where plantation slavery could never be established. He had reason to believe that the people of Santa Fé would shortly submit an application for statehood on behalf of New Mexico, and proposed that no action should be taken until they did so.

Unfortunately another boundary claim now became significant. The Texans claimed sovereignty over Santa Fé, and if the region was already part of a slave state the people could not take separate action. Taylor would have none of this. The Texans had never exercised authority in the Santa Fé region, had conspicuously failed to establish it in 1843, and could not now revive a dormant claim merely to legalize slavery in an area where it had never existed.

The principal weakness of Taylor's plan was that it ignored the intensity of Southern feeling. In January 1849 the *Richmond Enquirer*, which was not normally given to extreme language, defined the issue. It was "the sovereignty or vassalage of fifteen States of the American Union." If they were to avoid becoming "dependencies, or mere appendages of a combination (no longer a Union) of States hostile to their institutions . . . they must arouse their energies—prepare, consult, combine, for prompt and decisive action."[1] The call to action was not mere rhetoric, for the Southern Address of February 1849 had borne fruit in a call for a Southern Convention to meet at Nashville in June 1850 and the possibility that Southern moderates might then be

1. Quoted in *National Intelligencer*, 2 February 1850.

driven to enlist under Calhoun's banner hung as an ominous cloud over all the early deliberations of the Thirty-first Congress.

Southern Congressmen were aware of the popular pressure generated in their own states. The Wilmot proviso had transformed abstract discussion of Southern rights and hypothetical abolitionist designs into a genuine popular movement in defense of Southern society. A temperate letter in the *American Review* from a Virginian explained to Northern readers that if Southern leaders appeared "to conduct themselves occasionally in a very strange manner" it was not due to "genuine madness."

> A *politician*, of whatever clime, never loses his wits. They know that the community which they represent is impulsive, and they make their own demeanor to conform. The Congressman who is thus acting a part may appear ridiculous, but do not thence infer that an excited People will prove a spectacle to excite mirth. *Their* frenzy, if frenzy should seize them, will be of another sort.[2]

Some Northern politicians who met Southerners face to face became aware of the pressure on them. Francis Granger, the moderate New York Whig who had been a member of Tyler's cabinet, realized that the proviso had created a situation in which the Southerners must unite. "I know," he wrote, "that the ground having been taken, it cannot be abandoned—but better far better had it never been taken up. I so said at the time to those who put Wilmot up to it, soon after the game had opened."[3] From a distance it was more difficult to grasp the situation, and in February an experienced New York politician complained to Seward that "you gentlemen in Washington have pretty much all this agitation to yourselves." In the North there were "no public meetings, no alarming hand-bills, no loud talk, everything seems to be smiling around us."[4] Understanding was not helped by the *National Intelligencer*, which supported the President, circulated widely among Northern Whigs, tried to ignore the tension in Congress, and waited until February before providing its readers with an analysis of the question. Then it attributed "the excitement and the agitation, at the present juncture, of questions almost entirely geographical and sectional in their character" to anticipation of the

2. Letter signed "Tamen." *American Review*, New Series, V: 340.
3. To Thurlow Weed, 5 February 1850. Granger Papers, Library of Congress, Washington, D.C.
4. Simon Draper, 7 February 1850. Seward Papers. Rush-Rhees Library, University of Rochester, Rochester, N.Y.

1850 census which would show the growing preponderance of the North and the emergence of a new political power in the West. This tame explanation did nothing to reveal the intensity of Southern feeling.

In the North, the excitement of 1848 had died down and except in a few localities the Free Soil movement had left no legacy of crusading enthusiasm. Men of both parties assumed that, after the rhetorical points had been made, Southerners would recognize the impossibility of struggling against the tide of free settlement in the West. With this assurance a majority were now prepared to sacrifice the principle of the Wilmot proviso, and some Democrats went much further in their appeal to racial prejudice and contempt for Free Soilers. In July 1850 the *Democratic Review*, now under conservative control, warned that "The blacks already begin to aspire to a superiority over the whites, and Mr Giddings, the representative of Africa in the House, distinctly avows his preference for thick skulls and woolley heads."[5] The principal difference between the parties was that the Democrats would leave the choice to settlers on the spot, believing that white men in the territories had the right to enslave black men if they wished to do so; while Whigs believed that they could not do so without the authority of Congress (which was unlikely to be given). To avoid argument most Northern Whigs were ready to settle for Taylor's plan and get both California and New Mexico into the Union, as states, as quickly as possible.[6]

There was thus a marked contrast at Washington between the behavior of Southern and Northern politicians. The long debate over slavery in the South had terminated with emphatic proof that a substantial majority of non-slaveowners preferred slavery to any alternative, and the absurdity of any plan to remove free blacks by colonization or deportation was recognized. With slavery accepted as a permanent—and perhaps beneficial—institution, it became a point of great emotional significance to defend a slave society against imputations of inferiority. To this was added the great competitive advantage which slave property would give to migrant Southerners in a land where labor was scarce and dear. Southern politicians could not ignore the upsurge of popular resentment, and were bound to give it expres-

5. *Democratic Review*, XXVII: 1.

6. Robert C. Winthrop believed that the plan had "some difficulties" but seemed feasible (Winthrop to Everett, 30 January 1850, Everett Papers, Massachusetts Historical Society, Boston, Mass.); Horace Greeley was ready to organize New Mexico as a territory without the proviso, on the assumption that Southerners were not really concerned about slavery (*New York Tribune*, 1 February 1850).

sion in Congress. Religion and medical science appeared to back the Southern racial theories and the fact that these were endorsed by most Northerners lent support to the view that Northern attacks on slavery were not inspired by concern for black welfare.

By contrast, Northern politicians knew of divided counsels among their constituents or lack of recognition that a crisis was imminent. There was no clear majority view on the issues that Southerners insisted on bringing to the fore, and most Northerners would have much preferred to turn to normal business and the urgent problems presented by expansion and economic growth. Under these circumstances it was natural for Southerners to seize the initiative and lay down terms before the administration or Northern Whigs had an opportunity to present their case. The situation was made worse by the political inexperience of the President, the relative obscurity of his cabinet, and lack of leadership in Congress. As a soldier Taylor had been lucky rather than skillful, had had little success when he personally directed a battle, and relied most upon popularity and a reputation for determination. Shut up in the White House, without strong subordinates to direct affairs in Congress, popularity and determination were of no avail.

George W. Julian, a young protégé of Joshua Giddings, found the array of prominent Whigs singularly unimpressive. "Old Zack" was "an outrageously ugly, uncultivated, uninformed old man," who could not speak without "mispronouncing words, stuttering, stammering, and frequently making a break-down in the middle of a sentence." Daniel Webster was "the most intellectual man" he had ever seen, but was known to be "of weak integrity, wavering and uncertain principles, and never to be trusted when popular opinion is to be encountered." John M. Clayton had "a huge frame," was "very corpulent," and looked like "a man of talents . . . unaccompanied by moral principle." Judge McLean was "a timid, cowardly, old-fashioned politician, afraid the South will dissolve the Union, and almost ready to advise free soilers to surrender for the sake of peace." Clay alone made a favorable impression, but he was "quite old and shrivelled . . . and fast descending to the grave." Horace Greeley thought the cabinet "a horrid mixture, just such as a blind man (or one blindfolded) would probably have fished up, if turned in among three or four hundred would-be magnates of the Whig party and ordered to touch and take."[7] Altogether the Whig leadership looked elderly,

7. To Isaac Julian, 25 January 1850, Julian-Giddings Papers, Library of Congress, Washington, D.C.; Greeley-Colfax Letters, 17 March 1850, New York Public Library.

incompetent, unprincipled, or confused; which was, perhaps, an uncharitable judgment but too close to the mark to justify any optimism about political prospects.

The seriousness of the situation became apparent as soon as the House assembled and proceeded to ballot for a Speaker. The Whigs had a narrow nominal majority, but in their caucus Robert Toombs of Georgia moved a resolution condemning "all action in favor of the Wilmot Proviso and tending to the abolition of slavery in the District."[8] This was rejected, and as a result some Southern Whigs refused to support Robert C. Winthrop, first choice of the majority.

On the first ballot 221 voted and the rules required an absolute majority (111) of all the votes cast. Howell Cobb of Georgia, nominated by the Democratic caucus, received 103, and Winthrop 96. Eight Free Soilers voted for Wilmot, and Wilmot himself voted for Root of Ohio; six Southern Whigs voted for Gentry of Tennessee; Horace Mann received two Northern Whig votes, and six other members received one vote each. In subsequent ballots it became clear that the Free Soilers and the dissident Southern Whigs could not be moved, that other Southern Whigs would not vote for a Democrat, and that two or three Calhounites would not vote for Cobb. For a wearisome succession of ballots the stalemate continued. Winthrop rose to 102, but with the arrival of four more members, 114 was required for a choice. On the fortieth ballot William J. Brown, Democrat of Indiana, was within two of a majority, but Southern members became suspicious when he received Free Soil votes and withdrew support when it became known that he had promised them representation on the committees on Territories and the District of Columbia. Finally it was agreed that if no majority could be found after three more ballots, the man with the largest number of votes would be Speaker. On the final ballot the voting was almost exactly what it had been on the first, with Cobb chosen by 103 against 96 for Winthrop. Wilmot had eight, Gentry four, and five others one each; four Representatives were absent by accident or design.

The Free Soilers had had an opportunity to make Winthrop Speaker on the final vote, and have been blamed for allowing the prize to go to a Southern Democrat. Arithmetic does not tell all. If Free Soilers called early in the viva voce vote had supported Winthrop, this might well have caused Southern defections later in the roll. Moreover

8. N. W. Hilliard (Representative from Alabama) to Appleton, 4 December 1849. Appleton Papers, Massachusetts Historical Society, Boston Mass. It is not possible to reconcile the voting figures with the totals given in *Historical Statistics of the United States*, 691 (Series Y204–209).

the new party was drawn from both older parties, and Wilmot, a lifelong Democrat, would have found it as repugnant to support an orthodox Whig as Joshua Giddings to vote for a Democrat. Future growth could be assured only by sticking together in isolation, and if they supported a Whig or Democrat the price must be recognition of their independent existence and assignment to committees. This was political logic for men who looked to the future, but widened the breach with anti-slavery Whigs who could not willingly cooperate with men who had prevented their party from organizing the House, and had given the Speakership to a young, vigorous, ruthless, and partisan Democrat. Cobb gave the committees of the House a strongly Southern character; his rulings sanctioned Southern obstructionist tactics, prevented the House from voting on the admission of California, and effectively stifled the will of the majority in both parties. He also cooperated with Southern members to prevent a vote on the vexed Texas boundary, though a House majority was opposed to Texan control of Santa Fé. In effect the House was virtually deprived of its due influence throughout one of the longest sessions on record.[9]

The paralysis of the House of Representatives was symptomatic of the condition into which the country had drifted. The great question of slavery in the territories was insoluble by normal processes of debate and majority votes, and blocked the way to discussion of every other issue. Matters that interested large numbers of American citizens had to be shelved while both Houses of Congress endlessly discussed the sectional crisis. Among the neglected problems were reform of the public land system (to make free or cheaper land available to settlers), the proposed railroad to the Pacific, land grants to other railroads, adjustments to the tariff, and such minor but important questions as the abolition of flogging in the Navy. The Senate did find time to ratify the Clayton-Bulwer treaty with Great Britain, but gave brief consideration to the important principles involved. Under more favorable circumstances it would have been possible to find time for other business even in a congested timetable, but most Senators felt impelled to deliver set pieces of not less than two and sometimes of four or five hours' duration, while in the House Speaker Cobb found it

9. Holman Hamilton, "The Cave of Winds," *Journal of Southern History*, Vol. 23 (1957). The key figures, apart from Cobb, were Linn Boyd of Tennessee (chairman of the Committee on Territories and of the Committee of the Whole House), Thomas H. Bayly of Virginia (chairman of Ways and Means), and John McLernand of Illinois, a lieutenant of Senator Stephen A. Douglas.

expedient to recognize dozens of speakers on the Southern side and to connive at procedural moves that prevented territorial questions from being brought to the vote.

These considerations underline the handicaps of the thirty-first Congress as it approached the crisis; yet it was, in many ways, the most distinguished of the century. The wealth of old and new talent in the Senate is well known. The House, which never had a real chance to show its quality, contained, in the opinion of some observers, an unusually high proportion of able and eloquent men. In February a Washington correspondent of the *New York Tribune* wrote,

> I become more and more sensible every day that this Congress, whether it may achieve little or much, might stand an advantageous comparison as respects talents, intellect and oratorical power, with any contemporary legislative body in the world. I was favourably impressed with the appearance of the House of Representatives as a whole, when I came here, but had no idea of the mental repasts that were in store for me.[10]

Indeed, the close rivalry between the major parties, together with intense public interest, may have brought forward candidates of higher than average attainments and ability. The weakness of Congress did not lie in its members but in the rupture of the system of informal understanding on which successful government depends.

In both houses the party leaders hoped to achieve their objectives by ignoring the extremes, but in the event this tactic offered further impediments to the conduct of business. The Speakership contest had been concerned as much with the composition of committees as with personalities. It was normal practice for the Speaker to appoint committees, with his own party holding the chairmanships and major representation, but there was also an expectation that he would give fair representation to the minority party. The Free Soilers had contended for recognition in the allocation to committees, had failed to win their point, and could therefore expect nothing, but in view of the unusual circumstances attending his election Cobb might have been more scrupulous than usual in recognizing Northern Whigs. In fact his appointments were heavily weighted toward Southern Democrats, and some assignments were given to the Southern Whigs who had

10. Report signed "Roger Sherman," *New York Tribune*, 25 February 1850.

supported neither Winthrop nor himself. Committees so constituted were unlikely to command the confidence of the House, but their reports on major issues were not put to the test because their unacknowledged purpose was to hold up the legislative process until the territorial question had been settled to the satisfaction of the South. In the Senate committees were elected by ballot, but the slate was normally drawn up by the party caucuses, and a notable feature was the refusal of any assignments to Senators Chase, Hale, and Seward. Chase and Hale were Free Soilers, but both owed their seats to Democratic support in their state legislatures and might therefore have expected recognition. The omission of Seward was more serious. Though a new Senator he had been long in the forefront of Whig politics, and his friend Thurlow Weed was one of the leading strategists of the party. In New York both men had worked actively for Taylor before and after nomination, and Seward had become a close adviser to the President. His failure to receive a committee assignment was an insult to the administration, the state of New York, and the Northern Whigs who shared his anti-slavery views. It could have been no accident but a deliberate decision by the Southern and conservative Northern Whigs who dominated the party in the Senate.

\*    \*    \*

It is appropriate at this point to speculate on motives and expectations. While there were distinguished old men whose careers were drawing to a close, there were many younger men who looked beyond the crisis to the political world in which they wished to live. Fifteen years' experience had persuaded most men that the normal way to organize national political life was in two parties, so the question to be decided was their future character.

Howell Cobb, a man of great intelligence and character, was committed to a national Democratic party in which he expected to play a leading part. His conduct as Speaker is explained not merely by his wish to postpone votes on California and New Mexico, but also by the need to prevent the Democratic party from tearing itself apart. This had been threatened when the party split on the Wilmot proviso, and the division must not become permanent. In this Cobb was at one with Stephen A. Douglas, whose ambitions already embraced the presidency, and at home both men were fighting off threats to party unity. Cobb resolutely opposed the Calhounites, who now condemned alliance with any Northern group, while Douglas hoped to win back

Democrats who had deserted to Free Soil and to undercut the influence
of Thomas Hart Benton, who was increasingly unpopular with fellow
Southern Democrats. Both Cobb and Douglas were therefore trying to
steer the national party through the storms of sectional controversy,
and the prize would be the support of highly professional state organizations, with strong appeal to new voters, and traditional loyalty to
majority decisions. They foresaw, correctly, that the Van Burenites
would rejoin the party as soon as they could do so with honor. Paradoxically the sacrificial victims were likely to be the conservative Democrats of the Northeast, who had been anchormen of the national ticket
in 1848, for radicals would tolerate no reunion which confirmed the
ascendancy secured by Hunkers under Polk.

From his secure base in the West Douglas looked forward to
leading the party during a period of expansion on the Great Plains,
consolidation on the Pacific coast, exploitation of American natural
resources, and a vigorous foreign policy. To this Cobb may have added
thoughts of expansion in the Caribbean by the extension of economic
spheres of influence, if not by acquisition. Neither man looked with
favor on the presidential ambitions of James Buchanan, who was
safely out of range as minister in London, and hoped to rally enough
support in the South and West to neutralize his control of Pennsylvania and influence among Eastern conservatives.

The Whig problem was difficult but not insoluble. The party
had held together remarkably well through all the trials of Tyler's
presidency, Texan annexation, and Mexican war, but too many men
had different ideas about its future. Henry Clay's presidential ambitions were almost if not quite exhausted. He would be seventy five in
1852 and even his most devoted adherents could hardly contemplate a
four-year term. Nevertheless Clay regarded the party as his own and
wished to leave upon it the imprint of his personality. This meant
holding together in alliance large planters and merchants from the
lower South, small farmers from the white counties of the upper
South, manufacturers and men interested in internal improvements
from all parts of the Union, conservative merchants and bankers from
New York and Boston, and anti-slavery Whigs from the small towns
and rural districts who were unconditionally opposed to the extension
of slavery. This coalition of diverse interests required a delicate balance of power at the center and a nationwide network of personal
arrangements and understandings. In 1850 Clay was aware of the obvious harm inflicted by sectionalism to this alliance, and believed that
Taylor was doing as much as anyone to wreck it. It followed that some

formula must be found on which Northern and Southern Whigs could cooperate, and the President isolated from the congressional party. He did not exclude the possibility of attracting some Democrats into this alliance, but did not anticipate that the outcome of all his efforts would strengthen the Democratic and fatally weaken the Whig party.

Daniel Webster's presidential ambitions were not entirely exhausted and, even if he could not win the prize, he hoped to bequeath a handsome legacy to younger followers such as Winthrop and Rufus Choate. His base was the commercial and industrial interests of New England, but he had failed to build a national political structure on the foundation of economic association between North and South, and lacked support west of the Appalachians. He still hoped to attract Southern support for a Massachusetts leader, and with skilful handling the crisis of 1850 might yield unexpected dividends. A threat to the Union would rally support from both North and South, and provide the nucleus for a truly conservative national party. One option was to support Zachary Taylor, and some of his closest friends expected him to do so. On February 18 Edward Everett wrote to Webster about a report that he had been consulted by the President, and added "I cannot but congratulate him on recovering from the extraordinary delusion under which he entered office, that there were times when the government of the country could be administered with the assistance of Second-rate men."[11] And as late as March 3 Winthrop told Everett that he had no idea what line Webster would take in the speech announced for March 7 but had "every reason to think that it will look to the President's plan." Nevertheless in his famous speech Webster accepted the principle—anathema to the President—that the South must be compensated for the admission of California and, in addition, threw in support for a new Fugitive Slave Law. Perhaps the truth is that by March, Taylor was so alienated from the Southern Whigs that support for him would have closed the door on a national conservative Whig alliance.

A man who watched the movements of the two great compromisers with considerable interest was Vice-President Millard Fillmore. In his own state he could make little headway against Seward and Weed, but the situation might alter if he could inherit the conservative interests which had looked to Clay or Webster for leadership. The attractiveness of this prospect increased when Seward quickly established close relations with Zachary Taylor, and the

11. Everett Papers, 18 February 1850; 3 March 1850.

Vice-President found himself with little influence on New York patronage. Success by the new alliance might mean Fillmore's political extinction.

William Henry Seward had no intention of letting the leadership of the party go by default. He was strong but not unchallenged in New York; he had won political credit in Ohio when he campaigned for Taylor in 1848; and through his influence with the administration hoped to gain further allies in Washington. But how could a Northern Whig, of known anti-slavery opinions, hope to win a national constituency? Early in 1849, when building up support for his election to the Senate, he had defined his position with characteristic sensitivity. In a letter intended for circulation he wrote that he would never defend or apologize for slavery, would do all in his power to prevent its extension, and looked "confidently to its ultimate removal from the face of the earth." But these aims could not be achieved "by disorganizing action but by the lawful action of those to whom responsibility belongs." He would not break down "any barrier that the Constitution had erected between the Federal authority and the States," but he would insist that the Constitution gave free states the right to refuse responsibility for slavery.[12] A year earlier Thurlow Weed had described Seward as uncompromising in opposition to the extension of slavery, and "looking to the action of Whig principles for the accomplishment of all that can be done for freedom."[13]

In the context of 1850, Whig principles, as understood by Seward and Weed, meant that when all safeguards had been duly observed and constitutional limitations respected, the national majority must determine the course of policy. One point was secured when, in his first annual message, Taylor declared that he would not use the veto except to protect his own constitutional rights or when there was clear evidence that Congress had acted with undue haste. The next and more difficult point was to convince enough Southern Whigs that they could not expect to preserve slavery indefinitely against the declared opinion of the national majority. Once this was realized all could be asked to share responsibility for its gradual elimination. It was to persuade Southerners to accept these arguments that Seward applied his efforts in the Senate; he may have been influenced by Palfrey's argument that anti-slavery represented the true interests of the Southern whites, but his arguments were addressed to Southern leaders and not over their heads to the plain people. He failed in his effort.

12. Draft letter to J. Watson Webb, 1 February 1849, Seward Papers.
13. *Ibid.*, 28 January 1848.

This was partly because his political enemies succeeded in isolating him in the Senate, and partly because of his unfortunate facility for expressing temperate and far-sighted views in a way that sounded uncompromising and radical.

\*    \*    \*

To an extraordinary degree Southerners seized the initiative in Congress. Early in February the *New York Tribune* complained that

> The South . . . governs in good measure both Houses of Congress, and under their management the time of the country is wasted, public business retarded . . . and the wheels of government all but stopped.[14]

It became clear that the normal processes of government could not be resumed until Southern demands had been satisfied. It was a vital element in the situation that Howell Cobb was able to prevent the House from passing a bill for the admission of California, which would have also enjoyed the full weight of executive favor. Lewis Cass wrote privately that he would have voted for unconditional admission if a bill had reached the Senate "for it is exactly the ground for which I have contended."[15] Other Northern Democratic senators would have found it difficult to avoid the same conclusion, and a bill would certainly have had the votes of Benton, all the Northern Whigs, perhaps the two Senators from Delaware, and would, of course, have been promptly signed by Taylor. In default of an admission bill from the House, Southern Senators had ample opportunity to stake their claims and state their case.

  With the time thus gained Southerners in both houses developed the argument that they had grievances which must be met before California could be admitted or the territorial question settled. During January the attack was fairly launched. In the House Thomas L. Clingman proclaimed that disunion was being forced by the Northern majority, and such vehemence—coming from a North Carolina Whig—was particularly disturbing. In the Senate Andrew Butler of South Carolina spoke at length on Southern grievances, and particularly on Northern aid to runaway slaves. James B. Mason proposed a bill on fugitives which placed responsibility collectively on the na-

14. From an editorial dated 4 February 1850.
15. J. S. Bagg Papers, Huntington Library, San Marino, Calif., 20 February 1850.

tional government and individually on every citizen of the United States. Jeremiah Clemens of Alabama was particularly violent in denouncing the North in general and Free Soilers in particular. Henry S. Foote of Mississippi seemed to be the most excited and certainly the most active of all the Southern Senators; he was "a sharp little bald man, with gray hair and whiskers . . . up and down all the time like a Jack in a box"; his extreme audibility made matters worse, for he intervened frequently, repetitively, and at length.[16] More weighty than Foote was Jefferson Davis, also of Mississippi, and with Calhoun too unwell for frequent participation in debate, he attracted attention as the principal spokesman for Southern intransigence. Calhoun himself was in Washington, and his brooding presence kept waverers in line, while the major contribution (which he was known to have in preparation) was eagerly awaited.

The President's policy became the principal target for Southern attacks in January, and Northern Whigs—who saw in it either the best alternative to the Wilmot proviso, or a convenient way of avoiding the troublesome question—were thrown on the defensive. Northern Democrats were equally uneasy at the inferences drawn by Southern speakers from the campaign of 1848. Lewis Cass went further than ever before in denying the right of Congress to prohibit slavery in the territories, but protested that this did not mean that decision must be postponed until slavery had been established.

Given the strength of Taylor's case, it is extraordinary that it received so little overt support in Congress. Neither spokesmen for the administration nor anti-slavery men entered the forum of debate until the fury of controversy had run for weeks. Seward did not make a set speech until March 11, though he was both anti-slavery and a frequent caller at the White House. He could sometimes be diffident and liked time to mature his ideas, but it is possible that he was kept from the floor of the Senate by the same influences that had kept him off all committees. Chase and Hale were not able to make their major contributions until March 12. This meant that neither the administration policy, nor moderate anti-slavery opinion, nor the more uninhibited doctrines of Free Soil had a chance to counter the vehemence of the Southern onslaught. When a new initiative came it was not from the administration but from Henry Clay whose plan for compromise admitted that the prosecution had a case before defense witnesses had been heard.

Though Southerners seemed united in the debates of January and

16. Report signed "Alpha" in the *New York Tribune*, 2 February 1850.

February, a practiced political ear could distinguish nuances which indicated deeper divisions. Unrepresented in the Senate and barely represented in the House were avowed disunionists who would welcome any developments that forced their compatriots toward secession. In Congress a more influential group, led by Calhoun and Jefferson Davis, believed that the Union ought to be preserved but was about to be destroyed by Northern action. What was required was not compromise but permanent guarantees for Southern interests. Jefferson Davis said that the minimum requirement was extension of the Missouri Compromise line to the Pacific, with slavery legalized in all land—occupied or subsequently acquired—to the south of it. Calhoun was known to favor still more drastic constitutional changes. The suggestion that the Union could be preserved only by insisting upon conditions which no Northern majority would accept alarmed the third group of Southerners, including some Whigs but led by Jacksonian nationalists such as Cobb and Foote, who believed that a settlement was possible by normal legislative processes. They interpreted the Democratic platform of 1848 to mean that slaveowners would be free to enter territories during the crucial period of settlement, and expected support from Northern Democrats on that point. In addition they wanted a Fugitive Slave Law which would deal with a troublesome problem in the upper South and make symbolic recognition that slavery was a national responsibility. Finally there were Whigs who were strong for Southern rights, apprehensive about the economic consequences of a breach with the North, intensely suspicious of Calhoun and all his works, and ready to settle for any solution that rejected the Wilmot proviso without resort to such a geographical monstrosity as statehood for New Mexico as a barrier to Southern expansion. They also believed that Texas must not lose her western lands without compensation.

The reality behind the rhetorical facade inspired Clay to offer his plan for compromise. The essential points were the immediate admission of California, the organization of New Mexico and Utah with the legislatures free to decide on slavery, an adjustment of the Texan boundary to exclude all parts of New Mexico, the assumption by the United States of Texan debts as compensation, the abolition of the slave trade in the District of Columbia, and a more effective federal law for the recovery of fugitive slaves. There is no need to question the sincerity of Clay's unionism but, as in so many of his political gestures, there was a strong element of personal vanity. He had hoped for the position Taylor now occupied, and his rejection by the party might have been easier to bear if the nomination had not gone to a man whose political inexperience emphasized the scant gratitude for his own devoted service to the party. As in 1841 he intended to demonstrate that he was still the real leader despite opportunists who had denied him his rightful place. He would give Taylor a chance to follow but not to lead. After announcing his compromise proposals he allowed time for the Administration to offer support, and explained them at first as supplement rather than as a substitute for the President's plan. Indeed Clay proposed to admit California; so did Taylor. He proposed to adjust the Texan boundary excluding the upper Rio Grande; so did Taylor. He proposed the assumption of the Texas debts, but this was an amendment to administration policy, not a rejection. He proposed to go ahead with the territorial organization of New Mexico, but merely because civil government was preferable to military. He opposed the congressional prohibition of slavery as inexpedient, but so did Taylor. He would give the territorial legislature a free hand, which did not greatly differ from the procedure in California that Taylor had approved. The President had made pronouncements on neither the Fugitive Slave Law nor the slave trade in the District of Columbia, so the inclusion of these proposals in Clay's plan was in no sense a rebuke to Taylor.

It was therefore open to Taylor to pass the word to the Whigs in Congress that while his own proposal was in some respects preferable (because less complicated), he would accept Clay's plan if Congress so willed. In fact this did not happen. While Clay's plan was criticized in the Senate by Southern "ultras," the Administration newspaper in Washington came out with a strong attack on his compromise resolutions. Thereafter it was assumed that the President would oppose compromise, and Clay now aimed to generate so much support in Congress and the country that Taylor would not dare to risk a veto; or, if he did, would stand condemned as a mere obstructionist.

The reasons for Taylor's rejection of Clay's plan are readily explained. He objected, in principle, to the theory that any part of the Union should be given compensation because another part appeared to gain some advantage. In the long run every part of the Union derived benefit from the progress of all, and interference with the flow of events could bring advantage to none. The Constitution provided all the safeguards needed by any minority interest; it was wrong and superfluous to adopt a system of political trading. The President's objections were reinforced when Clay agreed to combine California, the organization of New Mexico and Utah, the Texan boundary, and the assumption of the Texas debt in a single "omnibus" bill. If this precedent were set the admission of any new state might become impossible without the encumbrance of conditions and compensations. On a less abstract plane the principal supporters of the Administration in Congress were Northern Whigs who were committed in principle to the prohibition of slavery in the territories but were prepared to support the President's plan as a second best. If he now endorsed Clay's plan, his already weakened administration would lose what support it had.

The initial reception of Clay's plan in the North was not promising, and illustrated various facets of Northern opinion. Horace Greeley observed editorially in the *New York Tribune* that it had been immediately rejected by the men whom it was intended to conciliate. "No Southern Senator stands up with Mr. Clay. Enough said, gentlemen! Let the struggle go on."[17]

From Michigan the editor of the *Detroit Tribune* wrote that Clay's resolution on the slavery question, "knocks our position in regard to it all to the winds." He said that many Free Soilers had been joining the Whigs and accessions were expected from anti-slavery Democrats following the action of the Democratic majority in the state legislature in rescinding instructions to Cass to vote for the Wilmot Proviso. These hopes must be abandoned.[18] In New York one politician feared that Clay would divide the Whig party. He added,

> The Whig Masses and the people generally here are well satisfied with the President's recommendations and will sustain him. Still they *demand* that the proviso shall be incorporated into any Territorial Government created by Congress.[19]

In Rochester, Clay's resolutions "found little favor."[20] Anti-slavery resolutions were carried through the New York legislature, and Thurlow Weed believed that it would be possible to sustain the President provided the federal office holders were kept in line.[21] On February 27 the *New York Tribune* was affecting a puzzled attitude; things were really quite straightforward—"What *is* the difficulty? What *need* is

17. *New York Tribune*, 25 January 1850.
18. Josiah Snow to Seward, 7 February 1850, Seward Papers.
19. Anthony C. Brown of Ogdensburg to Seward, 21 February, Seward Papers.
20. *Ibid.*, Lewis Henry Morgan to Seward, 2 February.
21. *Ibid.*, Weed to Seward, 19 February.

there of Compromise?" Four days earlier the *Tribune* had observed
(with a show of dispassionate judgment)

> Of the two evils, Disunion or Slavery Extension, we prefer
> the former; of the two perils we consider the latter more im-
> minent.

But the *Tribune* also concluded that if the free states stood firm, all
would be well.[22]

Injunctions to stand firm were of little avail unless opinion was
really unified. In both parties there was considerable confusion, and at
first it seemed that the Democrats would feel the greater strain. The
Barnburners could not be easily forgiven by the regular Democrats,
and the Free Soil had given control of the New York party to Tammany
and conservatives or Hunkers. In February Barnburners and Hunkers
were doing most of the arguing over resolutions against the extension
of slavery, and it seemed that men such as Senator Daniel Dickinson
would go to any lengths to avoid offending the South. The *Democratic
Review,* now completely pro-Southern in opinion, published an article
in July linking all hostility to slavery with abolitionism, and the latter
with all the subversive doctrines that were abroad.

> It is not a mere dissolution of the Union and a war between
> two great races of mankind that is contemplated by the
> abolitionists, who are gradually approaching to, if they have
> not already arrived at, union with socialism and infidelity.[23]

The foundations of social order were being undermined. "Itinerant
lecturers are everywhere prowling about, gathering together female
audiences, to whom they propound the most crude, yet mischievous
doctrines." The rights of women, including suffrage, were being

22. *New York Tribune,* 23 February.
23. *Democratic Review* XXVII (July 1850): 3. The tone of the *Review* became increasingly
violent during 1850. One can sometimes sympathize with those who lost patience with William
Lloyd Garrison, but the following comment went beyond the limits expected in a periodical
with intellectual pretensions:

"We are convinced that this hybrid, half-breed, is a mere puppet, whose wires are pulled in
England, and who probably knows no more what he is about than Punch and Judy at a fair. He
will do very well for a leader among the females enamoured of amalgamation, and who, it seems,
are forming a union of the gown and the petticoat, to usurp the breeches; but it is sufficiently
evident that he is nothing more than a wooden sword in the hands of an expert harlequin, and
that his intrepidity is not derived from a clear conviction of right, but is merely the violent
presumption of ignorance." *Ibid.,* 4.

preached, so that not only was racial conflict threatened but also a movement which "would at once array the two sexes against each other in political strife."[24]

Clay was exceedingly anxious to generate support for his initiative. He wrote to Daniel Ullman of New York City that outside support would do much good.[25] On February 1 Ullman assured him that "our private organization is in full action," and had already secured control of the senior and junior Whig committees of the city; but on February 5 he was less optimistic because it was difficult to arouse interest. "There is little or no excitement on the subject in this community." Nevertheless it was decided to go ahead with a call for a Union meeting, and on February 15 Clay expressed the hope that it would do much good "if it be large, imposing, attended without distinction of party," and appear as "a local and spontaneous assemblage." The *Tribune* reported that the move had "strength in the Commercial interests of our city." The meeting seems to have been a moderate success, though one of Seward's supporters described it as "got up by a few individuals who intend to vote for Mr Clay one term after his decease and others who were apprehensive that the sale of Negro Kerseys was in jeopardy."[26]

Calhoun's celebrated speech of March 4 was a further incentive for Northern conservatives (as it was for Southern Democrats) to rally to the cause of compromise.[27] He began by asserting "the belief of the people of the Southern states . . . that they cannot remain, as things now are, consistently with honor and safety in the Union." The causes were twofold. Agitation of the slavery question had eroded away the foundations of mutual respect on which a political society must rest; churches had divided, parties were going, and soon there would remain no associations to give life to the political body. Secondly, the equilibrium between slave and free, which had made the Constitution possible, was now being destroyed. The admission of California would destroy equilibrium in the last institution where it still existed —the Senate of the United States. As there was no way of stopping the growth of Northern population, a constitutional amendment must be sought which would guarantee the minority against oppression. "A single section, governed by the will of the numerical

24. *Ibid.*, 15.
25. The correspondence is in Ullman Papers, New York Historical Society, New York, N.Y.
26. *New York Tribune*, 25 February; Chandler Starr to Seward, 26 February, Seward Papers.
27. *Congressional Globe*, 31. 1. 451ff.

majority, has now, in fact, the control of the Government and the entire powers of the system." A constitutional and federal republic "is now converted, in reality, into one as absolute as that of the Autocrat of Russia, and as despotic in its tendency as any absolute Government that ever existed."

Shorn of its more extreme statements Calhoun's speech meant that there no longer existed any community of interest or body of shared beliefs to bind the Union together. The thesis rested on the assumption that slavery was so fundamental to Southern society that it must be protected forever against even remote possibilities of interference by the government of the Union. There was the further implication that even an amendment protecting the slave-owning minority could not be effective unless the Northern people changed their whole way of thought about slavery.

For conservative Northerners the conclusion was shocking and the assumptions unsound. They believed that Northerners and Southerners shared the same history and still spoke the same political language; moreover, in the world of commerce and finance, community of interest remained a fact of life. Philip Hone, the diarist, expressed a typical view of Calhoun's speech.

> It is a calm, dispassionate avowal that nothing short of absolute submission to the slave-holding States will be accepted; there is no compromise proposed, no conciliation offered. The prosperity of the North—the natural fruit of industry, perseverance and skill—is a mortal offence to South Carolina.[28]

Surely there must be some truth yet in the old Whig belief in an American System that would distribute to all states the benefits of agriculture, trade, and industry? Surely some way must be found to renew the mutual respect with which Northern and Southern men had once regarded each other?

Thus while the Northern Whigs in Congress showed by silence their disapproval of the compromise plan, there was a strong undercurrent among their wealthiest and socially most distinguished supporters to abandon the President and offer the South some quid pro quo for the admission of California. This would mean dropping the Wilmot proviso for which they had never had much enthusiasm once

28. Philip Hone, *Diary,* ed. Allan Nevins (New York, 1927), II: 887.

its politically explosive nature was revealed. This was the background against which Daniel Webster prepared the massive and moving speech that he delivered on March 7.[29]

Webster knew how desperately the men who looked to him for leadership wanted to end the crisis, yet he also realized their political peril if they allowed their critics to retain the moral initiative. His aim in his March 7 speech was to lift compromise from the level of a political auction to the heights of pure patriotism. Positive action to save the Union not retreat to safeguard profits must guide the conservative choice. At the same time abolitionists and Free Soilers must be put in their place, as well-meaning but short-sighted men whose imagined call of conscience endangered the world's best hope. The third aim was to provide an argument that would enable Northern men to abandon the Wilmot proviso with a clear conscience.

The association of compromise with the highest ideals of American civilization was accomplished with an oratorical skill of which Webster was alone the master. The argument that anti-slavery, though not perhaps mistaken, was politically inept was tackled with considerable delicacy. He referred to Calhoun's point that the national churches were dividing, and expressed the great concern he himself had felt over the separation of the Methodist Episcopal Church. "The result was against all my wishes and against my hopes." None of the arguments advanced on either side seemed to justify the decision, and no one was in any way the better for it. From this he insinuated that the political and social problems of slavery had become unfortunately entangled with religious conviction.

> When a question of this kind takes hold of the religious sentiments of mankind, and comes to be discussed in religious assemblies of the clergy and laity, there is always to be expected, or always to be feared a great degree of excitement.

This kind of controversy induced convictions that destroyed forbearance. On such occasions there were always those who "deal with morals as with mathematics, and think that what is right may be distinguished from what is wrong with the precision of an algebraic equation." A philosophic view might suggest that eighteen hundred years

29. The speech is in *Congressional Globe*, 31.1. 476ff. and a revised version is in the Appendix, 269ff. The version in *The Writings and Speeches of Daniel Webster* (National Edition, Boston, 1905), X: 56ff. is taken, with some additional notes, from the second edition of the speech published in Boston as a pamphlet.

after the Christian revelation there were still many evils in the world, and that it was an error to fasten on one as so unique that all other considerations should be sacrificed in order to eradicate it. "They prefer the chance of running into utter darkness to living in heavenly light, if that heavenly light be not absolutely without any imperfection."

This oratorical argument had considerable force, but it remained to dispose of the specific case for the prohibition of slavery in the territories. Here one did not deal with a generalized hatred of slavery as sin, but with the precisely stated case that slavery did not exist in the acquired territories, that Congress had power to prohibit it, and ought to follow the sound precedent set in 1787. Webster dealt with this by an appeal to climate and terrain as effective checks to the extension of slavery. The law of nature "settles forever, with a strength beyond all terms of human enactment, that slavery cannot exist in California or New Mexico." Why then insist upon a law to prohibit it?

> The use of such a prohibition would be idle, as it respects any effect that it would have upon the territory; and I would not take pains to reaffirm an ordinance of nature, nor to re-enact the will of God.

This was by far the weakest part of Webster's argument. It is clear from the context that he thought only of plantation slavery, and no attempt was made to deal with the argument that slaves could be used in mining, in construction work, or by small settlers. As Seward would observe later: "The discovery of a few flakes of gold, or of a few grains of silver, or even a few clumps of coal in the unexplored recesses of New Mexico, would be followed by a new revelation of the will of the Almighty in regard to it."[30] Yet even this flaw exposed less weakness than might be expected. The high-minded might be opposed to the legalization of slavery in any form, but for many (perhaps a majority) the major objection was not to slavery *per se* but to plantations and the thousands of blacks necessary to maintain them. He asked "Who expects to see a hundred black men cultivating tobacco, corn, cotton, rice, or anything else on lands . . . made fertile only by irrigation?" If the main objective was to prevent the establishment of a society based on mass slave labor, the question had force. A wedge

30. *Congressional Globe*, 31. 1. Appendix, 1021.

was driven between those for whom slavery was an absolute wrong and those who condemned it for the power which it gave to the Southern planter class.

Webster had provided Northern conservatives with a complete answer to free soilers, but there remained one awkward corner to turn. Calhoun had argued that the equilibrium had been destroyed by inexorable forces, and now Webster demonstrated that the South could gain nothing from the territories even if the law was on their side. Calhoun had spoken of population and wealth, Webster had thrown climate into the balance and declared that he would support no further acquisitions of territory. It was therefore necessary to assure Southerners that they had nothing to fear in a Union where they must be content with a minority position. A symbolic gesture was necessary and the means was to hand in Mason's Fugitive Slave Bill. Webster's precise words are not clear, and a comma and a relative pronoun made a considerable difference to his meaning. The *Congressional Globe*, published the day after the speech, reports him as saying, "My friend at the head of the Judiciary Committee has a bill on the subject, with some amendments to it, which I propose to support, with all its provisions, to the fullest extent." This sentence is repeated in the revised version in the *Appendix* to the *Globe*, but in the pamphlet edition, dedicated to the people of Massachusetts, it reads "a bill, which, with some amendments to it, I propose to support, with all its provisions, to the fullest extent." One amendment, already moved, guaranteed trial by jury in the state from which the fugitive was alleged to have escaped. On May 15 he wrote a letter to a group of citizens at Newburyport in which he agreed that the Constitution guaranteed trial by jury in criminal cases but observed that "the reclaiming of a fugitive slave is not a criminal prosecution."[31] On June 3 he himself moved an amendment guaranteeing jury trial for fugitives at the place of arrest,[32] but he must have known that there was not the slightest chance that this would be accepted by the Southerners, and his move can be seen only as a face-saving response to the savage criticism of his support for a bill which could deprive a black of his freedom without due process of law.

31. George Ticknor Curtis, *Life of Daniel Webster* (New York, 1870), 424.
32. *Congressional Globe*, 31. 1. 1111. Curtis *op cit*. 422 states that "when Mr. Webster declared it to be his purpose to support Mr. Mason's bill, he did so with the qualification that he should seek to amend it." Curtis knew many of the leading men of Massachusetts who had been active in 1850, and this is probably what Webster's defenders wished to believe. When the Fugitive Slave Bill was debated Webster was no longer a member of the Senate, but his amendment was moved by Dayton (N.J.), supported by Winthrop, and lost 11–27.

Why did Webster go so far? Even his closest supporters were alarmed. Winthrop told Everett that he could have said all that was necessary but "by a few omissions and qualifications, have left us with a safe New England platform."[33] Winthrop thought that "the speech would have killed any Northern man except himself," and Everett told Webster that it should have been possible to get an extradition law "less likely to incite the North than that which Mr Mason has reported." Everett also thought that Webster should have insisted more strongly that Southern states must give up their practice of imprisoning free black seamen who went ashore from Northern ships. In a scathing review of the speech Wendell Phillips noticed that in the second pamphlet edition Webster's condemnation of this Southern practice had been strengthened for Northern consumption.[34]

Webster himself was apprehensive. Before March 7 Winthrop had written to Everett, probably at Webster's suggestion, that after its delivery a meeting should be called in Boston "to give encouragement to our Senators and Representatives . . . in pursuing a conciliatory and temperate course," and on March 10 Webster wrote to Everett, "If you can conscientiously defend my speech I beg of you to go to Faneuil Hall and do so." Everett warned him that the early telegraphic reports of the speech had emphasized everything likely to give offense in the North, and "as disapproval is always more active than approval, a good deal of dissatisfaction was expressed," though he hoped that reasonable men would be satisfied.

Everett's mild doubts were amply justified. Conscience Whigs were certain to condemn support for compromise in any form, but the speech enabled them to fasten upon precisely the points most likely to trouble Northern minds. The price of compromise was dubious argument and a denial of human rights when their possessor was black. In June Horace Mann produced a reasoned attack in public letters which were first read and amended by Charles Sumner.[35] Mann pointed out that the climatic argument drew a moral conclusion from physical premises. "It is arguing from physics to metaphysics. It is determining the law of the spirit by geographical phenomena. . . .

33. Everett Papers, 17 March 1850. Quotations in this and the following paragraph are all from the same source during the same month.

34. Wendell Phillips, *Review of Webster's Speech* (Boston, 1850), 36. In the first edition imprisonment was "altogether impracticable and oppressive," in the second "exceedingly unjustifiable and oppressive."

35. Sumner to Mann, June 1850, Houghton Library, Harvard University, "You must strike Webster hard; but carefully; but hard." On jury trial he wrote (9 June), "I wonder if you let him off too lightly on this point. You might have tossed him in a blanket very well."

Slavery depends not on climate but on conscience." In any case, Mann argued, the climatic argument was fallacious. If slaves could not be used on plantations, there was housework to be done or perhaps mining. There was "an opening for a hundred thousand slaves today in the new Territories for the purpose of domestic labor."[36]

In the short run Webster's arguments prevailed, but attacks darkened his declining years and in the eyes of many high-minded New Englanders his reputation was permanently destroyed. More important than the personal repercussion was the way in which the eminently praiseworthy hope to save the Union was linked with arguments which were factually unsound and morally vulnerable. By alienating so many vigorous and articulate men in the North Webster contributed powerfully to the long-run forces which were weakening the Union he sought to save.

On March 11 William Henry Seward finally obtained the floor of the Senate, but words that might have seemed realistic in January could now be represented as attempts to throw fuel on flames that were about to subside. He had neither the reputation nor oratorical skill of Clay or Webster. He often made points in a minor oratorical key, with little appeal to the emotions and had an unfortunate knack for coining phrases that sounded extreme when quoted out of context. In 1850 it was the famous "higher law" which his critics saw as an attempt to justify resistance to the law of the land. Thomas Hart Benton omitted the speech from his "Abridgment of Congressional Debates" though including many trivial and time-consuming efforts. James Ford Rhodes and Allan Nevins made slight and slighting reference to it; Holman Hamilton deals with it in a single page mainly devoted to the "higher law." Yet read with the care that it deserves, Seward's speech emerges as the most profound of the controversy.[37]

He began by dealing somewhat conventionally with the arguments for the admission of California, but toward the close of this section he drew an implied contrast between the Unionism of Webster—who wanted no more acquisition—with the vision of an expanding civilization.

> If . . . the American people shall remain an undivided nation, the ripening civilization of the West, after a separation growing wider and wider for a thousand years, will, in its circuit meet again, and mingle with the declining civiliza-

36. Horace Mann, *Letters on the Extension of Slavery* (Boston, 1850).
37. *Congressional Globe*, 31. 1. Appendix, 260ff.

tion of the East on our own free soil, and a new and more
perfect civilization will arise to bless the earth, under the
sway of our own cherished and beneficent institutions.

Having argued the case for the admission of California whole and
immediately, he referred to the claim that this must be accompanied
by compromise. With great emphasis he declared: "I am opposed to
any such compromise, because . . . I think all legislative compromises radically wrong and essentially vicious."

The joining of separate questions prevented their proper consideration, and committed men to decisions which were premature.
"They involve a relinquishment of the right to reconsider in the future
the decisions of the present, on questions prematurely anticipated;
and they are a usurpation as to future questions of the province of
future legislatures."

So far Seward had not done more than translate Taylor's policy
into the close texture of a closely argued brief, and he might have been
expected to go on to the other limb of the President's policy: the
deferment of all action on New Mexico. Instead he went on to consider
the abstract question of equilibrium raised by Calhoun. Tackling the
heart of Calhoun's argument against majority rule, he concluded that
his real demand was to "alter the Constitution so as to convert the
Government from a national democracy, operating by a constitutional
majority of voices, into a Federal alliance, in which the minority shall
have a veto against the majority." The hope was, however, illusory, for
even if the equilibrium could be restored by some constitutional
sleight of hand, it would soon be lost, for no one would wish to curb
immigration or impede the natural increase of free men.

Turning to the proposed compromises he argued that they could
not work. The Fugitive Slave Law would be condemned by the Northern people.

> You will say that these convictions of ours are disloyal. Grant
> it for the sake of argument. They are, nevertheless, honest;
> and the law is to be executed among us, not among you; not
> by us, but by the Federal authority. Has any Government
> ever succeeded in changing the moral convictions of its sub-
> jects by force?

Moral convictions were not disloyal; the Northern people rever-
enced the Constitution but could not accept an implied power forcing
them to assist in the recapture of fugitives. "We are not slaveholders.

We cannot, in our judgment, be either true Christians or real freemen, if we impose on another a chain that we defy all human power to fasten on ourselves." If Southern owners wished to recover slaves, they must provide their own police and conform with the normal laws safeguarding the rights of freemen. This was not an incitement to resist the law, but a plain statement that a law would not work if unacceptable to public opinion.

On slavery in the District of Columbia Seward admitted that there was as yet no majority for abolition. Even the legislature of his own state had stopped short with a demand for ending the slave trade; yet it would be great folly to erect a barrier against the action of a future majority. He applied the same argument briefly to slavery in the territories; though there might be no majority in the Senate to prohibit it now, the future could not be bound. "I cannot too strongly express my surprise, that those who insist that the people of the slave States cannot be held back from remedies outside of the Constitution, should so far misunderstand us of the free States, as to suppose we would not exercise our constitutional rights to sustain the policy which we deem just and beneficent."

Seward then turned once more to the problem of equilibrium and observed that while Calhoun talked of "North" and "South" he meant "Free" and "Slave." The idea that there must be an equality between them derived from the accident that this had been so in 1787, but nowhere was this made a condition of Union. Indeed, when the Constitution was made, Virginia had already ceded her western lands and agreed to exclude slavery from them under the Northwest Ordinance. Nor could a permanent system be based on an institution which many Southerners themselves had once wished to change and might do so again. "The principle of this compromise gives complete ascendancy in the slave State, and in the Constitution of the United States, to the subordinate, accidental, and incongruous institution over its paramount antagonist." Applied to the public domain this principle of equality between slave and free ran counter to the principles of civilized society. It was true that the new lands had been acquired by all, but conquest did not confer arbitrary power and looking to the future it was a duty to safeguard the interests of those to come.

The Constitution regulates our stewardship; the Constitution devotes the domain to union, to justice, to defence, to welfare, and to liberty. But there is a higher law than the Constitution which regulates our authority over the do-

main, and devotes it to the same noble purposes. The territory is a part—no inconsiderable part—of the common
heritage of mankind, bestowed upon them by the Creator of
the Universe. We are his stewards and must so discharge our
trust as to secure, in the highest attainable degree, their
happiness.

Seen in this light he believed that no one could maintain that there
was a duty to establish slavery in the domain or even to allow this to
happen. "The most alarming evidence of our degeneracy, which has
yet been given, is found, in the fact that we even debate such a question."

Seward then dealt severely with the climatic argument. "There
was no climate uncongenial to slavery, and few where it had not
existed in one form or another. There was no 'law of God' limiting its
expansion, but if there was, why not write it into the law of the land?
Slavery might be less profitable than free labor, but men thought of
their immediate needs rather than the long-term consequences. "It is
the indolence of mankind, in any climate, and not the national necessity, that introduces slavery in any climate."

Clay had attributed the crisis to the violence of party spirit; Seward replied that "it is not the fierce conflict of parties we are seeing and
hearing, but on the contrary, it is the agony of distracted parties." The
parties had become weak because they had attempted to rest their
foundations on compromises, and in consequence now suffered from
paralysis. Finally Seward dealt with the threat of disunion. He agreed
that there could be no such thing as peaceable secession, and that an
attempt to separate would be revolution, but there were no signs of
revolution in the country. "This revolution began in this Senate
chamber a year ago, when the Representatives from the Southern
States assembled here and addressed their constituents on what were
called the aggressions of the North," and all that had happened since
was the passage of resolutions by legislatures as "conventional re-
sponses to the address which emanated from the Capitol." In the
United States a revolution could not be made at the center, as in
France. Yet the pressure existed, and a crisis had been precipitated.

The fearful issue [is] whether the Union shall stand, and slavery, under the steady, peaceful action of moral, social, and
political causes, be removed by gradual voluntary effort, and
with compensation, or whether the Union shall be dissolved,

and civil wars ensue, bringing on violent but complete and immediate emancipation. We are now arrived at that stage of our national progress when that crisis can be foreseen, when we must foresee it.

The only sure way out of the crisis was for slaveowners themselves to resolve on gradual emancipation, and for Congress to assist them—financially and in other ways—to carry out this plan. Slaveowners need not fear that the pace would be forced, nor should Northern men hope for a rapid collapse of slavery. Turning in his final passage once more to the Union, and to alarms for its future among timid men:

> The failure of a legislative body to organize itself is, to their apprehension, a fearful omen; and an extra-constitutional assemblage, to consult upon public affairs is, with them a cause for desperation. Even Senators speak of the Union as if it existed only by consent, and, it seems to be implied, by the assent of the legislatures of the States.

Originally the Union had been a necessary response to national changes and national interests. Increasing population, wider territory, and more varied interests made government more necessary than ever before. It was because so many men realized instinctively the need for and benefits from government, that the Union would survive. If the Union were broken down, some other government would have to take its place and what better government had been proposed? Seward concluded that fear for the Union arose because men had not properly considered its nature, and it was folly "to compromise one sentiment—one principle of truth or justice—to avert a danger that all experience teaches . . . is purely chimerical."

This long, closely argued speech was one of the most sensitive discussions on the character of the United States presented during the nineteenth century. By comparison with its intellectual texture Clay was a confused rhetorician and Webster an utterer of splendid platitudes. Seward himself was justly proud of it, and said that he would not wish to change a single word.[38] The core of his argument

---

38. In reply to criticism by Weed (see below) he said that with a single exception "it is the only speech I ever made that contains nothing that I could afford to strike out or qualify." Frederic Bancroft, *The Life of W. H. Seward* (New York, 1900) I: 264.

was that any political society must rest on the moral sentiments of its members. Southerners must reconcile themselves to the fact that slavery now stood condemned by the majority of civilized men, and no compromises or laws would alter this fact. Men who argued that concessions to slavery were necessary to save the Union had mistaken both the nature of the Union and the responsibility of those in temporary authority over a great nation. The paramount duty was to men of the future and not to write the mistakes of the past into permanent laws and new compacts. The decision to recognize that this destiny placed slavery under condemnation must be made in the South, but once made, the implementation of this decision should be a national responsibility. Yet most of the logic was too subtle to be readily grasped by excited men.

It was perhaps this that caused Seward's mentor, Thurlow Weed, to read the speech "with a heavy heart." He said that "it pointed out 'appalling evils,' but suggests no remedies, and following the temporary calm [created?] by Webster's speech, raises a storm, leaving you responsible for the consequences." He believed that Seward's pointed attack on Webster "makes for him, what he had lost—a Party in the North." He regretted that Seward had not given support to the President. At least he should have included a personal tribute to "the good and faithful and fearless Man who has incurred the hostility of the South by his devotion to the North."[39] A few days later he still believed that it would "divide the Whig party in New York, giving the power back to our opponents."[40] He also depreciated Seward's lack of consideration for Clay. On the other hand Schuyler Colfax, a future Republican Speaker and Vice-President, wrote enthusiastically of opinion in Indiana "as to your noble speech." Late in April he reported that this "opinion is strengthening and deepening." Horace Greeley was also enthusiastic, and Seward received many congratulatory letters (though Webster received far more).[41]

Seward replied to Weed's criticism in a letter that illuminates further the depth of his feeling and reflection. "This thing is to go on to an end, near a revolution. While it is going on, could I, with consistency or safety, be less bold or less firm?"

39. Seward Papers, 14 March 1850.
40. *Ibid.*, 17 March.
41. *Ibid.*, 26 March, 22 April. Lewis H. Morgan wrote, "I have just risen from the perusal of your noble speech—noble in its eloquence, noble in its strong positions and declarations for freedom."

If people carp at the recognition of the fear of God as the beginning of wisdom, or the truthfulness with which I have shown the cruelty of compacts between white men to oppress black ones, what could I have said that would not have provoked more just and severe censure? I *know* that I have spoken words that will tell when I am dead, and even while I am living, for the benefit and blessing of mankind; and for me this is consolation enough.[42]

On July 2 he had a further opportunity of speaking. This time, perhaps taking some account of Thurlow Weed's criticism, he gave more positive approval to the President's policy. On California he emphasized Taylor's insistence upon unconditional admission and—while still professing his own preference for the Wilmot proviso—suggested that the President had foreseen the impossibility of carrying it in the Senate and had therefore recommended non-intervention. He believed that Taylor would have "his triumphant vindication" when it would be said of him that "never did he do more for harmony and for freedom then when to dull and prejudiced apprehensions he seemed to be doing nothing."

In this July speech Seward also included a more sympathetic appeal to Southerners to face their own predicament.

Let those who have this misfortune entailed upon them, instead of contriving how to preserve an equilibrium that never had existence, consider carefully how at some time—it may be ten, or twenty, or even fifty years hence—by some means of their own, and with our aid, without sudden change or violent action—they may bring about the emancipation of labor and its restoration to its just dignity and power in the state. Let them take hope to themselves, give hope to the free states, awaken hope through the world. They will thus anticipate only what must happen at some time, and what they themselves must desire if it can come safely, and as soon as it

42. Frederic Bancroft, *The Life of W. H. Seward,* I: 264. Lewis Tappan approved of the speech, and told Seward that the American and Foreign Anti-Slavery Society would publish an edition of 10,000, and would add to this if Seward would provide a corrected copy. However he took issue with Seward's implied criticism of immediate abolitionists. "The great body of abolitionists do not expect that any power except the people of the Slave States can abolish slavery. . . . The emancipated would be badly off if their former masters were not reconciled to the change." (Seward Papers, 19 March 1850).

can come without danger. Let them do only this and every cause of disagreement will cease immediately and forever.[43]

This surely was the path of wisdom; if followed there would have been no Civil War, and though no magic could have obliterated the heritage of slavery, there would have been brighter prospects for the future relationship between the races.

In the days of March two other anti-slavery senators were able to speak. Salmon P. Chase, former member of the Liberty party and representing Ohio as a Free Soiler with Democratic support, was closer to abolitionism than Seward and was more likely to stress the populist element in Northern anti-slavery. Where Seward had spoken of moral convictions, Chase said,

> This is a Government of the people, and the voice of the people must be heard and respected in its administration. The States also are governments of the people, and must be administered in conformity with the popular will.[44]

Legislation, within constitutional limits, must conform to the will of the people, and in 1848 it had been hard to find in the North a candidate who was not opposed to the extension of slavery. These sentiments must finally control policy. "Here and there the arts or the fears of politicians or capitalists may suppress their utterance; but they live, and will live, in the hearts of the masses." The bulk of Chase's speech was, however, occupied with a long and somewhat tedious account of the way in which the slave power had succeeded in dominating the national government.

John P. Hale, until this session the only spokesman of outright anti-slavery in the Senate, attacked the equilibrium theory and poured scorn upon the alleged danger to the South from abolitionists who had already paid for their temerity. Indeed, said Hale, "There has

---

43. *Congressional Globe*, 31. 1. Appendix, 1024. Weed was very pleased with this speech; he wrote to Mrs. Seward that the first had exposed her husband to "bitterness and rancour without securing to him the greatest amount of regard which he deserved. But of *this* I would not change or spare a word. All is perfect."

44. *Ibid.*, Appendix, 473. To Sumner, Chase explained why he had not spoken before—"A junior Senator, especially of my stamp, has hardly a fair chance." He believed (and a study of the debates confirms his view) that men of known anti-slavery opinions were not able to get the floor of the Senate until both pro-compromise and Southern extremists had had their full say. *Diary and Correspondence of Salmon P. Chase*, American Historical Association Annual Report (1902) II: 204.

never been a sect . . . that has been met at every turn, on every hand, on every side, and by all parties, with more bitter, violent, unrelenting persecution." The only way in which they could gain influence would be by insistence upon such a measure as the proposed Fugitive Law which "proceeds entirely upon the assumption that there are no rights in the Constitution except the right of slavery" and deliberately denied protection to any man who might be wrongfully seized.[45]

Thus during the month of March the Senate explored the courses open to them, and with due deliberation chose to move in the wrong direction. In the short run Thurlow Weed's instinct was correct, and Seward's speech reinforced the compromisers at the moment when they seemed to be on the brink of collapse; if some Southerners such as Foote were pushed toward adjustment when they contemplated the bleak future envisaged by Calhoun, even larger numbers of Northerners in and out of Congress were frightened by Seward's condemnation of all compromise.

More than anything else this reaction was fostered by a distortion of Seward's "higher law" doctrine, which had never been intended to justify individual disobedience. He had emphasized the practical difficulty of executing a law which offended against moral sentiments because men would not willingly help to carry out a law they believed to be wrong. It is true that he suggested that the clause in the Constitution on the rendition of fugitives from labor had arisen from necessity, had no counterpart in the law of nations, and was now repugnant to civilized conscience, but his advice was that it should be allowed to fall into disuse, not actively resisted. A law could not execute itself, and if moral obligation were not recognized it would not be effective. The "higher law" passage occurred later in the speech, in the course of his discussion of the idea of trusteeship for the future in administering the domain. The Constitution, he said, "regulates our stewardship . . . [and] devotes the domain to union, to defence, to welfare and to liberty," but a higher law also "regulates our authority over the domain, and devotes it *to the same noble purpose*." The higher law did not override the Constitution, but provided the rule for interpretation when it was silent or ambiguous. There was no clear rule on the extent of congressional power over the territories and it was therefore reasonable to introduce the great universal principles proclaimed in the Preamble to the Constitution and reinforced by the higher law.

45. *Congressional Globe*, 31. 1. Appendix, 1054.

The *Tribune* understood Seward correctly in an editorial on March 19, but on the previous day George Badger of North Carolina had already given currency to the interpretation which has since been accepted even by acknowledged authorities on the period.[46] Quoting Seward's remarks on fugitive slaves and on the higher law, but without indicating any gap between them, Badger angrily accused Seward of justifying resistance to the Constitution by individuals. Thereafter this became the accepted interpretation of the higher law doctrine and was repeated in countless speeches and pamphlets. This abuse reached its apotheosis in an article in the *Democratic Review* which proclaimed that

> Should this new doctrine of the supremacy of individual opinion over constitutional enactments become general, and conscientious scruples supersede the law of the land, not only the Constitution, but the most sacred of all pledges to support it would be blown to the winds. If such should be the case, and Mr. Seward's conscience become despotic in the United States, we would seriously advise all good people, with the exception of abolitionists, socialists, and their various affinities to get out of the way as soon as possible.[47]

It must have been particularly galling to Seward that this interpretation originated with a respected Southern Whig representing a state with a large number of non-slaveowners. In his remarks on party, and elsewhere, Seward had expressed his own hope for a revival of national parties, and particularly, of course, for a reunion of Northern and Southern Whigs. As Kentucky was wholly dominated by Clay, the best hope for a response was from the Whigs of North Carolina, Tennessee, and western Virginia. Many of the Whigs in these states were small planters or farmers—owning few slaves—and here surely was the best ground on which to cultivate the idea that the Whigs could unite nationally on the understanding that slavery was a dying institution and its gradual replacement a national responsibility. Badger's speech was a blow to any such plan, and it soon became apparent that nowhere in the South would there be any response on other lines. Neither Seward nor other anti-slavery leaders understood

46. *New York Tribune*, 19 March, observed that the higher law did not override but reinforced the Constitution. Badger's speech is in *Congressional Globe*, 31. 1. Appendix, 387.

47. *Democratic Review* XVII (July 1850): 13.

that it was precisely among the smaller slaveowners and non-slaveowners that the greatest fear of emancipation existed, or that resentment at the idea that a Southern man should be prohibited from taking slaves with him into new settlements was greatest among the "plain people."

If the hope for the emergence of a Southern response to the invitation to cooperate with Northern anti-slavery was vain, the extent of Northern hostility must have shocked Seward. Yet it remains a puzzle why he did not take steps to correct the erroneous interpretation of the higher law. He could have risen to make a personal explanation when misrepresented by Badger and others, but he deliberately refused an opportunity when presented to him. During Hale's speech Cass intervened to say:

> The sentiment of the Senator from New York was, that a person who is sworn to support the Constitution, if he believes the Constitution countervails the law of God, is under no obligation to support the Constitution, and that he is to judge of his obligations after having taken the oath to support it.

To which Seward replied laconically,

> I stand by every word that I uttered on that occasion as it is recorded, and I have no explanation to make here or elsewhere. I have only to say that my conscience is in my own keeping, and the conscience of others in theirs. They will take care of theirs, and I of my own.[48]

It may be that Seward believed that politicians and people would read his speech rather than accept the version of hostile critics, but this was too much to expect from contemporaries or subsequent writers.

When Seward made his July speech there was hope that the compromise would fail. By this time the California, Texas, Utah, and New Mexico bills had been thrown together in one omnibus bill, so that a man who wished to admit California must either vote for other measures of which he disapproved or vote against statehood because so encumbered. Yet if all were contained in one bill, one veto would kill

---

48. *Congressional Globe*, 31. 1. Appendix, 1062, 19 March. It is possible that at this time Seward did not understand the interpretation given to his argument; Badger's speech had been delivered but not yet printed.

it. This knowledge encouraged the *Tribune's* Washington correspondent, a vigorous supporter of Taylor, to write in the middle of May that "The President commands the field and recruits and reinforcements from all quarters are hourly flocking to his standard."[49] It may have been this which persuaded Seward not to enter into controversy over the higher law, and his omission of this argument in his second speech can be seen as a preliminary to the expected veto, which would clear the ground, leave only the presidential recommendations before Congress, and permit his supporters to take the initiative in presenting his plan as the only one that could be effective. Then, on July 9 the situation altered completely with Zachary Taylor's sudden death. According to Horace Greeley the sixty or so Southern secessionists had been held in check by the knowledge that a proclamation by him "would paralyze their efforts to raise troops throughout the South," but after his death it would be "a mercy scarcely less than a miracle if the horrors of civil war shall yet be averted." Millard Fillmore, his successor, could not hope to exert the same personal authority in a crisis, and deeply resented the domination of the Whig party by Seward and Weed in his own state.

There is no need to deny the extreme difficulty of the situation facing the new President. A deep division in the country existed, and though the Nashville convention had been less well attended and less extreme than feared, the threats of Southern extremists were loud enough. Fillmore, a Northerner of mild anti-slavery sentiments, was particularly vulnerable. Southerners who had supported a Virginian Vice-President a decade earlier, were now unlikely to accept a Northern "accidency" as a representative man. Even if his own inclinations had not leaned in that direction it was therefore political sense for Millard Fillmore to join the conservatives in the North and thus win some support in the South. Having made his decision, he spared no effort to beat the anti-compromise Whigs on their own ground. In the fall elections in New York City "Down with Seward" was the cry in all the hotly contested wards, and federal officials were active against him.[50] In Detroit, government advertising was withdrawn from the *Daily Tribune* "on account of Sewardising," and the census takers took the opportunity of their visits to extend the circulation of the rival *Advertiser* which now enjoyed administrative favor.[51] Seward's lieutenant in New York, Simeon Draper, reported that "any man who does

49. *New York Tribune*, 13 May.
50. *Ibid.* 30 September.
51. Josiah Snow to Seward. 16 September, Seward Papers.

not swear eternal vengeance at you and Weed is to be quartered, hung up and spit upon." The Collector and Surveyor of the Port were "charged from Mr. Fillmore himself to demand obedience to their edicts, which are death to all who have heretofore, or once hereafter mention your name."[52]

With executive influence employed in this way the question was not whether the compromise would pass, but the precise form that it would take, and the modifications that Southern or anti-slavery Northerner senators could obtain. Even so the omnibus could not pass; extreme Southerners believed that it took too much from Texas while remaining ambiguous on the status of Mexican law in the territories. At the same time Seward and the Free Soilers were pledged to oppose any measure which exacted a price for the admission of California and opened New Mexico to slavery. July 31 saw the collapse of the omnibus, precipitated by a well-intentioned amendment from James A. Pearce, a Maryland Whig. Pearce first moved successfully to strike out the clause relating to New Mexico, but his substitute was then lost. Then in quick succession votes were obtained to strike out the Texas boundary clause, and finally the clause admitting California. This left only the Utah clause standing.[53]

If Taylor had been living this would have been the end of compromise, but Fillmore was prepared to back the passage of separate bills. With Clay temporarily out of action (wearied with the continual strain of controversy in the heat of a Washington summer), and Web-

52. Seward Papers, 17 September.
53. The Congressional maneuvers leading to the defeat of the omnibus were exceedingly complex. James Bradbury of Maine had proposed a joint commission from the United States and Texas to establish the boundary; this did not pass, but was then reintroduced by William Dawson of Georgia with an added clause giving Texas jurisdiction over the disputed area of New Mexico until the commission had adjudicated. This was carried, and meant that Texas would govern most New Mexicans until the commission had completed investigations and reached agreement. This might take years. It was to get rid of the Dawson amendment that Pearce moved to strike out the whole of the New Mexico clause. With New Mexico removed it was logical for Southerners (on the motion of David Yulee of Florida) to strike out the Texas clause. Then Pearce failed to get his substitute (the boundary commission without the Dawson amendment) adopted. With both New Mexico and Texas out, the retention of California would have produced the unconditional admission which Southerners had opposed all along, and David Atchison of Missouri succeeded in striking out the clause admitting California. Northern Whigs voted with Pearce (12 - 1), with Yulee (12 - 1), and (after some initial confusion) with Atchison (10 - 3). The last vote may seem surprising, but it was based on the reasoning that California could not wait, and that total wreck of the omnibus must be followed by a simple statehood proposal (for which a majority was known to exist). It is possible that President Fillmore had concocted with Pearce the initial move to get rid of the Dawson proposal which would have been resisted in New Mexico. The inconclusive evidence for this is discussed in Holman Hamilton, *Prologue to Conflict* (Lexington, 1964), p. 113, n. 26.

ster in the cabinet, the compromise forces became an alliance between Northern Democrats, Southern Unionists of both parties, and a handful of conservative Northern Whigs. It was now a foregone conclusion that no bill on the compromise agenda would be vetoed, and the only remaining problem was to get through a series of complex and controversial bills before Congress adjourned. The masters of compromise were Stephen A. Douglas in the Senate and the Speaker and Democratic leaders in the House.[54] Playing a mysterious but possibly significant role were the lobbyists acting on behalf of creditors for whom the assumption of the Texas debt was a vital part of the compromise. By skillful management an informal understanding was reached by which the key measures could be brought to the vote in the Senate, though on each separate measure some members of the compromise alliance were free to abstain or oppose. The abandonment of the omnibus enabled men opposed to the general principle of compromise to vote for separate bills. In the House liberal use was made of the procedural means to curtail discussion and force a vote. Thus the controversial Fugitive Slave Bill was pushed through the House on the previous question without allowing any debate, and the Speaker ruled consistently against those who introduced delaying motions.

In the Senate the bill for the admission of California came up on August 5 and passed on August 13. A Texas boundary and debt bill was also introduced on August 5 and, with its passage accelerated by a message from the President threatening to use force if Texas acted unilaterally, passed on August 9. The Texans were able to obtain more generous boundaries than had been offered in Clay's omnibus. The bill for the organization of New Mexico was passed on August 15 after an amendment adding the Wilmot proviso had been voted down. The Fugitive Slave Bill was taken up in the Senate on August 15 and passed, after considerable debate, on August 26 (the crucial vote being taken on August 23). Finally the bill to suppress the slave trade in the District of Columbia was taken up on August 28, postponed on September 4, and passed on the 16th.

The legislative history of the Fugitive Slave Bill deserves some attention. It was introduced by James A. Mason of Virginia on

54. Lewis Cass, who might have been expected to lead the Democrats, failed to rise to the occasion. Though earnestly working for compromise, he lacked the energy or insight to assume command. On 8 August he wrote, "The defeat of the compromise bill may be considered as a national misfortune. What are we to do? . . . I do not know. There is such a contrariety of feeling . . . that the ordinary rules of calculation do not assist us." To S. Beardsley, Cass Papers, Huntington Library, San Marino, Calif.

January 4, printed, and referred to the Committee of Judiciary, whose chairman was Senator Butler of South Carolina. On January 16 the committee reported the bill favorably. In this form the claimant of a fugitive could appear before any federal judge or official (down to postmasters), and if he produced satisfactory proof of ownership, a certificate would be issued giving him the right to reclaim the fugitive. The claimant would then apply to a federal commissioner appointed for the purpose, who would in turn issue a warrant to a federal marshal to arrest the fugitive. Anyone attempting to conceal or harbor a fugitive slave would be liable to a fine of $1,000. On January 28 Seward proposed an amendment giving the fugitive the right to jury trial in the place of arrest; Mason countered by extending the $1,000 fine to anyone obstructing arrest and barring testimony by the alleged slave. Neither amendment was passed, and in March the bill went to the Committee of Thirteen which did not, however, report on it in specific terms until May 8.

The Committee of Thirteen proposed two additions to the original bill: the claimant had to obtain, from a court in his own state, a record of the escape and description of the slave, and also to lodge a bond that he would bring the fugitive before a court in his own state where the case would be tried by jury. In presenting the report Henry Clay supported, but did not subsequently press, the proposal to give the fugitive an unconditional right to jury trial in his own state but not (as Seward had proposed) at the place of arrest.

On August 19 the committee's bill was dropped, but Mason then proposed his original bill plus the committee's requirement for preliminary investigation by a court in the claimant's state but without the right of trial by jury. A slave could, of course, sue for his freedom under existing law, but would require confidence and skill to take this initiative, and would be even less likely to do so if, after wrongful arrest, he found himself in an unknown community. Senator Pratt of Maryland wanted the United States to indemnify claimants who failed to recover after a legitimate claim had been lodged, but this was rejected by the majority as too open to fraud and opposed by Jefferson Davis on the ground that it gave dangerous strength to federal authority. Davis, however, added to the bill the right of a claimant to bring civil action for $1,000 per slave against anyone obstructing recovery, and requiring the federal marshal to deliver the fugitive to the claimant (thus preventing an unsympathetic marshal from arresting a fugitive and then keeping him in protective custody). With these additions the bill passed the Senate on August 24. In the House, as Joshua

Giddings later complained, "no discussion of its provisions was allowed. The feelings of the North were not expressed nor represented. Our lips were hermetically sealed, in order that it might pass and assume the force of law."[55] It was not, however, true that the North was unrepresented in the vote; a substantial majority of Northern Democrats combined with Southerners to give the bill a safe passage by 109 to 76, with 36 not voting. Thus, with minor amendments and with broad congressional support, was passed the law proposed by a Virginian, reported by a South Carolinian, and which all supporters of the compromise were pledged to defend and obey.

The compromise bills passed through their ordeal in the House during September, and in an incredible two weeks' work the compromise leaders were able to get all passed. Both the Fugitive Slave Law and the prohibition of the slave trade in the District of Columbia were passed immediately after their reception from the Senate. In the course of debate the Texas and New Mexico bills, joined in Clay's omnibus but separated in the Senate, were reunited. The real climax of the House debate came on September 6, when this "little omnibus" was passed 108–98. On Saturday, September 7, the House quickly passed the bills admitting California and organizing Utah, and that night men took time out to celebrate in appropriate fashion the preservation of the Union. On the Monday morning (while a good many sore heads were still being nursed in Washington) Philip Hone wrote in his Diary:

> There is rejoicing over the land; the bone of contention is removed; disunion, fanaticism, violence, insurrection are defeated. These horrible slavery questions, which have suspended the public business for more than eight months, are settled. . . . The lovers of peace, the friends of the Union, good men, conservatives, have sacrificed sectional prejudices, given up personal predilections, given up everything for Union and peace; and for this sacrifice the Lord be good to them.[56]

Men who rejoiced at the compromise thought primarily of the preservation of the Union, and hoped that the slavery questions would

---

55. *Congressional Globe*, 31. 2. 15, 9 December 1850. It was passed after the majority accepted a motion for the previous question (i.e., agreed to vote on the bill without debate).

56. Hone, *Diary* II: 902, 9 September 1850.

now cease to agitate politics. By inference public men hoped that it would now be possible to restore the network of understandings— within parties, between parties, in Congress, and between legislature and executive—which made government possible. Yet too many harsh things had been said and too many men nursed profound disappointment for things ever to be the same again. To his panegyric on compromise, quoted above, Philip Hone added this note of wise disquiet:

> Although all good men rejoice that the affair is settled, none are satisfied. It all comes of that crowning curse of national legislation, the annexation of Texas; and did not Daniel Webster warn the Loco-Focos of all this? Did not Henry Clay sound his admonishing trumpet?[57]

Whether one traced the disease to Texas or to some other cause, it was clear that damage had been done to the political system which could not be easily repaired. Even in the closing days of controversy, when the majority of men looked anxiously for an end to it all, the evidence of deep-seated bitterness was too plain to be ignored.

57. *Ibid.*

## Chapter 11

# POLITICAL CONSCIENCE
# AND THE END OF A
# PARTY SYSTEM

The national two-party system was a casualty of the events that culminated in the Compromise of 1850. Though Whigs and Democrats still competed in every state of the Union in 1852, the Whig party soon became victim to wasting disease. The Democrats survived until 1860—preserved by efficient local organization rather than by national purpose and leadership—but the few initiatives taken by the administrations of Pierce and Buchanan widened existing rifts and prepared the way for the break of 1860.

The direct links between the intrusion of slavery into the political arena and the end of the national two-party system are clear. If the extension of slavery had not become an issue, party leaders would have been able to devote time and energy to developing new policies, cultivating support, and neutralizing divisive factors. Yet inherent weaknesses may have been as important as the questions which were the immediate cause of collapse. The parties failed because they were unable to meet the expectations of the men who had supported them. The failure of the Whigs was quicker and more conspicuous because they had been able to fulfill few of the promises of 1840, and had shown themselves incapable of developing new policies to meet the changing times. The failure of the Democrats was at first less obvious because they had taken their stand on nonintervention by government, so that inaction could be interpreted as victory. In many states the traditonal concerns of the party—banks, improvements, privilege, and equal rights—continued to give meaning to local conflicts. There is, however, a sharp contrast between politics after 1850 and the hopes of the Jacksonian period inspired by equal rights and the vision of a free, dynamic, and self-regulating society. The defense of negations is a dispiriting business, and the Democrats found no new issues to fire the imagination. The failure of Stephen A. Douglas to give the party a new and progressive character was the symptom of the condition in which conservative Democrats dominated the party, feared new ideas, and trembled as soon as they heard distant thunder in the South.

The end of the two-party system was caused by failure of nerve, will, and imagination as much as by disputes over slavery. Paralysis of the will occurred because the bodies were too weak to resist infection. This was not inevitable. In 1852 the Democrats showed that their organizations were in excellent working order, while the defeated Whigs secured more popular votes than ever before. With the exception of the Calhounites and dedicated anti-slavery men, no one wished to break up the parties. Conscience Whigs had hoped to direct their party, not to ruin it, while Van Buren's followers had wished to transform their party into new-style deomocracy. Both dissident groups had hoped to attract mass support in the South once the slave-owning oligarchy had been isolated and defeated; while conservatives in both parties hoped to continue association with the Southern establishment. The crucial facts were that Northern Whig leaders had nothing to offer the plain people of the South, while deference to the South meant that Democratic administrations in the North had little to offer their Northern and Western supporters.

The bankruptcy in political policies was in part a consequence of constant arguments over slavery. There was little time, between 1848 and 1850, to talk about anything else, and even the apparent conclusion of the great debate did not get slavery out of politics. Southern demands that the compromise should be a "finality" kept the question to the forefront, while in 1851 the spectacular rescue of an alleged fugitive in Boston kept controversy alive.

A Northern writer deplored the end of constructive political debate. "The tariff, post-office reform, internal improvements, private claims, and the Cuba expedition have been almost lost sight of, in the deep excitement." Reporters had written of little else, and commercial and political newspapers were clogged with arguments for and against slavery. "Divines, editors, lawyers, and merchants, too, are entering the field," and slavery was the constant topic of discussion "in cars, steamboats, hotels, in the shop, at the fireside, upon the farm—wherever newspapers are read, or the claims of humanity felt."[1] Toward the end of February Salmon P. Chase complained that nothing had been done in 1850, during a ten-month session, and even in the new year as the end of Congress approached "hardly any measure of any considerable importance had been considered."[2]

Meanwhile in the South many were convinced that damaging concessions had been made. Though compromise and union won in the state elections of 1850 and 1851, the grievances remained. "California is by nature peculiarly a slaveholding State," declared the *Southern Quarterly*. If there had been no interference "thousands of young, intelligent, active men . . . would have been in that region, having each carried with them from one to five slaves; their own property or the advances of others to work upon shares." Slave labor in the mines would have been so successful that Northern immigrants would have been anxious to buy and thus their value in the South would have been increased by demand.[3] The *Southern Quarterly* also understood the significance of Northern refusal to legalize slavery south of 36°30′, and argued that an advantage of separation would be freedom for large slaveowners to move southward. "No pressure of the black population will ever then threaten us with its evils, for the slaveholder would make his patriarchal migration downwards to the tropics, and civilization be established on the banks of the mighty Amazon and Orinoco, by the same institutions which wrested the fertile delta of the Mississippi from its primitive wilderness."[4]

\*     \*     \*

On August 14 ten Southern senators entered a solemn protest against the admission of California as a justification and a memorial "to posterity, which even in its most distant generations may feel its consequences." They asserted that the statehood bill recognized illegal action by a portion of the inhabitants of California "by which an odious discrimination is made against the property of the fifteen slaveholding States of the Union, who are thus deprived of that position of equality which the Constitution so manifestly designs, and which constitutes the only sure and stable foundation on which this Union can rest." The greatest offense was that "this Government in effect declares, that the exclusion of slavery from the territory of the United States is an

1. Rufus Clarke, *Review of Professor Moses Stuart's Pamphlet on Slavery* (Boston, 1850).
2. *Congressional Globe*, 31. 2. 2.
3. *Southern Quarterly*, N.S. III (January 1851): 199.
4. *Ibid.*, 225.

object so high and important, as to justify a disregard not only of all the principles of sound policy, but also of the constitution itself." This conclusion "must lead, if persisted in, to the dissolution of that confederacy, in which the slaveholding States have never sought more than equality, and in which they will not be content to remain with less."

On September 3, while the Senate was debating the abolition of the slave trade, Seward moved an amendment abolishing slavery in the District. Senator George E. Badger was instantly on his feet to say that if passed "it would unsettle the foundations upon which the institutions of this country rest, and loosen the cement by which they are maintained and united." Badger was a Southern advocate of compromise; he had voted for the Utah and Mexico bills, and abstained on California; yet for him the future of the Union now depended upon the willingness of the national majority to retain slavery in the capital. Even more significant was an outburst during the same debate from Willie P. Mangum, his fellow senator from North Carolina. Mangum had been one of the least verbose but most influential members of the Senate; he was a key member of the Southern Whig group and a mainstay of the party. Speaking on the prohibition of the slave trade in the District of Columbia he remarked that "there has been no period for five and twenty years, when, if brought forward under proper auspices" he would not "with great cordiality and pleasure" have voted in favor; but he went on,

> I have now changed my course. I shall not vote for it. I am satisfied, from developments that are made, that it is impossible to satisfy certain gentlemen. To attain their objects they would wade through the blood knee-deep of the whole South, and over the wreck of this Union. The further discussion of such objects as this, in my judgment, only tends to operate as an entering wedge to enable these gentlemen to attain the object which they have sought at all times, hazarding the existence of this Union and the safety and liberties of the South.[5]

Mangum seems to have said more than is revealed by the sober pages of the *Congressional Globe,* for an unfriendly reporter for the *New York Tribune* wrote that he had been called to order for improper language

5. *Congressional Globe,* 31. 1. Appendix, 1643.

"such as might come from too much patriotism or peach brandy." However stimulated it was a sad comment on the months of argument that, as the controversy drew to a close, a man of Mangum's standing and former moderation should speak in this way.

In its January number the *Southern Quarterly* launched a bitter attack on the abolition of the slave trade in the District. It was "one of the worst acts of the session." The penalty for trading was the forfeiture and freeing of the slave offered for sale, and this established the fact that "by act of Congress a slave can be made free." The conclusion was that "the government of the United States is now an anti-slavery government,"[6] and that the North was hostile to the South. "You cannot speak, you cannot think of the South without slavery. *It is included in her ideas.*"[7] Imminent danger had been seen in a proposal of the Committee of Thirteen (subsequently dropped) that a fugitive slave should be guaranteed trial by jury in the district from which he was alleged to have escaped, and argued that "when the day arrives, on which a slave is to usurp his master's rule, and openly appeal to a jury to defend him, whatever may be the voice of the jury, a precedent will have been established, by means of which the doom of the South will be sealed." Abolition would be accomplished in all but name.[8]

Turning from dangers averted to prospects for the future, the *Southern Quarterly* contemplated a glorious future for a South freed from Northern shackles.

> If we are true to ourselves, the noblest of destinies is ours. Our ample area will be filled with a civilization marked by a stability which will excite the wonder and admiration of the world. If, as it is often asserted, it should prove that the career of the American race is to sweep over the whole continent, it must spread towards the tropics by the energies of the South, and the expansion of their institutions.[9]

Most plain people were unmoved by this heady rhetoric, and a majority gave their votes for compromise and union; but manifestos of separatism and slave expansion in a responsible journal would have been unthinkable five or even two years earlier. Francis Lieber, the distinguished German emigré and philospher who grew increasingly

6. *Southern Quarterly*, N.S. III: 225.
7. *Ibid.*, 199.
8. *Ibid.*
9. *Southern Quarterly*, N.S. III: 225.

unhappy with academic exile in Charleston, wrote to a Northern friend that "every son of a fool here is a great statesman, meditating on the relations of State sovereignty to the U.S. government, but as to roads, common schools, glass in the windows, food besides salt meat, as to joining in the general chorus of progress—what is that for Don Ranudo de Colobrados of S. Carolina—out of his elbows, to be sure, but then, what of that?"[10] Preoccupation with the great issue raised since 1846 was virulent in South Carolina but not confined to that state, and it was difficult to contemplate cooperation with Northern enterprise in material betterment.

In a more philosophic mood than the *Southern Quarterly* Jefferson Davis explained the real bonds and present weakness of the Union.

> The Union is held together by mutual attachments and common interests. It is held together by social links, from the fact that fathers and sons, mothers and daughters, brothers and sisters, and boyhood friends, live in extreme ends of the Union. These States are held together by so many unseen, close, and daily increasing points of contact, that it can only be rent in twain by something which loosens these rivets, and permits the use of a lever as powerful as that which has been recently introduced. When it depends upon politicians to manufacture bonds to hold the Union together, it is gone —worthless as a rope of sand.[11]

Yet paradoxically many Southerners came to regard that political contrivance, the Fugitive Slave Law, as the condition upon which all these mystic bonds of Union depended. At the opening of the second session of the Thirty-first Congress James A. Pearce, the moderate Maryland Whig who had inadvertently wrecked the omnibus, presented resolutions of a state Constitutional Convention with a request that they should be printed by Congress. The concluding resolution asserted that

> The repeal of [the Fugitive Slave] law or the failure to enforce its provisions, could only be regarded as evidence of a deter-

10. To George Hillard, May 1851. Francis Lieber Papers, Huntington Library, San Marino, Calif. Southern writers were not oblivious to the backward condition of the poorer whites. In an editorial article in *De Bow's Review,* Vol. III (February 1850) it was asked "Shall we pass unnoticed the thousands of poor, ignorant, degraded white people among us, who, in this land of plenty live in comparative nakedness and starvation?" The writer advocated manufactures, but as in other similar pleas Southern effort is seen as a bid for independence not association.

11. *Congressional Globe,* 31. 2. Appendix, 326. The debt to Edmund Burke's 1775 speech on conciliation with the American colonies seems to be clear.

mined purpose . . . to violate the sacred charter of our rights, or want of ability in the General Government to enforce the laws made for our protection, and in either event there would be a failure to comply with the solemn obligations which give to the Constitution its chief value and binding force, and which could not be violated or deliberately evaded without leading to a dissolution of the Union.[12]

Sentiments of this kind became commonplace throughout the South, and in many eyes the future of the Union depended upon the way in which the small number of fugitives who crossed into free states were treated by the few Northerners who encountered them.

At this point some aspects of the Southern case should be emphasized. There was nothing illogical or immoral in the proposition that the South should separate from the North, nor in the qualification made by those who agreed that secession might be necessary but that a further trial of union should be made before making an irrevocable decision for independence. If the modern age rejects Southern assumptions about race, they were endorsed, at that time, by a large majority in all white societies. The Southern claim that they could best handle their own problems was not groundless and an independent South might have made better progress than is sometimes imagined. The movement for secession may have been unwise, but there is a lingering suspicion that the world would not have been altogether a worse place if it had succeeded. On this point at least the *Southern Quarterly* and William Lloyd Garrison were agreed, and when extremes are found to coincide there may be some merit in the idea. The degree to which subsequent historians have accepted the view that a dissolution of the Union was the ultimate evil should therefore be questioned. In the delicate scales of human happiness there is no knowing whether the greatest number would not have been better off if Southern disunionists had carried their point and if the Northern majority had decided to treat as mere rhetoric the assertion that peaceable secession was impossible. The Southern case became impractical —and in a way which many in the North would also regard as immoral—when Union was held to imply a national commitment to protect and promote slavery. Political conscience in the South might reasonably demand freedom from a government which had ceased to command confidence; political conscience in the North could not for long accept the defense of slavery as a national obligation.

12. *Ibid.*, 77.

\*     \*     \*

In the North support for the compromise united two very different kinds of American: the rank and file Democrats and the commercial élite of the East. There were many traditionally minded politicians in both parties who had strong practical reasons for repairing the national party system by the avoidance of troublesome issues, and Democrats were in the best position to do this. They had provided the bulk of support for legislative compromise in both houses, and the majority had little sympathy with anti-slavery. Arguing the case for leaving slavery alone the *Democratic Review* said that the alternatives were emancipation and disunion on one hand, or abiding by the Constitution on the other. Emancipation was "impracticable and absurd."

> Prudence, indeed, would dictate that we should co-operate, by a patient and persevering line of conduct, with the interests of the slaveholder, which are gradually elevating the condition of the slave, until, in the course of time, he may become capable of freedom, which by the way we doubt, or else to labor for the same time, patiently and perseveringly to carry out a colonizing system which might relieve us of our slave population.[13]

With varying degrees of emphasis most Democrats were content to take the same line. It is true that most of them retained their dislike of the society created by slavery, but they were persuaded that there was no opening in the West for Southern planters. Nor, in most Democratic strongholds, was the Fugitive Slave Law seen as an offense; it was more likely to be welcomed as evidence that federal authority was cooperating with the states to prevent blacks from infiltrating into white society. As Stephen A. Douglas said in February 1851 in explanation of his support for the law,

> We claim to be a white people; we claim that our State is composed of a white community; we will protect the negroes that have been born within the State, or that were there before this provision was made; but we hold out no inducement, no encouragement for a negro to come into it, whether he be slave or free.

13. *Democratic Review* XXIX (1851): 392.

Illinois was, he said, threatened with fugitives from three sides,and a provision in the new Constitution would forbid the entry of any Negro. Further, he drew an alarming picture of violence and disorder if the spirit of the law as well as its letter were not observed. Abolitionists had been arming blacks in the free states, and "go where you will, and you can scarcely find a free negro that is not armed with pistols and bowie knives."[14]

A writer in the *Democratic Review* summed up the case in 1851:

> The people of the North cared nothing . . . what terms of compromise should be concocted, so long as the terms would restore peace. . . . In truth the North had . . . no surrenders to make, but a relinquishment of their own unwarrantable interference with the domestic relations of other men, as free as themselves, and as capable of self-government.[15]

For another writer in the same journal non-interference with slavery was an illustration of "the fundamental principle of the philosophy of democracy," which was to secure justice "and then leave all the business and interests of society to themselves, to free competition and association—in a word, to the VOLUNTARY PRINCIPLE."[16]

Whig defenders of the compromise had a harder task. In the party ranks were large segments of anti-slavery opinion, and many would fight to the last for the Wilmot proviso—not so much from fear of slavery's extension as from a conviction that the national government must not incur additional responsibility for it. The compromise opened the possibility that federal authority might be invoked to protect slavery where it had spread under "the voluntary principle," and imposed upon all citizens an obligation to assist in the capture and return of fugitive slaves. Compromise Whigs had to accept these innovations as the price of Union, and so jeopardized their claim to represent the conservative conscience of the nation.

The compromise yielded its most robust fruit when its Boston supporters gathered for a great Union meeting held in Faneuil Hall in November 1850.[17] In an open letter, David Henshaw, leader of the

14. *Congressional Globe*, 31. 2. Appendix, 312.
15. A. B. Johnson, "The Philosophy of the American Union," *Democratic Review* XXVIII (1851): 23.
16. *Ibid*, 296.
17. The quotations which follow are taken from *Proceedings of the Meeting at Faneuil Hall* (Boston, 1850).

Democratic party in Massachusetts, explained that the "slave power" was a fiction, or at least "as intangible as that of the landed interest, the money interest, or the commercial interest." The federal ratio, which gave three-fifths representation to slaves, was really a diminution of the slave power when the free states were allowed to count women, children, and paupers. On the Fugitive Slave Law he argued that it was really in the interest of the Northern people to enforce it: "Do we want in any way to encourage the immigration of colored people," particularly as Massachusetts was committed to giving them political rights? In phrases which had long been commonplace in the South he added that "experience teaches that the two races cannot exist together on terms of equality—equality of numbers and of rights." In another speech B. R. Curtis, a prominent Whig lawyer, asserted that Massachusetts had no concern with the rights of slaves; it was "enough for us that they have no right to be here." Blacks had natural rights, but "this was not the soil on which to vindicate them."

> This is *our* soil—sacred to *our* peace—on which we intend to perform our promises, and work out, for the benefit of ourselves and our posterity and the world, the destiny which our Creator has assigned to us.

The *tour de force* of the Faneuil Hall meeting was a speech by Rufus Choate, one of the most celebrated lawyers and orators of New England. Like other Northern Whigs Choate had previously condemned the extension of slavery, but he now pronounced that

> Henceforward every man according to his measure, and in his place, in his party, in his social, or his literary, or his religious circle, in whatever may be his sphere of influence, [must] set himself to suppress the further political agitation of this whole subject.

Men had misguidedly seen it as their moral duty to attack slavery, but now a higher duty supervened to "discourage and modify the further agitation of this topic of slavery, in the spirit in which, thus far, this agitation has been conducted." Rufus Choate asked whether there had ever been "a development of sheer fanaticism more uninstructed, or more dangerous than that which teaches that conscience prescribes the continued political, or other exasperating agitation of this subject." Answering his own rhetorical question, he posed the alternative of a higher moral duty

> To America—to our America, we are united by another tie,
> and may not a principled patriotism, on the clearest grounds
> of moral obligation, limit the sphere and control the aspira-
> tions and prescribe the flights of philanthropy itself?

To win the "mighty good summed up in the pregnant language of the preamble to the Constitution," it was necessary to "surrender the privilege of reviling the masters of slaves."

Without using the odious phrase Choate was appealing to a "higher law." The Constitution promised "such good as man has not on this earth been many times permitted to do or dream of," but pursuit of this aim implied restraint on customary freedom. The Constitution did not forbid speech on certain topics, but the collective good imposed an obligation to remain silent. This was a fragile argument, for it depended upon one's interpretation of the Preamble to the Constitution. In 1852 Charles Sumner would use similar logic with very different effect in arguing that the wording of the Constitution made freedom national and slavery sectional, and that it was not only justifiable but imperative to resist any attempt to reverse the sequence and make slavery national. In 1850 Choate's rhetoric was an effective reassurance for conservative Whigs. Deeply involved in the national economy and politically anxious to wrest the initiative from Conscience Whigs and Free Soilers, it was natural instinct for educated New Englanders to outmaneuver their opponents by seeking higher moral ground.

In studying the arguments used to support the compromise one is struck by the deterioration which had taken place in the terms of debate. A great many men had been frightened and were running for cover to whatever refuge seemed to offer a prospect of safety. Eagerness and moral confidence were no longer apparent; expediency and interest were the guiding principles. All was justified by devotion to the Union and respect for the Constitution, but these became empty phrases when no one dared to ask what kind of Union or how the Constitution was to be understood. National interest has been the excuse for much injustice in the modern world, and the compromisers sacrificed older values when they appealed to patriotism, with the implication that slavery was a national and permanent institution so long as Southerners chose to retain it and that slaveowners had a right to compensation if their political weight was reduced.

The Pennsylvanian counterpart to the great Boston meeting assembled at Philadelphia on November 21, 1850, and, though drawn from both parties, the political character of the city made it very much

328	Parties and Political Conscience: American Dilemmas, 1840–1850

a Democratic occasion. Philadelphians knew a great deal more about fugitive slaves than Bostonians, and had close commercial ties with the South. The principal speaker was George M. Dallas, who eulogized the Union and declared that the Fugitive Slave Law was legally binding, constitutional, and expedient. Josiah Randall was more explicit when he said that "the wilful harboring of a fugitive slave is a grave offence in morals as well as law," and though some abolitionists were men of exemplary private life "their purity of character is of no value when they jeopardize all that is dear to us." Joseph R. Ingersoll lamented that "the demon of strife comes among us in the white robes of peace and goodwill," professing humanity and scattering discord. A letter from James Buchanan attacked the Wilmot proviso for defeating every attempt to provide government for the territories, and had placed the "two divisions of the Union in hostile array." Emancipation had been making headway in Maryland, Virginia, Kentucky, and Missouri; now it had lost all the ground gained.[18] There was considerable force in this argument.

\*     \*     \*

Caught between upper class support for compromise and popular enthusiasm for the Union, the men who had regarded themselves as keepers of the nation's conscience felt themselves betrayed. In September 1850 Theodore Parker complained bitterly that

> The controlling men of Boston love almost wholly but two things: Money and Respectability. The latter is . . . a sort of Miasma which exhales from money and mixes compliance with public opinion.[19]

Charles Francis Adams deplored "the consummation of the iniquities of this most disgraceful Session of Congress," wondered how much the people would bear, and confessed that his faith in their good sense was much shaken. They rejoiced at the saving of the Union but "they have been so often debauched by profligate politicians that I know not whether a case of breach of promise will lie against their seducers."[20]

18. *The Great Union Meeting in Philadelphia* (Philadelphia, 1850).
19. Parker to Palfrey, 9 September 1850, Palfrey Papers, Houghton Library, Harvard University, Cambridge, Mass.
20. Adams to George W. Julian, 14 September 1850, Julian-Giddings Papers, Library of Congress, Washington, D.C.

Ministers of religion who had hitherto stood aside from the fray were roused by the assumption that the price of harmony was national responsibility for slavery. Henry Ward Beecher, the fashionable and eloquent preacher of Brooklyn, wrote that "the law may heap injustice upon me, but no law can authorize me to pour injustice on another."[21] His words on the Fugitive Slave Law may have moved the spirit of his still more famous sister, Harriet Beecher Stowe, with whom he corresponded frequently.

> Who with power, which even God denies to Himself, shall by compact foreordain me to the commission of inhumanity and injustice? I disown the act. I repudiate the obligation. Never while I have breath will I help any official miscreant in his base errand of recapturing a fellow man for bondage.[22]

The British minister, Robert Baird, who published in 1853 a book on Christianity in America, wrote that while Northern ministers preached obedience to the laws, "there is not one of them . . . that approves of the Fugitive Slave Law." The law was odious and no Christian man would willingly assist in its execution, though he would not obstruct it if he had "proper views of his duty to the government."[23]

Joshua Giddings, the veteran anti-slavery politician, did not speak for "the North" but his words would be echoed by the most articulate makers of opinion. Slavery was, he said, the curse of the Southern states: "Your fugitive law shall not compel us to share it." Northern men, he said, had not ceased to respect the Union "but one thing is certain, that they do not feel the reverence for it which was once so prevalent among us. . . . They now speak of dissolution without hesitation."[24] John A. McClernand, a supporter of Douglas from Illinois, intervened to disavow this disunionist sentiment and state that the question was not whether slavery was right or wrong, but whether constitutional obligations should be honored. In speaking

---

21. William C. Beecher and the Rev. Samuel Scoville, *A Biography of Rev. Henry Ward Beecher* (New York, 1888), 241. He amplified this argument by saying that "every citizen must obey a law which inflicts injury upon his person, estate, and civil privilege, until legally redressed; but no citizen is bound to obey a law which commands *him* to *inflict* injury upon another." (*Ibid.*). He ridiculed those who professed sympathy for the fugitive while insisting upon obedience to the law. "They give the Union Committee money to catch the slave, and then give the slave money to escape from the Committee." *Ibid.*, 244.

22. *Ibid.*, 237–38.

23. Robert Baird, *Christianity in the United States* (Glasgow, 1853), 53.

24. *Congressional Globe*, 31. 2. 14.

thus McClernand undoubtedly represented a majority of the Northern people, but an increasing number felt themselves betrayed by the government which they had learned from their youth to regard as the world's best hope.

"It is a time of trial for the friends of freedom ," wrote Salmon P. Chase to Charles Sumner on August 13, 1851. "The short-lived zeal of many has waxed cold. Hunkerism everywhere rallies its forces, and joins them to those of slavery." And again, on September 8, "Clouds and darkness are upon us at present. The slaveholders have succeeded beyond their wildest hope twelve months ago."[25] Edward A. Stansbury expressed widespread revulsion against the politicians, when he had news of a projected joint action in Massachusetts between Free Soilers and Democrats and wrote that he abominated such fellowship.

> If those men, the leaders I mean, were really *Democrats* in the large and noble signification of the term, then I should like nothing better than to mix with, and be one of them. But all possibility of sympathy with the odious, selfish, bruted, hypocritic Hunkerism of Dickinson, Cass, Douglas and such like was quite taken out of me at my birth. I loathe these libels on humanity, these blots on the face of creation, almost as intensely as I do the smooth, "respectable," oily, "moderate," perjured scoundrelism of Webster, Fillmore & Co., which contrasts so disgustingly with the professions of their past lives.[26]

Yet for the next decade the "Hunkers," abetted by the "respectable" and "moderate" would attempt to govern the United States. Their failure has been explained in many ways but a fundamental cause was the distrust with which they were regarded by so many intellectuals. No regime can long endure when condemned by the intelligent, active, and articulate. It was not merely that some intellectuals condemned the system established in 1850, but that so few could be found to defend it. For the first time the men of books and ideas— whose pervasive influence is so easily ignored—felt that they had no part in their government nor respect for those who administered it.

25. Chase to Sumner, 13 August and 8 September, *Diary and Letters of S. P. Chase,* 215.
26. Stansbury to Julian, 30 October 1850, Julian-Giddings Papers. The alliance he deplored secured a seat in the Senate for Charles Sumner, and gave anti-slavery its best-known advocate at Washington.

Their confidence would not be restored until a new party emerged, and they would then reward the Republicans with all the eloquence and literary skill they could command.

Men who had believed themselves to be upright and prudent defenders of the truth, found themselves assailed as enemies of society. "Already," one of them complained, "do we find the terms 'conscience' and 'higher law' used by a time-serving and venal press, to bring into contempt that class of our community who are under the influence of moral principle, humane feelings, and an honorable patriotism."[27] Political leaders led the way in their anxiety to repudiate all connection with the higher law. In New York President Fillmore strove to get a favorable verdict from the state Whig convention, and wrote privately to Francis Granger soliciting his support and assuring him that he had consistently voted for him against Seward when the latter was nominated for governor in 1838.[28] Although the majority of New York Whigs had supported the Wilmot proviso, and none had voted for the Fugitive Slave Law, Granger was chosen as convention chairman and a motion was passed rescinding (as obsolete) opposition to the extension of slavery. Friends of Seward were not, however, disposed to abandon their leader, and demanded a vote congratulating him on his conduct as a Senator. After an angry debate the motion was carried 75–40, but the minority, led by Granger, then withdrew, disassociated themselves from the proceedings, and pledged support for the compromise. If a former governor, ally of the most skilled political manager of the day who had recently led his party to victory in his state, came under this kind of fire, the fate of lesser men can be imagined.

In Pennsylvania the Democratic party gave unequivocal support to the compromise, and in 1851 made an issue of events at Christiana, where the claimant of a fugitive slave had been killed in a riot; this brought them heavy gains in the state elections. In August 1851, G. W. Julian, the Free Soil representative from Indiana, lost his seat though supported by many Whigs who had voted against him in 1849.[29] E. A. Stansbury wrote to Julian in a mood of despair.

> The whole battle against slavery is yet before us. The past has witnessed only skirmishes. And yet the anti-slavery men are

27. Rufus Clarke, *Conscience and the Law* (Boston and Portsmouth, N.H., 1851), 7.
28. Granger Papers, Library of Congress, Washington, D.C., 17 October 1850.
29. Julian-Giddings Papers, 22 August 1851.

subsiding, like children overcome with sleep, into drowsy indifference to the portents of the future. The Whig party is hopelessly given over to slavery. It will, more and more, grapple the Slave Power to itself, and slough off all but despots and the partizans of despotism.[30]

A true democracy should be organized, but "if this should fail, and democracy persists in abasing itself at the feet of slavery, then all is lost, and absolutism will soon possess the new, as it does the old world." There was, indeed, no doubt that on both sides of the political fence the people seemed to be deserting those who had offered themselves as men of the future.

Despite the evidence of popular support, and the optimism of those in authority, anti-slavery politicians and intellectuals continued to believe that the compromisers had made a catastrophic error. In Seward's scathing analysis "compromise implies a mingling of truth and error, right and wrong"; the nation had missed its best opportunity to rest its system on justice tempered by forbearance, and his retrospective view showed how deplorably weak the various aspects of compromise had been.

> One of these affiliated measures denied the admission of New Mexico, because she had determined to come in as a free state, and remanded her with permission to come back in the habiliments of slavery. Another distinctly intimated to the Mormons the consent of Congress that they should, if they would, plant a slave state in the very recesses of the continent. A third abolished a public slave-mart in the city of Washington, without abating either the extent or duration of slavery in the District of Columbia. A fourth obtained peace on humiliating terms from one of the youngest and feeblest members of the Confederacy in an attitude of sedition. While a fifth only reluctantly admitted California as a free state, when she had refused to contaminate herself with slavery.[31]

So even without the iniquity of the Fugitive Slave Law a rising generation of Northern men learned to regard compromise as a synonym for weakness and ineptness which brought no permanent gain while sacrificing both principle and common sense. The memory was still fresh

30. *Ibid.*, 7 September 1851.
31. W. H. Seward, *Works*, ed. George E. Baker (New York, 1853), III: 446.

when compromise and conservatism became ugly words to the Republican majority in 1861.

*     *     *

The travail of anti-slavery conscience was illustrated by Ralph Waldo Emerson. In common with most Northern intellectuals Emerson had hitherto combined a rejection of slavery with a vague expectation that time and the advance of civilization would work a cure. Slavery could not endure in a civilized world, but the realization would have to be made by slaveowners for themselves, rather than forced upon them. Emerson was an exceptional man, not a "representative man," but he saw himself, like the dominant historical figures of whom he had written, as drawing out and expressing, in word or action, the spirit of the age. If he could not rise to the heights of philosophy or prophecy, he could nevertheless distill into pontifical phrases the general ideas of his age. He began by explaining individuals to themselves, and by 1850 was pondering the momentous task of explaining nations to their people. His second trip to England in 1847 had inspired him with the ambition to interpret American civilization by writing an extended essay on English civilization. After several years this would emerge in 1856 as *English Traits*.

By 1850, therefore, Emerson had developed an acute sensitivity to the problems of American civilization, was evolving a historical theory about the destiny of races, and considering how each came to express itself in national character with a course to run and a mission to fulfill. For an American—even a highly educated American such as Emerson—the answer had already been given. America *was* the best hope of mankind, and had therefore incurred a special obligation to take the lead in everything that was noble and true. The compromise came upon him as a shock and a sudden revelation that the truth did not always triumph and that wrong principles could prevail.

In 1849, in a private note on Macaulay's *History of England* Emerson wrote,

> One sad reflection arises on all the course of the narrative, of wonder, namely, at the depravity of men in power, and at the shocking tameness with which it is endured. One would think the nation was all tailors, and mincepie makers.[32]

32. Ralph Waldo Emerson, *Journals*, ed. Edward Waldo Emerson (Boston and London, 1913), VIII: 29.

Yet he had given little deep thought to the problems of American government, but remained convinced that somehow, in spite of fallibility and failure, public men would help Americans fulfill their destiny. Throughout 1850 (partly because he was traveling in the West and engaged in a heavy lecture program) he paid little attention, so far as can be judged from his letters and journals, to events in Washington. In October 1850 he seems to have become interested in the problem of the higher law, and must have turned up several authorities on the subject. In his journal he transcribed passages from Fuller's *Worthies,* Campbell's *Lives of the Chief Justices,* Blackstone's *Commentaries,* Bacon's *De Fontibus Juris,* and quotations from Lord Coke, the famous seventeenth century Chief Justice. The most pertinent extract was from Blackstone:

> This law of nature being coeval with mankind, and dictated by God himself, is of course superior in obligation to any other. It is binding all over the globe in all countries and at all times. No human laws are of any validity if contrary to this; and such of them as are valid derive all their force and all their authority, mediately or immediately, from this original.[33]

Also, from Campbell's *Lives* he noted a dictum of Coke that "common law should control acts of Parliament . . . for where an act of Parliament is against common right and reason, the common law should control it and adjudge it to be void."[34]

It is therefore evident that Emerson had been reflecting on the law of Congress and the higher law, but his scholarly comments were private and, as yet, displayed no anxiety. Then in the spring of 1851 there was a sudden explosion of outrage and activity. He may have been stirred to anger by the spurious arguments of Rufus Choate and Edward Everett, supporting the compromise and advocating obedience to the Fugitive Slave Law, but it was against Daniel Webster that he turned his largest guns. More than a year after March 7, the *Journals* were suddenly filled with denunciations of Webster. On May 3, 1851, he delivered a speech in Concord against the Fugitive Slave Law, and from that day onward was openly enlisted in the anti-slavery cause.[35] Eight years later he would be delivering a eulogy on John Brown.

33. *Ibid.,* p. 134.
34. *Ibid.,* p. 133.
35. Sumner fully understood the importance of this speech. He wrote to Palfrey, "I have

As Emerson understood it, Webster had been guilty of the basest kind of betrayal. He had "undone all that he has spent his years in doing—he has discredited himself."[36] Though Webster was not the author of the Fugitive Slave Law, thousands now acquiesced in it because the great oracle of New England had declared it to be necessary and, in a sentence of dramatic brevity, "The fame of Webster ends in this nasty law."

The professional classes of New England had honored Daniel Webster, Rufus Choate, Edward Everett, and Henry Clay; but what now remained, asked Emerson, except "disgusting obsequiousness"?

> Their names are all tarnished; what we have tried to call great is little; and the merely ethnographic fact remains that an immense external property is possible, with pure cowardice and hollowness in all the conspicuous official men.

Rufus Choate had learned too much as a trial lawyer defending the guilty. Everett had formerly delivered splendid orations on the liberty of ancient Greece, "but one of his scholars cannot but ask him whether there was no sincerity in all those apostrophes to freedom and adjurations of the dying Demosthenes; was it all claptrap?"

Emerson acknowledged the emotional force of appeal to the Union, but "the worst mischiefs that could follow from Secession and new combination of the smallest fragments of the wreck were slight and medicable to the calamity your Union has brought us." "Union is a delectable thing, and so is wealth, and so is life, but they may all cost too much, if they cost honor." Of all the iniquities perhaps the worst was the way in which public men had turned against those who attempted to maintain ethical standards in public life.

> Webster and Choate think to discredit the higher law by personalities; they insinuate much about transcendentalists and abstractionists and people of no weight. It is the cheap cant of lawyers and of merchants in a failing condition and of rogues. These classes usually defend an immorality by the practice of men of the world, and talk of dreamers and enthusiasts.

---

heard with true satisfaction of Emerson's address at Concord. His voice will reach many corners not easily penetrated by our cry." Palfrey Papers.

36. Emerson, *Journals*, VIII: 185. The quotations in this and the following paragraph are all from pp. 182–89.

In this way Emerson proclaimed himself a prophet of the alienated intellectual; and his reaction to the Fugitive Slave Law was
symptomatic of the shock that ran through the world of the Northern
intelligentsia. It was not merely that the law was judged to be bad but
that a whole scale of values had been suddenly reversed. The American
future had once been linked with the promotion and perpetuation in
the world of a system of belief based on the idea of a superior morality.
Independence had been justified by an appeal to self-evident truths,
and only five years before Emerson had claimed with complete assurance "that here, here in America, is the home of man" and, though
one had to discount the conduct of politicians, America offered "opportunity to the human mind not known in any other region." How
could this faith be reconciled with the discovery that the Constitution
was incompatible with the higher law of morality, that compromise
was more important than justice, and that men who thought otherwise should be assailed as disunionists? The men who were foremost in
demanding acquiescence in the compromise were those who had
claimed to stand at the head of New England society and Emerson
thought that the triumph of cotton over conscience had some compensations.

> There is one benefit derived from the movement lately. The
> most polite and decorous Whigs, all for church and college
> and charity, have shown their teeth unmistakably. We shall
> not be deceived again. We believed, and they half believed,
> that they were honest men. They have been forced to take
> prematurely their true and ignominious place.

One consequence of this was that the intellectuals could stand
aside no longer. The men of wealth and position had been guilty of a
shameful betrayal; politicians, whose errors had been tolerable so long
as their capacity for evil had been limited, could no longer be allowed
to close the ring against outsiders in the contest for power. The success
of Charles Sumner in winning a seat in the Senate was seen as one
portent of the coming struggle. Emerson looked gratefully toward
Horace Greeley, and thought his career "one of the most encouraging
facts in our Whiggish age."[37] This "white-haired man in the city of
New York" had "adopted every benevolent crochet and maintained it,
until he commands an army of millions now in the heart of the United
States." New England idealists had been timid and neglectful; with

37. Emerson, *Journals,* VIII: 229.

the energy of a Greeley they might have dominated Boston long ago. And if conservatism was now too strongly entrenched to be easily overthrown, there were millions in the other free states who would respond. Conscience had to become political conscience if the nation was to be saved.

The combination of betrayal by those in authority, moral purpose abused, and experience of political failure, is more likely to breed radicalism than acquiescence. Indeed the seeds of radicalism within the future Republican party were sown during the frustrations of 1851 and 1852, when all the world seemed to have turned its face against righteousness. Indeed there was one further and significant ingredient. With all their disappointments the anti-slavery minority still felt that history was on their side. When Seward made his forlorn bid to amend the District Bill to abolish slavery, the correspondent of the *New York Tribune* made significant comments. In the long run the people would not be satisfied "while there is a slave on the national domain"; and Seward was safeguarding the interests of posterity, for "without this movement every future attempt in that direction would have been met by the charge of a breach of compromise." He would be supported only by Chase and Hale, but it was better to "stand with them, looking to the future, than with the overwhelming majority against them."[38] This sense of destiny, of fulfillment in the future, is essential if radical causes are to be sustained through dark days. Despite contemporary failure the anti-slavery men had a reason for confidence in the long-term forces molding opinion. One of them explained:

> Those who suppose that the American mind and the American conscience are to be controlled by contempt, have fallen into an egregious error. They who would stifle conscience and shatter the moral sentiment of the community, must aim their blows at our schools, churches, literature, and the various means that are employed to elevate the intellectual and moral character of the people. They must effect an entire change in our education, habits of thoughts and religious sentiments, before their work is accomplished.[39]

In 1850 the men who hoped to prevent the extension of slavery and deny national responsibility for the institution had suffered a

38. *New York Tribune,* 13 September 1850.
39. Rufus Clarke, *Conscience and the Law,* 7.

symbolic defeat. Government, parties, and popular opinion had
turned against them. Their failure resulted in part from the strength
of the forces arrayed against them but also from uncertain purpose,
confused motives, and a dependence on sentiment at the expense of
constructive thought. Many separate streams of thought had flowed
into the Free Soil movement and they were not yet fused together,
Northern Whigs who had stood apart from Free Soil were still resentful of the damage done to their party, Seward's attempt to create a new
consensus for all moderate men who were prepared to admit that slavery was a dying institution had been misrepresented by his critics and
hardly understood by his friends. Yet the experience of 1850 wrought
a transformation in the character of the anti-slavery movement; from
being diffuse, generalized, abstract, or too narrowly concerned with
particular points of policy, it had been forced to seek a place in the
broad current of middle-class liberalism. "The times are developing
our real strength," wrote the veteran Joshua Giddings, "the real
strength of freedom. Those who stand by us now are reliable at all
times."[40] The number might be reduced, but the issues had been
defined in a way that was most likely to gather support in a
nineteenth-century society, and in the following years more and more
became opposed not merely to a party or an administration but to the
whole spirit in which government was conducted. Though affected by
all kinds of political aspiration this movement of the mind owed little
to material forces. In the deep springs of national character an ideology was forming which would draw in all the restless spirits of the
age. This was the explosive legacy of the decade which closed with the
celebrated but ill-fated Compromise of 1850. When events were approaching a crisis in April of that year Charles Francis Adams noted
with disgust that a letter, with some 800 signatures approving Webster's course, had been published in the Boston *Daily Advertiser*. Most
of the signers were from "the commercial classes," not many from the
clergy, medical and legal professions; but even so it was "a deep and
damning spot on the good name of Massachusetts." A few days later
he added:

> The weakness and corruption is general among all sides. I
> confess I draw but little hope from anything but a revolution
> which shall be the result of accumulated wrongs. Perhaps
> such an event is silently and slowly breeding.[41]

40. Giddings to Julian, 27 August 1851, Julian-Giddings Papers.
41. Diary of C.F. Adams, 2 and 10 April 1850. Adams Papers, Massachusetts Historical
Society, Boston, Mass.

Two months earlier Henry Ward Beecher, who had recently taken the pulpit at the Plymouth Church in Brooklyn and was already winning a reputation as a leading preacher of the age, wrote in the *Independent,*

> It is time for good men and true to gird up their loins and stand forth for God and humanity. No compromises can help us which dodge the question; certainly none which settle it for slavery. [42]

In October he wrote "Let no man stand uncommitted, dodging between daylight and dark on this vital principle. Let every man fearlessly and openly take sides."[43] In the debate that followed the compromise, men were forced to take sides and the conservatives won, but men such as Emerson and Beecher, who had been stirred to public utterance by the compromise, were unlikely to let the matter rest.

In some notes for a lecture, probably made in 1854, Beecher reflected upon the great gulf that had opened between North and South. "It was not a commercial quarrel. We are interdependent and mutually benefitted"; nor was it a quarrel over political or religious principles, for both shared the same traditions; it was not even antagonism between races for both came predominantly from the same stock. The "one root from which all this trouble springs is the radical diversity of ideas North and South upon Labor."[44] From the Southern adhesion to slavery flowed every difference that set it in conflict with the North. Southerners were no longer republican or democratic, and their insistence on national recognition of slavery threatened the health of the nation.

"Once let it be settled slavery is right—and Moral Apostasy is inevitable," wrote Beecher. The struggle was "as deep as human nature can go," but it had begun with a compromise "contrary to the whole pulse and heart of the North." The North had "loved the Union too much . . . loved it beyond religion . . . had again and again yielded Conscience for the sake of Union." It was now a paramount duty to propagate "the truth of manhood and Human Rights, as found in the Gospel. . . . Above all, raise a conception of manhood

---

42. Beecher and Scoville, *A Biography of Henry Ward Beecher*, 237.
43. *Ibid., 242.*
44. Beecher-Scoville Papers, Series II, Sterling Library, Yale University, New Haven, Conn. From a file of undated notes. The quotations in this and the following paragraph are all drawn from notes for the same lecture or article.

which shall silence the miserable apology for slavery." This was the authentic voice of political conscience which neither parties nor institutions could for long withstand and before which politicians would be powerless. "The theory of freedom and slavery are utterly irreconcilable. . . . A community cannot hold both."

The energy and ideals that had once flowed into the two party channels now sought other courses. Could this condition have been avoided? The parties might have provided civilized and sophisticated means for the adjustment of political differences, and their failure to do so arose partly from the need to work within an institutional framework that was nicely calculated to wring compromise or acquiescence from conflicts over minor or material issues, but rejected the intrusion of basic questions about national purpose or character. Mainly, however, the failure came about because political leaders lacked statesmanship to imagine what lay beyond the horizon of their time.

The two-party system, as it had taken shape by 1840, provided a complex but potentially effective means by which conflicts could be formalized and decisions obtained. Within parties across the nation, and between parties at Washington, the process was sensitive enough to provide satisfaction for those who gained a point without alienating those who had to concede. Even on the momentous question of slavery in the nation the two parties came to offer a clear choice, but with enough common ground to suggest that decision by a majority might be accepted. Under pressure a majority of party leaders abandoned these positions, achieved superficial success in compromise, but mortgaged the future by failing to satisfy the most active and high-principled men of both sections. For the North the lesson of 1848 was ignored; for the South no attempt was made to come to grips with the formidable problems of a biracial society. The seeds of weakness had been planted during the previous decade. The Whig party had failed in 1841, and thus diminished the incentive to develop stronger central institutions; the experience had also thrown doubt on the ability of a party that had won an election to provide government. Democratic cohesion had been weakened by determined but insensitive executive leadership. At a time when all advanced societies experienced the explosive forces of economic change, rationalist thought, romanticism, and religion, the parties were unable to satisfy the men who expected most from political action. In 1840 the parties had seemed to be the instruments of political conscience; by 1851 it was clear that they could not perform this function.

# SOURCES AND BIBLIOGRAPHICAL ESSAY

## UNPUBLISHED COLLECTIONS

(listed in alphabetical order of family names).

Charles Francis Adams
Massachusetts Historical Society,
Boston, Mass.
Nathan Appleton
Massachusetts Historical Society,
Boston, Mass.
J. S. Bagg
Huntington Library,
San Marino, Calif.
George Bancroft
New York Public Library,
New York, N.Y.
Beecher-Scoville
Sterling Library, Yale University,
New Haven, Conn.
J. M. Berrien
Southern Historical Collection,
University of North Carolina,
Chapel Hill, N.C.
Blair Family
Library of Congress,
Washington, D.C.
Brock Collection
Huntington Library,
San Marino, Calif.

James Buchanan
Historical Society of Pennsylvania,
Philadelphia, Pa.
Lewis Cass
Huntington Library,
San Marino, Calif.
Salmon P. Chase
Library of Congress,
Washington, D.C.
Historical Society of Pennsylvania,
Philadelphia, Pa.
J. F. Clarke
Houghton Library, Harvard
University, Cambridge, Mass.
Henry Clay
Library of Congress,
Washington, D.C.
G. M. Dallas
Historical Society of Pennsylvania,
Philadelphia, Pa.
R. W. Emerson
Houghton Library, Harvard
University, Cambridge, Mass.
Edward Everett
Massachusetts Historical Society,
Boston, Mass.

Millard Fillmore
  Buffalo Historical Society,
    Buffalo, N.Y.
Joshua Giddings
  Library of Congress
    (Julian-Giddings Papers),
    Washington, D.C.
Horace Greeley
  Library of Congress,
    Washington, D.C.
Greeley-Colfax Letters
  New York Public Library,
    New York, N.Y.
S. G. Howe
  Houghton Library, Harvard
    University, Cambridge, Mass.
R.M.T. Hunter
  University of Virginia,
    Charlottesville, Va.
Francis Lieber
  Huntington Library,
    San Marino, Calif.
John McLean
  Library of Congress,
    Washington, D.C.
James G. Palfrey
  Houghton Library, Harvard
    University, Cambridge, Mass.
Theodore Parker
  Massachusetts Historical Society,
    Boston, Mass.

J. R. Poinsett
  Historical Society of Pennsylvania,
    Philadelphia, Pa.
Thomas Ritchie
  William and Mary College,
    Williamsburg, Va.
Epes Sargent
  Boston Public Library,
    Boston, Mass.
W. H. Seward
  Rush-Rhees Library, University of
    Rochester, Rochester, N.Y.
Charles Sumner
  Massachusetts Historical Society,
    Boston, Mass.
  Boston Public Library,
    Boston, Mass.
Zachary Taylor
  Library of Congress,
    Washington, D.C.
John Tyler
  Library of Congress,
    Washington, D.C.
Daniel Ullman
  New York Historical Society,
    New York, N.Y.
Martin Van Buren
  Library of Congress,
    Washington, D.C.
Gideon Welles
  Huntington Library,
    San Marino, Calif.

## PRINTED SOURCES

### THE FEDERAL GOVERNMENT

*Congressional Globe*
*House Executive Documents*
*Journal of the House*

*Journal of the Senate*
*Senate Documents*
*Senate Executive Documents*

### NEWSPAPERS

Albany *Argus*
Albany *Evening Journal*
Boston *Whig*
*National Intelligencer*
*New York Tribune*

Washington *Union*
*Annals of Cleveland* (Works Progress
    Administration in Ohio: A digest
    and abstracts of the Newspapers of
    Cleveland)

## CONTEMPORARY PERIODICALS

De Bow's Review
Hunt's Merchants' Magazine
Niles' Register
North American Review
Southern Quarterly Review

United States Magazine and Democratic
  Review (usually known as Democratic
  Review)
Whig Review (also published as
  American Whig Review)

## CONTEMPORARY PAMPHLETS

This was, above all, the age of the pamphlet as a means of disseminating views and conducting controversy. In addition to pieces first written in this form, hundreds of other speeches, sermons, and newspaper articles were reprinted as pamphlets. Any list can, therefore, be no more than a sample of a vast number of ephemeral publications and others intended as more permanent contributions to debate. The titles themselves may provide an interesting commentary on current controversies.

### Intellectual and Political Controversy
### before 1840

George Bancroft. *Oration delivered to the Democracy of Springfield, 4 July 1836.*

Lyman Beecher. *A Reformation of Morals practicable and indispensable.* New Haven, 1812.

F. Byrdsall. *History of the Loco-Foco or Equal Rights Party.* New York, 1842.

William Ellery Channing. *A discourse on the Life and Character of the Rev. Joseph Tuckerman.* Boston, 1841.

————— *The Evidence of Revealed Religion: a discourse before the University of Cambridge.* Boston, 1822.

—————. *The Obligation of a City to care for and watch over the Moral Health of its members with remarks on the life and character of the Rev. Dr. Tuckerman.* Boston and Glasgow, 1841.

—————. *The Present Age: an Address delivered before the Mercantile Library Company of Philadelphia, 11 May 1841.*

William Gouge. *A Short History of paper-money and Banking, together with an Inquiry into the Principles of the system with consideration of its effects on morals and happiness.* New York, 1833.

### Anti-Masons

John Quincy Adams. *Letters on the Masonic Institution.* Boston, 1832.

*Address of the Anti-Masonic Convention to the People of Massachusetts, 5 and 6 September,* Boston, 1832.

*Address of the Anti-Masonic Convention of the State of New York, 17 February,* New York, 1831.

*Proceedings of the Anti-Masonic Convention of Massachusetts, 19 and 20 May,* Boston, 1831.

## 1840–41

The election produced a very large crop of pamphlets, mostly of little but polemical interest. Harrison's speeches, especially those at Dayton and Fort Meigs, were widely circulated and appear in several editions.

Among the few of more than passing interest are:

Anon. *The Crisis Answered*. New York, 1840.
Anon. *Whiggery is Federalism*. Boston, 1840.
> Identifies the personal links between the Federalists and Whigs in Massachusetts.

Nathan Appleton. *Remarks on the Currency and Banking*. Boston, 1841.
John A. Dix. *Address before the Democracy of Herkimer County*. New York, 1840.
"Junius" (Calvin Colton). *The Crisis of the Country*. New York, 1840.
A Kentucky Democrat (Samuel S. Nicholas). *Letters on the Presidency . . . addressed to Daniel Webster*. Louisville, 1840.
> Argues against direct election to the presidency; proposes a reform of the electoral college, from which seven will be chosen by lot, and the President chosen by ballot from among them. In the event of a tie, the Speaker or Chief Justice will decide. A single term and limitation on veto power.

John G. Miller. *The Great Convention . . . held at Columbus on 21 and 22 February 1840*. Columbus, 1840.
> Referred to in the text.

## 1844 and Texas

Charles Francis Adams. *Texas and the Massachusetts Resolutions*. Boston, 1844.
––––––. *An Oration delivered before the City Council and Citizens of Boston*. Boston, 1843.
*Address of J. Q. Adams and others to their Constituents*. Boston, 1843.
*Address of the American Republican Party of the City of New York*. New York, 1844.
*Address of the Executive Committee of the American Republicans of Boston to the People of Massachusetts*. Boston, 1845.
John M. Clayton. *Speech at the Delaware Whig Convention*. Wilmington, 1844.
"Hamden" (Jabez B. Hammond). *Letter to the Hon. John C. Calhoun*. Cooperstown, N.Y., 1844.
"Junius" (Calvin Colton). *Democracy*. New York, 1844.
Mirabeau Bonaparte Lamar. *Address to the Citizens of Macon, Georgia*. Macon, 1844.
*Proceedings of a meeting to consider the annexation of Texas*. New York, 1844.
> Includes a speech by Albert Gallatin against annexation.

Charles Sumner. *An Oration before the City Council and Citizens of Boston*. Boston, 1845.
"Veto" (Theodore Sedgwick). *Thoughts on the Annexation of Texas*. New York, 1844.
Robert J. Walker. *Letter Relative to the annexation of Texas*. Washington D.C., 1844.
> (Reprinted Frederick J. Merk, *Fruits of Propaganda in the Tyler Administration*. Cambridge, Mass., 1971.)

## Slavery

(in chronological order)

### Debate in the North

A Citizen of Massachusetts (James T. Austin). Remarks on Dr. Channing's Letter on Slavery. Boston, 1835.

A Citizen of Massachusetts (George F. Simmons). Review of the Remarks on Dr. Channing's Slavery. Boston, 1836.
> A reply to the above.

William E. Channing. Remarks on the Slavery Question in a letter to Jonathan Phillips, Esq. Boston, 1839.

"An American." *The American Churches, the Bulwarks of American Slavery*. Newburyport, 1842.

James Freeman Clarke. *Slavery in the United States—a sermon on Thanksgiving Day, Nov. 24, 1842*. Boston, 1843.

American and Foreign Anti-Slavery Society. *Letters respecting a book dropped from the Catalogue of the American Sunday School Union in compliance with the Dictation of the Slave Power*. New York, 1843.

William Jay. *A view of the action of the Federal Government in behalf of slavery*. With an appendix by Joshua Leavitt. Utica, 1844.
> Jay's well-known pamphlet was first published in 1839. Recounts all federal laws and action that favored slavery. Reprinted in 1844, with Leavitt's appendix, as Liberty party campaign literature.

Gerritt Smith. *Letter of Cassius M. Clay to the Mayor of Dayton, Ohio, with a review of it by Gerritt Smith of Peterboro, N.Y.* n.p., 1844.
> Answering an appeal by C. M. Clay to support Henry Clay.

J. Blanchard and N. L. Rice. *A Debate on Slavery held . . . in October 1845 in the City of Cincinnati*. Cincinnati, 1846.
> Both were Presbyterian ministers. Rice opposed slavery but argued for mitigation rather than immediate abolition. He was invited to debate "Is the practice of slave-holding in itself sinful?" The organizers included William Birney and S. P. Chase. The debate is of considerable interest.

Samuel Brooke. *Slavery and the Slaveholder's religion as opposed to Christianity*. Cincinnati, 1846.

John Gorham Palfrey. *Papers on the Slave Power*. Boston, 1846.
> Referred to in the text.

Albert Barnes. *An Inquiry into the Scriptural Views of Slavery*. Philadelphia, 1846.
> A scholarly refutation of the argument that "servant" in the Bible always means "slave."

Lysander Spooner. *The Unconstitutionality of Slavery*. Boston, 1847.
> Discussed in the text.

Wendell Philips. *Review of Lysander Spooner on the unconstitutionality of slavery*. Reprinted with additions from the *Anti-Slavery Standard*. Boston, 1847.
> Argues at great length the Garrisonian case. "We undertake the distasteful task of proving the Constitution hostile to us and to the slave."

Henry C. Wright. *Slaveholders or Playactors: which are the greater sinners?* Dublin, 1847.
> A rebuke to the Society of Friends for accepting £2,500 for the relief of

the Irish poor from Baltimore and Charleston, while rejecting the proceeds of a benefit performance at the Queen's Theatre in London.

William Wilson. *The Great American Question. Democracy versus Doulocracy*. Cincinnati, 1848.

By the pastor of the Church of the Covenanters and Chancellor of the
Protestant University of the United States. An argument against government by slaveholders.

## Debate in the South

James H. Hammond. *Letter . . . to the Free Church of Glasgow on the subject of slavery*.
Columbia, S.C., 1844.

Anon. *Slavery: a treatise showing that slavery is neither a moral, political, nor social evil*.
Penfield, Ga., 1844.

A Southern Baptist. *A Calm Appeal to Southern Baptists in Advocacy of separation from the
North in all the Works of Christian Benevolence*. n.p. n.d. (?1846).

Matthew Estes. *A Defence of Negro Slavery as it exists in the United States*. Montgomery,
1846.

A Slaveholder of West Virginia (Henry Ruffner). *An Address to the People of West Virginia*. Lexington, Va., 1847.

Referred to in the text.

George A. Longstreet. *A Voice from the South, comprising letters from Georgia to Massachusetts*. Baltimore, 1848.

H.B. Bascom, A.L.P. Greene and C. B. Parsons. *Brief Appeal to Public Opinion in a
series of Exceptions to the course and action of the Methodist Episcopal Church from
1844 to 1848, affecting the rights and interests of the Methodist Episcopal Church
South*. Louisville, 1848.

John G. Fee. *An Anti-Slavery Manual*. Maysville, Ky., 1848.

Elwood Fisher. *Lecture on the North and South delivered before the Young Men's Mercantile
Library Association of Cincinnati, Ohio*. Washington, 1849 (also Richmond,
1849).

This lecture was widely noticed. It was given a long and very favorable
review by J. B. Hammond in the *Southern Quarterly Review*, July 1849.
The copy in the Huntington Library belonged to Francis Lieber and has
critical notes by him on the endpapers.

Osgood Mussey. *Review of Elwood Fisher's Lecture on the North and the South*. Cincinnati,
1849.

Demonstrates Fisher's misuse of statistics.

James Shannon. *The Philosophy of Slavery as identified with the Philosophy of Human
Happiness*. Frankfort, Ky., 1849.

Shannon was President of Bacon College, Harrodsburg, Ky. The lecture
was first delivered in 1844; a second edition, with additions and
amendments, appeared in 1847; this third edition was issued to influence the debate on emancipation. It drew a reply from Cassius M.
Clay.

Edward R. Bryan. *The Rightful Remedy: Addressed to slaveholders of the South*. Charleston, 1850.

The title page reads "The Disunionist; or Secession the Rightful Remedy."

Iveson L. Brookes. *A Defence of the South against the reproaches and Incroachment of the North: in which slavery is shown to be an institution of God intended to form the basis of the best Social State and the only safeguard to the Permanence of a Republican Government.* Hamburg, S.C., 1850.

Francis E. Brewster. *Slavery and the Constitution. Both sides of the Question.* Philadelphia, 1850.

A Southerner (George Fitzhugh). *Slavery Justified.* Fredericksburg, 1850.
      Subsequently printed as an appendix to *Sociology for the South* (see below).

William H. Barnwell. *Views upon the Present Crisis. A discourse delivered in St. Peter's Church, Charleston, 6 December 1850, being the day of fasting, humiliation and prayer appointed by the Legislature of South Carolina.* Charleston, 1850.

George Fitzhugh. *Sociology for the South or the Failure of Free Society.* Richmond, 1854.

## Religion and Reform 1846–48

James Freeman Clarke. *Charge at the Ordination of T. W. Higginson.* Newburyport, 1847.

William Henry Channing. *The Gospel for Today: a discourse delivered at the Ordination of T. W. Higginson.* Boston and Newburyport, 1847.

Samuel J. May. *Jesus the Best Teacher of Religion.* Boston, 1847.

## 1848 and Free Soil

*Address of the Whig Legislature of Massachusetts to the Whigs of the Union.* Boston, 1848.
      Supports Webster for nomination by the Whigs as President.

Anon. *General Taylor and the Wilmot Proviso.* Boston, 1848.

Nahum Capen. *The Republic of the United States . . . including a review of the late war . . . and of those measures which have characterized the Democracy of the Union.* New York and Philadelphia, 1848.
      Dedicated to James Buchanan.

Oliver Dyer. *Phonographic Report of the Proceedings of the National Free Soil Convention.* New York, Philadelphia, and Buffalo, 1848.

Oliver Cromwell Gardiner. *The Great Issues or the Three Candidates.* New York, 1848.
      The author had been Associate Editor of the *Democratic Review.* He now backed Free Soil. Prints numerous speeches, especially those given at the Herkimer and Utica Conventions.

William Bowditch Ingersoll. *Cass and Taylor on the Slavery Question.* Boston, 1848.

Preston King. *Oration delivered at Canton, N.Y., July 4, 1848.* Ogdensburg, 1848.

*Proceedings of the State Independent Free Territory Convention of the people of Ohio, at Columbus, June 20 and 21, 1848.*

*The Utica Convention—The Voice of New York.* 16 February 1848. Albany *Atlas Extra.*

Cornelius P. Van Ness. *Letter to the Public upon Political Parties, Caucuses, and Conventions.* Washington, D.C., 1848.
      Written to support Taylor as a "no-party" candidate.

## The Compromise and After

Rufus W. Clarke. *Conscience and the Law: a discourse preached in the North Church, Portsmouth, New Hampshire on April 3, 1851.* Boston and Portsmouth, 1851.

———. *Review of Professor Moses Stuart's Pamphlet on Slavery.* Boston, 1850.

*The Great Union Meeting in Philadelphia.* Philadelphia, 1850.
*Proceedings of the Constitutional Meeting at Faneuil Hall, Nov. 26, 1850.* Boston, 1850.
Moses Stuart. *Conscience and the Constitution with remarks on the recent speech of the Hon. Daniel Webster.* Boston, 1850.
> A defense of Webster by a former professor of Andover Theological Seminary.

## DIARIES, REMINISCENCES AND COLLECTED PAPERS OF PUBLIC MEN

There are modern editions of some Diaries, but none of the great editions of collected papers—the pride of American scholarship—has so far covered the 1840s. The historian is therefore forced to rely on older editions, and in nineteenth-century collections the standards of selection and accuracy are often suspect.

Charles Francis Adams
> *Diary* (Aida Di Pace Donald, David Donald, Marc Friedlander, and Lyman H. Butterfield, eds.) 4 Vols., 1964–68.

George Bancroft
> *Life and Letters*, by Mark A. De Wolfe Howe. 2 Vols., 1908.

Thomas Hart Benton
> *Thirty Years View* 2 Vols., 1854–56.

James Buchanan
> *Works* (J. B. Moore, ed.) 12 Vols., 1908–11.

John C. Calhoun
> *Works* (R. K. Crallé, ed.) 6 Vols., 1853–55; reprinted 1968.
> ———. *Letters* (J. F. Jameson, ed.) American Historical Association. Annual Report, 1899. Vol. II. Part I, Letters from Calhoun; Part II, Letters to Calhoun.
> ———. Correspondence addressed to Calhoun, 1837–49 (Chauncy S. Brooks and R. P. Brooks, eds.) 1930.

Salmon P. Chase
> *Diary and Correspondence* American Historical Association. Annual Report, 1902. Vol. II.

Rufus Choate
> *Works: with a memoir of his life* (S. G. Brown, ed.) 2 Vols., 1862; reprinted 1977.

Cassius M. Clay
> *Writings* (Horace Greeley, ed.) 1848.

Henry Clay
> *Speeches and Correspondence* (Calvin Colton, ed.) 1855.

Howell Cobb
> *See* Robert Toombs.

George M. Dallas
> "Diary and Letters" (Roy F. Nichols, ed.) *Pennsylvania Magazine* Vol. LXXIII (1949), No. 3, 349 ff.; and No. 4, 475 ff.

John A. Dix
    *Memoirs of John Adams Dix*, by Morgan Dix. 2 Vols., 1883.
Stephen A. Douglas
    *Letters* (Robert W. Johannsen, ed.) 1961.
Ralph Waldo Emerson
    *Journals* (E. W. Emerson and W. E. Corbes, eds.) 10 Vols., 1909–14.

    *Journals and Miscellaneous Notebooks* (William H. Gilman *et al.*, eds.) 10 Vols. to date, 1960–76.
Albert Gallatin
    *Writings* (Henry Adams, ed.) 3 Vols., 1879.
William A. Graham
    *Papers* (J. G. de Roulhac Hamilton, ed.) 4 Vols., 1957–61.
Philip Hone
    *Diary* (Bayard Tuckerman, ed.) 2 Vols., 1889.
    *Diary* (Allan Nevins, ed.) 1927.
Andrew Jackson
    *Correspondence* (J. S. Bassett and J. F. Jameson, eds.) 7 Vols., 1926–35.
Willie P. Mangum
    *Papers* (Henry T. Shanks, ed.) 5 Vols., 1950–1956.
Theodore Parker
    *Collected Works* (Frances Power Cobbe, ed.)
    *Life and Correspondence*, by John Weiss. 2 Vols., 1864.
James K. Polk
    *Diary* (Milo M. Quaife, ed.) 4 Vols., 1910
    *Polk: The Diary of a President* (Allan Nevins, ed.) 1929.
    *James K. Polk,* by Eugene I. McCormac. 1922.
William H. Seward
    *Works* (G. E. Baker, ed.) 5 Vols., 1853–54.
Alexander H. Stephens
    *See* Robert Toombs.
Robert Toombs
    *Correspondence of Robert Toombs, Alexander H. Stephens, and Howell Cobb* (Ulrich B. Phillips, ed.) American Historical Association. Annual Report, 1911. Part II.
John Tyler
    *Letters and Times of the Tylers*, by Lyon G. Tyler. 3 Vols., 1884–96.
Daniel Webster
    *Writings and Speeches* (J. W. McIntyre, ed.) 18 Vols., 1903.

## SECONDARY WORKS

The admirable *Harvard Guide to American History*, ed. Frank Freidel, 2 Vols., (Cambridge, Mass., 1974) renders unnecessary a lengthy bibliography of secondary works. However, as my debt to other writers is not noticed in the text or footnotes, some explanatory notes and comments are necessary. I have followed the practice of the *Harvard Guide* in giving the date but not the place of publication.

## PARTIES

To anyone familiar with the literature on political parties in this period it will be clear that my interpretation differs in important respects from that of Richard P. McCormick. Nevertheless my interest in the subject was first aroused by his important articles "Suffrage, Classes and Party Alignments: a study in voting behavior" (*Mississippi Valley Historical Review*, XLVI (1959), 297 ff.) and "New Perspectives on Jacksonian Politics" (*American Historical Review*, 65 (1960), 288), and I profited greatly from his *Second American Party System: Jacksonian Era* (1966). McCormick's general views on party were challenged by Robert E. Shalhope, "Jacksonian Politics in Missouri" (*Civil War History*, 15 (1969), 210), and McCormick replied briefly (*Ibid.*, 16 (1970), 92–93). I accept McCormick's argument that Shalhope's figures do not support his conclusion, but I agree with the latter's statement that "to view the Whig and Democratic parties simply as electoral machines obscures the fact that they did represent two separate 'persuasions,' which, whether altogether conscious or not, were very real to the men of the day." Missouri was also the subject of a detailed study on *The Whig Party in Missouri* by John Vollmer Mering (1967), which confirms, for this state, the hypothesis advanced by Charles J. Sellers, "Who were the Southern Whigs" (*American Historical Review* 59 (1954)) to which reference is made in Chapter 1 above. Further contributions to this subject have been made by Grady McWhiney, "Were the Whigs a class party in Alabama?" (*Journal of Southern History*, XXIII (1957), 510 ff.), Thomas B. Alexander *et al.*, "Who were the Alabama Whigs?" (*Alabama Review*, XVI (1963), 5–10), and W. Wayne Smith, "Jacksonian Democracy on the Chesapeke: Class, Kinship and Politics" (*Maryland Historical Magazine*, LXV (1970), 55 ff.). Ronald P. Formisano, *The Birth of Mass Political Parties: Michigan 1827–1861* (1971) is an important challenge to the belief that grass-roots politics can be understood in terms of elite aims and national issues. He shows that small, independent farmers were not universally Democratic but strongly Whig in many areas; some frontier counties were Whig; and more Democrats than Whigs were engaged in promotional activities. He emphasizes religion as a major determinant of party allegiance. Elliott R. Barkan's unpublished Harvard Ph.D. dissertation "Portrait of a Party: The Origin and Development of the Whig Persuasion in New York" (1968) contains useful material, particularly on the influence of the Anti-Masons and Whig links with reform movements. William H. Adams, *The Whig Party of Louisiana* (1973) is a straightforward account. Other histories of state parties are listed in the *Harvard Guide* II, 807–08, but special mention should be made of Lee Benson, *Concept of Jacksonian Democracy: New York as a test case* (1961) which broke new ground, both in the analysis of campaign literature and in the use of census material to study ethnic factors in party support. A student of this period must regret that so little space was allocated to the antebellum Democrats and Whigs in *The History of United States Political Parties*, A. M. Schlesinger, Jr. (ed.), 4 Vols., (1973). Some interesting documents are printed, but do not seem to have been selected on any systematic plan. Everyone studying political history must be grateful for the data on county voting in Walter Dean Burnham, *Presidential Ballots, 1836–1922* (1955). Two valuable studies using quantitative methods to demonstrate party solidarity, both published in 1967, are Thomas B. Alexander, *Sectional Stress and party strength: a study of roll-call voting patterns in the United States House of Representatives, 1836–1860* and Joel H. Silbey, *The Shrine of Party: Congressional voting behavior, 1841–1852*. There are essays and documents on each election in Arthur M. Schlesinger, Jr., and Fred L. Israel (eds.), *History of American Presidential Elections*, Vol. I (1971). Individual authors are Joel H.

Silbey (1836), William Nisbet Chambers (1840), Charles Sellers (1844), Holman Hamilton (1848), Roy and Jeannette Nichols (1852). Recent books which throw light on the development of the party system are David B. Cole, *Jacksonian Democracy in New Hampshire* (1970), William G. Shade, *Banks or No Banks: The Money Issue in Western Politics 1832–65* (1972), Sydney Nathans, *Daniel Webster and Jacksonian Democracy* (1973), Matthew A. Crenson, *The Federal Machine: Beginnings of Bureaucracy in Jacksonian America* (1975), Peter Temin, *The Jacksonian Economy* (1970), and John McFaul, *The Politics of Jacksonian Finance* (1972). Continuing interest in the politics of the Jacksonian period is also demonstrated by an unusually large harvest of articles in recent periodical issues. Among them the following deserve special notice: H. Ershkowitz and William G. Shade, "Consensus or Conflict? Political Behavior in the State Legislatures during the Jacksonian Era," *Journal of American History* 58 (1977), D. J. Russo, "The Major Political Issues of the Jacksonian Period and the Development of Party Loyalty in Congress," *Transactions of the American Philosophical Society* n.s. 62 (1972), L. Marshall, "The Strange Still-birth of the Whig Party," *American Historical Review* 72 (1967), Richard Latner, "A New Look at Jacksonian Politics," *Journal of American History* 61 (1975), K. T. Phillips, "The Pennsylvania Origins of the Jacksonian Movement," *Political Science Quarterly* 91 (1976), and Donald J. Ratcliffe, Politics in Jacksonian Ohio: Reflctions on the Entrepreneurial Politics Interpretation," *Ohio History* 88 (1979).

## INTELLECTUAL FRAMEWORK OF POLITICS

I owe much to David Levin, *History as a Romantic Art: Bancroft, Prescott, Motley and Parkman* (1959). If one wishes to grasp the wide range of William Ellery Channing there is no substitute for browsing in his voluminous articles, lectures, and sermons (a one-volume edition was published in 1875), but he has attracted the attention of several modern biographers: Arthur W. Brown, *William Ellery Channing* (1961), David P. Edgell, *William Ellery Channing* (1955), Madeleine H. Rice, *Federal Street Pastor: William Ellery Channing* (1961), and Jack Mendelsohn, *Channing: the Reluctant Radical* (1971). The conservative face of Unitarianism is described in Elizabeth M. Geffen, *Philadelphia Unitarianism 1796–1861* (1961). The anti-mission movement is analyzed by Bertram Wyatt-Brown in "The Anti-Mission Movement in the Jacksonian South," *Journal of Southern History* 36 (1970). There is a brief but perceptive account of Anti-Masonry by Michael F. Holt in *History of United States Political Parties*, Arthur M. Schlesinger, Jr. (ed.), Vol. I, 575 ff. Albert F. McLean, Jr., *William Cullen Bryant* (1964) is somewhat stronger on his literary career but provides useful insights into Bryant's political views and influence. Marvin Myers, *Jacksonian Persuasion* (1957) remains the best short study of Jacksonian ideas. Milton S. Heath, *Constructive Liberalism: Role of the State in the Economic Development of Georgia to 1860* (1954) is a good study of public responsibility in a key state of the South.

## The Whigs in 1841–42

There is no full-scale study of the Whig debacle in 1841. Oliver P. Chitwood, *John Tyler* (1939) is naturally well disposed to his subject but not unfair to the Whigs. Robert J. Morgan, *A Whig embattled: the Presidency under John Tyler* (1954) is more critical of the President. There are two good studies of Henry Clay: Clement Eaton, *Henry Clay and the Art of American Politics* (1957), and George R. Poage, *Clay and the Whig Party* (1936). The treatment in Glyndon G. Van Deusen, *Jacksonian Era, 1828–1848* ('New American Nation' Series, 1959) is necessarily brief, but balanced and—as one might expect from the biographer of Henry Clay (1937), Thurlow Weed (1947), and William H. Seward (1967)—sympathetic to the Whigs.

## ANNEXATION, WAR, AND THE WILMOT PROVISO

Justin H. Smith, *Annexation of Texas* (1911) remains a standard work. Carl M. Wiltse, *John C. Calhoun*, Vol. III (1951) discusses annexation at length but David M. Pletcher, *The Diplomacy of Annexation: Texas, Oregon, and the Mexican War* (1973) is the fullest and most reliable study of the issues in their international setting. Kinley J. Brauer, *Cotton versus Conscience* (1967) deals with the anti-Texas movement in Massachusetts. There is, unfortunately, no authoritative study of Van Buren and the anti-Texas Democrats, but John A. Garraty, *Silas Wright* (1949) is useful. Elgin Williams, *The Animating Pursuits of Speculation* (1949)—a somewhat neglected book—provides an account of the seamy side of annexationist pressure (Texas bonds, land scrip, and commercial speculation). The nomination of James K. Polk is described in detail by Charles G. Sellers, *James K. Polk*, 2 Vols. (1957–66).

The books mentioned above continue the study of Texas to the final achievement of annexation. Sellers, *James K. Polk*, Vol. II, and James P. Shenton, *Robert J. Walker* (1961) deal with domestic policy. For general studies of the war with Mexico see the *Harvard Guide* II, 817. The standard biography of David Wilmot (which needs revision at some points) is by Charles B. Going (1924). Champlain W. Morrison, *Democratic Politics and Sectionalism: Wilmot Proviso Controversy* (1967) is a detailed account of the political repercussions of the proviso.

## RESPONSE TO THE WILMOT PROVISO

The literature on the first phase of the American Party is meager, but the best survey is in Ray A. Billington, *Protestant Crusade, 1800–1860* (1938). Holman Hamilton, *Zachary Taylor* (1951) Vol. II, describes the Taylor movement and his nomination; see also his "Election of 1848" in Arthur M. Schlesinger, Jr. and Fred L. Israel (eds.), *History of American Presidential Elections, 1789–1968* (1971) Vol. II. The conscience Whigs are given detailed treatment in Kinley J. Brauer, *Cotton versus Conscience* (1967), David H. Donald, *Charles Sumner* (1960) Vol. I, Martin J. Duberman, *Charles Francis Adams* (1961) and *James Russell Lowell* (1966), and Frank O. Gatell, *John Gorham Palfrey and the New England Conscience* (1963). Henry Steele Commager, *Theodore Parker* (1936) is surprisingly unsympathetic to Parker's antislavery activities. Robert C. Albrecht, *Theodore Parker* (1971) is short but perceptive.

Frank B. Woodford, *Lewis Cass: the last Jeffersonian* (1950) is adequate but does not go fully into the views of Cass on slavery and expansion. Joseph C. Rayback, *Free Soil: the Election of 1848* (1971) and Frederick J. Blue, *The Free Soilers* (1973) together provide a full history of the movement. An important work which sets Free Soil in the full context of political antislavery is Richard H. Sewell, *Ballots for Freedom: Anti-Slavery and Politics 1837–1860* (1976). Jonathan Messerli, *Horace Mann* (1972) describes the political interlude in the life of this distinguished educational reformer.

Two books are of outstanding interest in the interpretation of the South: David M. Potter, *The South and Sectional Conflict* (1968) and Eugene D. Genovese, *The World the Slaveholders Made* (1969). William R. Taylor, *Cavalier and Yankee: Old South and American National Character* (1961) is concerned mainly with literary culture but contains many striking analyses of Southern thought. Clement Eaton, *Growth of Southern Civilization, 1790–1800* ('New American Nation' Series, 1961) and Charles S. Sydnor, *Development of Southern Sectionalism 1819–1848* (1948) are distinguished surveys. The later chapters of Charles M. Wiltse, *John C. Calhoun,* Vol. III, and the early chapters of Robert W. Johannsen, *Stephen A. Douglas*, describe the political stalemate of 1849.

The works already cited on the South are relevant. William S. Jenkins, *Pro-Slavery Thought* (1935) remains a good survey of the subject, and some further points are made by Ralph E. Morrow in "The Pro-Slavery Argument" (*Mississippi Valley Historical Review* 48 (1961), 79) with special emphasis on the way in which it was addressed to a Southern audience. Some interesting illustrative documents are collected by Eric L. McKittrick in *Slavery Defended: Views of the Old South* (1963). The numerical strength of the slaveowning interest is examined by Otto H. Olsen, "Historians and the Extent of Slave Ownership in the Southern United States" (*Civil War History* 18 (1972), 101). An important work, pointing the way to new areas for research, is Frank L. Owsley, *Plain Folk of the South* (1949), but some may find his picture of the "plain people" too idealistic. A far-sighted work is Roger W. Shugg, *Origins of the Class Struggle in Louisiana: a social history of White Farmers and Laborers during Slavery and After, 1840–1875* (1939).

## THE COMPROMISE AND AFTER

Holman Hamilton, *Prologue to Conflict: the Compromise of 1850* (1964) is the best general history; it supplements at several points the account in Allan Nevins, *Ordeal of the Union,* 2 Vols. (1947). Some pertinent questions are raised in Robert R. Russel in "What was the Compromise of 1850?" (*Journal of Southern History* 22 (1956), 292); he stresses the importance of the legal provisions for carrying slavery cases from the territories to the federal courts. David M. Potter, *The Impending Crisis* (1976), chaps. 5 and 6 provides a balanced and reflective account. Major L. Wilson in *Space, Time, and Freedom* (1974) discusses the compromise in relation to ideas about history and national destiny. For other articles on the compromise see the *Harvard Guide* II, 836. Glyndon G. Van Deusen, *William Henry Seward* (1967) examines and defends Seward's course. The biographies of Clay, Calhoun, and Douglas already cited give much space to the compromise. Robert F. Dalzell, *Daniel Webster and the trial of American Nationalism, 1843–1852* (1973) supplements other biographies (for which see *Harvard Guide* I, 266) and will provide a corrective for those who find my treatment of the March 7, 1850, speech too abrasive.

Avery O. Craven, *The Growth of Southern Nationalism 1848–1861* (1953) gives a good analysis of Southern reactions. The works already cited by David Donald (*Charles Sumner*), Martin Duberman (*Charles Francis Adams*), and Richard H. Sewell (*Ballots for Freedom*) provide perceptive comment on Northern views of the compromise and the Fugitive Slave Law.

# INDEX

Colton, Calvin, 21, 50
 "Junius" tracts, 61
Compromise of 1833, 82, 103
Compromise of 1850, xiii, 276–316
  passim, 332, 388
  reception of, 324–28
Congregationalists, 51
Congress
 lack of continuity in, 28
 procedure in, 74–75
 *See also* House of Representatives;
  Senate
Conscience Whigs, 184–207 passim,
  218
Constitution, xiv, 36, 259
 and "higher law," 302–3, 308
 and instructions to Senators, 8
 and slavery, 263–64
Corwin, Thomas
 on Mexican War, 171–72
 on Whig principles, 10
Counties, election records (1836–48),
  24–25
Crittenden, John J., 29
 condemns anti-war meeting, 187
 supports Taylor, 187
Curtis, B. R., supports Compromise,
  326

Dallas, George M.
 casting vote on 1846 tariff bill,
  173–74
 on character of Polk, 165–66
 supports Compromise, 328
Davis, Jefferson, 239–40, 289
 on character of Union, 322
Davis, John, talks out Wilmot proviso,
  182
Dayton, William L., 245, 298n
De Bow, J. B. D., 235
*De Bow's Review*, 235
Democratic party, 10
 Barnburners and, 213–14
 and Catholic voters, 25
 condition in 1846, 151, 208
 counties carried by (1836–48), 24–25
 elections
  1840, 21–22

1844, 154–56
1848, 213–14, 228
geographical distribution, 26–28
image of Whigs, 20
Loco-Focos and, 59–60
National Conventions
 1844, 136–39
 1848, 212
party principles, 7, 11
in the South, 16
strength in Congress, 27
and Texas, 154
*Democratic Review*
 article on Bentham, 57
 on Compromise, 325
 condemns Van Buren in 1848, 231
 and crisis of 1850, 293–94
 on danger of black political power,
  279
 on Democratic doctrine, 18–19, 49,
  147
 on economics of slavery, 231–32
 on "higher law," 309
 on national destiny, 143
 on parties, 6–7, 19, 22
 repudiates egalitarianism, 65
 on Texas, 147
Depression, effects of in 1840, 10–11
Dewey, Orville
 on civil liberty, 45
 on moderation, 193–94
Dickinson, Daniel, 251
 opposes legislation on slavery in territories, 210–11
Distribution Act, 102–4
District of Columbia
 abolition of slave trade, 313
 slavery in, 245
 Southern views on abolition of slave
  trade, 320–21
Dix, John A.
 on banks, 61
 on expansion of slavery, 209, 251–52
 on party conflicts, 40
Douglas, Stephen A., 149, 175
 and Compromise bills, 313
 plan for California and New Mexico
  statehood, 243–45, 248–52
 political aims (1850), 284–85